Reinventing Functional Finance

Reinventing Functional Finance

Transformational Growth and Full Employment

Edited by

Edward J. Nell

Malcolm B. Smith Professor of Economics, Graduate Faculty, New School University, USA

Mathew Forstater

Director, Center for Full Employment and Price Stability, University of Missouri–Kansas City, USA

Edward Elgar

Cheltenham, UK • Northampton, MA, USA

Published by
Edward Elgar Publishing Limited
Glensanda House
Montpellier Parade
Cheltenham
Glos GL50 1UA
UK

Edward Elgar Publishing, Inc.
136 West Street
Suite 202
Northampton
Massachusetts 01060
USA

A catalogue record for this book
is available from the British Library

Library of Congress Cataloguing in Publication Data

Reinventing functional finance: transformational growth and full employment/edited by Edward J. Nell, Mathew Forstater.
p. cm.
Papers presented at a conference held in the spring of 1998 at the New School for Social Research.
Includes index.
1. Fiscal policy—Congresses. 2. Monetary policy—Congresses. 3. Full employment policies—Congresses. 4. Inflation (Finance)—Congresses. I. Nell, Edward J. II. Forstater, Mathew, 1961–

HJ192.5.R48 2003
339.5—dc21 2002035303

ISBN 1 84376 111 4 (cased)

Typeset by Cambrian Typesetters, Frimley, Surrey
Printed and bound in Great Britain by MPG Books Ltd, Bodmin, Cornwall

Contents

Contributors

Per Gunnar Berglund is a Ph.D. candidate in economics and a Research Fellow at the Center for Economic Policy Analysis (CEPA) at New School University in New York. His main fields of work are the theory of aggregation and index numbers, national accounting, macroeconomic modeling, monetary theory, and the political economy of full employment.

David Colander is the Christian A. Johnson Distinguished Professor of Economics at Middlebury College.

James S. Duesenberry is Professor Emeritus of Economics at Harvard University.

Walter A. Eberstadt, Limited Managing Director, Lazard Freres and Co. L.L.C.

Robert Eisner (1922–1998) was William R. Kenan Professor Emeritus of Northwestern University and a fellow of the American Academy of Arts and Sciences and the Econometric Society. He is well known for his contributions to understanding investment, consumption behavior, macroeconomic theory, and fiscal and monetary policy. He published extensively in academic journals such as the *American Economic Review*, *Review of Economics and Statistics*, *Quarterly Journal of Economics*, *Econometrica*, *Economic Journal*, *Survey of Current Business*, *Review of Income and Wealth*. Eisner is the author of many books including *Social Security: More Not Less* (1998), *The Misunderstood Economy: What Counts and How to Count It* (1994), and *The Total Incomes System of Accounts* (1989). He also wrote frequent columns on economic affairs for the *Wall Street Journal*, *Los Angeles Times*, and other general media.

Mathew Forstater is Assistant Professor of Economics and Director of the Center for Full Employment and Price Stability at the University of Missouri–Kansas City. He is also a Research Associate with the Jerome Levy Economics Institute of Bard College and an Affiliated Faculty Member with the Missouri Institute for Public Policy. Forstater's scholarly articles have appeared in the *Journal of Economic Issues*, *Journal of Post Keynesian Economics*, *Review of*

Political Economy, *Review of Social Economy*, *Economic and Labour Relations Review*, *Economie Appliquée*, *Eastern Economic Journal*, and a number of edited volumes. He is also the co-editor (with Aaron Warner and Sumner Rosen) of *Commitment to Full Employment* (M.E. Sharpe, 2000) and (with Edward Nell) of *Functional Finance and Full Employment* (Edward Elgar, 2000). Forstater received an M.A. (Honors) and Ph.D. in Economics from the New School for Social Research and a B.A. (*summa cum laude*) in African American Studies from Temple University.

Philip Harvey is Associate Professor of Law and Economics at Rutgers University. He is the author of *Securing the Right to Employment: Social Welfare Policy and the Unemployed in the United States* (Princeton University Press, 1989) and co-author with Theodore Marmor and Jerry Mashaw of *America's Misunderstood Welfare State* (Basic Books, 1990).

Robert Heilbroner is the author of some 20 books, perhaps the best known being *The Worldly Philosophers*, just out in its seventh edition. He has taught for many years at the Graduate Faculty of the New School for Social Research.

Raymond Majewski is currently Chief Economist at the New York City Council Finance Division. From 1997 until 2000 he was the Assistant Director of the Transformational Growth and Full Employment Project at the New School University. He received his Ph.D. from the New School in 1997 and has taught at Seton Hall and Monmouth universities. His research areas include public finance, macroeconomics and economic history.

Perry Mehrling is Professor of Economics at Barnard College, Columbia University. His work on the foundations and history of monetary economics has been published in numerous scholarly articles, yet uncollected, and one book, *The Money Interest and the Public Interest: American Monetary Thought 1920–1970* (Harvard, 1997). His major current project is a book entitled *The Price of Risk: Fischer Black and the Revolution in Modern Finance*.

William F. Mitchell is Professor of Economics and Director of the Centre of Full Employment and Equity at the University of Newcastle, Australia. His research is primarily in the areas of macroeconomic policy, labor economics, with a particular emphasis on unemployment, inflation and large-scale macroeconometric models.

Richard A. Musgrave is H.H. Burbank Professor of Political Economy Emeritus and Adjunct Professor of Economics at the University of California, Santa Cruz.

Edward J. Nell is the Malcolm B. Smith Professor of Economics in the Graduate Faculty of the New School University, in New York. He was born and grew up in the Chicago area, and then attended Princeton as an undergraduate, going on to Oxford as a Rhodes Scholar. After teaching at Oxford, he joined the faculty of Wesleyan, later moving to the University of East Anglia. He has spent most of his career at the Graduate Faculty of the New School, where his research carried on the critical and interventionist traditions of Adolph Lowe and Robert Heilbroner, which he ultimately developed into the Transformational Growth approach. This is presented in his principal work, *The General Theory of Transformational Growth*. He has lectured and taught in many parts of the world, including Cambridge, London, Paris, Nice, Montreal, Frankfurt, Rome, Siena, Sydney, and Melbourne, among others.

Ingrid H. Rima is Professor of Economics at Temple University in Philadelphia.

Louis-Philippe Rochon is the Stephen B. Monroe Assistant Professor of Economics and Banking at Kalamazoo College, MI, where he is also the Director of the Center for Policy Studies. He is the author of numerous articles on credit and endogenous money, and the author/editor of *Credit, Money and Production* (Edward Elgar), *Credit, Interest Rates and the Open Economy* (Edward Elgar), *Modern Theories of Money* (Edward Elgar), *Financial and Monetary Integration* (Routledge), *Dollarization* (Edward Elgar) and *The Keynesian Multiplier* (forthcoming, Routledge). He has received financial grants from *The Ford Foundation* and *The Mott Foundation*.

John Smithin is Professor of Economics in the Department of Economics and Schulich School of Business, York University, Toronto, Canada.

Hans-Michael Trautwein is professor of international economics at Carl von Ossietzky Universität, Oldenburg, Germany. He has published widely on various issues of macroeconomic theory, in particular Wicksellian approaches to money, credit, business cycles and employment.

Lynn Turgeon was Professor Emeritus of Economics at Hofstra University.

L. Randall Wray is Professor of Economics at the University of Missouri-Kansas City as well as Senior Research Associate, the Center for Full Employment and Price Stability (at UMKC), and a senior scholar at the Jerome Levy Economics Institute. He is a past president of the Association for Institutionalist Thought (AFIT) and member of the board of directors of the

Association for Evolutionary Economics (AFEE). Wray has focused on monetary theory and policy, macroeconomics, and employment policy. He is currently writing on full employment policy, modern money, and the monetary theory of production.

Preface

In 1941, Professor Abba Lerner of the University of Kansas City (later the University of Missouri–Kansas City) laid out the principles that he believed should guide the government's budgetary policies. These principles, spelled out in his article, 'The Economic Steering Wheel,' which appeared in the *University of Kansas City Review*, were offered as an alternative to the orthodox principles of so-called 'sound finance.' Lerner later moved to the New School for Social Research where he elaborated his ideas in 'Functional Finance and the Federal Debt,' published in 1943 in the New School's Graduate Faculty journal, *Social Research*.

The New School's Program on Transformational Growth and Full Employment, under the direction of Edward J. Nell, Malcolm B. Smith Professor of Economics, has revived the tradition that Lerner began. Part of this revival, a conference on 'Functional Finance and Full Employment,' was held in the spring of 1998 at the New School, attracting economists from around the globe. The conference re-examined monetary and fiscal relationships – both in theory and policy – in the light of Lerner's prescient principles.

Among the participants were Harvard University Professors Richard Musgrave, the father of modern public finance, and James Duesenberry, best known for formulating the relative income hypothesis, an alternative to the permanent income and life-cycle theories of consumption. The late Robert Eisner of Northwestern University, former President of the American Economic Association, and the late Lynn Turgeon of Hofstra University both presented papers at the conference. This would be the last such activity for both of these important scholars of fiscal and budgetary policy. David Colander of Middlebury College, who collaborated with Abba Lerner, presented a paper, and the New School's own Robert Heilbroner, whose book on the deficit influenced President John F. Kennedy, gave a talk, and both took part in the roundtable discussions.

In 'Functional finance and the federal debt,' Lerner proposed his principles of functional finance, which he believed the government should implement to bring about full employment:

> The central idea is that government fiscal policy, its spending and taxing, borrowing and repaying of loans, its issue of new money and its withdrawal of money, should all be undertaken with an eye only to the results of these actions on the economy, and not to any established traditional doctrine about what is sound and what

> is unsound. This principle of judging only by effects has been applied in many other fields of human activity, where it is known as the method of science opposed to scholasticism.
>
> The principle of judging fiscal measures by the way they work or function in an economy we may call Functional Finance. . . . Government should adjust its rate of expenditure and taxation such that total spending in the economy is neither more nor less than that which is sufficient to purchase the full employment level of output at current prices. If this means there is a deficit, greater borrowing, 'printing money,' etc. . . . then these things are neither good nor bad, they are simply the means to the desired ends of full employment and price stability.[1]

These extremely simple ideas differ greatly from both the 'deficit hawk' and the 'deficit dove' views of budgetary policy. The deficit hawks argue that deficits cause inflation and high interest rates, that public spending 'crowds out' private spending, that the national debt will burden future generations – all in all, that deficit spending is virtually immoral. Deficit doves see problems in the views of hawks, finding little or no empirical support for their claims, and weakness, even confusions, in their theories. This particularly affects issues of the measurement of deficits and national debt, and also how we understand the impact of fiscal policy. But doves tend to agree that deficits are generally undesirable. By arguing that deficits are not really as big as they look, or that a larger economy can afford bigger deficits, they give too much credence to the views of the hawks, and nothing at all to Functional Finance.

Lerner was not alone among the New School's Graduate Faculty in promoting counter-cyclical fiscal policies to achieve full employment with price stability. Adolph Lowe, Hans Neisser, Gerhard Colm, Alfred Kaehler, and other New School economists advised President Roosevelt on policies combating unemployment. With a message that was not simply Keynesian, these graduates of the 'Kiel School' were perhaps described best as 'friendly critics' of Keynes. They were never completely comfortable with the framework offered in *The General Theory*, where Keynes considers neither technical change nor income distribution. Lowe, Neisser, and Kaehler all did important work on technological unemployment and the relation of technical change, income distribution and effective demand. Labor-displacing technical change, resulting in a shift in income distribution away from wages and towards profits, could result in a weakening of effective demand if capitalist propensities to consume are lower than those of workers. But the economists at Kiel in the late 1920s and 1930s, and at the New School's University in Exile (now the Graduate Faculty), in the 1930s and 1940s, admired Keynes's commitment to a policy-relevant economics focused on the business cycle and dedicated to eliminating unemployment.

1. From Lerner, Abba P. (1943), 'Functional finance and the federal debt', *Social Research*, 10, February, pp. 38–51.

But Keynes's economics was not developed in the direction supported by Lerner and his colleagues. Instead, the profession applied its developing tool box to grounding Keynes's macro in neoclassical microfoundations. The 'Grand Neo-Classical Keynesian Synthesis' – as Samuelson first dubbed these efforts that would later become known simply as 'the neoclassical synthesis' – sought to reconcile the rational maximizing agents of neoclassical theory with *some* of Keynes's insights. The real balance–effects arguments of Patinkin and his peers dealt with aggregate variables, included money in the analysis, recognized the multiplier and even acknowledged liquidity preference while still maintaining a picture of market economies as eliminating unemployment through the price mechanism. By insisting on the validity of the price mechanism, however, even if only in theory, they sacrificed what for many was the overarching theme of Keynes's contributions – the paradoxical nature of macroeconomics. Lerner called it 'topsy-turvy' economics. When the economy reaches equilibrium, or at any rate a steady position, in which there is still involuntary unemployment, then saving, labor-saving technical progress and imports all will *reduce* the performance of the economy and increase social costs. However when the economy comes to equilibrium only at full employment, these aspects all improve the economy's performance and are socially beneficial!

The important point is that we do live in a topsy-turvy world, not in a world of rational choices and smooth equilibrium. So deficits may be helpful and surpluses dangerous, saving may slow us down and technical progress can make us poorer. It is not, however, a matter of 'realistic assumptions.' All theorizing has to abstract and simplify. The point is to identify and understand the actual mechanisms and market forces that govern our economic relationships. Then we can devise policies to adjust these mechanisms and forces, to make them work better and put the topsy-turvy arrangements right side up. That was not only Lerner's program, it was also that of the New School, and it still is today, as the contributions of this conference show.

Mathew Forstater

Acknowledgments

Marsha Lasker Nell took on the chief responsibility for organizing and running the conference and for obtaining the manuscripts. She did a fine job. Louis-Philippe Rochon also helped ensure a well-run conference. Ray Majewski organized the contributions from the Program on Transformational Growth and Full Employment. Natalia Filippova ably assisted in difficult editorial responsibilities and helped Luca Fiorito research the New School heritage in social economics. Pavlina Tcherneva and Fadhel Kaboub provided first-rate editorial assistance in the final stages of the project. Janet Cavallero performed excellent editorial work and handled the complex job of pulling the final manuscript together with grace and efficiency.

We are particularly grateful to Richard Musgrave and James Duesenberry for attending and participating. We note with sorrow that the conference was the last occasion of academic participation for both Robert Eisner and Lynn Turgeon. They both will be sorely missed.

Finally, we thank the Graduate Faculty of Political and Social Science of the New School for Social Research, now New School University, which has served as the intellectual base for many of the participants, as well as being the home of the originator of functional finance, Abba Lerner. We also thank the Center for Full Employment and Price Stability, at the University of Missouri–Kansas City, for providing generous resources and support, which also enables the Program on Transformational Growth and Full Employment at the New School's Graduate Faculty to continue its important work on real-world macroeconomics.

Edward J. Nell
Mathew Forstater

PART I

INTRODUCTION

1. Transformational growth and functional finance

Edward J. Nell

> 'There is no such thing as Society,' said Margaret Thatcher, 'there are only individuals.'

Margaret Thatcher seems to have captured the perspective of modern macroeconomics. Whether 'New Keynesian' or 'New Classical,' everything can be reduced to the actions of individuals. Macro is simply micro, aggregated. Or further, macro is micro writ large – the working of the economy can be examined by looking at the (rational) actions of a representative agent. (Or the agent's limited but almost rational behavior in imperfect circumstances.) Macro is based, then, on microfoundations. These may take the form of a neo-Walrasian general equilibrium, or a 'partial' version may be considered adequate. The markets may be perfect or imperfect, but the focus is on how rational, or nearly rational, agents in them interact.

Such 'foundations' are timeless. Agents are (nearly) rational and generally well-informed; their preferences are clear and consistent, and they are endowed with given supplies of factors, including labor, which they allocate optimally to producing goods, which they exchange – also optimally – in more or less competitive barter trades. Whether in ancient Egypt or modern America, this is the way the world works.

But this is not how the early developers of the macro approach saw it. For them, macro was about the way the *system* adjusted, where 'system' referred to the interaction of business firms, banks, labor and government. They studied a system of interacting *institutions* that developed and changed over time. The short-term problem was to analyze the forces determining its levels of output, employment and inflation; the long term concerned its productivity and growth. Both were cast in terms of institutions, that is, money and the banking systems, corporations, labor, households, capital markets and government. Further, these institutions were not established givens but were the products of historical development. Particularly, the early macroeconomists noted in this regard that the monetary system had changed and so had government.

In the recent New Keynesian/New Classical (NK/NC) approach[1] (Mankiw and Romer, 1993), the economy reflects the choices and actions of given, independent individuals under various conditions. In the older version, the choices were understood to be made by bureaucracies following standard (and perhaps arcane) procedures, with actions carried out by agents 'just following orders.' In the NK/NC case, independent individuals, consulting their preferences, are modeled as acting to supply and demand in barter markets. By contrast in the older vision, output is produced by large business corporations, who also set prices, sell the products for money and distribute a portion of profits in money dividends, and retain another portion for investment. Demand comes in money form from households, businesses and government, reflecting their respective obligations and plans, and resting in part on debt creation. Employment in the first case is a matter of choice: 'Labor can hire capital just as easily as capital can hire labor.' In the second, employment means being hired for a job, where the job is defined by the personnel department. In the recent picture, government is not a major player – the economy reaches an optimal position without any involvement at all on the part of government. By contrast, in the early post-war picture, government is a major player, its taxes and spending driving a major part of the economy. Finally, in the NK/NC world, inflation is assumed to be a uniform rise in all prices – product and factor both – caused simply by excess money creation. In the earlier picture, inflation could be wage inflation or price inflation, and any difference between the two would have distributive implications. The early macroeconomists were very conscious of the varying roles of different kinds of debt – household, business and government debt. The later system downplays debt, and even denies that the debt–equity ratio of a firm matters (in equilibrium).

WHAT IS MACROECONOMICS?

Macroeconomics is generally taken to mean the study of the determination, in the short run, of aggregate employment and output together with the rate of inflation. This is a practical definition, useful for policy-makers. Output, employment and inflation are determined through the interaction of business firms – who set their current activity and make plans for future capacity – with households, who are concerned to ensure their incomes and provide for their normal consumption, all mediated by the monetary and credit system that helps to finance various aspects of both business and household activities. The employment offered will operate the existing technology and produce the corresponding style of output, and the whole process will be regulated, monitored and adjusted in various ways by government.

It is a crucial feature of the economy that it is monetary. Were it not it would be difficult to understand 'entry' and 'exit,' and the shifting of capital from low-profit or slow-growth sectors to more attractive ones. In a money economy, contracts will be written in money terms and businesses can be capitalized and sold for money; employment and output will be determined in monetary terms by forces acting in monetary form. Businesses offer employment for money and expect to make a profit in money terms; households need work to provide incomes to support consumption spending – again, all in money terms. By contrast, a European serf in the Middle Ages would exchange work for grain from the lord's granary; a nineteenth-century US farmer on free land on the Western frontier would, in effect, exchange his own work for his own crops, and might well barter products for clothes or tools or exchange work with his neighbor. In neither case would money or capital be involved. But in a modern capitalist economy, workers produce profitable goods by working for money wages with which they purchase consumer goods from suppliers who must also make a normal profit in the transaction.[2]

INSTITUTIONS AND INDIVIDUALS

Surely, it must be difficult to object to the preceding remarks. Yet, though in a sense obvious, they have an important implication: firms, households, the monetary system, capital markets and employment practices are all institutions or arrangements of institutions. So is government. Employment and output, and also the rate of inflation, are determined, then, by the interaction of institutions.

And what are institutions, one might ask? Are they not, as Margaret Thatcher implied, 'just people' behaving? 'Methodological individualism' would explain institutions away, 'reducing' them to the patterns of individuals interacting. Individuals are the basic building blocks of society; institutions are simply conveniences that individuals construct, to enable them to pursue their goals more efficiently.

This sounds very hard-nosed and practical: 'Away with all the metaphysics about structures and functions! It is people we see and deal with, people make up society, and that's that.' Yet this is a very superficial view. People cannot perform social actions unless they are *in a position to do so*. No one can vote who is not a citizen or sell what he or she does not own. No one can perform a marriage unless invested with the appropriate powers.

It can be thought of in this way: to obtain or hold a position in an institution one must be appointed to it, as with a job or office; or win it in a competition, as for example, in becoming the leader; or, as with marriage, go through a public ceremony; or be sworn in, as in becoming a judge. One may also acquire an institutional position at birth, or on coming of age. Taking on such a position confers rights and privileges, and also imposes duties and obligations. The institution is the arrangement of such roles or positions to accomplish certain tasks or achieve certain goals. The discipline of economics studies *production* institutions (firms, banks); *exchange and distributive* institutions (markets, payment systems); *regulatory* institutions (government agencies, etc.); and to some extent *reproductive* institutions (families).[3]

THE TEXTBOOK APPROACH

As opposed to what? The alternative approach most commonly pursued today asserts that employment and output are determined by the rational choices of representative agents, agents typically considered in abstract form, though the circumstances in which they operate may contain various kinds of imperfections. There are highbrow and middlebrow versions of the story, where the latter, often termed a 'parable,' is supposed to be a simpler, more easily understood version of the former.

The highbrow story is usually given in a general equilibrium format, although partial equilibrium versions are sometimes presented, highlighting the main features of the full-dress model. But in either version the story starts from a set of agents with given preferences variously endowed with given, initial supplies of factors, all having access to the same technology, who then produce, using the factors optimally, and swap the resulting goods, also optimally. Competition will ensure optimality. The system will settle down to an equilibrium set of swapping ratios – prices – and outputs. If a factor is fully utilized, it will have a positive price; if it is not fully utilized, it is not scarce and will, therefore, have a zero price. The startling implication, therefore, is that if real wages are positive in equilibrium, labor must be fully employed! That is, if employed labor is getting paid, there can be no involuntary unemployment.[4]

A 'middlebrow' version of the story goes as follows: The ability to produce output depends on technology and 'inital endowments,' as summarized, for instance, in an aggregate production function. Employment then depends on the supply and demand for labor; it will settle at the point where marginal product and marginal disutility curves intersect. Aggregate employment and output are dominated by 'supply' considerations, that is, by technology and endowments, with preferences entering into the determination of the composition of output and into the supply of labor, while inflation is seen as determined by nominal demand, which is believed to rest wholly or in large part on the money supply. Supply and demand for labor determine the real wage and the level of employment. Output then can be read off the production function for the equilibrium level of employment.

But the IS and LM curves may not intersect at this level of output. So much the worse for them; in the 'idealized' version of the model they will have to adjust.[5] If the level of aggregate demand is too low, then wages and prices would have to be lower, so that the real value of cash balances – and government bonds – would become higher, shifting the LM down and out and the IS up and out. When the IS/LM intersection occurs at the equilibrium level of output, the pressure on wages and prices will cease. (The story is often told as if there were 'movement'; in fact it is only a static story that happens to be comparative.)[6]

Of course, in practice, the world does not live up to the ideal case. As a practical matter, therefore, wages and prices will not adjust in disequilibrium, so wealth will not move countercyclically and long-term unemployment will be possible. In *theory*, the system is self-regulating; in *practice* there is a strong case for interventionist policy.

DIFFICULTIES

There are many well-known difficulties here, but perhaps two sets of partly empirical, partly conceptual problems stand out.[7] The first concerns labor and wages, the second prices and demand.

First with regard to labor and wages, the approach depends quite fundamentally on diminishing returns to labor. According to marginal productivity theory, the real wage is a scarcity price; it measures the scarcity value of labor, in the same way as any other factor. As more labor is employed, its marginal product falls or, put another way, marginal costs rise. But in fact all the evidence shows that, in general, in modern economies, this is not the case. Marginal costs do not rise; they are either constant or falling. Returns, in other words, are constant or increasing in both the short and long run. This reality calls for a re-casting of the way the labor market is modeled.

A second, fundamental point arises in connection with labor: The scarcity approach to value itself implies that if employed labor is getting paid, there cannot be any involuntary unemployment. The very problem to be examined – Why the system settles into periods of long-lasting unemployment? – is ruled out of court! For if labor is unemployed, it is not scarce. But factor prices reflect relative scarcity; if labor is not scarce its real wage should be zero. Since the real wage is not zero, labor must be scarce, and so there cannot be any involuntary unemployment. To get around this requires a strong appeal to 'imperfections' or to institutions that keep wages positive in the face of chronic unemployment.

The second set of difficulties begins with the ways in which prices have behaved. Percentage capacity utilization over the post-war period has averaged in the mid-to-low 80s; this would seem to indicate that demand, typically, has fallen significantly short of capacity output. So if markets are competitive in the textbook sense – even imperfectly competitive – we should have seen a general tendency for wages and prices to drift downwards over the last 50 years. At the very least, we should have seen some clear evidence of periods of downward drift. In fact, however, we have always had inflation at varying rates.

In any event, there is a problem with the proposed adjustment mechanism, the real balance or wealth effect. When wages and prices fall, because of a decline in demand, the real value of cash balances is supposed to rise, stimulating spending. But a fall in wages and prices also raises the burden of debt, which is fixed in nominal terms. This is the 'Fisher effect' and it implies that a substantial decline – enough to raise the real value of cash balances/government bonds, enough to influence spending – will lower profits sufficiently to leave some businesses with a problem in meeting debt-servicing. This will entail a decline in the value of *both* their bonds and their stock, and it will also require that businesses cancel their capital spending plans. In other words, a general decline in wages and prices implies a decline in money profits, and with given nominal debts and contracts, this could well lead to cumulative debt-deflation rather than to expansion. (Financial institutions, the chief holders of government bonds, do not tend to spend on capital expansion. Moreover, they also hold private bonds and stocks, some of which will be losing value because of the Fisher effect.)

There are other problems as well. The textbooks have not developed their treatment of the capital market. They tend to analyze portfolios containing only bonds and money, suggesting that all capital is borrowed and leaving us with the impression that, no one having equity, there is no trading of equity! This cannot be an adequate picture of a modern capitalist system.

Finally, the textbooks tend to treat the money supply as exogenous. Of course this was quite reasonable at one time. When reserves consisted of precious metal, the monetary issue was constrained by the reserve ratio and reserves were exogenous, at least in the short run. Moreover the supply and demand for reserves was important in determining the interest rate. But in the Post-World War II dollar economies, reserves are created by the Federal Reserve Bank, the 'Fed', and supplied to the banks that need them. They might still be considered exogenous if the Fed were able to control them at will, but this is not the case. For the most part, the Fed *must* supply reserves, otherwise the system will behave in undesirable ways, or the Fed will be unable to meet its other policy objectives. But while the Fed is obliged to provide reserves, it does control the overnight interest rate, and can also control other rates, though it chooses not to. The usual model of 'the money market,' showing the Liquidity Preference Curve intersecting a vertical Supply of Money, has to be considered highly misleading.

So, in spite of its widespread popularity, Aggregate Demand–Aggregate Supply analysis rests on remarkably problematical foundations. Both its reliance on the real balance effect and on marginal productivity theory suggest that it is not suitable for the analysis of advanced capitalist economies.

NEO-WALRASIAN THEORY

But 'middlebrow' theory does not have to stand on its own; it is developed – like the 'Surrogate Production Function' – as a parable to present and explain the implications of 'highbrow' theory, in a form that will allow for empirical studies and for the drawing of policy conclusions. So even if Aggregate Demand–Aggregate Supply theory is flawed, it might nevertheless be useful as a shorthand way of allowing us to draw on the implications of full-blown neo-Walrasian theory. This was surely what many had hoped.

But these hopes have not been fulfilled. Indeed an unkind critic might suggest that neo-Walrasian theory seems almost to have self-destructed. It aims at establishing general equilibrium; agents form their plans on the basis of their preferences, the technologies available and in the light of the given initial endowments. Preferences and technologies are assumed convex. There are complete futures markets, so plans encompass the distant future as well as the immediate. Nothing happens until all plans are reconciled; there is no 'false trading.' Once plans are reconciled and action begins, everything that happens follows the script; there is no room for learning, for innovation or for changing one's mind. It can be shown that, in general, an economically meaningful equilibrium exists in conditions of perfect competition.

Unfortunately it is usually the case that more than one exists, often infinitely many more. And it has not been possible, in general, to demonstrate stability except on extremely restrictive and implausible grounds. How can multiple equilibria – some or all of which may be unstable in fully competitive conditions – provide a basis for understanding the economy or a foundation for macroeconomics? And it is plainly *not* the case that Aggregate Demand–Aggregate Supply theory is just a simple version of highbrow General Equilibrium theory. On the contrary, AD–AS models tend to have unique and stable equilibria, even if they have other imperfections of various kinds.

Nevertheless a defender of the approach could argue that non-uniqueness and instability represent technical problems. Sufficiently strong assumptions can be found to assure uniqueness and stability, but they lack economic justification. More work is needed to find the right assumptions. Success may seem unlikely after so many decades, but it was also unlikely that Fermat's Last Theorem would be proved. So let us suppose that these 'technical' problems can be overcome, rendering neo-Walrasian theory capable of providing us with a unique and stable set of equilibrium prices and quantities – our 'microfoundations.' What kind of macro theory can be built on these foundations?

Institutions in Neo-Walrasian Theory

In fact, it will not be easy to build anything useful. Earlier we provisionally defined macroeconomics in terms of the interaction of firms, households, capital markets and the monetary system, all regulated by government. But neo-Walrasian theory is hard-put to make room for any of these. They are institutions; neo-Walrasian theory deals with abstract agents. This in itself is not necessarily a problem. The difficulties come when we try to introduce the characteristic features of these institutions into the neo-Walrasian model. Let's take them one by one, starting with what is possibly the most egregious failing – money.

Money

Neo-Walrasian models simply have no role for money. All transactions are 'pre-coordinated' by the auctioneer; no trades take place until equilibrium has been established. When the time comes for transactions, suppliers deliver goods to the 'chamber of settlements,' where demanders pick them up. Accounts are kept and, since in equilibrium all budget constraints are satisfied, the accounts will always balance. There is no need for a unit of account, since any good can serve as numeraire, and prices in any one numeraire can readily be converted to any other. There is no need for a medium of circulation, since nothing circulates; goods are simply delivered and picked up. There is no need for a special store of value, since anything durable stores value, and no value need be stored, except as determined by intertemporal optimizing. There is no evident need for credit.

If paper money were to be issued either by a bank or a government, there is no reason to suppose it will attain a positive value in the market (Hahn, 1985).

Firms

Next consider firms themselves. In competitive equilibrium the market allocates optimally and ensures the best use of resources. Why then should some resources be allocated bureaucratically by managers of firms when every activity that is coordinated by management should ideally be coordinated by the market? The answer that has been given, of course, is that, because 'transactions costs' would be too high, it would not pay to break firms up. While transactions costs are important and undoubtedly part of any explanation of firms, they can hardly be the full or only explanation. How do transactions costs explain a multi-divisional hierarchy? Have these hierarchies begun to change because transactions costs have been changing, or because of changes in management technology, for example, in communications and computers? In any event, how do we account for industries in which there are a few large firms and many small ones? How do transactions costs explain the (approximately) log-normal distribution of firm sizes?

The idea that firms are 'explained' by the existence of 'transactions costs' – to a large extent postulated, rather than measured – amounts to saying that firms and corporations, large and small, are the consequence of a more or less unavoidable *imperfection* in the market.

Households

Households might seem to pose similar difficulties. If the members of a household transact with each other, they must either prefer domestic inefficiency to the rigors of market competition, or there must be sufficient transactions costs to make it worth while. But here we face a new issue. Time series data for many countries over many decades has established the validity of Engel Curves; it is probably the best confirmed relationship in the whole area of household budgets. Yet conventional preference theory offers no useful insight whatsoever into this phenomenon. Moreover the relationships that conventional theory tries to justify, making up the life-cycle theory or the related permanent income theory, do not appear to be confirmed by the data. The simple 'stripped-down' versions are clearly wrong; more elaborate versions contain many ad hoc modifications. The whole approach is problematical. In fact as we all know from our own experience, 'wants' are complex: households have to *learn* to consume, people must learn how to use complex products. (For example, we are licensed to drive; we have electricity, gas and plumbing installed in the home by licensed technicians; we must learn to use computers and VCRs.) Only after we have acquired the appropriate skills can we decide how a complex product fits into our 'preferences.'

Production technology

In general, microfoundations are grounded on convex technologies; in 'middlebrow' models it is usual to assume diminishing returns. 'Highbrow' models may feature fixed coefficient techniques – constant returns though the normal assumption is that switches of technique will trace out a relation of rising capital intensity associated with falling rates of return. Diminishing returns at the margin may well have been a feature of craft technologies, but they do not figure in mass production. High-tech sectors of today's advanced economies are characterized by network externalities and increasing returns. But even constant returns cause difficulties in neoclassical models; increasing returns cannot be brought in without giving up central aspects of the scarcity framework.

Moreover, it is arguable that the entire approach misinterprets and understates the true flexibility of the system. Productive capacity is not 'given' once and for all. Production and productivity both respond to pressure. Like a great athlete, the system delivers when the chips are down, when the pressure is on. The more that is demanded of it, the more it produces – and the greater the pressure, the lower, not the higher, the unit cost. This is arguably what is captured in the Verdoorn–Kaldor Laws.

Labor and employment

Unions are an imperfection, or the result of imperfections. In a fully competitive neoclassical market, 'Labor can hire capital just as easily as capital can hire labor.' Everything turns on prices. So if wages were perfectly flexible downward, there would be and there could be no unemployment. This implies that there are no firm-specific skills, no long-run employment and no established teamwork. There are no employees who are part of the firm. That is, the market works through workers being hired for wages; there are no issues of promotion and transfer, no 'internal' labor markets.

Capital markets

According to conventional neo-Walrasian thinking, the value of a firm is independent of its debt–equity ratio. The composition of its capital does not matter. But this implies that no useful purpose is served in equilibrium by having different kinds of securities, such as bonds and stocks and, presumably, derivatives. The requirement that borrowers have independent collateral cannot be explained in neo-Walrasian theory. In the neoclassical framework, savings are assembled from households by banks and channeled to investors through the capital market. In fact most investment is internally financed. Buy-backs outweigh new equity issues.

Government

Neo-Walrasian theory must find it difficult to provide a purpose or justification for government. The system reaches equilibrium, which is optimal, without considering government, although presumably some protection for property and some way of enforcing contracts is implied. But there is nothing explicit, so there is no basis on which to develop an explanation for the size of government or the composition of its activities. 'Public choice' theory tries to explain government by the presumed maximizing activities of bureaucrats, but fails to explain why these succeed more in some eras than in others.

To pose the challenge in a nutshell: Mainstream theory, based on the neo-Walrasian approach, cannot explain why the size of government in relation to GDP increased dramatically, perhaps fivefold, all over the advanced world in the middle of the twentieth century.

Thus it seems that neo-Walrasian 'microfoundations' cannot be provided. To put it another way, the normal working of contemporary economic institutions cannot be accommodated within that approach, and since those are the institutions that interact to determine macroeconomic outcomes, macro theory cannot be 'grounded' on neo-Walrasian micro.

The Appeal to 'Realism' and Market 'Imperfection'

This seems a drastic conclusion. Perhaps we could just 'improve' the neo-Walrasian approach by 'adding' institutions or making more realistic assumptions?

The basic problem, however, seems to lie in the approach itself, the underlying vision of scarcity and optimal allocation. If equilibrium – of prices and quantities – is defined by the optimal allocation of scarce resources, then unemployment is impossible in equilibrium. The market is supposed to reach equilibrium; hence if markets were working properly, they would tend to eliminate unemployment, automatically. But they do not. Yet it seems unreasonable to say that markets are never working properly and that the only way this picture could be improved or made more 'realistic,' while remaining within the neo-Walrasian framework, would be to introduce 'imperfections' – which would then imply that markets do *not* work properly.

Moreover, the idea of 'adding' institutions to the neo-Walrasian model is a little strange. *Without* them the competitive market reaches an optimal position. So it would seem that they cannot be added for economic reasons – it's hard to improve on optimality! Institutions seem to be defined as market imperfections, arangements entered into for non-economic reasons that will prevent markets from adjusting optimally.

Nevertheless it may be that there are some costs, overlooked by the model, that institutions might plausibly be thought to manage. Transactions costs are often invoked at this point, and it is claimed that institutions make it possible to reduce or avoid these costs (although at the expense of introducing imperfections into the market). Yet this idea is awkward. It suggests that small family firms develop into giant corporations because the bureaucracy can reduce transactions costs. Surely bureaucracies are themselves costly. Is the implausible claim that small government grows into big government in order to manage transactions better? To take the objection one step further: Imperfections and transactions costs were surely larger in the era of the craft economy, when communications were poorer and transporation slower, than they are today. But government was smaller then and business was conducted largely by family firms, rather than giant corporations (Nell, 1998a, 1998b).

The appeal to 'realism' is not likely to offer much help either. If it is taken seriously, the entire set of assumptions will have to be revised. Corporations will replace small family firms; internal labor markets will have to be considered; everything will have to be set out in money terms, with a banking system based on Chartalist money; household preferences will depend on learning; government will be large and important. As for the basic data of endowments, technologies and preferences – endowments, themselves dependent on the state of technology, will be endogenous in the long run; technology will show constant or increasing returns, and will depend on investment in education and innovation; preferences will depend on learning and technology; networks will be important for both consumption and production. Moving towards realism appears simply to undermine the whole approach. But perhaps it was not always so.

The True Role of Neo-Walrasian Theory

As a result of its assumptions, Neo-Walrasian theory *must* determine employment and output from the supply side. Its chosen problem is the determination of the optimal allocation of resources from the preferences, endowments and available technology for a given number of agents. In this framework, underutilized resources or involuntary unemployment simply represent a misallocation; they are a logical mistake. Similarly inflation *must* be due to excess nominal demand, since there is no way that it can be the outcome of an optimal allocation. But if the supply of money is given at the outset, it will be properly allocated so that, given the factors that fix velocity, the price level will be fixed. Hence it appears that the only source of inflation must be exogenously created money.

Assumptions and approach largely fix the outcome. Yet the neo-Walrasian approach can be seen to lack any foundation in reality. The Walrasian model, as we have just seen, is inconsistent with the basic institutions of the modern economy, so it cannot provide 'foundations' for a macro theory of today's economy. But this was not always so. There was a time when its assumptions and functions as a model corresponded rather well with the way the world worked. Most output, for example, was produced in small family firms or on small farms[8] (Nell, 1998b). Markets were competitive. Households had simple preferences. Returns did diminish. Prices were flexible. Output and employment were less flexible than prices or wages. Real wages moved inversely to employment and output. Money was exogenous (in the short run); the Classical Dichotomy held. There was little or no inflation. Governments were small. Indeed these assumptions provided a reasonable description of the system in the time of Walras and Marshall, the time when the theory was first developed.

Thus at one time it may have been that the price mechanism did work, more or less. The basic textbook assumptions are reflective of their era. The textbooks assume, just as once was the case, that the market consists of many small firms, each facing diminishing returns in production, and selling to independent households with endowments. Just as there once were many small self-sufficient farmers who traded with and also worked for each other, and businesses whose profit income was distributed, saved and invested, rather than retained and ploughed back. The textbooks assume universal access to credit, that is, no credit rationing. This was never the case, but self-sufficient farmers have land, and craftsmen have their place of work and tools, which can provide collateral. The textbooks assume that labor markets are external matters of supply and demand, not internal matters of competing for promotions. All these features of the system – competitive markets, the price mechanism, small government, neutrality of money, the Classical Dichotomy, simple well-defined preferences – make some sense as a simplified description of nineteenth-century capitalism, although they are wholly inappropriate in the late twentieth century, let alone in the twenty-first century.

Implications of the Change from Craft-based to Mass Production

In short, macroeconomics must be understood as based on such institutions, but, in addition, it is important to see that these institutions themselves have changed and developed over the past century. Particularly important to acknowledge are the changes in a technology that developed from a craft-based system with diminishing returns to a system of mass production, based on constant or sometimes increasing returns. Moreover, it appears perhaps to be changing again.

In particular, demand fluctuations lead to profit fluctuations in craft-based systems, for craft technology tends to have inflexible employment – all workers have to be present in order for anything to get done. There are only two feasible operating positions – full-out, or shut down. Thus there are strong incentives to make this much more flexible. And this is one of the features of mass production: flexible employment. Many different levels of operation are possible; start-up and shut-down costs are small (Nell, 1998a, 1998b). This leads to multiplier-accelerator adjustments through patterns of 'cumulative causation.' For example, layoffs of workers reduce household spending, which, in turn, reduces business receipts, leading to further layoffs and further reductions in household spending. With unused capacity increasing, businesses will cut back on investment spending, leading to further layoffs, and so on. The same process will work more or less the same way in an expansion.

The change from craft to mass production brought about new developments in every one of the above areas. Here it is possible only to sketch the changes, but the implication should be clear. The neo-Walrasian assumptions are close to the actual conditions of the craft economy of the period in which Marshall and Walras developed their ideas. But the modern economy is very different, and its markets adjust according to different principles. The craft economy adjusted through a price mechanism, the mass production economy adjusts through a multiplier-accelerator process. Now we can consider the list of institutions reviewed earlier.

Money

The monetary system changed from one based on the intrinsic value of precious metals in which bank credit was constrained by reserves, to one in which a mixture of government fiat and bank credit serves as the medium of circulation, with no anchor, and where reserves chiefly function as clearing balances.

Firms

The business system changed from one dominated by family firms and family farms to one dominated by modern corporations. Small firms remained, but accounted for an ever-decreasing percentage of GNP.

Households

Households evolved from nuclear families embedded in kinship networks performing considerable domestic production, to isolated nuclear families performing little domestic production.

Technology

In the craft economy, diminishing returns probably prevailed over a wide range of activities, both in regard to the short and the long run. Skills were learned at home and passed on from generation to generation. Under mass production, constant returns apply to utilization over a wide range, while constant or increasing returns probably apply to new construction. Network externalities are widespread in some sectors, learning is important everywhere and technology is as important in household and consumer activities as anywhere else.

Employment

Employment in craft conditions tended to be fairly stable, except in times of severe crisis when the firm would close its doors. Output varied more, implying that productivity rose in booms and fell in slumps. Under mass production the 'layoff' system developed in which firms would systematically vary output, at roughly constant productivity, by varying employment, laying off employees in reverse order of seniority, hiring back in order of seniority.

Capital markets

In the craft era, capital markets were dominated by government and railroad bonds; the stock market was small. Initially issuing equity was an alternative way to raise funds. With the rise of mass production, the stock market grew and changed character, while bonds diversified greatly. Today, the equity market is primarily concerned with corporate control, and securitization has led to the proliferation of derivatives.

Government

In the craft era, governments were small, near or even under 5 per cent of GNP, apart from wartime. Transfers were small, apart from war pensions. Under mass production, government spending at all levels, including transfers, has greatly increased to over a third of GNP, and even higher in other advanced economies. The activities of government have grown and diversified.

The Classical Long-run Price Equations as a Setting for Macro

So neo-Walrasian theory is unsuited for today. But macro theory is concerned with quantities and monetary demand. Where, then, should we turn for an understanding of prices?

The first question is, why do we need a theory of prices? Partly, of course, because of aggregation: quantities of disparate goods have to be added up and value streams from different sectors have to be compared. But there is a deeper level, too. In the long run, given normal conditions, employment will be offered only if it is expected that resulting production can be sold profitably. Profits, however, depend among other things on wages and prices. How are we to account for profits, wages and prices?

Certainly not with models with no focus on the relevant variables. The basic neoclassical general equilibrium model is short run and does not contain a variable for the rate of profit! More aggregate models take a long-run perspective and explain the rate of profits as the marginal product of capital, the wage as the marginal product of labor. Though this at least addresses the problem, the approach has been shown to be hopelessly defective[9] (Laibman and Nell, 1977; Nell, 1992; Garegnani, 1970; Kurz and Salvadori, 1995).

To understand the way the economy works in the long run we need to relate exchange to production and distribution. Goods and services are produced, using goods and services as inputs. More goods and services are produced in a given period of time than are used up or consumed in the (directly and indirectly) necessary processes of production. Such 'surplus' goods and services may serve to provide public services, might be turned into support for the poor or made into luxuries for the few or could be invested to expand the system. But an effective model of these basic long-term relationships will provide the stage for the drama of the short run and the business cycle.

To put the issues of employment, inflation and effective demand in a proper setting, we need a theory of *reproduction*; we need to know how the system will be able to maintain and reproduce itself. What material conditions have to be filled for an economy with given institutions to be able to carry on for another period? What has to be done for capital to remain intact, for firms to avoid bankruptcy, for households to survive at the same standard of living, for banks to stay afloat? And what must be done if this system is to expand at a certain rate? We have defined macroeconomics as the way a given set of economic institutions interact in the market to determine employment and output. Fine. But what conditions on relative prices and relative outputs does the system have to meet in order for it to continue operating in the same way? (Note that many of these conditions are likely to be embedded in money contracts, so the question is not fanciful.)

The answer will lie in a set of relative prices and quantities, derived from the classical equations (the neo-Ricardian system), which will provide relatively stable values by which to form macroeconomic aggregates. These relative values and relative quantities, however, still leave the Keynesian question of the *scale* of employment and output open. Hence they form a solid foundation for macroeconomics.

But a theory of *reproduction*, combined with markets, implies that the system will evolve. For reproduction will not ever be exact. At the very least, there will be accidental variations. And there will be a drive to improve products and reduce costs; this will be ensured by competition. Then the market will act as a selector, picking the best innovations. So the system can be expected to evolve over time.

Far from macro being based on the more 'fundamental' micro, the two might better be considered pictures of different market systems. 'Micro' describes the ways that craft markets operate, 'macro' the ways mass production markets adjust. But production systems must reproduce themselves, and in doing so they change; so over time the craft economy has developed into mass production, and the price mechanism has given way to the multiplier-accelerator.

SUMMING IT UP

Neither conclusions about how the system works nor policies to regulate it can be derived from Walrasian models. The picture the Walrasian system presents is *fundamentally* misleading: the modern macro economy does not adjust through a price mechanism. Indeed it has no self-regulating features at all – except in the government budget! And its monetary system is no longer based on any kind of 'backing,' except the 'full faith and credit' of the US Government. There are no longer any real reserves; reserves are created by the Federal Reserve as needed. Policies have to be based on these facts; it has to be understood that the size and character of the government are fundamentally different from what they were in an earlier era.

To put it briefly, for the purposes of this volume: Sound finance and balanced budgets were appropriate policies in the craft economy, but Functional Finance is appropriate to the economy of mass production and big government. Small government made sense in the older system; big government is necessary in the Post-World War II era. Sound money required backing in the older system; money is created and managed in the modern world.

All this is well known. It was first set out and developed by the early Keynesians, notably Abba Lerner, Alvin Hansen and their successors, such as Robert Eisner, Richard Musgrave and James Duesenberry. One might think it should hardly need repeating today. Yet not so long ago the Secretary of the US Treasury declared in a talk here at the New School that deficits were dangerous because they would drive up interest rates and crowd out productive investment. Now we hear from Democrats that the surplus must be defended, and from Republicans that government must be downsized. The message has been lost, buried under an avalanche of misspecified macro models. It is time, now, to rescue these insights and reinvent the approach.

NOTES

1. Lumping New Keynesians together with New Classicals? Stiglitz with Lucas? Well, of course not. They differ in all sorts of ways. But there are certain respects in which their models are similar. They share assumptions about individual agents and rationality and they agree that macroeconomics must rest on 'microfoundations.' Hahn and Solow (1995) advance devastating criticisms of the New Classical approach – but they do so within a modeling framework that permits almost no institutional detail.
2. 'Capitalism' therefore should not be treated as simply an 'ideological' word, devoid of serious analytical meaning. On the contrary, it designates a systematic way of arranging rights, claims and obligations with regard to production and distribution, a different way from that of feudalism, or mercantilism or indeed, socialism, with which it is most often compared. The employment relationship is crucially different in capitalism, a point that can be overlooked when skittishness about ideological words has turned investigators away from exploring the differences between alternative systems of arranging production and distributing claims.
3. Methodological individualism, of course, claims with Lady Thatcher, that institutions can be 'reduced to,' that is, explained in, terms of individuals. The truth of this claim is certainly not obvious and many attempts to demonstrate it have failed. One important reason to dismiss it is that 'individuals' are themselves *produced by* institutions, namely families. People are born into families, and are raised and socialized by them, and by other institutions like schools and churches (Lawson, 1998; Nell, 1998a, Chs 3 and 4).
4. In addition to the well-known technical problems discussed above, there are severe conceptual difficulties in this approach. Preferences depend not only on technology, but also on previously acquired skills. Think of driving, of programming a VCR, of using a computer. Preferences for kitchenware depend on cooking skills. Endowments also depend on technology. Technical progress therefore is difficult to handle.
5. There is a 'highbrow' version of these wealth effects, developed by Patinkin (1965). The claim is that when utility functions are redefined to include them, the resulting model 'integrates' value theory and monetary theory, overcoming the 'Classical Dichotomy.' The ambition is laudable, the execution less so (see Lloyd, 1964; Nell, 1992 pp. 606–7 for critical discussion).
6. This version of the story suggests that Aggregate Supply is a vertical line; a substantial body

of analysis has been devoted to justifying an upward-sloping supply relationship between output and the price level or employment and the price level. Virtually all of the suggestions depend on one or another kind of 'market imperfection' and could easily strike a disinterested observer as ad hoc.

7. A purely logical problem may be worth mentioning: when a level of employment has been determined, the production function and marginal productivity theory imply a rate of return on the capital stock, its marginal product. The rate of interest, however, is equated to the *marginal efficiency of capital*, that is, to the rate of return expected on new investment. There is nothing in the model to bring these two rates together – in the short run we might expect them to differ. Yet if they do differ, then we should expect *funds* to flow to purchase *titles* to the more profitable types of capital assets. This is consistent with short-run adjustment. Suppose the marginal product of existing capital is greater than the marginal efficiency of new. Then new saving and depreciation funds will flow to finance the purchase of shares in existing companies, rather than to finance the setting up of new; in the opposite case, funds would flow to new investment, and the scrapping rate would rise. This is inconsistent with short-run equilibrium (Nell, 1992, Ch. 25; 1998, Ch. 12).
8. Such firms were seldom bureaucratic. The proprietor decided to 'hire capital,' since he was optimistic about his abilities. But given appropriate circumstances, he might shut down his own firm and offer his services to another.
9. The inverse relationship between the rate of profit and the value of capital cannot, in general, be constructed given a set of alternative techniques of production and alternative divisions of income between wages and profits. For a recent discussion, including reflections on why the economics profession has tended to try to sweep this anomalous and unsettling result under the carpet, see Pasinetti (2001).

REFERENCES

Garegnani, Piero (1970), 'Heterogeneous capital, the production function and the theory of distribution', *Review of Economic Studies*, 37: 407–36.

Hahn, Frank (1985), *Money, Growth and Stability*, Cambridge, MA: MIT Press.

Hahn, F. and Solow, Robert (1995), *A Critical Essay on Modern Macroeconomic Theory*, Cambridge, MA: MIT Press.

Kurz, H. and Salvadori, N. (1995), *Theory of Production*, Cambridge: Cambridge University Press.

Laibman, D and Nell, Edward (1977), 'Reswitching, Wicksell Effects, and the neoclassical production function,' *American Economic Review*, 63: 100–13.

Lloyd, Cliff (1964), 'The real balance effect and the Slutsky equation', *Journal of Political Economy*, 72 (June).

Lawson, Tony (1998), *Economics and Reality*, London and New York: Routledge.

Mankiw, N.G. and D. Romer (1993), *New Keynesian Economics*, vols. 1 and 2, Cambridge, MA: MIT Press.

Nell, Edward (1992), *Transformational Growth and Effective Demand*, New York: New York University Press.

Nell, E.J. (1988a), *The General Theory of Transformational Growth*, Cambridge: Cambridge University Press.

Nell, E.J. (1988b), *Transformational Growth and the Business Cycle*, London and New York: Routledge.

Pasinetti, L.L. (2001), 'The principle of effective demand and its relevance to the long run', *Journal of Post Keynesian Economics*, **23**(3) 383–90.

Patinkin, Don (1965), *Money, Interest and Prices*, 2nd edn., New York: Harper and Row.

Interlude I

OPENING REMARKS

Richard A. Musgrave

I have been asked to say a few words about my life in public finance, an addiction that by now has extended for over 70 years. Throughout I have drawn on three diverse traditions: German *Finanzwissenschaft*; British thought from Smith, to Mill to Pigou; and Wicksell's and Lindahl's Scandinavian model. When I came to the United States from Germany in 1933, I had already studied economics for three years in Munich and Heidelberg. The former was a city I chose in anticipation of opera and skiing and the latter was the site of a then recent renaissance in fiscal thought. The classical German *Finanzwissenschaft* of Stein and Wagner, with its emphasis on the state as decision maker, had reached its high point in the 1880s and 1890s but thereafter had gone dormant. At that time, that tradition was revived in Heidelberg's INSOSTA Institute. Gerhard Colm's work continued the Wagner tradition; Pfleiderer brought national income analysis into the picture; Sultan resumed Joseph Schumpeter's interest in fiscal sociology; and Ritschl related back to Müller's and Spann's very German concept of a romantic vision of community. So as a student in Germany I was well aware of the German public finance tradition.

That tradition was not unfamiliar to earlier American authors, such as Adams and Seligman who had both studied in Germany, but it was quite alien to the English fiscal theorists from Smith on. Most important, English authors were unfamiliar with the Austrian and Scandinavian contributions of Sax and Wicksell who, in the 1880s and 1890s, linked marginal utility theory with fiscal process. Knowing these various traditions, while still being young enough to come to the States and combine them with English fiscal theory, gave me a comparative advantage unavailable perhaps to older immigrant scholars who had to leave behind their well-formed past and adapt to a new world.

In America my interest in the micro aspects of public finance continued, along with the key role assigned by Keynesian economics to the macro function of fiscal policy, a new concern that soon came to dominate the stage of economics during my years as a graduate student. That side of public finance was quite new to me and I responded with great interest and enthusiasm. As you may gather from my writings, I have always considered public finance to have multidimensions distributed between three major functions: provision for public goods in its Allocation Branch; concern with equity and distributive justice in its Distribution Branch; and responsibility for maintaining full employment and price stability in its Stabilization Branch.

Prior to Hitler's coming to power, I had the good fortune of being awarded a fellowship from the German Student Exchange, and was thus able to leave for the United States just in time. I spent my first year at the University of Rochester where I read Mill, Marshall, and Pigou. In 1934 I went on to Harvard where I was given a Holtzer Fellowship. Apart from the standard graduate work, my continuing interest and thesis theme focused on how individuals as citizens could best join in common pursuits not manageable by the market, and how this could be accomplished through the budget. The nature of public goods was at the core of the problem and the opportunity to discuss it with Paul Samuelson, a fellow graduate student, was most helpful. I also like to think that my interest in that theme and acquaintance with the European literature contributed to the seminal articles on the theory of public expenditures that appeared in the mid-1950s.

My central concern with the micro aspects of the budget extended into my thesis, but I shared equal interest in the new aspects of fiscal theory that had been raised by the Keynesian model. That side of public finance was something quite new. Alvin Hansen, who arrived at Harvard the following year, became my main mentor in that field, but before discussing that relationship, let me add a word about Schumpeter's unique presence. He was a great and fascinating figure but, in those years at Harvard, out of his time and place. I was impressed with his sweeping perspective on the scenes of economics and social issues. And though he was always very kind to me, I always felt a bit *unheimlich* in his presence – a bit like Wagner the student when addressed by Mephistopheles posing as Professor Faust. Schumpeter was a middle European intellectual who did not understand the New Deal world around him that, in turn, did not understand him. His time would have to wait for today's world, but he occupied that territory too soon. Not surprisingly the closest person to him was Paul Sweezey who, as a Marxist, could communicate with Schumpeter's reciprocal image of that creed. While Schumpeter admired Samuelson's brilliance, he never became a close part of our intellectual circle.

I respected Schumpeter, especially in his lectures on economic doctrine, but the person I admired most was Alvin Hansen. If Schumpeter was the European intellectual, Hansen was the American pragmatist and reformer, a totally different type that I found most appealing. When coming from Germany, I had left behind me many hopes with the breakdown of the Weimar Republic.

Thinking back to my high school years in the 1920s and into the early 1930s, I realize that my friends and I had been dreaming of a democratic Germany instead of the failure which is now remembered. Rather, the Weimar Republic seemed to us a time of promise for German democracy and perhaps one of the most creative periods in Germany's cultural history. Leaving, therefore, was not easy, but coming to share the spirit of America's New Deal years offered the promise that had been lost.

Roosevelt's leadership was a great experience. There was great enthusiasm and a sense that things could be done and progress made. The thought was that economics should be about meeting people's needs and improving their welfare. Hansen, with his straightforward and down-to-earth approach to policy problems, precisely fit that image. Whether or not all the policies would prove successful, I greatly admired the spirit in which they were approached, without vanity and without viewing economic analysis as an intellectual exercise to be enjoyed for its own sake. Twenty years later, when teaching at Michigan in the 1950s, I joined a painting group once a week, led by various members of the Art Department. One evening when I was not doing serious work, the professor came behind me and said, 'I don't play around with your economics, so don't play around with my medium.' I never forgot that counsel, and that was precisely the way Hansen was – there was no playing around with economics. It was there to solve problems as was the spirit of Keynesian economics that had just arrived in Cambridge.

Along with this atmosphere, I had the company of an outstanding group of graduate students assembled in Hansen's seminar on fiscal policy. The leading member was Samuelson who had a genius for driving economics forward and setting things straight – one by one – seemingly, right through the whole science. He was generous with his fellow students even if equally ungenerous with his teachers, especially when they were not as smart as he. Lloyd Metzler was another figure who, had he not become ill, might have had a great impact. There were many other notable people as well – the two Salants, Henry Wallich, Abe Bergson, Ben Higgins, Robert Triffin: an outstanding group.

John Williams, then Dean at Littauer, also attended, bringing with him his contact with monetary policy from his association with the New York Federal Reserve Bank. Though not a Keynesian, he served as a constructive critic, as did Professor Haberler. There probably has never been so fruitful a time and place to be a graduate student in economics (except perhaps the Chicago of Frank Knight!) as those years at Harvard. It was as though economics had been set straight and reinvented. First there came Joan Robinson, followed by Ed Chamberlin with their analysis of perfect markets, and then came Keynes who did the same on the macro level. There also was the introduction of the social welfare function, showing that Robbins, after all, had not quite buried the idea of welfare economics when questioning the validity of interpersonal utility comparisons. Everything in the field seemed in the process of being fixed up and we were part of it. This is the way you want to feel as you complete your doctorate, with plenty of time later on for reconsideration.

Understanding Keynes at that time was a challenge, unlike later when its core was reduced to a few textbook pages. The notion of an equilibrating macro system that could be reduced to a relatively small number of key functions and need not come to rest at full employment was new. The new tools of consumption function, liquidity preference and investment functions – later neatly joined in Hick's IS–LM model – had to be sorted out and understood. How would this equilibrating process move, seen from *ex ante* and *ex post* perspectives? Even the multiplier concept was a somewhat mysterious creation, not to mention Samuelson's addition of the accelerator. All this was very novel and fascinating and not self-evident.

These concepts were discussed and worked through very carefully, mixed in with the urgency of policies to overcome the Depression. Pending policy developments were explored, including the appearance of the Beveridge Report and the creation of the Social Security system. Hansen was closely associated with the questions as to whether Social Security should be based on a pay-as-you-go or a vested system. Behind all of this were a few key relationships that moved the macro economy. Derived from individual behavior, the system was far from lacking a micro foundation, as later argued by its critics. That foundation existed but its working out in an optimal fashion might be interfered with by the shapes of these functions and other snags in the system.

The mistake, rather, was to see key functions as locked into a form yielding continuing stagnation of employment and economic growth. Keynes, from his earlier years on, might well have enjoyed showing that the market need not function that nicely, a view that could be corrected later on. But this was not true of Hansen who then viewed a stagnationist future as embedded in population decline and lack of technical progress, an unavoidable consequence that conditioned the future of the economic system. This, in turn, limited Hansen's view of the Keynesian system. As restated later in the neoclassical version of the 1950s and 1960s, a model very similar to that used with a depressed setting could be used to deal with an economy of high employment and inflation. In fact, much the same model – but with more attention to expectations and wealth effect on consumption – continues to provide the foundation for the present conduct of a macro policy conditioned by a fiscal policy determined by the politics of budget size.

After receiving my degree at Harvard in 1937 and teaching there for several years, I moved to Washington DC and spent the 1940s at the Federal Reserve Board as a fiscal economist. Hansen was also there, as well as Haberler, Machlup and Harris who served as regular consultants. There was an elevator in the building that went from the first floor to the cafeteria and it was joked that the war effort was held up when Haberler and Machlup, in their Viennese politeness, could not decide who should enter first. Economists are helpful but not in all ways.

Seymour Harris arranged for frequent Fed seminars, Keynes and Hicks being among the visitors. I recall Keynes, in an exchange with Abba Lerner and Evsay Domar, taking an upbeat, non-stagnationist outlook on the postwar scene. Towards the end of my Fed years, I worked as special assistant to Marriner Eccles, the controversial Chairman of the Board, amateur Keynesian and a major New Deal figure. Helping write his testimony and going with him to hearings gave me a vivid impression of interaction with the congressional scene. In all, the Fed years offered the hands-on experience essential to any academic concerned with public policy.

But I wanted to return to teaching and to my work on tying together the various aspects of fiscal theory in a coherent view of the public sector and a theory of public finance. The decade of the 1950s, spent at Ann Arbor's University of Michigan, offered a splendid haven for that purpose. I returned to thinking about the nature of public goods and how it had to be developed along two lines – one, Samuelson's efficiency conditions, and the other, Wicksell's concern with how to overcome the free rider problem and secure preference revelation, thereby linking fiscal theory to voting and the political process. This offered a first look at what was to be dealt with 70 years later under the heading of 'public choice,' although in a rather less positive spirit than Wicksell's. Another major focus of my work was the structure of the income tax: the definition of a broad base in the Henry Simons tradition of accretion and vertical equity in setting the rate structure. A further important development of that period was the emergence of cost–benefit analysis and project appraisal, indicating the important contribution made by technicians to the design of public policy. My guiding thought through all this was the search for a consistent logic of public policy as applied to its fiscal process, a logic that would differ from that of the market but nevertheless offer a consistent and complementary system. I was not aware of the difficulties and imperfections that public policy, as conducted in practice, would encounter. My main concern was to show how consistent and meaningful policy could be developed, and how essential is its contribution to the democratic process. Unless correct solutions are understood, not even errors can be adequately identified.

The appearance of my book on the theory of public finance in 1959 was followed by a few years spent at Johns Hopkins and Princeton University. I returned to Harvard in 1964. My writing and teaching continued along its earlier lines, combined with the conduct of tax missions in various parts of the world. The rise of optimal taxation in the 1970s, with its more rigorous focus on the efficiency aspects of taxation, offered a new perspective on tax equity and distributive justice. Though restraining the case for progressive taxation, it remained only one of the factors to be considered in the design of a social welfare function. The fiscal policy seminar, which I then offered jointly with Martin Feldstein, returned me to an old setting though in a rather different analytical and political climate. My interests also returned to the broader issues of the fiscal system and the role of the state, involving sociological dimensions and the linkage of fiscal equity to the broader philosophical problems of distributive justice raised in the early 1970s so challengingly by John Rawls. I can report that a seminar that I offered along these lines was not just an aging scholar's return to an old fancy, but a rather successful venture in the closing years of my teaching. Along with this, my joint appointment with the Law School at Harvard kept me in contact with the technical aspects of income taxation, as well as with the emerging doctrine of economics and law.

In closing, you will not be surprised to hear me say that the present state of fiscal thought is not altogether to my liking. The size of the budget, as I see it, must not be minimized and apologized for but established at the right level. Issues of distribution inherently involve conflicts, but these should be met rather than shunned. Placing the active use of fiscal policy in cold storage involves a lost instrument and 'paying off the debt' is not the ultimate goal. Was all our work, though stimulating and fun, of that little consequence? I do not think so. Lasting contributions were made and their presence will continue to be felt. Moreover, even if this is not the case, it is worth while as a matter of intellectual history for good thoughts to have been thought.

INTRODUCTION

Robert L. Heilbroner

I

It is a pleasure as well as a privilege to be asked to say a few words at this cerebration – (a glance into *Webster's Dictionary* will make it clear that my spelling is not in error) – of Edward Nell's pioneering work on transformational growth. I say this not because I am qualified as a judge with respect to all the matters on which Nell has shed light, but because I have had some experience in dealing with the problem of economic conceptualization itself, a problem that is also part of Nell's larger contribution, including, not least, that of growth that transforms.

Let me then begin by describing briefly how I came to have such an odd interest in economics in 'itself.' My education began at Harvard University, not quite two-thirds of a century ago, when I found myself in the midst of what seemed to be an explosive change in the basic concepts that defined the very field I was trying to understand. I have never forgotten an impassioned intra-departmental debate at Harvard's Dunster House with regard to Keynes's *General Theory*. I was, of course, an all-out Keynesian, along with the greater part of the student body, but it was apparent that the ground on which the faculty stood was shaking under its feet.

Yet in retrospect, it is clear that what seemed an unbridgeable conceptual leap was not so definitive as we then thought. Indeed, within a few years, Keynesianism had taken on the plain clothes of macroeconomics, cheerfully sharing virtually every textbook with a distillation of the economics I had learned five years earlier, now called microeconomics.

To be sure, while learning about supply and demand and *ex post*, *ex ante*, I had become aware that there did exist other conceptions of 'economics,' some of which traveled under the name of Political Economy. This was a description that the faculty, almost without exception, made clear did not pertain to our classroom readings. There were a few exceptions: I had Paul Sweezy as my tutor for a semester and we read Thorstein Veblen because Paul quite rightly said I was not ready for Marx. And of course, I knew Adam Smith's name and intended one day to read his book. I had also heard of Ricardo, peeked into Mill, and read *The Manifesto* behind Paul's back.

Yet I think it is fair to say that I was quite blind to a control feature of classical political economy – namely its lurking sense – I would not quite say 'acute awareness' – of the involvement of the 'economy' with the structure of the larger society of which it was obviously – but not altogether clearly – a part. As a result, the very economy itself appeared to us then, as I think it still does to the great bulk of students and their professors, as a 'given' rather than a problematic; a point of view that then carries over to the subject matter of economics itself, which is memorized rather than examined in a spirit of curiosity as to why it is part of economics rather than some other field of inquiry, such as sociology or political analysis. This question, I should add, leads to the view of economics that will dominate these pages – namely, a search for the ways in which primal behavior patterns are harnessed to fulfill the needs for social formations of many kinds to provide the foodstuffs and other materials needed for their continuance.

Marx takes this problem for granted, perhaps from a viewpoint of 'succeed or perish.' But I find that the relation between what I see as the fundamental behavior-shaping forces of human activity and their social employment to differ from one socio-political formation to the next. Although I distinguish among only three such formations, I believe that this somewhat un-Marxian relegation of the deep behavioral forces of society to its basement, rather than to its immediately visible workings, will be useful in thinking about our subject – namely, how to conceptualize economics itself.

II

What turned me to this view of the altered placement of the economy within the larger entity of society? The answer is a growing awareness that all groups of living beings – from insects through humankind – assure their collective continuance through a reliance on order-bestowing behavioral influences that set the stage, so to speak, for the performance of the many and varied tasks necessary to this end. In the case of insects and still 'lower' organisms, this all important assurance is entirely provided by instincts; in the case of animals, by a mixture of instinctual promptings and experience gained in early life.

And in the case of human beings? I believe the necessary discipline is acquired – I will not say 'learned' – in early infancy as the obedience to authority, which is its deepest, if most resisted, lesson. As adults that deep-planted propensity is translated into the strong appeal of tradition as a venerable, as well as trustworthy, guide to action; and all these fundamentally psychological sources of obedience are given additional strength by structures of law, formally established practice and pressures of conformity, each with its punishment for disregard. Collectively, these pressures assure the normally strong endorsement of the existing structures of social and of political and, as a result, of economic life.

Further as I see it, there have been only a handful of these order-providing societal architectures. The first, and longest lasting, were the hunting and gathering bands, tribes and people (e.g., Native Americans) that held stage for uncountable millennia under the aegis of obedience-become-tradition. Thereafter, dating from perhaps the fifth millennium, tradition gives way to command, embodied in near-absolute power at the apex of the social pyramid and abject obedience of slaves, prisoners of war, and impoverished workers below – again supported by infantile experience or fantasy. In Europe, command now evolves into the mixed disciplines of feudalism – part tradition, part command – and that in turn yields, most markedly in England, to the guidance of a social formation that would not be formally called capitalism until Marx's work in the mid-nineteenth century.

Living as we do in the historical formation of capitalism, we should recognize its order-bestowing forces. The most familiar is the presence of a market that serves as both a disciplinary constraint and a restless setting for the exercise of aggressive impulses – again rooted in childhood, but now directed to the pursuit of money, or at a higher level of operation, the accumulation of capital. Thus in my view, capitalism is essentially a social formation in which always-present infantile drives find expression in a new institutional setting, with dramatic, but also explainable, consequences to which we give the name of economics.

Added to these two identifying features are another one-and-a-half. The first is the division of production and distribution into two separate sectors or spheres of responsibility – one private, in which all activities are undertaken by business; the other public, in which government produces and distributes such items as military equipment, roads, health care and scientific research – a sector that has steadily grown in size and importance, to become, along with the enormous contribution of technology, perhaps the most important influence in shaping capitalism's future.

That leaves the 'last half' order-bestowing element. I would identify it as the culture(s) of capitalism: the socio-political views – some national, some regional – that endow all capitalisms with distinctive national and, within that, local, ways of conducting business, treating employees, relating to political authority and vice versa, all of which endow capitalism with its distinctive properties from one nation or region to the next.

There remains to be considered only one last form of social-political architecture. It is socialism, characterized by its extensive government planning of production and distribution and, its consequence, a heavily bureaucratized economic order. Once the repository of great hopes for social progress, socialism today is viewed with little enthusiasm, either in economic or social-political terms. Perhaps this can change if socialism moves in the direction of socialization rather than 'socialism.' But now I must turn to the task of economics, given the not very laudatory way in which I have depicted it.

III

Whatever the conception of economics – classical, Marxian or neoclassical – it must fulfill a common task: that is, examine systems of production and distribution to explain how the economy 'works.' I mean by this crucial word making clear how the social order seen 'under the microscope' organizes the all-important processes of production and distribution and, beyond that, how the larger patterns of economic life arise from these essential processes.

For precapitalist societies this is not a difficult task. Tradition-and-command societies, however complex from a socio-psychological view, pose no particular problems from an economic one: tradition leads to, or toward, patterns of production and distribution that continue those of the past; command gives rise to patterns desired by the commanding class or person.

Both outcomes require no special explication, unusual attributions of nature or patterns of behavior aside.

It is with nascent capitalism that the task of economic clarification takes on a new complexity and importance. Tradition and command both begin to give way to the drive of private capital expansion and the currents of the marketplace. Thereafter production/distribution systems rapidly gain in complexity and, with them, would-be economic clarifications. We enter the world of the early economic theorists, such as the Physiocrats in the court of Louis XV where we might meet a visitor from England, Adam Smith.

This puts us in touch with the first great chapter of economic thought: Classical Political Economy – (kindly note the adjectival modifier). Unlike the conventional and very useful consideration of the evolution of the Smithian model through its Ricardian, Millian, Marxian, Marshallian, Schumpeterian, and climactic Keynesian successors, I propose we look for another identifying aspect of this still-dazzling two centuries of economic clarification. This is its lurking awareness – often more sensed than seen – of political and social roots beneath the 'economic' trials and tendencies that provide the focus, but perhaps not the ultimate depth, of their insights.

Here I shall do no more than point in the direction of the insights on which I place such importance, as it would take a shelf of books to describe them in depth and detail. But even a casual acquaintance with this literature can reveal its authors' awareness of the political and social pressures whence spring the motivations behind the dramas of economic life – the insatiable capitalist, the parasitic landlord, the helpless worker, the indifferent government. I say, please note, 'can reveal' not 'will reveal.' These fundamental elements of *political* economy are conscious perceptions for Marx and likely Schumpeter, but no more than a kind of naïve awareness for Smith and Malthus or a more sophisticated one for Keynes. Nonetheless what else lies behind Adam Smith's intuitive perception of the ill-effects for the laborer of the generally much celebrated division of labor, or Ricardo's grasp of the self-destructive aspects of the drive for capital that he so much favors, other than an awareness of what we would call a socio-political framework that blindly produces economic movements from which some parts of society suffer and others benefit?

More to our point, why is this unmistakable sense of socio-political involvement absent from virtually all contemporary economic analysis, save that small fraction that announces its Marxist or other radical base? If my perception is correct, the answer lies in a twentieth-century aversion to a recognition of the very socio-political underpinnings of economic analysis that were so directly, if perhaps unknowingly, embraced by its eighteenth- and nineteenth-century precursors. *Why* this is so is less clear than that it *is* so, but for that very reason I can think of no more suitable conclusion to this contentious chapter.

IV

I shall put forward two I hope plausible, but I know unproveable, suggestions – the first, political; the second, societal. The first will hardly come as a surprise. As I mentioned above, there has been one exception to the general aversion of contemporary economics to socio-political explications: namely, Marxian or other radical perspectives.

Here a persuasive answer to our overriding question lies in the widespread decline in the esteem in which such thought has been held since I was introduced to it in college. The collapse of the Soviet economy and of the dictatorial climate of communist regimes everywhere have seriously damaged the high standing once accorded to outspokenly leftist views. Whether this will continue I cannot say, but I have no doubt that a powerful reason for the aversion of modern day economics to 'radical' thought lies in the unfortunate reputation earned by its vocabulary as well as by its ideas. As an instance I note that most modern day economists shy away even from such terms as capitalism, preferring 'market,' or 'free enterprise' system. It is not a trivial matter when historically and contentually rich terms are shelved in favor of bland, half-accurate, but 'safe' ones. Consider only that the word *Capitalism* appears in very few indices to economic textbooks these days, an unbelievable assertion I shall leave to my readers to test.

This brings me, finally, to a more substantial explanation for the political primness that I find an identifying property of 'scholarly' economic thought today. Here to explain the apoliticality that is my main target I look in a quite different direction toward the 'scientificality' (to coin a word) that has become the model to which economics now aspires. When I say 'now' I do not mean that earlier economic inquiry was indifferent to the standards of convincing demonstration, avoidance of rhetoric and testable procedures that are among the most laudable standards of science. I mean, rather, that the conscious pursuit of science as the model for economic inquiry removes such considerations as Power, which is central to all social dynamics, but absent from those in the worlds of non-human nature that are the sole objects of scientific explanation.

Let me be more direct. What can a physicist, a chemist, an astronomer tell us about the forces that drive firms, or consumers or workers? Worse, does not the quite proper exclusion from scientific inquiry of such 'things' as social classes, or acquisitiveness or motivation suggest that a scientific vocabulary may be inadequate to specify some of the most important elements in the landscape of economic life? And finally, how can a field of scholarship, which sedulously avoids that which is political or social, be equal to the task of clarifying the faults and possibilities of the capitalist order whose past has been, and whose present and future must be, the central privilege as well as purpose of economic inquiry?

PART II

FUNCTIONAL FINANCE: THE BACKGROUND

This section presents the foundations of the Functional Finance approach to policy. Although Keynes in his *General Theory* provided a theoretical background, the central ideas of Functional Finance were already present in the thinking of leading German émigrés at the New School by the mid-1930s or earlier. Abba Lerner was a key figure in the development of the radical implications of the Keynesian approach, Adolph Lowe provided the historical context, Hans Neisser developed an interventionist policy framed in terms of the Quantity Theory, and Gerhard Colm – not represented here, but discussed at the Conference – worked out the principles of fiscal policy, not only writing an early and successful textbook, but also becoming a member of Truman's Council of Economic Advisors.

The principle ideas of Functional Finance, developed by Abba Lerner in the late 1930s and early 1940s and then laid out in a famous article while he was at the New School, can be summed up in a few slogans:

> Governments have to intervene; the economy is not self-regulating.
>
> The principal economic objective of the state should be to ensure a prosperous economy.
>
> Money is a creature of the state; it has to be managed.
>
> Fiscal policy should be directed in the light of its impacts on the economy, and the budget should be managed accordingly, that is, 'balance' is not important in itself.
>
> The amount and pace of Government spending should be set in the light of the desired level of activity, and taxes should be levied for their economic impact, rather than to raise revenue.
>
> Principles of 'sound finance' apply to individuals. They make sense for households and businesses, but do not apply to the governments of sovereign states, capable of issuing money.

Lerner, Lowe, Neisser and Colm all came to the New School after leaving Europe prior to World War II. Lerner's ideas on Functional Finance are presented here by David Colander who relates them to developments in macroeconomics. Colander traces the theoretical developments that undermined the Keynesian approach, especially the insistence on Walrasian microfoundations. If macro rested on a scarcity theory of value, then steady unemployment would be impossible in any conditions in which wages were stable. Rational Expectations took this a step further; the new approach argued that active policy could have no impact even in the short run. 'New Keynesians' offered only palliatives in reply: If there were significant 'imperfections' it would be possible for policies to work, and many of these imperfections are unavoidable. By contrast, Colander wants to ground macro in the work on complexity, which he sees as providing a new foundation for both theory and policy, one very compatible with Lerner's approach. Mat Forstater also considers recent developments that echo Lerner, especially in the consideration of 'endogenous' money. These as well reflect the historical approach of Lowe, leading Forstater to examine the connections and complementarities between Lerner and Lowe, Lowe's approach proving to be more historical with less use for conventional microeconomic thinking. Like Lerner, Lowe also supports activist intervention, but he justifies it on the grounds that the historical changes have left markets less able to stabilize themselves. Neisser worked in a different tradition, that of the Quantity Theory, but within that framework he developed a case for activist government, and studied the impact of technological change on unemployment. Hansen's changing thinking on the role of government in regulating the economy is traced by Perry Mehrling. He began with the idea that government should provide social insurance, then came to the view that it had to jump-start the economy, and ended thinking that it had to act as a 'balance wheel,' a stabilizer. Each of the approaches examined leads to a different emphasis in specifying the role of the state. The question for today is how can Functional Finance help us cope with the crisis of the welfare state.

2. Functional finance, new classical economics and great-great grandsons

David Colander

At sea Septr. 1944.

My dear Lerner,

Your book arrived in London whilst I was away at Bretton Woods. But now again I am on the sea for yet another visit to the USA, and the sea voyage has given me an opportunity to read it.

It is a grand book worthy of one's hopes of you. A most powerful piece of well organized analysis with high aesthetic qualities, though written more perhaps than you see yourself for the cognoscenti in the temple and not for those at the gate. Anyhow *I* prefer it for intellectual enjoyment to any recent attempts in this vein.

In the second of the two books which you have placed within one cover, I have marked with particular satisfaction and profit three pairs of chapters – chap 20 and 21, chap 24 and 25, and chap 28 and 29. Here is the kernel of yourself. It is very original and grand stuff. I shall have to try when I get back to hold a seminar for the heads of the Treasury on Functional Finance. It will be very hard going – I think I shall ask them to let me hold a seminar of their sons instead, agreeing beforehand that, if I can convince the boys, they will take it from me that it is so![1]

The above letter from John Maynard Keynes to Abba Lerner celebrating his book *The Economics of Control* (1944) contains the essence of my view of functional finance: It is grand stuff, worthy of much more serious attention than it currently receives.

The generation before me – the sons whom Keynes spoke of – knew it was grand stuff, but their sons – my generation and their grandsons – began to lose the vision. It is now fair to say that their great grandsons have come full circle – back to where the heads of Treasury were in the 1930s, and I sometimes wonder whether they might not be even a little bit behind that. In reading the economics journals and talking with newly minted PhDs, it is as if Keynesian economics never existed.

There are two exceptions to this blanket observation. The first concerns policy makers. While most policy makers now tell a Classical story, their practice still reflects many of the ideas of functional finance; the expectation of government intervention is still giving stability to the economy and allowing policy makers' talk to be stronger than their actions. The second exception is in cutting-edge macroeconomic theory. The new work on multiple equilibria macro, selection mechanisms and complex dynamics is beginning to touch on ideas that can once again make functional finance relevant. When that work has progressed and diffused through the profession, I believe the profession will see once again why functional finance is grand stuff.

In this chapter I will try to shed some light on why functional finance fell out of favor, and why, I believe, it will come back into its own as the recent developments of modern macro theory progress a bit further. Specifically I will argue that the rules of functional finance, as developed by Lerner, are fully consistent with assumptions of rational expectations placed in a context of a realistic economy and that, theoretically, the rules of functional finance are as relevant now as they were when Lerner first developed them in the 1940s. There are limitations, some serious, about their use in practice, but when supplemented by an inflation rule and seen as a general structural guide to macro policy, they are a good first step and worthy of being a focal point in the teaching of macroeconomics.

THE RULES OF FUNCTIONAL FINANCE

I will first specify what functional finance is. 'Functional finance' is the name given by Lerner (1941) to the theory of financing government according to the following three rules:

1. The government shall maintain a reasonable level of demand at all times. If there is too little spending and, thus, excessive unemployment, the government shall reduce taxes or increase its own spending. If there is too much spending, the government shall prevent inflation by reducing its own expenditures or by increasing taxes.
2. By borrowing money when it wishes to raise the rate of interest and by lending money or repaying debt when it wishes to lower the rate of interest, the government shall maintain that rate of interest that induces the optimum amount of investment.
3. If either of the first two rules conflicts with the principles of 'sound finance' or of balancing the budget, or of limiting the national debt, so much the worse for these principles. The government press shall print any money that may be needed to carry out rules 1 and 2.

In proposing these rules of functional finance, Lerner's purpose was to shift thinking about government finance from principles of sound finance that make sense for individuals – such as a balanced budget – to sound finance principles (now designated as functional finance) that make sense for the aggregate economy in which government spending and taxing decisions affect levels of economic activity. These two differed because the secondary effects of spending decisions and savings decisions – what Lerner and I called macro externalities – had to be taken into account in the aggregate economy. By introducing functional finance, Lerner's goal was to get economists to focus on the *consequences* of government financing, not on the then generally accepted, but little considered, rules of sound finance and the quantity theory of money.

Lerner's stark presentation of these rules of functional finance caused much of a stir in the 1940s and 1950s when most Keynesians, including Keynes, were politically more circumspect about Keynesian ideas for government fiscal policy than they were in the 1960s. Thus the letter quoted above was written, in part, to atone for a tongue-lashing that Keynes had given Lerner at a Federal Reserve seminar for saying that deficits did not matter, a comment that caused Evsey Domar to lean over to Lerner and say that Keynes should read *The General Theory*.

Through the debates over functional finance (and Lerner's ability to win them), the concept of functional finance became well known. In the 1950s and 1960s, Lerner's functional finance rules became both the basis of most textbook presentations of Keynesian economics and the basis for policy. Thus when Keynesian policy came under fire in the late 1960s and early 1970s, it was Lerner's functional finance that most people were attacking.[2] That fire intensified through the 1970s, became a full frontal attack in the 1980s and by the late 1990s, Keynesians, like the Scots in the fourteenth century – had become a diverse set of clans, often fighting among themselves and meeting each other clandestinely in various retrospective conferences such as the one where these papers were first presented.[3]

THE DEMISE OF FUNCTIONAL FINANCE IN POLICY

The rules of functional finance lost favor as a basis for policy because, empirically, they did not seem to lead to the desired state of the economy. Specifically, initial interpretation of the rules of functional finance concluded that the target rate of unemployment should be approximately 3 per cent. This was based on an implicit assumption that inflation would only become a problem at lower rates of unemployment. If unemployment rose above 3 per cent, the government should increase spending or lower taxes; if unemployment fell below 3 per cent, the government should increase taxes or lower spending. So too with the interest rate: if unemployment were above 3 per cent, the government should lower interest rates by increasing the money supply. Conversely if unemployment were below 3 per cent, the government should raise interest rates by decreasing the money supply.

It is important to note that the initial interpretation of a 3 per cent target rate of unemployment is not inherent in the functional finance rules. Rule 1 does not state what is meant by excessive unemployment. Nor does it state what to do if both a zero level of inflation and the desired rate of unemployment cannot be achieved. Thus, depending on how they are interpreted, the rules of functional finance can be compatible with many different types of government spending and taxing rules.

As the rules were interpreted, however, they became synonymous with significant deficit spending. Functional finance was seen as having an expansionary and inflationary policy bias. As modern Keynesians gave up their belief that they could specify the desired inflation and unemployment rates independently of the actual functioning of the economy, they simultaneously abandoned the functional finance policy prescriptions. As a result, in the 1990s, the rules of functional finance are little discussed. This is unfortunate because there is still much sense in the rules. Specifically they lead to the policy questions of why a 3 per cent unemployment rate is inconsistent with a stable price level and whether institutions could be changed to make it consistent. Only a few outspoken Keynesian economists – Robert Eisner and Bill Vickrey come to mind – have been vocal in pointing out the problems with the new emphasis on balanced budgets.

Actually the giving up of the rules of functional finance by policy makers occurs much more in words than in deeds. Despite what central bankers may say their policy is, and despite the rhetoric of policy-oriented macroeconomists, the actual policy reaction to recessions is now quite different than it was in pre-Keynesian times. When presenting fiscal policy to voters, governments talk about balanced budgets; but the benefits of government deficits in a recession are recognized.[4]

At times, however, the policy rhetoric of modern macroeconomics is written down as a framework for policy, as in the structure of the new European Monetary Union where member countries are required to have budget deficits no larger than 3 per cent regardless of the state of the economy. Such a requirement precludes the use of functional finance rules and thus could present serious problems for the European Union. My suspicion is that ways around these rules will be found because, while the rhetoric of functional finance is not used, the lessons of functional finance – you don't try to reduce the deficit when the economy is heading into a recession – are still understood by most policy makers (even though they are not understood by many young theoretical macroeconomists).

THE DEMISE OF FUNCTIONAL FINANCE IN THEORY

Somewhat less important from society's standpoint, but more interesting from the standpoint of most economists, is the demise of functional finance on the theoretical front. This decline is closely tied to major developments in theoretical macro – the rise to power of neo-Keynesianism, the micro foundations revolution, the New Classical revolution and the New Keynesian flash in the journals. A brief review of these developments will explain how the theoretical demise of functional finance came about.

From Keynesian to Neo-Keynesian Macroeconomics

The seeds of the theoretical loss of favor of functional finance were sown early in the Keynesian revolution when the formal development of the Keynesian model was tied to the Walrasian unique equilibrium general equilibrium model. This grafting of the two lines of research led to neo-Keynesian economics that placed Keynesian economics in a unique equilibrium aggregate framework. This Walrasian framework was devoid of the institutional characteristics that underlay Keynesian economic reasoning. It was at that point that Keynesian economics entered a theoretical end-play leading, ultimately, to its almost total demise.

One of the aspects of the decision to structure the Keynesian argument within a Walrasian model was the long, unproductive debate about the role of wage and price level flexibility in macro. Having, in my decadent youth, taken part in some of that debate, I try now to avoid it entirely. In reality wages and prices are not, and cannot be, perfectly flexible in any institutional structure that resembles our own and thus that debate about price level flexibility is irrelevant for policy and for understanding how our real-world economy works.[5]

My basic working premise is that our type of monetary system requires a relatively stable price level. Financial institutions and contracts are based on the prescription of reasonable price level stability and cannot operate efficiently without far more stability than is required by any formal, theoretical, classical price level adjustment story.[6] Unexpected changes in the price level bring about changes in the terms of contracts. Since full price-level-contingent contracts are too complicated to design, the very functioning of our economic system relies upon the price level not varying 'too much.' Since the Walrasian theory assumes a functioning economy, to the degree that the models require significant price level flexibility to maintain equilibrium, they embody a fundamental inconsistency.

Effects of variations in the price level are asymmetric; inflation can actually provide a temporary stimulus as wealth is redistributed from creditors to debtors who include most entrepreneurs. Deflation, however, will redistribute money from debtors to creditors and can undermine the financial stability of many businesses. If the government does not step in as that happens, the economy, its institutional structure undermined, will fall apart.[7] A significant fall in the price level as required by modern adjustment mechanisms that underlie textbook macro models and give rise to what those texts call 'the aggregate demand curve,' would undermine existing financial institutions and, by extension, the institutional structure underlying our economy. As Keynes said, 'Having regard to human nature and our institutions it can only be a foolish person who would prefer a flexible wage policy to a flexible money policy.' Such common sense is not based on money illusion. It is based upon our institutions' dependence on a relatively fixed price level and the need to maintain institutions as a foundation to the existence of markets.[8]

Why were the neo-Keynesians willing to agree to such a synthesis that theoretically precluded Keynesian economics? As I argued in *The Coming of Keynesianism to America* (Colander and Laudreth, 1996) their primary interest was policy; theory for them was something that led to a model with acceptable policy conclusions. The fact that one could develop a model requiring the policy they wanted within a fixed-wage Walrasian structure led them to accept a synthesis based on that structure in order to avoid unending, and quite irrelevant, arguments with Classicals over logical debating points with little relevance on the checkerboard of real life.

From Neo-Keynesian to Micro Foundations

Like many compromises based on short-run policy concerns, the neo-Keynesian compromise had within it the seeds of destruction of neo-Keynesian economics. The destruction of neo-Keynesianism began with the work in micro foundations that led to the rise of Phelps's and Friedman's concept of the natural rate of unemployment. That micro foundations work changed the name of the theoretical game. It was no longer acceptable to develop comparative static macro models and then talk about how to relate those models to policy. Instead to be taken seriously in macroeconomic theory, one had to structure one's model within a Walrasian system and relate one's equilibrium concept to a steady state equilibrium framework.

The acceptance of the need for micro foundations had two effects: first, it undermined many of the Keynesian models as being without micro foundations and second, it created a split between long- and short-run analyses. The long-run domain was given to the Classicals, since wages and prices were assumed flexible in the long run and the neo-Keynesians had already agreed that with flexible wages and prices the economy would gravitate to its long-run equilibrium. For policy-oriented Keynesian macroeconomists, these new terms of synthesis were still acceptable, since there was still a short-run role for their primary policy concern: stabilization policy. Functional finance was still possible, as long as it was kept to a stabilization role around a predetermined natural rate. However the stage was also set for the next theoretical development in macro that was to undermine neo-Keynesian analysis and place it in the dustbin of history.

From Micro Foundations to New Classical Macro: the Rational Expectations Revolution

The next step in the burial of Keynesian economics was the rational expectations revolution. This hypothesis was first suggested by John Muth in 1961 when, while working on a project on institutions and process in economics, he extended some ideas originating from the Stockholm expectational school. Muth suggested an improvement to the ad hoc method by which expectations were analyzed in discussing price movements. Before Muth's article, the contention was that individuals average past and present prices as predictors of future prices. It was not clear how weights were chosen, nor was there any clarity as to the validity of this entire method. This led Muth to raise two fundamental questions: (1) What kind of information is, in fact, used and how is it processed to estimate future conditions? (2) How can change in expectations be predicted according to alterations in the amount of available information or with a change in the structure of the system?

Muth's answers to these questions were delightfully simple: Assume that since expectations are the informed predictions of future events, they are essentially the same as those that would be derived by the relevant economic theory. This answer became the basis for the rational expectations hypothesis in macro.

There are two things to note about this revolution. The first is that while Muth wrote his paper in 1961 about an individual market, his idea was not taken up because it was felt that its informational requirements in an individual market were too great to be useful in practice. It only became widely used when in 1969 Lucas and Rapping applied it to macro where, ironically, the informational requirements were infinitely more complicated than in an individual market.

The second point to raise about rational expectations is that to call the expectations rational was a marketing coup. The issue had nothing to do with rationality; it had to do with consistency. As Allen Walters (1971) pointed out, Muth's contribution actually concerned modeling. Muth argued, quite reasonably, that it would be desirable for a model to assume that individuals in the model understand that model and base their actions upon that understanding. For unique equilibrium models, this would mean that the model should assume that individuals know the solution to the model and act accordingly. Such expectations would more appropriately be called 'model-consistent expectations.' Muth argued that any model should have the property that its solution be consistent with modeling individual's expectations within that model.

This assumption put neo-Keynesians on the floor because it undermined the basis of the compromise they had had with Classical economists. It essentially tied together the long run and the short run and made it so that anything that could happen in the long run would be anticipated in the short run and, therefore, short-run policy could not be effective unless based upon real cost differentials.

The result of combining rational expectations with the market clearing assumptions that underlay the neo-Keynesian/neoclassical synthesis was the New Classical economics revolution. New Classical economics took rational expectation and used it in conjunction with the Walrasian unique equilibrium model to arrive at the proposition that, assuming competitive markets, if macro policy were irrelevant in the long run it was also irrelevant in the short run. Thus the fact that Keynesian economics had conceded the long run to the Classicals meant that, to be logical, they should also concede the short run. This proposition was much debated; implicit contracts, staggered contracts and a variety of nominal and real imperfections were raised by New Keynesians, creating the possibility of some role for stabilization policy in the short run despite rational expectations. But these were rearguard actions. With the development of rational expectations, neo-Keynesian economics as we knew it was essentially theoretically dead.

The Rules vs. Discretion Addendum

Along with the development of New Classical economics, there was simultaneously the related development of Kydland and Prescott's time-inconsistency argument for rules over discretion. This was used to argue against the short-run role for Keynesian policy that still remained. The time-inconsistency argument goes as follows: Discretion at each moment in time is the optimal policy; rules are the consistent policy. Following the optimal policy in each time period – following discretion – can lead to dynamic suboptimality and is hence a worse policy than a consistent policy. Ergo, conclude Kydland and Prescott (1977): Rules are preferable to discretion.[9]

They 'prove' their case with mathematics, but they attempt to convince the reader with the following metaphor:

> Suppose the socially desirable outcome is not to have houses built in a particular flood plain, but given that they are there, to take certain costly flood-control measures. If the government's policy were not to build the dams and levees needed for flood protection and agents knew this was the case, even if houses were built there, rational agents would not live in the flood plains. But the rational agent knows that if he and others build houses there, the government will take the necessary flood control measures. Consequently in the absence of a law prohibiting the construction of houses in the flood plain, houses are built there and the army corps of engineers subsequently builds the dams and levees.

In this example, building the dam is the optimal policy; not building the dam is the consistent policy; and most people can easily see the problem with following the optimal policy. The time-inconsistency argument did not kill neo-Keynesian economics – rational expectations had done that. The time-inconsistency argument nailed the coffin shut so that neo-Keynesians could not rise from the dead.

BEYOND NEW CLASSICAL ECONOMICS

Recent Developments and the Revival of a Theoretical Role for Functional Finance

If the New Classical revolution were the end of the story, functional finance would belong in the dustbin of history. But it does not. The New Classical revolution brought about some serious rethinking about the neo-Keynesian/Classical synthesis. Specifically the tying together of Keynesian macroeconomics with Walrasian economics was questioned.[10] That rethinking sets up the possibility of a more meaningful theoretical macroeconomics in which the rules of functional finance can play a central role in the conception of macro policy.

All of the policy conclusions of the New Classicals are based upon the assumption of the unique equilibrium Walrasian model. If the Walrasian unique equilibrium underpinnings are removed, the rug is pulled out from New Classical economics and macroeconomics is thrown into chaos, or at least into complexity, the precise location from which new developments are coming.[11] Why has it taken so long for economics to face up to this complexity? It is an interesting question about the sociology of the profession, but I think Joseph Schumpeter (1954) spelled out the central reason when he wrote:

> Multiple equilibria are not necessarily useless, but from the standpoint of any exact science the existence of a uniquely determined equilibrium is, of course, of the utmost importance, even if proof has to be purchased at the price of very restrictive assumptions; without any possibility of proving the existence of (a) uniquely determined equilibrium – or at all events, of a small number of possible equilibria – at however high a level of abstraction, a field of phenomena is really a chaos that is not under analytical control.

Since economics wanted to be and still wants to be an 'exact science,' it had to assume away the possibility of multiple equilibria. In doing so the intuitive logic that supports multiple equilibria is also assumed away. Standard economics simply avoided such issues. Recently, however, with the development of the science of complexity and major developments in non-linear systems theory, more and more economists have been willing to give up the sense of economics as an 'exact science' and, happily, see it as an intuitively sensible, empirical science and deal seriously with the economy's complexity. Herein lies, for me, the further development of macro theory and the potential resurrection of the rules of functional finance within theory. They are institutionally specific rules that embody important lessons from history. They are not theoretically derived and immutable rules.

Within multiple-equilibria models there is a potential theoretical role for both monetary and fiscal policy. Although economists are a long way from formally specifying that role, it is possible to specify it informally and to outline the general argument for functional finance in a complex multiple-equilibria world. Functional finance is a method of affecting the equilibrium-selection mechanism so that the economy chooses a more desirable equilibrium. Before I turn to this issue, let me discuss briefly how multiple-equilibria theory undermines the central tenets of New Classical economics.

Multiple Equilibria and Rational Expectations

As I stated above, rational expectations are really model-consistent expectations. If one has a multiple-equilibria model, where many outcomes are possible, then just about any set of expectations consistent with one of those potential equilibria is possible.[12] Used within a multiple-equilibria model, there is no inconsistency in the combination of rational expectations and Keynesian economics. Consider Keynes's (1936) famous 'expectations' passage:

> The social object of skilled investment should be to defeat the dark forces of time and ignorance which develop our future. The actual private object of the most skilled investment today is 'to beat the gun' as the Americans so well express it, to outwit the crowd, and to pass the bad, or depreciating, half crown to the other fellow. . . . We have reached the third degree where we devote our intelligence to anticipating what average opinion expects average opinion to be and there are some, I believe, who practice the fourth, fifth, and higher degrees. . . .
>
> There is no clear evidence from experience that the investment policy which is socially advantageous coincides with that which is most profitable. It needs more intelligence to defeat the forces of time and our ignorance of the future than to beat the gun. Moreover life is not long enough.

This quotation is completely consistent with individuals holding rational expectations in a multiple-equilibria world. Initially, however, macroeconomists, tied up in a Walrasian unique equilibrium model, did not see this.

With multiple equilibria the long run and the short run are interconnected but neither dominates the other. Short-run considerations play a role in choosing which long-run equilibrium we arrive at and, hence, short-run policy can affect the long-run equilibrium. As a practical matter, since many of the long-run paths are unknowable, practical policy will often focus on the short run. After all, as Lerner said, the long run is simply a collection of ongoing short runs and, in the long run, we find ourselves in another short run. In a multiple-equilibrium model, policy is not only affecting stabilization around a stable long run path; policy is also affecting the economy's choice as to which of the multiple growth paths to take.

Time-inconsistency in a Complex Economic Environment

Let me now turn to the time-inconsistency argument. The problem with the argument is not with the mathematical proof – that is almost logically trivial. The problem is with the interpretation Kydland and Prescott and others, such as Robert Barro, give to it. These New Classical economists equate rules with consistent policies and discretionary action with optimal policy, concluding that rules are preferable to discretion because of problems that develop if people can expect government to follow an optimal policy.

While theirs is one possible definition of rules, it is not a meaningful one when there is uncertainty about the future in a complex, multiple-equilibria environment. A rule in the Kydland–Prescott definition involves full specification of what will be done in every possible contingency; their rules are what I would call 'full contingency rules.' Given this definition, any proof of the superiority of rules over discretion is trivial. The very definition of rules includes all possible discretionary action. It is totally possible within the Kydland–Prescott definition of rules to say that the rule that the government should follow is to act optimally, subject to a well-specified social welfare function. This rule is not the rule that most individuals consider when they speak of rules. Most definitions of rules are of limited contingency and there is no a priori case for the superiority of limited contingency rules over discretion.

My objection to Kydland and Prescott is that they jump from their mathematics demonstrating the superiority of a full contingency rule to a discussion of policy that suggests a very simple monetary rule. That a simple monetary growth rule is incorrect can be seen in the following example:

> Say the rule states that the government will increase the money supply by 3 per cent regardless of circumstances. Then, in the second period, half the world sinks into the sea because of some shift in the underlying geostructure of the earth. Most economists would argue that the money supply should be reduced to prevent inflation in such a situation but, if the simple 3 per cent rule is followed, that cannot be done if the rule is to be upheld.

Rejection of the Kydland and Prescott argument does not imply that discretion is preferable to rules: it only implies that one cannot a priori prove the superiority of either discretion or rules in an operational sense. Specific rules and specific discretionary actions must be compared by calculating the expected loss function under both. The steady-state rule will usually be followed, but the possibility of discretionary actions remains for sufficiently unanticipated contingencies that are optimal to build into the rules. So time inconsistency does not theoretically preclude functional finance – nor any policy – in a complicated world where all contingencies cannot be specified.

Multiple Equilibria and Functional Finance

Let me now turn to the potential theoretical role of functional finance in a multiple-equilibria economy. Above I stated that functional finance's theoretical role was to influence the equilibrium selection process of the economy. But cannot the same questions be asked as was asked by the Classicals in a unique equilibrium world?: Why should the government have any role in guiding the economy to an equilibrium? Why doesn't the same '$20 lying on the pavement' argument work for multiple-equilibria economies? The answer to these questions is a simple one: With multiple equilibria there is no presumption of global optimality of the equilibrium chosen by the market. Everyone can know of the existence of a preferable equilibrium but may not be able to achieve it by private actions. We can only say something about that question when we have a theory of equilibria selection mechanisms. Currently we have none. Thus there should be no general presumption that the private economy, given its institutions, arrives at an equilibrium preferable to one achieved with government guidance.

Another way to express that same idea is to say that the '$20 on the pavement' argument concerns profit while the multiple-equilibria argument concerns rent. Competition eliminates profit; it does not eliminate rent. If one can show empirically that government has a comparative advantage in adjusting to short-run fluctuations, then it can have a positive effect even though there is no potential profit available to private individuals. Here enters Lerner's and my macroeconomic externality argument. The effects of individual decisions on the aggregate level of spending and inflation are too small for individuals to take into account separately; it only makes sense for people to take those effects into account collectively. Since people have collectively organized through government already, the logical agent to internalize those externalities is government. Thus the reason that there is a potential role for government is that comparative advantage implies that rent, not profit, exists.

Notice I have said 'potential role.' Theory will not prove or disprove a role for government; it simply provides a framework for thinking about the issue. Built into the rules of functional finance is the implicit assumption that government has a comparative advantage in achieving steady-state stabilization.

Keynes and Lerner gave plausible reasons why government did have a comparative advantage; they did not *prove* it did have a comparative advantage. That position can only come from historical observation.

In my view, the past 60 years have shown both the limits and strengths of functional finance. Its strength is in providing a guide for handling major swings in aggregate demand such as those caused by the financial crises we recently saw in Asia. (This is what Axel Leijonhufvud refers to as 'out of the corridor' swings.) Even when functional finance is not used, its role is central to the efficient functioning of our economy; *it is the expectation that government functional finance policy will be used when crises occur that gives stability to our economy, keeping it in the corridor*. This allows the economy to expand much more than it otherwise would and thus provides a necessary foundation for growth. This means that the expectations of the policy often make it unnecessary for the policy to be used.

But history has also shown us the limits of functional finance. The first limit of functional finance policy involves fine tuning. Government policy is not a finely tuned instrument – Lerner's steering wheel analogy is misleading; government policy is more like steering a 200,000 ton super tanker that takes 20 miles to make a full turn. This limitation is now generally agreed upon.

The second limit involves the level of unemployment that can be aimed for given existing institutions. The initial interpretation that 3 per cent unemployment could be the target has proven far too ambitious, and it now seems clear that there is a range of between 3 and 8 per cent unemployment in the United States where the policy directives flowing from Lerner's functional finance rules are ambiguous. Within this range, inflation and unemployment occur simultaneously and therefore functional finance gives two alternative policy directives.

The Fourth Rule of Functional Finance

Lerner quickly recognized the problem, at least as it related to the problems of inflation and unemployment, and started early on to revise his theory of macro to directly take into account the possibility of multiple equilibria. He did this in two ways: (1) He distinguished two equilibria the economy could achieve – a high level and a low level of full employment; and (2), he specified a new form of inflation – sellers' inflation – which operated as a separate phenomenon, quite apart from demand pressures. Depending on how sellers' inflation was dealt with, there could be either high full employment or low full employment. Sellers' inflation resulted from existing institutional realities; it was not part of the perfectly competitive model, but Lerner was quite willing to relinquish the perfectly competitive model when he found that it did not fit reality.

His reaction to the ambiguous range was not the conventional one. Conventional wisdom has been to forget the unemployment target and simply aim for the inflation target. Thus the standard rules have government concerned only with inflation under the belief that the economy will gravitate to some long-run equilibrium that is independent of government policy. For Lerner inflation that occurred before 3 per cent unemployment was a product of faulty institutions, not a problem inherent in markets. Thus he refused to accept that the target level of unemployment should be raised to whatever level required to stop inflation.

Lerner found the implications of sellers' inflation so important that, beginning in the 1960s, he changed his research program to center on finding cures for sellers' inflation. Initially he toyed with various administrative wage and price control policies, but he found those lacking and soon gave them up. He replaced them, first, with a tax-based incomes policy and ultimately, a market-based incomes policy in which property rights in prices are set and individuals have to buy the right to change prices from others who change their price in the opposite direction. It was this idea that formed the basis of our market anti-inflation (MAP) book (Lerner and Colander, 1980). Under MAP, rights in value added prices would be tradable so that any firm wanting to change its nominal price would have to make a trade with another firm that wanted to change its nominal price in the opposite direction. Thus, by law, the average price level would be constant but relative prices would be free to change.

Three features of MAP should be pointed out. First, it is a totally market-oriented plan. Second, practically, it is implemented through a value added per unit input concept not an output price concept. While there are measurement problems with both capital and labor input, they are far less severe than with output prices. Moreover this measurement assigns the property rights of general productivity increases to the consumer, not to the producer. To emphasize this point, Lerner and I have called MAP a form of synthetic competition. Third, MAP credits will have a zero price in a purely competitive society with no inflationary tendencies, yet most economists' intuition fails to lead them to that view.

To integrate the necessity of dealing with the institutional problem of sellers' inflation by changing institutions rather than accepting whatever unemployment was required to stop inflation, Lerner and I arrived at a modification of the rules of functional finance. Specifically, we added a fourth rule: 'The government must establish policies which stabilize the price level and coordinate both the money supply rule and the aggregate total spending rule with this stable price level at the unemployment level it prefers.'[13] With this fourth rule the rules of functional finance can once again be relevant to modern economic problems.

CONCLUSION

In conclusion, let me make some general comments about Lerner's contribution to economics. As Keynes suggested in the letter I quoted at the beginning of the chapter, Lerner operated in two different worlds – one of micro and one of macro. Lerner is best known for his contribution to microeconomics, specifically his contribution to setting up the foundations of modern welfare economics in *The Economics of Control.* That contribution is still seen as major and his contribution in macro is seen as minor. I suggest that it should be precisely the opposite. True he did make contributions to unique equilibrium general equilibrium theory, but that theory is not especially interesting. His major contribution is in macro where he spelled out some important operating rules of thumb – functional finance – that can serve as a solid guide to policy makers.

When commenting on the difficulties of the first three rules of functional finance Lerner (1951) writes:

> These problems . . . will make life difficult for the administrators of the economy. . . . [B]ut there is no reason for supposing that life will be any more difficult than in any other financial system which does not give the society the benefits of Functional Finance. . . . Functional Finance will not inaugurate a problemless world. Life will not be effortless. There will still be struggles and conflicts and defeats. . . . But it is an important step forward.

The conflicts and struggles for functional finance have been much more difficult than Lerner expected they would be, but if we make the same deal with policy makers today that Keynes wanted to make with the Treasury in the 1940s, I think functional finance can once again move to center stage in discussions of macro policy.

NOTES

1. The complete letter is reprinted in Colander and Landreth, *The Coming of Keynesianism to America* (1996).
2. See Colander, 'Was Keynes a Lernerian?' (1984) for a discussion of this issue.
3. The much touted new principles textbook by the 'New Keynesian,' Greg Mankiw (2001) goes so far as to push Keynes and stabilization policy to an end chapter of the book as something for students to learn as an afterthought to Classical economics.
4. The difference between rhetoric and action is not new. Abba liked to recount the following story of a conversation he had with the president of the Bank of Israel in the corridors of the Treasury in Jerusalem. The president came up to him and said, 'Professor Lerner, once more the government is pressing me to create more money, but I shall resist it till the last ditch.' To which Abba's answer was, 'I see you're getting ready for the last ditch.' Abba concluded the story by pointing out how the central bank always had to submit to the government's pressure, just as the government had to submit to social (and political) pressure (see Lerner and Ben-Shahar, 1975).

5. Lerner shared that view and that is what he meant when he distinguished instantaneous price adjustment from fast, but less than instantaneous, price adjustment.
6. The formal stories rely on wealth effects, international effects and Keynes effects. There are also informal stories that are much more intuitively plausible, but these are not part of the formal system and are much more like Keynesian economic adjustment stories with a different political twist.
7. This view is not novel to me. As Jim Tobin points out, Irving Fisher suggested that these effects would be significant. However they have been largely ignored in the literature.
8. Elsewhere (Colander 2001) I have argued that the production function must include a coordination variable and the effect that price level flexibility would have on institutional coordination as a necessary analytic aspect of the core model we present to students.
9. This is the New Classical extension of a longstanding debate in economics. The monetarists' argument for rules was an empirical one. They based it on the limited availability of information about the magnitude and timing of monetary effects, emphasizing the lags in recognizing the need for policy changes in the uncertainty in predicting short-run effects. The New Classicals – Kydland and Prescott – made a stronger claim: that the superiority of rules over discretion is a deductive truth, not an empirical argument.
10. I should point out that many Keynesians did not accept the neo-Keynesian position. Various groups, such as Post Keynesians, Clowerians and many others, refused to accept the basic neo-Keynesian position. But their view was in the minority and did not show up in the textbooks. Thus when the 'grandsons' learned Keynesian economics, they learned neo-Keyesian economics.
11. Complexity refers to the work of individuals associated with the Santa Fe Institute; they are attempting to model macroeconomics following their intuition, rather than letting the mathematical modeling requirements guide their assumptions. The result is extraordinarily complex models that come to no specific policy conclusion, at least not yet. This, to me, is a significant result; when one models the economy reasonably, one does not come to any specific macro policy conclusions. Policy conclusions are only arrived at when one combines theory with a knowledge of institutions in the art of economics. The world is too complex, given the current state of our understanding of the economy, to draw definitive policy conclusions from a model (see Colander, 1999).
12. Generally the formal models that are workable on this level are game-theoretic models; see the work of John Bryant (1996) or Russell Cooper (1999).
13. For the arguments for this rule see Colander (1979).

REFERENCES

Bryant, John (1996), 'Team Coordination Problems and Macroeconomic Models,' in David Colander (ed.), *Beyond Microfoundations: Post Walrasian Macroeconomics*, Cambridge: Cambridge University Press.

Colander, David (1979), 'Rationality, Expectations and Functional Finance,' in James Gapinski (ed.), *Essays in Post Keynesian Inflation*, Cambridge, MA: Ballinger.

Colander, David (1984), 'Was Keynes a Lernerian?,' *Journal of Economic Literature*, December.

Colander, David (2001), 'A Post Walrasian Explanation of Wage and Price Inflexibility and a Keynesian Unemployment Equilibrium System,' in Mark Setterfield (ed.), *Essays in Honour of John Cornwall*, New York: Macmillan.

Colander, David (ed.) (1986), *Incentive Based Incomes Policies*, Cambridge, MA: Ballinger.

Colander, David and Harry Landreth (1996) *The Coming of Keynesianism to America*, Cheltenham, UK and Brookfield, US: Edward Elgar.

Cooper, Russell (1999), *Coordination Games: Complementarities and Macroeconomics*, Cambridge: Cambridge University Press.

Keynes, John Maynard (1936), *The General Theory of Employment, Interest, and Money*, London: Macmillan.

Keynes, John Maynard (27 September 1944), personal correspondence to Abba Lerner.

Kydland, Fynn and E.C. Prescott (1977), 'Rules Rather than Discretion: The Inconsistency of Optimal Plans,' *Journal of Political Economy*, Vol. 85, No. 3 (June) pp. 473–92.

Lerner, Abba (1941), 'The Economic Steering Wheel,' *University Review*, June.

Lerner, Abba (1944), *The Economics of Control*, New York: Macmillan.

Lerner, Abba (1951), *The Economics of Employment*, New York: McGraw Hill.

Lerner, P. Abba and Haim Ben-Shahar (1975), *The Economics of Efficiency and Growth: Lessons from Israel and the West Bank*, Cambridge, MA: Ballinger Pub. Co.

Lerner, Abba and David Colander (1980), *MAP: A Market Anti-Inflation Plan*, New York: Harcourt Brace Jovanovich.

Mankiw, N. Gregory (2001), *Principles of Economics*, 2nd edn, Fort Worth: Harcourt College Publishers.

Schumpeter, Joseph (1954), *History of Economic Thought*, New York: Oxford University Press.

Walters, Alan (1971), 'Consistent Expectations, Distributed Lags, and the Quantity Theory,' *Economic Journal*, Vol. 81, No. 322 (June) pp. 273–81.

3. Toward a new instrumental macroeconomics: Abba Lerner and Adolph Lowe on economic method, theory, history and policy

Mathew Forstater

This chapter argues that the ideas of Abba Lerner and Adolph Lowe contain overlapping and complementary insights and themes that may contribute to the development of a new approach to macroeconomics, and that have rather specific practical policy implications. This approach might be called Instrumental Macroeconomics, after Lowe's instrumentalism, but it could be termed Functional Macroeconomics after Lerner's functional finance without changing the intended meaning.[1] Terminology aside, what is required today is a macroeconomics that considers macro policy goals at the ground level of theoretical practice – a *political* macroeconomics; a macroeconomics that recognizes that the system is dynamic and transformational, with major features changing over time – a *historical* macroeconomics; a macroeconomics that pays careful attention to institutional frameworks and arrangements – an *institutional* macroeconomics. What is required is a macroeconomics that, rid of neoclassical microfoundations, nevertheless considers sectoral as well as aggregate relations, technological change as well as monetary production – a *structural* macroeconomics that avoids the unacceptable mechanisms of aggregate models that bypass the complexities of human agency through their insertion of unacceptable motivational and behavioral assumptions.

The works of Lerner and Lowe serve as an interesting point of departure in thinking about such a new approach to macro theory and policy. While there are important areas of overlap in their work and thought, Lerner and Lowe diverge in their emphases, but, it shall be argued, in ways that are strikingly complementary. Lerner's functional finance deals with aggregate proportionality and balance, while much of Lowe's work emphasizes sectoral relations. While full employment and price stability were lifetime concerns for both, Lerner – following Keynes – focused more on monetary factors, while Lowe emphasized issues of structural and technological change. A Lowe–Lerner synthesis offers a powerful starting point for fleshing out an alternative approach to macroeconomic theory and policy, one which – because of its careful attention to historically changing social and institutional structures – is as fresh and relevant today as it was when Lerner and Lowe began formulating their historical and institutional approach to macroeconomic theory and public policy.

INSTRUMENTAL ANALYSIS AND THE METHOD OF FUNCTIONAL FINANCE

Lowe's investigations of the technological and structural features of contemporary capitalism from the 1920s to the 1950s led him to the position that modern industrial systems exhibit inherent macroeconomic instability, necessitating an abandonment of the traditional deductive method and its replacement with an alternative instrumental method for economic theory and public policy. Rather than taking only initial conditions as given and employing deductive analysis to predict and explain, Lowe proposed as also given, a vision of desired macro outcomes. These macro goals would not be determined by economic analysis but, rather, would be independently determined by democratic political process. Analysis would then 'work backwards' from the macro goals to the economic means for their attainment (Lowe, 1965; Forstater, 1999).

Such a conceptualization of the means–ends relation is also found in Lerner's functional finance. Functional finance was first put forward by Lerner in his article, 'Functional Finance and the Federal Debt' (1943) and in his *Economics of Control* (1944).[2] Sound finance confuses means and ends; a balanced budget seen as 'good' in and of itself is taken to be the end. In many cases it is even a politically stipulated goal. For Lerner what matters are the effects of the government budget and other fiscal and monetary policies: Is the current fiscal stance goal-adequate? Does it promote our macroeconomic goals?

Traditional economics would say that positive and normative economics are mixed here. But both Lowe and Lerner rejected the overly dichotomous positive–normative distinction. Lowe refers to the approach that begins analysis without consideration of macro outcomes as 'a radical positivism interested only in the explanation and prediction of movements "wherever they might lead" ' (Lowe, 1969: 7). For Lowe, the separation of the positive and normative 'can no longer be justified; . . . recent developments demand the conscious integration of the analytical and normative aspects' (1967: 180).

Lerner echoes this view when he distinguishes between 'objective' and 'normative' based not on whether one considers macro outcomes, but whether one does so openly and honestly: 'Objectivity turns out to be not the avoidance of concern with what is *desired* in a pure concentration on what *is*, but merely the avoidance of smuggling in an advocacy of desired objectives without making it clear that this is being done or making it clear whose are the desires being considered' (Lerner, 1969: 131, original emphasis).

In 1941, Lerner used the analogy of driving an automobile to defend the use of government controls to 'steer' the economic system onto the right path. While respecting market forces Lerner likened *laissez-faire* to a refusal to take hold of the 'economic steering wheel.' We may now add that it also helps to know your destination. In Lowe's instrumental framework, once we know our destination and from where our journey begins, we may consider suitable alternative routes for successfully completing the trip.

While Lowe claimed that 'the ultimate concern of [*On Economic Knowledge*] is not methodological,' certainly he deals explicitly with methodological matters and offers instrumentalism as an alternative methodological approach for economic theory and public policy. Lerner's outline of functional finance was not presented with regard to methodological issues, but it constitutes an important methodological position fully consistent with Lowe's instrumental method. In fact in his contribution to *Economic Means and Social Ends* – a symposium exploring issues raised in Lowe's *On Economic Knowledge* – Lerner explicitly and fully embraced instrumentalism, writing that: 'Only through the conscious application of instrumental analysis can there be any hope of further development or even survival of the economic or any other aspect of human society' (Lerner, 1969: 136).

Lowe and Lerner share some important methodological positions. By emphasizing the incorporation of macro goals at the beginning of their theoretical analyses they reject not only the traditional positive–normative dichotomy, but also the standard attribution of the state as 'outside' the economic system. Mainstream economics, as well as a number of heterodox traditions, have tended to analyse a pure market system or the logical operation of capitalism, before considering the role of the state. Instead, with Lerner and Lowe, the state is regarded as part of the economic system and therefore must be included in analysis from the start. Both Lerner and Lowe reject the view of the economic system – including both market and state – as static and unchanging, a position implicit if not explicit in all approaches based on universal economic 'laws' for all societies, or at least all stages of capitalism, throughout history. Failure to recognize fundamental change in the nature and role of the state has serious implications for the range of conceivable policies and their effectiveness. Thus constant, careful attention to historical, institutional, structural, technological and associated social and environmental change is fundamental to the Lowe–Lerner approach. Though they go to great lengths to expose the dangers of authoritarianism and the importance of defending precious freedoms, Lerner and Lowe simply do not accept the argument that economic policy by its nature violates individual freedom, or that the absence of policy guarantees that freedom is protected. While both support a democratic political process as the means for stipulating macro goals, it is clear that historical experience, study of the economy and legislation – such as the Full Employment Bill and the Humphrey–Hawkins Act – have led each to assume some basic set of macro goals as desirable: at the most fundamental level, full employment and price stability (for example, see Lowe, 1965, 1976; Lerner, 1943, 1951, 1972). They both also considered a decent standard of living for all as a fundamental and, in a sense, ultimate goal to be achieved by job creation and the maintenance of the purchasing power of income. Thus these goals serve as points of departure in their analyses.

FUNCTIONAL FINANCE AND MONEY AS A CREATURE OF THE STATE

Lerner's insight was a fundamentally Keynesian one: The economy is likely to find itself in an unemployment equilibrium with no inherent tendency to move to full employment. Lack of effective aggregate demand requires that the federal government run a deficit to exactly offset the shortfall so that there can be aggregate balance at the full employment level of output. This is based on fundamental accounting relations as represented in the national income accounts. Keynesian unemployment is due to lack of effective demand. Deficits are not one-time injections, but may have to be run continually, permanently. The size of the deficit depends on the relation of actual and desired net saving.

Lerner's policy prescription is thus firmly in the strong fiscal Keynesian tradition: Government should run a deficit that closes the recessionary gap. This not only rejects the 'deficit hawk' position, it also transcends the 'deficit dove' stance. The confusions regarding national budget deficits and the debt are important and real. There are measurement problems; mistreatments (or non-treatments) of capital budgeting; fallacies concerning 'crowding out' and the relation of deficits and interest rates (and of deficits and inflation); unfounded views on the 'burden' on future generations; and more (see, for example, Heilbroner and Bernstein, 1989; Eisner, 1994; Cavanaugh, 1996). As Bator (1962) pointed out some time ago, however, while these are all debating points, concentration on these areas maintains discussion at a level that actually concedes too much. For example it may be true that due to measurement and accounting problems, the deficit (or debt) is 'not as big as it looks,' but this line of attack implicitly condones the 'sound money' view that smaller is inherently better. Functional finance simply refers to an approach to public finance that sees the federal budget and the management of the national debt as a *means* to economic prosperity. This notion need not assume any particular a priori relation between government expenditures and revenues or set in advance a most desirable absolute or relative size of the national debt.

> The central idea is that government fiscal policy, its spending and taxing, its borrowing and repayment of loans, its issue of new money and its withdrawal of money, shall all be undertaken with an eye only to the *results* of these actions on the economy and not to any established traditional doctrine about what is sound and what is unsound. This principle of judging only by *effects* has been applied in many other fields of human activity, where it is known as the method of science opposed to scholasticism. The principle of judging fiscal measures by the way they work or function in the economy we may call *Functional Finance*. . . . Government should adjust its rates of expenditure and taxation such that total spending in the economy is neither more nor less than that which is sufficient to purchase the full employment level of output at current prices. If this means there is a deficit, greater borrowing, 'printing money,' etc., then these things in themselves are neither good nor bad, they are simply the means to the desired ends of full employment and price stability. (Lerner, 1943: 354)

Thus functional finance does not say anything about what the budget should be prior to economic analysis. If it is concluded that under particular circumstances a balanced budget describes the best means to economic prosperity, then even a balanced budget is not inconsistent with a functional approach to public finance. 'Sound money' is therefore only inconsistent with functional finance if the balanced budget is seen as an end in itself, rather than as a means to an end. If a balanced budget – or surplus in order to decrease the national debt – is insisted upon, even if it may be shown to have negative economic consequences (or be impossible), then this is not functional finance (it is, actually, 'dysfunctional finance'). Likewise, functional finance does not stipulate that bigger deficits are 'better' or that deficits are 'good' in and of themselves; it is the effects with which we are concerned.

Such an approach has an immediate implication that at first glance may appear shocking or surprising but which economists and policy makers would do well to consider: *neither taxing nor government 'borrowing' are funding operations*. Decisions concerning taxation are to be made only with regard to their economic effects in terms of the promotion of full employment, price stability or other economic goals, and not ever because 'the government needs to make money payments' (Lerner, 1943: 354). Likewise 'the government should borrow only if . . . the effects' of borrowing are desired, for example 'if otherwise the rate of interest would be too low' (Lerner, 1943: 355). These points of view were repeated and elaborated by Lerner in his 1951 book *The Economics of Employment*: '[T]axes should *never* be imposed for the sake of the tax revenues. It is true that taxation makes money available to the government, but this is not an effect of any importance because money can be made available to the government so much more easily by having some created by the Treasury' (1951, 131).[3] Likewise 'borrowing' is also not a funding operation for Lerner.

What are the purposes of taxation and borrowing, if not to fund government spending? The purpose of taxation for Lerner is, first, the role it plays in endowing otherwise worthless bits of paper with value and, second, its 'effect on the *public* of influencing their economic behavior' (Lerner, 1951: 131, original emphasis). Like taxation, borrowing is not a funding operation; rather, it is a means of managing reserves and controlling the overnight interest rate in the face of government spending and running budget deficits:

> [T]he spending of money . . . out of deficits keeps on increasing the stock of money [and bank reserves] and this keeps on pushing down the rate of interest. Somehow the government must *prevent* the rate of interest from being pushed down by the additions to the stock of money coming from its own expenditures. . . . There is an obvious way of doing this. The government can *borrow back* the money it is spending. (Lerner, 1951: 10–11)

Note here the crucial implication that 'borrowing' logically *follows*, rather than *precedes*, government spending. In fact, this analysis questions the accuracy and relevance of the term 'borrowing' itself for discussing government bond sales.

The role of taxation and borrowing, reserve management and interest rate maintenance will become clearer upon examination of another, less prominent Lerner article – 'Money as a Creature of the State' – an article that places Lerner squarely in the Keynes–Knapp Chartalist school and that is key to fully understanding the possibility and effectiveness of functional finance (Lerner, 1947). The ability of the government to conduct fiscal and monetary policy according to the principles of functional finance is made possible by the fact that, as the title of Lerner's paper states, 'money is a creature of the state':

> The government – which is what the state means in practice – by virtue of its power to create or destroy money by fiat and its power to take money away from people by taxation, is in a position to keep the rate of spending of the economy at the level required to fill its two great responsibilities, the prevention of depression, and the maintenance of the value of money. (Lerner, 1947: 314)

In adopting this view Lerner followed Keynes in accepting the main thrust of Knapp's 'State Theory of Money' (Keynes, 1930: 4, 6, n. 1; Knapp, 1924). Of course, the basic starting point can be traced back at least as far as Adam Smith who put forward the idea that 'a requirement that certain taxes should be paid in particular paper money might give that paper a certain value even if it was irredeemable' (Cannan, 1904: 312). The state has the power not only to tax but to designate what will suffice to retire tax obligations, that is, what it will accept at its pay offices. By determining public receivability, the state can create a demand for otherwise worthless pieces of paper, leading to general acceptability. The state can issue this currency, and use it to purchase goods and services from the private sector:

> The modern state can make anything it chooses generally acceptable as money and thus establish its value quite apart from any connection, even of the most formal kind, with gold or backing of any kind. It is true that a simple declaration that such and such is money will not do, even if backed by the most convincing constitutional evidence of the state's absolute sovereignty. But if the state is willing to accept the proposed money in the payment of taxes and other obligations to itself the trick is done. Everyone who has obligations to the state will be willing to accept the pieces of paper with which he can settle the obligations, and all other people will be willing to accept those pieces of paper because they know that taxpayers, etc., will accept them in turn. On the other hand if the state should decline to accept some kind of money in payment of obligations to itself, it is difficult to believe that it would retain much of its general acceptability. . . . What this means is that whatever may have been the history of gold, at the present time, in a normally well-working economy, money is a creature of the state. Its general acceptability, which is its all-important attribute, stands or falls by its acceptability by the state. (Lerner, 1947: 313)

Thus a variety of state powers, such as government's ability to tax, declare public receivability, create and destroy money, buy and sell bonds and administer the prices it pays for goods and services purchased from the private sector, constitute a menu of instruments with which full employment and stability of the value of the currency may be promoted.

We have cited Smith, Knapp and Keynes, but perhaps we would do well to examine more recent examples of this view. It can be found in other 'Post Keynesian' authors after Lerner (see, for example, Kurihara, 1950: 34–39; Bator, 1962).[4] But the skeptic will argue that these pronouncements from the 1950s and 1960s are of a day long gone by. It is thus constructive to note the following:

> In advanced societies, the central government is in a strong position to make certain assets generally acceptable media. By its willingness to accept a designated asset in settlement of taxes and other obligations, the government makes that asset acceptable to any who have such obligations, and in turn to others who have obligations to them, and so on. (Tobin, 1998: 27)

Goodhart has also used the 'Cartalist' framework to argue against the Mengerian–metallist–monetarist position on optimal currency areas (Goodhart, 1997, 1998).

Mosler (1997–98) and Wray (1998) incorporate these insights into a framework that draws on Post Keynesian monetary theory and a rigorous institutional analysis of the relation of the Treasury, the central bank and the banking system. The central bank does not control the money supply; it does, however, have significant ability to determine the short-term interest rate. The central bank is the lender of last resort, a necessary function for the stability of the financial system. Open market operations, government spending and lending, borrowing and taxation all affect reserves in the banking system. Excess reserves will cause short-term rates to tend to zero, while insufficient reserves will send rates toward infinity. Thus bond sales are essentially a reserve drain used to maintain a positive overnight rate of interest (interbank lending rate). Government borrowing is not to fund untaxed spending. Government spending comes first; then the government borrows what it does not tax in order to drain reserves and maintain interest rates. The national debt is 'the total number of dollars that have been drained from the banking system in order to maintain the fed funds rate [overnight rate]. A more appropriate name [for the national debt] would be the Interest Rate Maintenance Account (IRMA)' (Mosler, 1995: 14). Since money is a creature of the state, the Government does not need to tax or borrow to spend. Taxation is not to fund government spending; it is a means of creating a demand for fiat currency, while 'borrowing' is a reserve drain to support short-term interest rates. There is no problem 'financing' full employment. From the functional finance perspective, the goals are full employment and price stability, not any particular relation between either government expenditure and tax revenues or the sales and purchases of government bonds. Obsession with budget balancing for its own sake makes no sense whatsoever, but threatens the health of the economic system and blocks the way to full employment.

The importance of the Lernerian contributions of functional finance and money as a creature of the state are hard to overstate. There are two in some respects related problems, or areas, where this framework remains incomplete by itself. Lerner recognized one issue quite early on, and he dedicated a good bit of his life to it. In his early versions of functional finance, inflation was seen as the result of excess aggregate demand and therefore increasing taxation was seen as the cure. But as it became apparent that there were other sources of inflation, this simple policy for demand-side inflation was no longer sufficient for managing the value of currency. Thus Lerner dedicated himself to the study of stagflation and the evaluation and formulation of various incomes policies, market anti-inflation plans (MAPs), wage-price controls and so on. The second issue regards the meaning of full employment. In addition to other types of inflation, Lerner also began to notice that inflation did not begin at true full employment but well before that point. Thus he even began to use terms like 'low full employment' and 'high full employment,' neither of which actually meant zero involuntary unemployment (Lerner, 1951). For those who reject NAIRU and 'natural rates' of unemployment and who are interested in zero involuntary unemployment, these terms are not adequate. As Lerner admits, then, functional finance – as formulated, and by itself – is not capable of attaining and maintaining zero involuntary unemployment with price stability.

This brings us to the work of Lowe. Lowe did not believe that what he called 'primary interventions' (regular fiscal and monetary policies) were adequate to bring about true full employment. These were not sufficient by themselves because, even when the assumption is made that such policies can bring an economy to full employment, there is then the issue of *maintaining* full employment in the face of ongoing structural and technological change, that is, changes in the supply of labor and natural resources, capital- and labor-displacing technical changes and changes in the composition of final demand. Not only aggregate proportionality and balance must be considered, but sectoral relations as well. In addition to Keynesian unemployment, structural unemployment – meaning unemployment due to structural and technological change – must also be addressed. This was precisely the focus of Lowe's 'structural analysis.' Issues of structural rigidity and elasticity of the production system must be confronted, as well as technological unemployment and the reserve army of labor and issues of sectoral relations. All of which brings us back to issues of price stability.

LOWE'S FULL EMPLOYMENT PROPOSAL

Lowe's structural analysis is concerned with a realistic evaluation of the elasticity of the production system, its adaptability in the face of structural and technological changes, such as capital- or labor-saving technical innovations, changes in labor supply and the supply of natural resources and changes in the composition of final demand. A viscous system, having trouble with quick adaptation to such changes, may be characterized by bottlenecks in production, sluggish growth, inflationary pressures, significant structural, frictional, and technological unemployment and periods of plant and equipment underutilization. Conversely, the more elastic the production system, the better its ability to respond to structural and technical change without structural rigidities. Such an economic climate is more conducive to high employment economic growth without inflation.

Structural analysis highlights the impediments to rapid adjustment – structural disequilibria, the disproportionalities and the physical–technical consistency conditions for system viability (reproduction) – that confront in particular an economy brought to full employment by, for example, Keynesian demand management. In neoclassical theory there is a trade-off between flexibility and reality; in structural analysis there is a trade-off between flexibility and full employment of resources.

Lowe's proposal for full employment, which he called 'planned domestic colonization,' is what is better known as direct job creation by government. Lowe, while seeing a number of clear advantages to public employment programs, was very skeptical about the possibility of attaining or maintaining full employment through indirect means such as stimulating private sector demand: 'Unlike private investors, public investors are not hampered by uncertainties about future demand, because they themselves determine the purpose that investment and its final output is to serve, for instance, the items that make up the infrastructure' (1988: 107). Lowe saw in public works a degree of variability and flexibility not possible in the private sector where competitive pressures legislate methods of production, the composition of output and the types of capital equipment and natural resources utilized, and where private decisions governed by narrow economic motives may not be consistent with what is best for society as a whole (Forstater, 1998).

For Lowe, some of the major obstacles to full employment were rooted in the technological conditions of production. Employment of workers available as a result of labor-displacing technical change or increases in labor supply depends on the prior construction of real capital. But the public sector has the ability to vary the labor intensity of productive activity in ways that the private sector cannot. The public sector may choose to utilize a more labor-intensive method of production that would be 'inefficient' for a private firm but that is quite reasonable from the perspective of social well-being. For the purpose of altering overall capital–labor ratios, or easing the utilization of certain types of capital equipment or increasing the utilization of yet other types, the public sector may also vary public sector employment between different tasks. The spectrum of choices includes activities that approach the level of '*pure services* in the fields of health, education, and general welfare,' as well as activities that do not use or make more limited use of precious natural resources and that do not pollute (1988: 107). A public sector employment program can also deal with the unequal geographical distribution of unemployment, which highly aggregated demand stimulus programs do not necessarily address.

Functional Finance and Full Employment . . . and Price Stability

Lerner himself recognized the weaknesses of functional finance for attaining true full employment, and wrote of the role to be played by government direct job creation (Lerner, 1944: 315–16). His peers recognized the need to go beyond highly aggregated demand management to direct government job creation if true full employment were the goal (see especially, Pierson, 1945: 33ff). More recently a number of proposals along these lines have appeared (see, for example, Harvey, 1989; Collins et al., 1994; Gordon, 1997; Mosler,

1995, 1997–98; Mitchell, 1998; Papadimitriou et al., 1998; Wray, 1998). An important recent proposal for what Papadimitriou et al. have termed the 'job opportunity' approach, put forward around the same time as Lowe's, came from Hyman Minsky (1986). Like Lowe, Minsky believed full employment approaches based on 'subsidizing demand' are limited as they are likely to result in inflation, financial crisis and serious instability (1986: 308). He thus sought an alternative to reliance on schemes based on stimulating private sector demand:

> The main instrument of such a policy is the creation of an infinitely elastic demand for labor at a floor or minimum wage that does not depend on long- or short-run profit expectations of business. Since only government can divorce the offering of employment from the profitability of hiring workers, the infinitely elastic demand for labor must be created by government. (1986: 308)

While functional finance – again, as originally formulated and by itself – cannot provide for zero involuntary unemployment, it does provide the framework for making the question of how to pay for full employment a non-issue. Instead of government simply concerning itself with aggregate spending to close the gap between actual and potential employment, government closes the gap by hiring the unemployed. The figures look the same in the aggregate, but the composition, and not simply the amount, of government spending comes to the fore. Spending must be on job creation. Functional finance provides the rules for such spending and the rules for the management of reserves and control of interest rates under such a system.

In addition Lerner's recognition of money as a creature of the state, when combined with Lowe's employment strategy, provides a framework for price stability that draws on the ideas of Benjamin Graham. Graham (1937) outlines a program for price stability based on commodity buffer stocks. This is an idea made familiar to economists and policy makers through the work of such eminent figures as Nicholas Kaldor and A.G. Hart, among others. As put forward recently by Mitchell, Mosler, Wray and others, a Public Service Corps can be conceived as a buffer stock of labor. Thus the national currency itself can be defined by the wage paid to Public Service workers. Of course changes in the Public Service wage will constitute a redefinition of the currency. Nevertheless the Public Service wage may serve as a regulating anchor to which the currency is tied. Because labor is a basic commodity, employed directly and indirectly into the production of every other commodity, the job opportunity program offers a mechanism for regulating the value of the currency and thus controlling the price level.

There are a number of other reasons why the job opportunity program need not be inflationary. First, Public Service Corps workers may be engaged in public works such as infrastructure revitalization that promote private sector productivity growth. Second, such workers may be employed in activities that help reduce expensive social and environmental costs, such as environmental protection. Third, the increase in expenditure on Public Service workers will be at least partially offset by decreases in other forms of expenditure on the unemployed or the effects of unemployment. Expenditures on unemployment insurance and other forms of general assistance can be expected to decline with the job opportunity program. Savings may also be expected in the form of decreased expenditures on indirect costs of unemployment. These factors range from reductions in spending on crime prevention and prosecution, criminal justice related to unemployment, reductions in medical bills and savings on other social and economic costs of unemployment. Fourth, public works tend to be less inflationary than 'the dole' because the former increases both supply and demand, while the latter increases only demand. Fifth, as Lowe pointed out, government has a degree of discretion unavailable to the private sector in choosing between alternative methods of production and alternative productive activities, which can be used to avoid bottlenecks and structural rigidities without sacrificing employment.

CONCLUSION

The work of Lowe and Lerner challenges us to go beyond the received wisdom of current economic theory and policy to reconsider the methodology of economics and its relation to public policy. It also provides theoretical insights that may inform the crafting of a new macroeconomics – a political macroeconomics, an institutional macroeconomics, a historical macroeconomics, a structural macroeconomics. A Lowe–Lerner synthesis also provides a framework for incorporating both monetary production and structural and technological change, and for analysing both Keynesian and technological unemployment. Instrumental analysis and functional finance are more than oddities to be studied in history-of-thought journals, or worse, simply forgotten. These are approaches that must be carefully considered for their potential contribution to the formulation and implementation of effective practical policies for today and the future.

NOTES

1. Admittedly both terms are problematic, as 'instrumentalism' and 'functionalism' carry baggage that has nothing to do with either Lowe's instrumental analysis or Lerner's functional finance.
2. The basic principles of functional finance – though not the term – can be found in 'The Economic Steering Wheel,' published in 1941.

3. The details of this and related propositions under contemporary institutional arrangements in the US have been demonstrated by Bell (2000).
4. Likewise Samuelson, at least as late as 1961, fully and explicitly embraced functional finance (see Samuelson, 1966[1961]); A.C.L. Day is one example of an author whose analysis of the government's reserve management and interest rate control clearly echoes the Lernerian analysis (Day, 1957). Wray (1998) has additionally documented recent Chartalist tendencies in authors such as Minsky and Boulding, among others.

REFERENCES

Bator, Francis M. (1962), 'Money and Government,' *Atlantic Monthly*, April.

Bell, Stephanie (2000), 'Do Taxes and Bonds Finance Government Spending?,' *Journal of Economic Issues*, 34 (3), 603–20.

Cannan, Edwin (1904), 'Marginal Summary,' in A. Smith, *An Inquiry into the Nature and Causes of the Wealth of Nations*, New York: Modern Library.

Cavanaugh, Francis X. (1996), *The Truth About the National Debt*, Boston, MA: Harvard Business School Press.

Collins, Sheila D., Helen Lachs Ginsburg, and Gertrude Schaffner Goldberg (1994), *Jobs for All: A Plan for the Revitalization of America*, New York: Apex Press.

Day, A.C.L. (1957), *Outline of Monetary Economics*, Oxford: Clarendon Press.

Eisner, Robert (1994), *The Misunderstood Economy*, Boston, MA: Harvard Business School Press.

Forstater, Mathew (1998), 'Flexible Full Employment: Structural Implications of Discretionary Public Sector Employment,' *Journal of Economic Issues*, 32(2), 557–63.

Forstater, Mathew (1999), 'Working Backwards: Instrumental Analysis as a Policy Discovery Procedure,' *Review of Political Economy*, 11 (1) 5–19.

Goodhart, Charles (1997), 'One Government, One Money,' *The Prospect*, March, pp 1–3.

Goodhart, Charles (1998), 'The Two Concepts of Money: Implications for the Analysis of Optimal Currency Areas,' Working Paper, Financial Markets Group, London School of Economics.

Gordon, Wendell (1997), 'Job Assurance – the Job Guarantee Revisited,' *Journal of Economic Issues*, 31 (3), September.

Graham, Benjamin (1937), *Storage and Stability*, New York: McGraw-Hill.

Harvey, Philip (1989), *Securing the Right to Employment*, Princeton, NJ: Princeton University Press.

Heilbroner, Robert L. (ed.) (1969), *Economic Means and Social Ends: Essays in Political Economics*, Englewood Cliffs, NJ: Prentice-Hall.

Heilbroner, Robert L. and Peter Bernstein (1989), *The Debt and the Deficit*, New York: Norton.

Keynes, John Maynard (1930), *A Treatise on Money*, New York: Harcourt, Brace.

Keynes, John Maynard (1936 [1964]), *The General Theory of Employment, Interest, and Money*, New York: Harvest Harcourt Brace, 1964.

Knapp. G.F. (1924), *The State Theory of Money*, Munich: Duncker and Humblot.

Kurihara, Kenneth (1950), *Monetary Theory and Public Policy*, New York: Norton.

Lerner, Abba P. (1941), 'The Economic Steering Wheel,' *University of Kansas Review*, June.

Lerner, Abba P. (1943), 'Functional Finance and the Federal Debt,' *Social Research*,

(10), 38–51, reprinted in M.G. Mueller (ed.), *Readings in Macroeconomics*, New York: Holt, Rinehart, and Winston, pp. 353–60.

Lerner, Abba P. (1944), *The Economics of Control*, New York: Macmillan.

Lerner, Abba P. (1947), 'Money as a Creature of the State,' *American Economic Review*, 37 (2), 312–17.

Lerner, Abba P. (1951), *The Economics of Employment*, New York: McGraw-Hill.

Lerner, Abba P. (1969), 'On Instrumental Analysis,' in R.L. Heilbroner (ed.), *Economic Means and Social Ends: Essays in Political Economics*, Englewood Cliffs, NJ: Prentice-Hall.

Lerner, Abba P. (1972), *Flation*, Baltimore, MD: Penguin Books.

Lowe, Adolph (1935), *Economics and Sociology*, London: Allen and Unwin.

Lowe, Adolph (1965), *On Economic Knowledge*, White Plains, NY: M.E. Sharpe, expanded edition (1977).

Lowe, Adolph (1967), 'The Normative Roots of Economic Value,' in S. Hook (ed.), *Human Values and Economic Policy*, New York: NYU Press.

Lowe, Adolph (1969), 'Toward a Science of Political Economics,' in R.L. Heilbroner (ed.), *Economic Means and Social Ends: Essays in Political Economics*, Englewood Cliffs, NJ: Prentice-Hall.

Lowe, Adolph (1976), *The Path of Economic Growth*, Cambridge: Cambridge University Press.

Lowe, Adolph (1988), *Has Freedom a Future?*, New York: Praeger.

Minsky, Hyman P. (1986), *Stabilizing an Unstable Economy*, New Haven, CT: Yale University Press.

Mitchell, William F. (1998) 'The Buffer Stock Employment Model and the NAIRU: The Path to Full Employment,' *Journal of Economic Issues*, 32(2), 547–55.

Mosler, Warren (1995), *Soft Currency Economics*, West Palm Beach: III Finance, 3rd edn.

Mosler, Warren (1997–98), 'Full Employment and Price Stability,' *Journal of Post Keynesian Economics*, 20 (2), 167–82.

Papadimitriou, Dimitri, L. Randall Wray, and Mathew Forstater (1998), 'Toward Full Employment without Inflation: The Job Opportunity Program,' *Report*, Jerome Levy Economics Institute, 8 (3), August.

Pierson, John H. G. (1945), 'Fiscal Policy for Full Employment,' National Planning Association Planning Pamphlets, No. 45.

Samuelson, Paul (1966[1961]), 'Functional Fiscal Policy for the 1960s,' in E. Phelps et al. (eds), *Problems of the Modern Economy*, New York: Norton.

Tobin, James (with S. Golub) (1998), *Money, Credit, and Capital*, New York: McGraw-Hill.

Wray, L. Randall (1998), *Understanding Modern Money: The Key to Full Employment and Price Stability*, Cheltenham, UK and Lyme, US: Edward Elgar.

4. Neisser's unorthodox quantity theory of money

Hans-Michael Trautwein

1. INTRODUCTION

When Hans Neisser came to America in 1933 to become a professor of monetary theory at the Wharton School in Philadelphia, his works in that field had already earned him an international reputation of high stature.[1] His treatise on the value of money (*Der Tauschwert des Geldes*, 1928) was approvingly cited by Keynes, Hayek and other writers in those peak years of monetary theory. This is remarkable for several reasons. It was not only because they were written in German that Neisser's works were not an easy read.[2] They also contained painstaking dissections of the effects of capital accumulation and technical progress on the circuit flow of money; and they were based on Irving Fisher's formulations of the quantity theory of money. At first glance we might take these to be very orthodox approaches, and Neisser, in fact, never made any great claims to originality. Yet his methods and results were unorthodox, both for his time and from the vantage point of ours.

The first unorthodox feature of Neisser's approach lies in the fact that he took recourse to the quantity theory. The hyperinflation in 1923 may have made many Germans believe that changes in price level were directly and equiproportionally caused by changes in the volume of money. Among monetary theorists in the German language area, however, the quantity theory was quite unpopular. Under the influences of Knapp's chartalism, other types of nominalism and Austrian attempts to extend marginal utility theory to the determination of money prices, most of them had developed a predilection for the Tookean income approach, banking theories and a variety of monetary metaphysics (see Ellis 1934). As Neisser deplored (1936a: 109), the German literature was full of an 'invincible antipathy to any kind of the quantity theory, however modernized.' There were but few, like Schumpeter (1917/18) and Marschak (1924), who made use of the equation of exchange, at least as a heuristic device.

Neisser's second 'non-orthodoxy' relates to the Wicksellian tradition in the European interwar literature on money and the business cycle. Wicksell (1898) had meant to adapt the quantity theory to modern credit economies by considering the feedbacks between interest rates and the price level. However, nearly all writers with a Wicksell connection – such as Hayek, Lindahl, Myrdal, and the Keynes of the *Treatise* – struggled to free monetary theory from the 'tyranny' exercised by the conventional quantity concepts (Ohlin, 1936, xiv). Neisser has been ranked among the Wicksellians (see end-note 2), but he merits that label for different reasons. He, for one, shared Wicksell's interest in modernizing the quantity theory. Unlike most other Wicksellians, he did not confine his analysis to short-run disequilibria in business cycles. Appealing to classical concepts of the circulation of capital and money, he was more concerned with structural change in the 'real sphere' than with the potential to produce non-neutralities of money in the long run.[3]

Neisser's third 'non-orthodoxy' relates to his critique of Say's Law.[4] Neisser invalidated the classical dichotomy of the level and structure of prices by demonstrating that a general glut of markets can result from changes in the structure of production in a credit economy. Moreover he showed how overproduction can turn into equilibrium underemployment. With hindsight Neisser's refutation of Say's Law could therefore be taken to resemble, if not anticipate, the core message in Keynes's *General Theory* (1936). It differs, however, from the Keynesian orthodoxy insofar as it does not rely on a liquidity preference motive in the money demand function.

Finally, the first three 'non-orthodoxies' indicate some of the dividing lines between Neisser's monetary theory and the quantity-theoretical orthodoxies of our time. Neisser disputed the stability of full employment equilibrium in a monetary economy. For him, the long-run neutrality of money was not a natural outcome of the market process. Instead of taking a stock perspective on money, where income is conceptualized as discounted wealth and where the rate of return to money holdings is but one of many relative prices, he set the focus on the flow of money in the circulation of capital.

In the following sections, Neisser's unorthodox quantity theory will be discussed in greater detail. Sections 2 and 3 provide a summary discussion of his writings on the value and circuit of money published between 1928 and 1931. Section 4 connects these early works with Neisser's writings on business cycles and structural unemployment between 1931 and 1942. In concluding Section 5, I will identify a few areas in which Neisser's non-orthodoxies might prove to be useful for further research.

2. THE VALUE AND THE CIRCUIT OF MONEY

This section is a synoptic summary of Neisser's habilitation thesis on the exchange value of money (1928) and of a longer article on the circuit of money (1931a). In *Tauschwert des Geldes* (1928), Neisser examined the determinants of the value of money, which he defined as the inverse price level. He based his analysis on the 'deposits and income' version of Fisher's equation of exchange:

$$MV + M'V' = PY$$

where M is the volume of cash, V the velocity of cash, M' the volume of checkable bank deposits, V' the velocity of deposits, P the price level and Y the real national income. This equation differs from Wicksell's reformulation of the quantity theory in which deposits were captured as an accelerating factor of 'virtual' cash velocity. The Fisherine equation of exchange can nevertheless be used to make a Wicksellian connection between interest rates and the price level. Moreover Neisser emphasized that the scope of the equation is wider than suggested by the proponents of the 'naïve quantity theory' according to which P is exclusively and proportionally dependent on M (1928: 10f). The task of monetary theory is to show how *all* factors of the equation interact in the circulation of goods.

Neisser based his analysis of the equation of exchange on the benchmark of price level stability that implies a constant value of money. If the quantity theory is to hold, changes in the velocity of money and flow of goods require compensating changes in the volume of money. Neisser used the word *Geldbedarf* to denote this benchmark condition (1931a: 367). It should not be confused with money demand (*Geldnachfrage*) in the conventional understanding of 'real balances' (1931b: 367). I will translate *Geldbedarf* as 'deflationary gaps' wherever the focus is on the *causes* of deviations from the point of reference. These causes need to be described first before we can consider Neisser's position on the comparative relevance of *adjustment* mechanisms (prices, income or money stock).

Neisser developed his theory of the circulation of money in two stages. At the first stage, he distinguished between two types of money holdings in the economy: balance reserves and operating funds (1928: ch. II). Reserves represent the precautionary demand for money. From an individual point of view, they are hoarded to meet contingencies. In the aggregate they are nevertheless part of the circulation of money. They affect the size and composition of the monetary aggregate ($M + M'$) in so far as they support bank lending. Under normal circumstances, however, the velocity of balance reserves is close to zero. It will rise and affect the average total of velocity only when high inflation provokes a flight into real assets or when current income falls short of expenditures in severe crises (1928: 18). The total velocity of money is thus determined by two factors. One is the ratio of balance reserves to the operating funds that represent the transactions demand for money. The other is the velocity of the operating funds, which varies inversely with the length of the average period between the payments of income.

At the second stage (1931a), Neisser shifted the focus onto the circulation of capital by switching back to Fisher's basic equation:

$$MV = PT$$

with T as the volume of transactions. As the circulation of money largely takes place in interindustrial transactions, Neisser chose to replace income velocity by the broader concept of transactions velocity. Accordingly he set the focus on the operating funds, which he now described as 'active money' because they are regularly spent in the circular flow.[5] In this context, Neisser reintroduced the classical distinction between income money and business money, accounting for the fact that the total of payments cannot be fully disaggregated into factor incomes.[6] A certain proportion of payments serves to mediate the circular flow of capital goods in the production of capital goods. In addition to the outlays on variable capital (the v-fund in Neisser's Marxian terminology), there must be a fund of constant capital (c-fund) that buys machines, auxiliary goods and raw material. From this follows that the *income* velocity of money, or its circulation in the v-sphere, is determined by the length of the average period between payments in both spheres,[7] *and* by capital intensity.

In Neisser's view the secular increase in capital intensity is a stylized fact, a widely observable tendency that is part and parcel of the evolution of market systems. The intensification implies increasing flows of goods within the business sphere. As it tends to raise the net product, it generally also produces greater flows of goods within the income sphere. If the volume of money is constant and if *transactions* velocity is given by the technical and institutional determinants of the periods between payments, there must be a *double* tendency of prices to decline – unless income velocity increases – so that a greater proportion of money can circulate in the business sphere (1931a: 378ff).

In this context Neisser developed a fruitful classification of deflationary gaps (see Figure 4.1). Their causes and consequences can be conceptualized by defining the benchmark condition, an unchanged value of money, in terms of a dynamic transformation of the equation of exchange:[8]

$$p = (m + v) - t = 0.$$

If structural change increases the volume of transactions ($t > 0$) and if $(m + v)$ does not rise in proportion, the price level will fall ($p < 0$). There are cases in which deflation will not (necessarily) disturb the traverse of the economy to a new equilibrium position. In other cases structural change will lead to disrup-

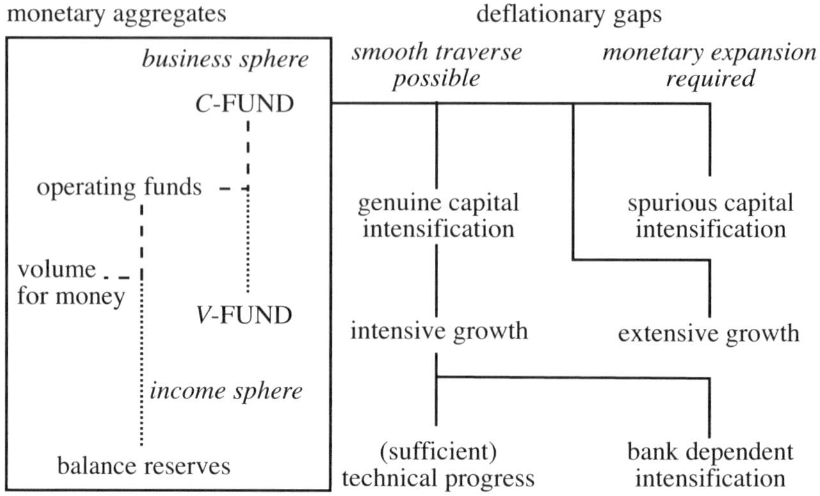

Figure 4.1 Neisser's concepts of deflationary gaps in the circulation of capital

tions of the market process or take place only if its effects on *t* are offset by monetary expansion (*m*) or by changes in velocity.

In his classification of transactions affecting structural change, Neisser made a first distinction between changes in the structure of production and the structure of circulation. *Genuine capital intensification* adds intermediate goods and stages of production to the process. This type of intensification requires real saving in terms of resource reallocation and therefore implies a redistribution of money from circulation in the *v*-sphere to the *c*-sphere. The redistribution may take place in the classical fashion, resulting from changes in time preference or the interest rate; or it may be effected by inflationary credit, in a process of 'forced' or 'unplanned saving.'[9] Genuine intensification is contrasted with changes in the degree of vertical integration. A 'slicing up' of the product chain into a greater number of firms (by way of intermediation, 'outsourcing,' etc.) may increase the volume of transactions without affecting the material structure of production. In these cases, capital intensification is *spurious*, and the demand for money can be satisfied only if the volume or the velocity of money is increased (1931a: 381).

A further distinction should be made between extensive and intensive growth. *Extensive growth* implies an increase in the inputs of capital and labour, normally without a corresponding lowering of unit costs in monetary terms (1931a: 393f). The velocities and proportions of the *v*- and *c*-funds remain unchanged. If the supply of money is constant, the transition to a new equilibrium position could be disturbed by contractual rigidities of nominal wages and interest. In general, however, such disturbances will be mitigated by a credit expansion that is induced by expectations of greater profit at the going rate of interest.

In the case of *intensive growth*, a deflationary gap is produced both by an increase in the ratio of capital to labour and by an increase in output. At this point, Neisser distinguished between cases of genuine capital intensification with and without *sufficient technical progress*.[10] If capital intensification comes with advances in technology that preserve or raise the marginal productivity of capital, the economy may make a smooth transition to an equilibrium position with higher output and lower prices (1931a: 394). In this limiting case, the rate of reduction in unit costs equals or exceeds the rate of increase in output. In all other cases, the increase in capital intensity can only be profitable for firms if banks lower their lending rates and other costs of credit. In those cases capital intensification becomes *bank-dependent*.

Neisser's classification of structural change in production and circulation clearly illustrates a variety of cases in which changes in the volume of transactions will affect the price level. With the exception of 'sufficient technical progress,' capital intensification and growth implies an invalidation of the classical dichotomy of real and monetary analysis.[11] The price level, and hence the value of money, would only remain unaffected if there were compensating changes in the velocity or the volume of money. In the cases of spurious intensification, extensive growth and bank-dependent intensification, deflation has the potential to feed back onto profit expectations and real activity.

With regard to compensating adjustments, velocity was counted out. Referring to German data of the highly inflationary and deflationary 1920s, Neisser proclaimed its relative invariance to be a stylized fact (1931a). At any rate he insisted that there is no mechanism that makes capital intensification, technical progress and the determinants of payment periods move in step. So if the quantity theory is to hold, there must be compensating changes in the volume of money. This raises two questions: Will the market process produce such changes automatically? And how does an autonomous increase in the volume of money affect prices and production? Both questions were beyond the scope of Neisser's essay on the circuit of money (1931a), but they were addressed in his treatise of 1928 and in his writings on the business cycle.

3. CREDIT MONEY IN THE STRUCTURE OF PRODUCTION

Most of the space in Neisser's early re-examination of the quantity theory was taken up by the analysis of the interaction between the components of the monetary aggregate, cash (M) and deposits (M') (1928: chs. III–VI). In modern terms, the argument can be put succinctly as follows:

$$M'/M = \{1/[b + r(1 - b)]\} - 1 \qquad \text{and} \qquad M = M(i_a)$$

where b is the ratio of cash in circulation to the monetary aggregate, r is the ratio of the banks' cash balance reserves to the aggregate, and i_a is the discount rate which is autonomously set by the monetary authorities, with $dM/di_a < 0$. The deposit/cash ratio is a simple transformation of the money multiplier that is routinely expounded in modern textbooks. Neisser observed that cash demand is rendered volatile by seasonal, cyclical and structural factors (including fiscal policy) that interact with a trend towards cashless payments (1928: chs. IV–V). Moreover he pointed out that the link between the discount rate and capital market rates may be loosened by speculative stock transactions.[12] These qualifications notwithstanding, Neisser firmly believed that central banks can control the total supply of money by setting the discount rate, and that they do so even when they *choose* to accommodate loan demand (1928: 91f).

For Neisser, the main rationale of central banking was to preserve an 'elasticity of the credit supply' that would help to keep the value of money stable. As the note supply should be regulated to meet this target, it should not be subject to the motive of profit maximization. The deflationary bias of capital accumulation and output growth should be counteracted by an expansion of bank credit beyond saving *ex ante* to prevent the paralysis of real investment by the real appreciation of debt contracts with fixed nominal interest (1928: 58f). Following Schumpeter and Hahn, Neisser assigned the banks a central role in directing progress in industrial production. Through their lending business, banks create additional purchasing power and intermediate savings. Contrary to the classical view, Neisser insisted that savings are, to a large extent, nothing but 'credit consolidated' by the income mechanisms of extensive growth or technical progress. In 1928 this was, however, only a hint in passing, because Neisser was more concerned with killing illusions about the scope for 'productive credit expansion.'

That discussion was likewise based on the benchmark of a constant price level. This time, however, Neisser dealt with the real effects of monetary expansion, not with the monetary effects of structural change in production and circulation; and the focus was shifted onto *inflationary* gaps (1928: Ch. VI). Under the condition of full employment, a credit expansion will promote an increase in productive capacity only if one or more of the following conditions are fulfilled:

(a) 'Forced' (or unplanned) saving exceeds the loss of voluntary (or planned) saving that results from the inflationary redistribution of purchasing power from the income to the business sphere. This could be the case if a significant part of the population receives fixed nominal incomes *and* if they have a low propensity to save.

(b) Genuine capital intensification is combined with 'sufficient' technical progress, or if technical progress does not raise the (expected) 'marginal productivity of capital' to a sufficient degree, the banks lower the market rate of interest.[13]

(c) Additional loans are extended only to producers of capital goods so that purchasing power is redistributed from the income sphere to the business sphere.

Even if these conditions are fulfilled, it is highly improbable that real growth will fully neutralize the inflationary tendency of a credit expansion. Neisser pointed out that velocity normally has a multiplying effect on prices requiring an overproportional increase in the net product (in absolute terms), or equal growth rates of national income and the money stock (1928: 134ff). He overstretched this argument, however, by applying it *in general* to cases of unemployed resources. In 1928 he did not yet see that the liquid(iz)ation of capital and hoarding of money in depressions tends to slow down velocity and that this, in combination with the discharge of bank debts (which reduces the volume of money), eliminates upward pressures on prices so that a credit expansion could promote real activity (see Section 4).

Nevertheless, Neisser acknowledged that monetary expansion can have lasting effects on production (1928). It should not be forgotten that, in his habilation thesis, he had set the focus on the value of money and not on the business cycle or on secular growth. Like Wicksell (1898), he therefore confined the real effects of monetary expansion to the small print. He arrived at the conclusion that it is plausible to assume that the determinants of the value of money are independent of each other (1928, Ch.VII). Velocity, income and transactions take more time to vary than the volume of money. In the short run the price level therefore reacts primarily to changes in the latter. Moreover, Neisser stressed that money is *the* representative of effective demand,[14] and that the creation of purchasing power (embodied in income) is limited by the supply of cash (1928).

At first sight, Neisser's conclusions do not seem to differ much from the Fisherine quantity theory that he had used as his point of departure. Neisser made, however, an important qualification. Unlike the standard interpretation, his quantity theory does *not* imply that the neutrality of money is a 'natural' outcome of real balance effects under full competition in the marketplace. On the contrary, it is a politically contrived elasticity in the money supply that helps to prevent feedbacks from the price level to real activity. In other words, changes in real income, transactions or velocity may cause movements in the price level that could be considered as macroeconomic coordination failures of the price mechanism. The elasticity of the money supply that prevents such failures from taking effect is a product of the discount rate policy of the central bank. This does not imply, of course, that monetary policy always can and will fulfill the task of neutralization. That is another matter to be taken up in the next section.

4. BUSINESS CYCLES AND STRUCTURAL UNEMPLOYMENT

Neisser had based his re-examination of the quantity theory on the assumption of an exogenous cash supply (1928). When he wrote about the business, he shifted the emphasis to the endogeneity of credit money cycle (1931b, 1934a, 1936b). The repayment of bank loans was a key factor in his theory of general overproduction and cumulative deflation. Moreover Neisser acknowledged that crises of those types cannot be counteracted by monetary policy alone if investors become so pessimistic that no reduction in nominal interest rates can make up for the fall in profit expectations. He did not consider his wide interpretation of the quantity-theoretical 'principle of causation' to be incompatible with such investment traps. On the contrary he emphasized that 'general overproduction is essentially a deflationary phenomenon' that can only occur in economies where the volume of money determines the price level (1934a: 440). Neisser's work on the business cycle was mainly directed at disentangling this causation theorem from the neutrality postulate, the 'fundamental principle of classical theory' according to which 'the absolute position of the general price level is a matter of indifference' (1934a: 435).

Neisser's analysis of cyclical growth and credit is rather complex, but my scheme of deflationary gaps (see Figure 4.1) helps to cut the argument short. The dynamic equilibrium benchmark for the classification of cyclical disturbances is provided by the case of genuine capital intensification with sufficient technical progress (bottom left). This 'moving equilibrium' is based on three conditions:[15]

1. The positive effects of technical progress suffice to balance the decline of 'marginal productivity' (or rate of return to real investment) that results from capital intensification.
2. The volume of money grows in accordance with the volume of marketed output; alternatively, deflation is so slow that contractual 'rigidities' do not affect the price structure.
3. The composition of additional net output matches perfectly with the spending schedule of the additional (real) income.

If these conditions are fulfilled, receipts equal costs including 'normal interest on owned capital,' which Neisser defined as the opportunity cost factor of real investors. When receipts equal costs, the economy is in the state of 'prosperity,' the phase in the cycle that coincides with the equilibrium benchmark. Prosperity does not, however, imply full employment. It is fully compatible with involuntary unemployment and unutilized capacity. Say's Law holds in the sense that there are no leaks in the circuit flow of purchasing power; and it holds in the 'complementary disequilibria' version of Walras's Law.[16]

In order to understand Neisser's notion of equilibrium unemployment it is helpful to take another look at the case of extensive growth (Figure 4.1). Even in prosperity:

> structural unemployment arises when the *physical* stock of capital either in the shape of fixed capital or of working capital is not sufficient to employ the total supply of labor . . .; owing to the harmony between the structure of expenditure and the structure of production, capital, but not labor, would be utilized optimally. (1936b: 63)

Structural unemployment is thus characterized as 'capital scarcity,' even though it results from the combination of technical progress and capital intensification. It can be cured by extensive growth if the rates of real capital accumulation and monetary expansion are high enough to close the deflationary gap that would otherwise make receipts fall short of costs.[17]

Quite contrary to this line of argument, 'capital shortage' or 'undersaving unemployment' is often associated with Austrian theories of the business cycle in which a purely bank-dependent capital intensification requires an unsustainable rate of monetary expansion. *Cyclical* unemployment is explained to arise from the inevitable disruption of the traverse to a more roundabout structure of production.[18] The 'Austrian-type' of crisis could be described as a deflationary gap arising from bank-dependent intensification (Figure 4.1), but neither Hayek nor Neisser would have put the argument this way. Hayek regarded the crisis as a cure that eliminates the distortions of the price structure generated by monetary expansion; neither his nor Neisser's explanations of crises turn on a lack of technical progress. In Neisser's theory, both undersaving and oversaving crises are caused by an overdose of technical progress. The character of the crisis is determined by the 'temporal distribution' of technical progress between the producer and the consumer goods' industries. Neisser's sectoral distinction has further implications for the validity of Say's Law.

In general, technical progress will raise the productivity of labour. In many cases the lowering of unit costs can be realized only at a greater scale of production. Hence technical progress also tends to raise capital intensity and output. If output rises to the extent that the above stated equilibrium conditions are violated, receipts fall short of costs. In his discussion of such discrepancies between the structures of expenditure and production, Neisser pointed out that the profitability of investment does not exclusively depend on the equality of marginal productivity and the (real) market rate of interest (1934a: 447). It depends just as much on effective demand, and Neisser's emphasis on this constraint brought him close to Keynes's notion of marginal efficiency.[19]

If technical progress and effective demand are out of step in the producer goods' industries, the crisis may be characterized as a consequence of undersaving and partial overproduction. Losses in these industries would not inhibit investment in the consumer goods' industries, whose costs of inputs tend to fall (1936b: 7). If this boosts profits or sales in the consumer goods' industries, derived demand and profit expectations in the producer goods' industries may recover sooner or later. Say's Law holds, in principle. In modern credit economies, however, the recovery could be prevented by a discharge of debts at the banks that reduces the volume of money. In this credit channel of transmission, widespread expectations of losses in the producer goods' industries may produce a monetary contraction that turns partial overproduction into a general glut. In that case receipts fall short of costs throughout the economy, and Say's Law no longer holds.

Risks of general overproduction and cumulative deflation are even greater if similar discrepancies between the structures of production and expenditure develop primarily in the consumer goods' industries. A lack of effective demand in that sector will negatively affect profit expectations in *all* industries. Hence Say's Law is invalidated by oversaving or underconsumption. Apart from that, Neisser noted that his underconsumption theory helped to account for the development of the Great Depression, which the undersaving theories failed to explain. This did not prevent him from criticizing traditional underconsumption theories for their stagnation hypothesis that ignored a monetary mechanism of self-stabilization in the market system. Neisser believed that the crisis will, sooner or later, force the dissolution of balance reserves, thereby accelerating velocity. Precisely those factors that first reduce the volume and velocity of money will induce a turn in the other direction: '[H]oarding, liquidation (in the form of bank deposits), and the payment of bank loans leads eventually to a condition of liquidity that almost forces the granting of new credit to those industries which have readjusted their cost or show profits for other reasons' (1934a: 446f).

Neisser pointed out that the new loans mainly help to finance the realization of cost-cutting techniques (1936b). Productivity is increased by investment in new machinery and by the scrapping of obsolete machinery. The displacement effects of labour-saving technical progress may easily transform cyclical unemployment into structural unemployment (1932, 1942). Along these lines, Neisser defined as capital shortage what is nowadays termed hysteresis in the rate of unemployment; and he endogenized technical progress by making it dependent on cyclical variations in the volume of credit money.

He did not share the conventional belief in automatic compensation by positive employment effects of technical progress. Instead he arrived at the pessimistic conclusion that 'successive waves of displacement, capital destruction, etc., might for a very long period, if not forever, hinder the absorption of all unemployed' (1936b: 64; see also Neisser 1942).

Five years earlier, when Neisser still could contribute to policy debates in Germany, he had already begun to plead for an anti-deflationary policy mix. As discount rates are bounded above zero, monetary policy might fail to counteract the larger demand failures that can develop into depressions. Therefore Neisser advocated public loans for railways and other projects that quickly stimulate consumer demand by way of income payments (1931b). Turning against the mainstream orthodoxy of his time, he closed his article with the following question: 'Does economic theory have nothing to offer to the German people but stones for bread?' (1931b: 84). There is some bitter irony of fate in the fact that Hitler, whose takeover forced Neisser into emigration, still gets the credit for 'having built the motorways' and thereby 'having given the German people bread for stones.'

5. CONCLUSION

Unorthodox thinking is a virtue only if it helps to widen the horizon. And the return to some old unorthodox thinker (who might not even have seen himself that way) will in general be considered worth while only if it helps to widen the horizons of our time. So in the end we may ask what we can make of Neisser's theory of the value and the circuit of money today.

First, it might be helpful to discuss why Neisser set his analysis in the orthodox framework of the quantity theory. First of all, his pronounced aim was to 'isolate the essential role of money in structuring the price and income relations in a capitalist economy' (1928, Ch.V). The quantity theory that nowadays is widely interpreted to imply the long-run neutrality of money does not seem to lend itself to that sort of exercise. At first sight, the results of Neisser's inquiry into the determination of the value of money are, indeed, not very spectacular. Starting from the Fisherine equations of exchange, he arrives at the conclusion that the volume of money is the causal determinant of the price level in the short run. In other words, the value of money (the inverse price level) is determined by its quantity.

However, the crucial difference is that Neisser turns the conventional method of inquiry upside-down. Instead of focusing on exogenous changes in the volume of money and their effects on the price level, he asks what happens to the price level if changes in the structures of production and market transactions (that is: changes in trade, income and velocity) are *not compensated* by changes in the volume of money. His focus on the secular processes of capital accumulation and growth of income makes him stress the potential for the development of deflationary gaps in the interaction of capital intensification, technical progress and market differentiation.

Neisser had little to say about financial markets and asset demand for money. He considered velocity to be the most invariant factor in the equation of exchange, not giving much attention to the demand for money *holdings*. In this respect, his flow approach clearly differs from the cash-balance approaches of his time, from their Keynesian critics and from modern monetarist versions of the quantity theory. Those who consider Neisser's neglect of these stock perspectives as 'so one-eyed' that he ought to be counted out should not forget that modern theories tend to be blind in the other eye. Whether or not the different perspectives of modern monetary theories and of Neisser's approach can be combined in one consistent framework is a matter that cannot be addressed in this chapter.

It is a standard result of quantity theory that monetary policy should play the role of preserving the *functional scarcity* of money ('fiat' and bank credit), in the sense of stabilizing the standard of value. Neisser's focus on the deflationary bias in capital circulation made him look the other way. His theory leads to the conclusion that money is neutral only if monetary policy eliminates the deflationary gaps. Thus Neisser can be said to have stressed the need to preserve the *functional plenty* of money. His later work on the business cycle shows that he was aware of the limits of monetary policy in achieving this aim. His critique of Say's Law is based on endogenous contractions in the volume of credit money. This smacks of reversed causation, so that some might say that Neisser was not a quantity theorist after all. We should not forget, though, that the quantity theory is essentially a theory of the long run. Even Fisher, Hawtrey and other quantity theorists in Neisser's time admitted the existence of reversed causation in certain phases of the business cycle (see Laidler 1998).

Among the most interesting points about Neisser is that he was one of the first to show how cyclical unemployment can turn into structural unemployment. As credit contractions tend to prevent the system from returning to the original equilibrium position, the causation theorem may hold in the long run, but the postulate of the neutrality of money does not even do that. Whether or not we consider Neisser's approach as a version of the quantity theory is therefore a matter of semantics rather than substance. We should acknowledge that more can be made out of the identity in equations of exchange than we have been accustomed to see.[20]

Neisser's approach helps us to take a fresh look at disinflation and stagnation in our times. Recent waves of outsourcing and differentiation in intermediation may, for example, have led to a 'spurious capital intensification' that requires more of a monetary expansion than the authorities tend to permit. In the same vein, one may ask whether technical progress is and has been sufficient to allow for intensive growth without (more) monetary expansion. To my knowledge there is little research on such structural issues. Neisser's unorthodox use of the quantity theory of money brings them back in sight again.

NOTES

1. Hans Philipp Neisser (1895–1975) had worked at the Kiel Institute of World Economics between 1927 and 1933. As an active Social Democrat with Jewish ancestors, he was one of the first German academics to lose his job when the Nazis came to power. During the war he served as Principal Economist at the US Office of Price Administration. In 1943 he moved from the Wharton School at the University of Pennsylvania to the New School for Social Research in New York, where he remained until retirement in 1965. For biographical notes and background information about the Kiel School and its 'transplantation' to the New School see Hagemann (1994) and Trautwein (1996a).
2. Keynes attested to these difficulties when in his *Treatise on Money* (1930: 178) he remarked that his own theory of the credit cycle was fairly close to those of the Austrian–German 'neo-Wicksell School' represented by Mises, Hayek and Neisser. In a footnote he added: '. . . (in German I can only clearly understand what I know already! – so that *new* ideas are apt to be veiled from me by the difficulties of language). I find Dr. Neisser's general attitude to monetary problems particularly sympathetic, and am hopeful that he may feel the same about my work.'
3. As is well known, Wicksell did not consider his theory of interest and the price level to be a business-cycle theory. In his view, the main cause of the cycle is found in asynchronies of technical progress and consumer demand; see Boianovsky (1995). As will be seen below, Neisser's approach can be read as a synthesis of central elements in Wicksell's real business-cycle theory and monetary theory.
4. This critique was developed in Neisser's writings on the business cycle published in his early American period (Neisser 1934a, 1936b). It was nevertheless well grounded in his earlier work on money and technological unemployment; see Section 4 below.
5. The use of 'inactive money' (reserves) is 'completely dependent upon the arbitrary decision of the holder' (1931a: 368). Neisser focused on the circulation of 'active money' in goods transactions and the transmission of savings. Unlike Holtrop (1928) and Keynes (1930), he paid little attention to stock transactions in the 'financial circulation.'
6. This distinction dates back to Smith (1776). Ellis (1934: 170f) compares Neisser's concepts with 'income deposits' and 'business deposits' in Keynes (1930: Ch. 3).
7. The technical duration of payments in the c-sphere is net of clearing that, according to Neisser, affects the size and composition of the monetary aggregate, but not velocity.
8. Lower case letters denote approximations of the growth rates in natural logarithms.
9. In his critical review of Hayek (1931), Neisser (1934b: 438f) pointed out that the transmission of *voluntary* saving at a given volume of money requires an additional reduction in income. This conclusion seems erroneous as it is based either on the unwarranted assumption of a concomitant rise in the price level, or on the exclusion of saving from the circulation of active money.
10. In cases of technical progress without capital intensification, the deflationary gap will arise in the income sphere and not in the business sphere (1931a, 392).
11. If technical progress is 'sufficient' (Figure 4.1), there may not be any feedbacks from the price level to the volume of transactions. This is the only case in which Neisser's combination of real and monetary analysis vindicates the classical dichotomy.
12. In Wicksellian terms, $dM/di_a < 0$ is valid only if the increase in the discount rate does not coincide with a further increase in the rate of return on real investment. This relation is not given any systematic treatment in Neisser (1928).

13. Neisser did not discuss the two ways in which this may happen: either the banks (or, rather, the authorities) lower the nominal rates of interest autonomously, or they do not adjust their lending rates to the rate of inflation.
14. See Neisser (1928: 155) and his accurate definition of the constraint that nowadays passes under the name of Clower: '[G]oods have not the purchasing power required to buy them tied around their necks.' (1934a: 444).
15. They have been extracted from Neisser (1931b, 1934a, 1934b, 1936b, Ch. I: 82).
16. The common distinction between Say's Identity and Walras' Law is of more recent origin. Neisser (1934a) spoke of 'the two classical principles,' the first being that purchasing power cannot be lost in circulation, and the second asserting that the price mechanism will eliminate partial overproduction. Hence unutilized resources could be a temporary consequence of partial overproduction, or: '[e]nterprises that have shut down and do not pay out costs at all could not be reckoned within the circular flow concerned' (1936b: 5).
17. The link between structural unemployment and cyclical unemployment, which arises when 'the existing capital stock could not be utilized optimally because of the absence of adequate demand at *cost price*' (Neisser 1936b: 63), will be explored below.
18. See Hayek (1929, 1931), whose approach I have discussed elsewhere (Trautwein 1996b).
19. 'According to [the] orthodox opinion, investment does not depend on the profitableness of the lowest stage of production, but on the rate of interest alone. In our opinion, the "orthodox" theorists neglect the importance of the *level* of the demand for capital, whereas the underconsumption school neglects the significance of [its monetary] *form*. On the whole, however, this latter school seems to be right, because shifts in the demand curve could easily wipe out all advantages from a declining interest-rate level' (Neisser 1934a: 447). For comparisons of Neisser and Keynes see Klausinger (1998) and Trautwein (1996a).
20. As Schumpeter (1954: 1109, fn. 3) remarked, Neisser has helped to demonstrate the compatibility of the cash-balance approach of the quantity theory and the income approach to the explanation of money prices: '[T]he most eminent of the sponsors of the income approach, R.G. Hawtrey . . . starts from Consumers' Outlay, which is 'proportional jointly to the unspent margin . . . and the circuit velocity of money.' He calls this 'a form of the quantity theory. Several German writers, however, refused to see this and had to be taught by Hans Neisser . . . (1928) that there is no contradiction between the income and the quantity theory.'

REFERENCES

Boianovsky, Mauro (1995), 'Wicksell's Business Cycle,' *European Journal of the History of Economic Thought*, 2, 375–411.

Ellis, Howard (1934), *German Monetary Theory, 1905–1933*, Cambridge, MA: Harvard University Press.

Fisher, Irving (1911), *The Purchasing Power of Money*, New York: Macmillan.

Hagemann, Harald (1994), 'Hayek and the Kiel School: some reflections on the German debate on business cycles in the late 1920s and early 1930s,' in *Money and Business Cycles: The Economics of F.A. Hayek, Vol. 1*, M. Colonna and H. Hagemann (eds), Cheltenham: Edward Elgar, pp. 101–120.

Hayek, Friedrich August (1929), *Geldtheorie und Konjunkturtheorie*, Vienna and Leipzig: Hölder-Pichler-Tempsky.

Hayek, Friedrich August (1931), *Prices and Production*, London: Routledge.

Holtrop, Marius (1928), *De Omloopssnelheid van het Geld*, Amsterdam (German translation in Beiträge zur Geldtheorie, edited by Friedrich A. Hayek, Vienna: J. Springer, 1932, pp. 115–209).

Keynes, John Maynard (1930), *A Treatise on Money*, vol. I: *The Pure Theory of Money* (*Collected Writings of John Maynard Keynes*, vol. 5, 1971), Basingstoke: Macmillan.

Keynes, John Maynard (1936), *The General Theory of Employment, Interest and Money*, Basingstoke: Macmillan.

Klausinger, Hansjörg (1998), 'German Anticipations of the Keynesian Revolution? The Case of Lautenbach, Neisser and Röpke,' *European Journal of the History of Economic Thought*, vol. 6, No. 3 (Autumn 1999), pp. 378–403.

Laidler, David (1998), 'The Wicksell Connection, the Quantity Theory and Keynes,' in Erich Streissler (ed.), *Knut Wicksell als ökonomischer Denker*, Berlin: Dunker and Humblot.

Lindahl, Erik (1930), *Penningpolitikens Medel*, translation as Part II in Erik Lindahl, *Studies in the Theory of Money and Capital*, London: G. Allen & Unwin, 1939.

Marschak, Jakob (1924), 'Die Verkehrsgleichung,' *Archiv für Sozialwissenschaften und Sozialpolitik*, 52, 344–384.

Myrdal, Gunnar (1931), 'Om penningteoretisk jämvikt: En studie över den "normala räntan" i Wicksells penninglära,' *Ekonomisk Tidskrift*, 33, 191–302, translation in *Monetary Equilibrium*, London: W. Hodge & Company (1939).

Neisser, Hans (1928), *Der Tauschwert des Geldes*, Jena: G. Fischer.

Neisser, Hans (1931a), 'Der Kreislauf des Geldes,' *Weltwirtschaftliches Archiv*, 33, 365–408.

Neisser, Hans (1931b), 'Ankurbelung oder Inflation? Eine Entgegnung,' *Der Deutsche Volkswirt*, 6, 80–5.

Neisser, Hans (1932), 'Lohnhöhe und Beschäftigungsgrad im Marktgleichgewicht,' *Weltwirtschaftliches Archiv*, 36, 414–55, translation with an introduction by Harald Hagemann: 'The Wage Rate and Employment in Market Equilibrium,' *Structural Change and Economics*, 1 (1990), 141–63.

Neisser, Hans (1934a), 'General Overproduction: A Study of Say's Law of Markets,' *Journal of Political Economy*, 42, 433–65.

Neisser, Hans (1934b), 'Monetary Expansion and the Structure of Production,' *Social Research*, 1, 434–57.

Neisser, Hans (1936a), 'German Literature on Money and Credit 1933–34,' *Social Research*, 3, 109–12.

Neisser, Hans (1936b), *Some International Aspects of the Business Cycle*, Philadelphia: University of Pennsylvania Press.

Neisser, Hans (1942), ' "Permanent" Technological Unemployment: "Demand for Commodities Is Not Demand for Labour," ' *American Economic Review*, 32, 50–71.

Ohlin, Bertil (1936), Introduction, Knut Wicksell, *Interest and Prices: A Study of the Causes Regulating the Value of Money*, New York: A.M. Kelley (Reprint 1985), vii–xxi.

Schumpeter, Joseph Alois (1917/18), 'Das Sozialprodukt und die Rechenpfennige. Glossen und Beiträge zur Geldtheorie von heute,' *Archiv für Sozialwissenschaft und Statistik* 44, 627–715, translation as 'Money and the Social Product' in *International Economic Papers*, 6 (1956), 148–211.

Schumpeter, Joseph Alois (1954), *History of Economic Analysis*, London and New York: Oxford University Press (Reprint 1994).

Smith, Adam (1776), *An Inquiry into the Nature and Causes of the Wealth of Nations*, 5th edn (1789), presented here, republished from Edwin Cannan's annotated edition, 1904, Methuen & Co., Ltd.

Trautwein, Hans-Michael (1996a), 'On "Dr. Neisser's General Attitude to Monetary Problems," ' forthcoming in Riccardo Bellofiore (ed.), *German Monetary Theory Revisited*, London: Macmillan.

Trautwein, Hans-Michael (1996b), 'Money, Equilibrium and the Cycle: Hayek's Wicksellian Dichotomy,' *History of Political Economy*, 28, 27–55.

Wicksell, Knut (1898), *Geldzins und Güterpreise. Eine Untersuchung über die den Tauschwert des Geldes bestimmenden Ursachen*, Jena: G. Fischer.

5. Functional finance, past and present

Perry Mehrling

FUNCTIONAL FOR WHAT?

Abba Lerner coined the phrase 'functional finance' as a label for his proposal to stabilize business fluctuation at full employment by allowing the government deficit, and hence the government debt, to fluctuate as needed in order to stabilize aggregate demand. At the time he wrote, the problem of stabilization was uppermost in everyone's mind, and Lerner was one among many who were thinking about how to make use of the apparatus of government finance to address, and maybe even solve, the problem.

In retrospect and in prospect, the apparatus of government finance is a powerful tool that has been and could be used to address any number of pressing social problems. The problem of stabilization is just one of many, and not always the most important. The answer to the question whether government finance is functional or not turns on the answer to the prior question of what problem we are trying to solve. What is functional at one time and place may well not be functional in another time and place. What seems functional to one group of people may not seem functional to another group. Functional finance is both an historical and a political question before it is a technical one.

IN RETROSPECT: ALVIN HANSEN

Alvin Hansen's thinking about what is the most functional use of government finance went through three successive stages: social insurance for spreading the costs of a dynamic economy; investment banker for jump-starting an economy suffering from secular stagnation; and balance wheel for stabilizing the postwar dual economy.[1] In each of these stages, Hansen identified a different problem as the most pressing, and so proposed a different model for the role of the state.

In the years before the Great Depression, Hansen was mainly a business-cycle theorist in the Continental vein. He believed that business cycles were caused by fluctuations in real investment spending that were themselves caused mainly by technological change. Technology, not money or credit, was the underlying cause. It followed that instability, and the unemployment caused by instability, was simply the price of progress in a dynamic economy. From a social point of view, that price was not too high because, in a rapidly growing economy, recessions are short and recovery rapidly pushes to full employment. In Hansen's view, the United States was just such a dynamic economy, and so could be depended upon to recover and forcefully to move toward full employment more or less without any intervention. The role of government was to spread the burden of cyclical unemployment through various mechanisms of social insurance. Hansen thought of the state as a kind of American analogue to the European cooperative movement. The government is just the way we band together to help one another collectively, and the financial dimension of that cooperation is insurance.

Hansen's first response to the Depression in the early 1930s was, therefore, to promote forms of unemployment insurance, initially at the state level. When it became clear that depression was differentially affecting the elderly, he went on to advocate for old age insurance in his role as chair of the technical advisory committee that established the Social Security system. Significantly, at the same time that he advocated expansion of insurance, he opposed the use of macroeconomic policy. In his mind, money was more effect than cause, so monetary policy could have little impact. As for fiscal policy, he worried that public works might tend to crowd out the natural tendency of private investment to recover.

As the Depression continued however, Hansen came to see that large-scale unemployment insurance might also play a macroeconomic role, not just alleviating the pain of the unemployed, but actually stabilizing aggregate demand. By 1934, two years before Keynes's *General Theory*, Hansen was arguing that unemployment insurance helped to put a floor under depression until revival, but he still thought revival was inevitable, so deep was his faith in the underlying dynamism of the US economy. The increase in unemployment in 1937 and 1938 shook that faith. How dynamic could the economy be if recovery was so anemic that it could collapse and retreat before ever achieving full employment? And if the economy had lost its underlying dynamism, then the palliative measures of social insurance were clearly not enough. But what would be enough?

After 1937 or so, Hansen no longer understood the Depression as a business cycle but rather as a problem of trend. The Depression was about the end of an era, the end of the dynamism that had been driving western economies since the advent of the Industrial Revolution. This is Hansen's famous thesis of secular stagnation. Hansen had earlier been an advocate for laissez faire coupled with social insurance because he thought it was the best way to ensure rapid diffusion of technological change, and hence, progress. When he came to believe that diffusion was more or less complete, however, laissez faire lost its justification. Laissez faire has costs and people were still bearing them, but without the formerly dependable benefits. Society could endure the costs of unemployment so long as the benefit was rapid growth, but no longer. Hansen came to see that the movement for social control of prices was not something to oppose as an obstacle to progress, but rather something to understand as the consequence of the end of progress. The price rigidities caused by cartelization of business and labor were freezing the western economies, but they were more effect than cause of stagnation.

Hansen's proposed solution to stagnation came at two levels. Domestically, the solution was to develop what he called the New Frontier as a replacement for the closing of the old frontier. (This was in 1944, twenty years before President Kennedy would adopt the phrase.) The idea was to use the government to promote resource development in both urban and rural areas. If private sector investment lagged, then government could and should step in to make investments of its own, without fear of crowding anything out. The Tennessee Valley Authority was an example of the kind of thing the government needed to be doing. It might be the end of one era – the era spawned by the Industrial Revolution – but it could be the beginning of a new era, the era of the dual economy of public/private partnership. The financial aspect of that possible dual economy was government as investment banker, not merely providing finance but also actively seeking worthwhile projects and making some part of the investment itself.

The second part of the solution, so Hansen argued, was renewed expansion of the old Industrial Revolution to the farther hinterlands that had not yet been reached. The financial dimension of this part was something he called the International Development Authority, which was to be an investment bank at the international level with the job of steering capital flows to develop the poor countries. This development, Hansen thought, would stimulate demand for goods from the mature economies and so help to generate a new dynamism in the world economy as a whole.

The dogma of sound finance was the chief obstacle to both parts of his proposed solution, and so he attacked the dogma. This is significant. Instead of spending time developing the technical details of his proposal, he focused on changing people's minds about what counts as functional finance for the problems facing the economy at that moment. He argued, in effect, that sound finance, meaning a balanced or surplus budget, was not functional for the times. Capital spending requires spending long in advance of receipts, and capital spending is what we need, so unsound finance is the more functional.

In a sense the postwar economy we got was the dual economy that Hansen proposed. It had more to do with military spending and investment in developing weapons systems than it did in slum clearance and resource development, but the end result was a definite resurgence of growth and the system got moving again. The burning question was therefore no longer how to restart the engine of growth for capitalism. For better or worse, the engine had been restarted and the period of secular stagnation was over. Focus consequently turned toward the smaller issue of stabilization by means of 'compensatory government expenditure' and away from developmental government expenditure. Compensatory government expenditure is of course more or less what Abba Lerner was advocating under the label 'functional finance.'

Surviving stalwarts of sound finance may have seen (and may still see) Lerner's proposal as wildly radical, but not Hansen. He still wanted the government to be an agent of economic development, and he was disappointed that society seemed to be settling for what he saw as a fundamentally conservative goal. But times change and Hansen ultimately changed with them. If people want to stabilize cycles, he thought, that's a reasonable thing to be concerned about and it does broaden the role of the state and put some institutions in place that later on might be useful for something else. He came out in favor of the Murray Full Employment Bill, which eventually got passed in a weakened form. And he came out in favor of the World Bank, even though it was not really the international development authority that he hoped it would be, nor did it play as central a role as he had hoped. In this third stage of Hansen's evolution, he thought the appropriate role of government was as a giant balance wheel, expanding during periods of recession through deficit spending and then contracting during periods of surplus in order to stabilize the economy.

The development of Hansen's thought shows three different views of functional finance depending on what problem is facing the economy. In retrospect, the question of functional finance is only incidentally about what is the appropriate macroeconomic policy to stabilize employment or to achieve full employment. The more fundamental question is how best to make use of this wonderful tool that we have: a legitimate state with the power to tax and spend and with the power to issue debt at the lowest terms in the economy. What is the appropriate use of that social resource?

IN PROSPECT: THE CRISIS OF THE WELFARE STATE

Turning now to the future, the question facing us today is not which of these three versions of functional finance we want to accept but, rather, what are the problems facing us today and how can we utilize government finance to help us address them? Looking around it seems clear that, although we face some problems of unemployment and instability, the more serious problems we are facing concern the maturing of the institutions like Social Security that were set up, partly by Hansen, during the Great Depression. It also seems clear that the future economic development of the United States will depend fundamentally on our success or failure with human capital resource development, which means capital formation through education and capital maintenance through health care provision. The question of functional finance for today is a question of how best to use the power of state finance to help us address these challenges.

In pondering the financial dimension of these issues, we need to be taking account of how the world of private finance has been transformed since the days of Hansen and Lerner. For better or worse, their world is not our world, and if they were alive today they would be taking account of the changes made in order to ensure effective intervention. The world we live in today is a world of money manager capitalism, and the game for functional finance today is to figure out how best to engage and operate in that world.

The slogan of today is that anything that can be securitized will be securitized, but the one thing that Wall Street cannot securitize is human capital. In a free society, we do not permit individuals to own other individuals. We do however permit individuals to own shares in the collectivity of all individuals, and we do permit the collectivity to own shares in each individual, through the intermediation of government. The power to tax is, from one point of view, an ownership claim on human capital. Here is a tremendous resource that the state has and Wall Street does not, a resource that can potentially be turned to help us solve the kinds of problems that we're facing in the realm of Social Security, in the realm of education finance and in the realm of health finance. One possible version of functional finance for today is to conceptualize the government as a kind of mutual fund.

Social Security is already in effect a kind of social mutual fund, although that fact is obscured by the accounting system currently in use.[2] Currently the retirement portion of Social Security receives about 10 per cent of the aggregate wage bill. The present value of this income flow is the principal asset of the system. (And a very large asset it is too, even though accounting practice treats the system as though it had no assets beyond a few government bonds that have been temporarily accumulated in a trust fund.) The difference between the private pension system and Social Security is not that the former is funded while the latter is unfunded pay-as-you-go, but rather that Social Security is funded with a class of assets that is unavailable to the private pension system. It may be that Social Security is under-funded, in the sense that the value of its assets may be less than the value of its promised benefit payment liabilities, but even that is by no means clear. We will not know for sure until we start valuing the assets and liabilities in accordance with the same valuation procedures we use for the private pension system. Maybe Social Security is even over-funded.

Whatever the value of Social Security's assets, the larger point is that through the Social Security system we all individually have an interest in collective human capital formation and maintenance. Understanding Social Security as a mutual fund in which we all own shares, we also see more clearly our interest, our narrowly financial self-interest, in collective education and health programs. Our retirement security in the future depends in a very direct way on the return to human capital investments that are being made right now. Social Security is already a social mutual fund *de facto*. Recognizing that fact *de jure* would help us to see more clearly the true nature of the challenges facing us as we go forward.

It would also help to bring the dialogue about government finance into the twenty-first century where it needs to be if it is to connect with the modern era of money-manager capitalism. Like generations before us, we ask what is the best use of the apparatus of government finance for addressing the problems of our own time. As we do, we need to be taking account of the enormous advances that have taken place in recent decades in the apparatus of private finance. Learning from private finance need not mean privatizing Social Security, or education or health. It can also mean learning how to make best use of that most vital of social resources, the apparatus of government finance.

NOTES

1. The discussion of Hansen draws on my study of his life and work in Perry Mehrling, *The Money Interest and the Public Interest, American Monetary Thought 1920–1970* (Cambridge, MA: Harvard University Press, 1997, Chapters 5–8).
2. The discussion of Social Security as a social mutual fund draws from unpublished work done under a grant from TIAA-CREF, 'The Future of Social Security' and 'The Social Mutual Fund.'

PART III

ASSESSING THE INFLATION BARRIER

Functional finance initially focused on bringing about and maintaining full employment, but it soon ran into trouble in the form of endemic inflation. It seemed that the only effective way to control inflation was to reduce demand pressure, which meant allowing unemployment to rise. The conventional wisdom quickly came to the conclusion that the economy could not be operated at full blast. The Phillips Curve showed the tradeoff between unemployment and inflation. However, the curve seemed to shift out over time, the tradeoff becoming progressively less and less favorable. Higher and higher levels of unemployment, it seemed, were required to control inflationary pressure. As a result, what began as a program to stabilize full employment, degenerated into a set of controversies over how best to control inflation.

Yet this tact was neither warranted by the problems nor called for by the facts. Robert Eisner shows that the econometrics of the conventional approach to unemployment and inflation are unsound; the facts do not support the 'NAIRU' hypothesis. Higher unemployment may lower inflation, but there is virtually no evidence that low unemployment increases inflation. Indeed, on these grounds, even the Phillips Curve is suspect. Lynn Turgeon surveys the development of postwar policy, showing how unfounded fears of excessive demand pressure weakened and undermined efforts to move to full employment and prosperity. In fact, the inflationary pressures almost always arose not from demand, but from the supply side. The problems were misunderstood. James Duesenberry surveys and re-examines decisions of policy-makers to 'trade off' moves towards full employment for reductions in inflationary pressure, and notes that many of these tradeoffs were unwarranted. Richard Musgrave notes that, along with the concerns of functional finance, a complete approach to the government budget must consider the proper tasks of government, and the distribution of benefits and burdens resulting from government activities.

6. The NAIRU and fiscal and monetary policy for now and our future: some comments

Robert Eisner

This chapter mixes something old and something new. The section dealing with NAIRU, using data up to 1997, simply updates and re-estimates the material on budget deficits and monetary policy from a number of my previous papers. I have long been denouncing NAIRU, the 'Non-Accelerating Inflation Rate of Unemployment.' The NAIRU is a dogma that has for too long undermined meaningful economic theory and paralyzed economic policy. Here I am offering some empirical results supporting the assertions that fiscal policy can work and that correctly measured budget deficits stimulate the economy and, reinforced by monetary policy, can significantly increase employment, saving and investment and economic growth.

I have documented the decline and fall of the NAIRU on many occasions.[1] For over three years, inflation has been going down while unemployment has been below the commonly supposed magic NAIRU number of 6 per cent. It has been difficult to avoid saying 'I told you so.'

The conventional NAIRU relies upon two basic assumptions: that (a) current and past inflation in equilibrium generates equal future expected and actual inflation; and (b) that for any given time, there is a specific NAIRU that generates an equilibrium. Unemployment above that rate brings continuously decreasing inflation, while unemployment below it continues to increase or accelerate inflation.

I should make clear just what the NAIRU means. Those who are not its cognoscenti, devotees or attackers may not appreciate its full implications. The NAIRU goes far beyond the old Phillips Curve, which I also never enthusiastically supported. But the Phillips Curve at least told us that we could use policy to reduce unemployment, although there was a price to be paid in terms of added inflation. By contrast the NAIRU tells us there is nothing to be done. Unemployment cannot be cut below this so-called natural or non-accelerating inflation rate of unemployment because if that attempt generates expectations of higher inflation, the old Phillips Curve, in effect, will move up. The NAIRU paints a specter of real disaster. It is not even possible to avoid that disaster by going back to the old NAIRU, to the natural rate of unemployment, whatever it might be. Going back to the previous level just leaves the higher inflation rate in place. The way to reduce inflation then, as Milton Friedman and others tell us, is to suffer future unemployment. If expected unemployment is high expected inflation will be low. At best it is only possible to have lower unemployment now in return for higher unemployment later; otherwise the economy will be destroyed by huge and accelerating inflation.

This is a dogma that has undermined meaningful economic theory and paralyzed economic policy. Fiscal policy can work and correctly measured budget deficits do stimulate the economy. Reinforced by monetary policy, they can significantly increase employment, saving and investment and economic growth. Let me offer some empirical results, old and new, supporting all of these assertions.

First, recall the two basic assumptions above: (a) current and past inflation at equilibrium generates equal future expected and actual inflation; (b) there is a particular NAIRU at any time, which generates this equilibrium and unemployment above it brings continuously decreasing inflation while unemployment below it brings continuously increasing or accelerating inflation. I illustrate this conventional version in Tables 6.1a and 6.1b, for the quarterly observations to 1997.4, beginning respectively in 1956 and 1976. The data begin in the first quarter of 1956 and extend to the fourth quarter of 1997. I have also done separate regressions for the period from 1976 to 1997, since there has been so much talk that perhaps the NAIRU always makes sense, but now has changed because something has changed in the economy. The estimating equation is:

$$IN_t = C + \Sigma\, b_i\, IN_{t-1} + \Sigma\, b_j\, U_{t-j} + \Sigma\, b_f\, FAE_{t-f} + b_p\, PRD_t + b_c\, NIXON_t + b_o\, NIXOFF_t \qquad (6.1)$$

The lagged inflation variables, *IN*, run from $t - 1$ to $t - 20$. The lagged unemployment variables, *U*, are taken from t to $t - 4$. FAE is a measure of inflation in food and energy prices. PRD is the difference between the rates of change of labor productivity in the non-farm business sector and segmented trends of labor productivity. *NIXON* is a dummy variable for the quarters of Nixon price controls, 0.8 for the five quarters between 1971.3 and 1972.3, and zero otherwise. *NIXOFF* is a dummy variable for the termination of wage and price controls in 1974, 0.4 in 1974.2 and 1975.1 and 1.6 in 1974.3 and 1974.4, and zero otherwise.

For all measures of inflation – the CPI-U, the GDP implicit price deflator, core inflation, excluding food and energy prices – the past inflation coefficients

Table 6.1a Inflation and unemployment conventional model, n = 168: quarterly observations from 1956.1 to 1997.4

Variable or statistic	Regressions coefficients and standard errors		
	CPI-U *INC*	GDP Implicit Price Deflator *INF*	Core Inflation *INR*
Constant	3.318 (0.863)	3.096 (0.544)	2.458 (0.459)
ΣIN_{t-I} Coef. (1 < = I = < 20)	0.980 (0.131)	1.032 (0.075)	1.183 (0.061)
ΣU_{t-j} Coef. (0 < = j = < 4)	–0.634 (0.175)	–0.609 (0.115)	–0.535 (0.103)
FAE_{t-f} (1 < = f = < 4)	0.156 (0.107)	0.097 (0.039)	
PRD_t	–0.058 (0.038)	–0.037 (0.024)	–0.001 (0.025)
$NIXON_t$	–1.189 (0.861)	–1.014 (0.537)	–1.341 (0.558)
$NIXOFF_t$	0.614 (0.829)	2.361 (0.529)	1.886 (0.522)
R^2	0.810	0.877	0.844
D–W	2.036	2.062	1.925

sum to unity or above, and the sums of the unemployment coefficients, are negative. The NAIRU would appear to be robust.

But as I have pointed out repeatedly, it is not robust against formulations that, reasonably, distinguish between periods when unemployment is above the NAIRU and unemployment is below the NAIRU. I have therefore estimated an equation permitting such asymmetric results. We replace equation (6.1) by:

$$IN_t = C + \Sigma\, b_i\, IN_{t-I} + \Sigma\, b_{jH}\, UH_{t-j+1} + \Sigma\, b_{jL}\, UL_{t-j+1} + \Sigma b_f\, FAE_{t-f} + b_p\, PRD_t + b_c\, NIXON_t + b_o\, NIXOFF_t, \quad (6.2)$$

$I = 1$ to 20, j = 1 to 5, f = 1 to 4,

$UH = U$ when $U \geq$ NAIRU and zero otherwise,
$UL = U$ when $U <$ NAIRU and zero otherwise.[2]

Table 6.1b Inflation and unemployment conventional model, n = 88: quarterly observations from 1976.1 to 1997.4

Variable or statistic	Regressions coefficients and standard errors		
	CPI-U *INC*	GDP Implicit Price Deflator *INF*	Core Inflation *INR*
Constant	6.467	2.967	2.705
	(2.209)	(1.063)	(0.802)
ΣIN_{t-I} Coef.	1.663	1.087	1.368
(1 < = I = < 20)	(0.342)	(0.114)	(0.102)
ΣU_{t-j} Coef.	–0.368	–0.588	–0.181
(0 < = j = < 4)	(0.444)	(0.211)	(0.103)
FAE_{t-f}	–0.251	0.060	
(1 < = f = < 4)	(0.233)	(0.054)	
PRD_t	–0.063	–0.033	0.053
	(0.083)	(0.036)	(0.037)
R^2	0.767	0.910	0.866
D–W	2.020	2.135	2.030

Table 6.2a presents the results of regressions with separate variables for *UH*, unemployment above the NAIRU and *UL*, unemployment below the NAIRU. The sums of *UH* coefficients are again negative, although considerably less in absolute value than when asymmetry is not allowed for. Increasing unemployment above the NAIRU does appear to lower inflation more and more rapidly.

But the sums of the *UL* coefficients are close to zero or even positive. Decreasing unemployment when it is below the supposed NAIRU does not accelerate inflation more; it may even reduce the acceleration or reduce inflation itself.

When we restrict ourselves to the observations from 1976 to 1997, we find the striking results shown in Table 6.2b . The sums of the *UH* coefficients are again negative but the sums for the *UL* coefficients are sharply positive, confirming what Wall Street, Alan Greenspan (happily), and economists belatedly, have finally been observing: lower unemployment, far from accelerating inflation in the past two decades, has contributed to decreasing it. All of this is confirmed in the results of the separate high-unemployment and low-unemployment regressions shown in Tables 6.3a and 6.3b.

The difference between the 6.3 tables and the 6.2 tables is that in the 6.2, I used dummy variables. I separated out the high unemployment and low unem-

Table 6.2a Inflation and unemployment, unemployment above NAIRU (UH) and unemployment below NAIRU (UL), n = 168: quarterly observations from 1956.1 to 1997.4

Variable or statistic	Regressions coefficients and standard errors		
	CPI-U *INC*	GDP Implicit Price Deflator *INF*	Core Inflation *INR*
Constant	0.205 (0.320)	0.184 (0.234)	0.039 (0.245)
ΣIN_{t-I} Coef. (1 < = I = < 20)	0.843 (0.146)	0.841 (0.081)	0.987 (0.056)
ΣUH_{t-j} Coef. (0 < = j = < 4)	–0.396 (0.321)	–0.277 (0.197)	–0.325 (0.185)
ΣUL_{t-j} Coef. (0 < = j = < 4)	–0.107 (0.330)	–0.202 (0.216)	–0.065 (0.204)
$\Sigma UL_{t-j} - \Sigma UH_{t-j}$ Coef.	0.290 (0.339)	0.075 (0.240)	0.260 (0.215)
FAE_{t-f} (1 < = f = < 4)	0.125 (0.134)	0.105 (0.049)	
PRD_t	–0.083 (0.038)	–0.048 (0.024)	–0.008 (0.025)
$NIXON_t$	–0.530 (0.955)	–0.498 (0.640)	–0.878 (0.627)
$NIXOFF_t$	0.246 (0.9269)	1.680 (0.603)	1.347 (0.560)
R^2	0.776	0.848	0.818
D–W	1.950	1.981	1.912

ployment observations, but restrained coefficients of the other variables, particularly the past inflation variables and the variables that were eventually put in for the price control period, food and energy prices and the like. For the high unemployment and low unemployment, separate regressions are not constrained to be the same. Now, these results are substantiated by comparisons . . . I hadn't tried this before . . . of core inflation, and changes in core inflation for quarters where unemployment was above and below the NAIRU, both for the entire period from 1956 on, and for the years beginning in 1976.

Table 6.2b Inflation and unemployment, unemployment above NAIRU (UH) and unemployment below NAIRU (UL), n = 88: quarterly observations from 1976.1 to 1997.4

Variable or statistic	Regressions coefficients and standard errors		
	CPI-U *INC*	GDP Implicit Price Deflator *INF*	Core Inflation *INR*
Constant	0.800 (0.773)	0.019 (0.428)	–0.490 (0.533)
ΣIN_{t-I} Coef. (1 < = I = < 20)	0.653 (0.319)	0.820 (0.113)	1.050 (0.095)
ΣUH_{t-j} Coef. (0 < = j = < 4)	–0.299 (0.532)	–0.419 (0.261)	–0.497 (0.236)
ΣUL_{t-j} Coef. (0 < = j = < 4)	4.090 (2.096)	1.137 (1.149)	1.558 (0.907)
$\Sigma UL_{t-j} - \Sigma UH_{t-j}$ Coef.	4.389 (2.140)	1.556 (1.116)	2.055 (0.886)
FAE_{t-f} (1 < = f = < 4)	0.179 (0.278)	0.127 (0.074)	
PRD_t	–0.089 (0.084)	–0.005 (0.041)	–0.043 (0.038)
R^2	0.741	0.859	0.848
D–W	2.054	2.013	1.906

These results are substantiated by comparisons of core inflation and changes in core inflation – eliminating food and energy prices – for quarters where unemployment was above and below the NAIRU, both for the entire period from 1956 on and for the years beginning in 1976. Looking first at Table 6.4a for the observations beginning in 1956, we find that inflation averaged 4.6 per cent in the high unemployment quarters but only 3.7 per cent in the low unemployment quarters. Of course, this kind of naïve comparison does not prove anything. Rather, the quarters and what was going on in these periods must be reviewed. But it does immediately raise some questions. If low unemployment is so inflationary, why, on average, over this whole 40-year period, did low unemployment correlate with less inflation than high unemployment? In the high unemployment quarters, inflation did decline at an aver-

Table 6.3a Core inflaton and unemployment, unemployment above NAIRU (UH) and unemployment below NAIRU (UL), separate regressions n = 168: quarterly observations 1956.1 to 1997.4

	Regressions coefficients and standard errors	
Variable or statistic	High unemployment regression *UH*	Low unemployment regressions *UL*
Constant	0.122 (0.209)	0.281 (0.199)
ΣIN_{t-I} Coef. (1 < = I = > 20)	0.968 (0.048)	0.928 (0.044)
ΣU_{t-j} Coef. (0 > = j = < 4)	–0.246 (0.162)	0.048 (0.182)
PRD	–0.016 (0.024)	–0.017 (0.024)
NIXON	–1.026 (0.603)	–0.751 (0.627)
NIXOFF	1.212 (0.542)	1.136 (0.545)
R^2	0.817	0.815
D–W	1.894	1.923

age rate of 0.12 per cent, while in the low unemployment quarters it increased at an average rate of 0.14 per cent.

Restricting ourselves to the 1976–97 observations, we still note in Table 6.4b that core inflation was higher in the high unemployment quarters, averaging 5.2 per cent, as against 4.3 per cent in the low unemployment quarters. While inflation fell on the average by 0.12 per cent in the high unemployment quarters, it rose on the average by only a negligible 0.04 per cent during low unemployment quarters. Now, that should hardly be enough to frighten the Federal Reserve or any fiscalist from trying to stimulate the economy because you cannot take these figures precisely. I am honest enough to offer you standard errors, which are usually substantial. But that is your best estimate, if you wish, 0.4 per cent per quarter? That means, in 25 quarters, you would raise inflation by 1 per cent, in six years? Then of course, if you really thought that was so terrible . . . that is what you would get presumably if you were in the low unemployment, unemployment below the NAIRU era. That hardly seems

Table 6.3b Core inflaton and unemployment, unemployment above NAIRU (UH) and unemployment below NAIRU (UL), separate regressions n = 88: quarterly observations 1976.1 to 1997.4

Variable or statistic	Regressions coefficients and standard errors: High unemployment regression *UH*	Low unemployment regressions *UL*
Constant	–0.837 (0.427)	0.289 (0.390)
ΣIN_{t-I} Coef. (1 < = I = > 20)	1.122 (0.075)	0.916 (0.072)
ΣU_{t-j} Coef. (0 > = j = < 4)	–0.533 (0.209)	1.957 (0.891)
PRD	–0.045 (0.037)	0.025 (0.037)
R^2	0.844	0.846
D–W	1.947	1.932

Table 6.4a Means of inflation and changes in inflation high unemployment and low unemployment, 168 quarterly observations from 1956.1 to 1997.4

Inflation Quarters	Mean	Standard error	t-statistic	Probability
High unemployment	4.594	0.264	17.426	0.000
Low unemployment	3.692	0.243	15.223	0.000
Difference	–0.902	0.358	–2.519	0.013
Changes in Inflation				
High unemployment	–0.115	0.163	–0.705	0.482
Low unemployment	0.135	0.150	0.900	0.369
Difference	0.251	0.222	1.128	0.261

such a great calamity. So we may conclude again, as I have concluded before, that while higher unemployment may mean lower inflation, there is hardly any evidence that low unemployment does increase inflation.

What we are finding is that high unemployment, as most of us have

Table 6.4b Means of inflation and changes in inflation high unemployment and low unemployment, 88 quarterly observations from 1976.1 to 1997.4

Inflation Quarters	Mean	Standard error	t-statistic	Probability
High unemployment	5.193	0.280	18.562	0.000
Low unemployment	4.283	0.370	11.575	0.000
Difference	–0.909	0.464	–1.960	0.053
Changes in Inflation				
High unemployment	–0.121	0.119	–1.011	0.315
Low unemployment	0.138	0.158	0.241	0.810
Difference	0.159	0.198	0.802	0.425

observed, does finally tend to reduce inflation because, for various reasons, it destroys the labor market. When people cannot get work, they are willing to work for less. With high unemployment there is a lot of excess capacity. Firms may be pressed by competition to sell their goods more cheaply. But with low unemployment, there is the converse, inflation does not seem to rise as unemployment gets lower. Some of my estimates even show that, as unemployment drops (up to at least some point or other), inflation will go down. I am not suggesting, as Bill Vickrey does, that bigger and bigger deficits should be run, more and more money printed, more and more roads built or that we should go to war and bid for all kinds of resources in an attempt to drive unemployment down. I do not entirely agree with Vickrey. He suggested that we drive unemployment down to 1 per cent. I am not sure we can do that because *that* might begin to cause inflation. In terms of what has happened in our economy in relation to unemployment – even at the height of the Vietnam War, when it went down to only 2.7 or 2.8 per cent for a few months – we do not have an experience where a lower unemployment rate raised inflation. That means that we should feel free to at least allow the economy to have lower unemployment.

Let us now turn to our favorite topics: budget deficits and monetary policy. My standard line is that budget deficits can be good or bad, but you cannot tell which unless you measure them correctly. The federal budget used by Congress and the Administration is inconsistent with standard private accounting and different from state and local government budgets. It is devoid of analytical content. In itself, it is not merely largely useless, but seriously misleading as a tool of economic policy. First, it does not distinguish between current expenditures and capital expenditures. All outlays, whether for new or real capital – let alone human capital – or acquisition and financial assets, contribute to the so-called 'deficit,' or to the reduction of the surplus. We could have eliminated the deficit a long time ago by selling off year by year (and leasing back) all government buildings and public infrastructure. I like to joke that we could begin with the Pentagon, and the Capitol building and the White House and then go on to the interstate highway system. If the federal government had rights to that, then a couple of hundred billion dollars each year could be sold off. Two hundred billion dollar deficits, for example, would be met because the yearly rent would be small. Of course, by the end of ten or twenty years, assets would run out, but in that event, we would figure out some new gimmick to get around things. I should suggest that this lack of a capital budget does play real havoc. The government in Washington tends to a great extent to rent public buildings, which is a very expensive practice. But it looks better in the current budget to rent for $50 million or so than to build a new building, which costs much more. In the long run, of course, rent is very much more costly to the taxpayer.

There is also the problem of financial assets. Purchase and sale of financial assets in the course of the Savings and Loan fiasco played such havoc with the accounts that the Congressional Budget Office (CBO) established separate lines to indicate the deficit with and without the Savings and Loan transactions. Further – as I hope is still taught in elementary economics classes – the economy impacts a deficit (or surplus) as much, and usually more, than the deficit affects the economy. Thus any measure of the impact of deficits on the economy must abstract from the effect of the economy on the deficit. Such a tool has long been available in the variously called 'full employment budget,' 'high employment budget,' 'cyclically adjusted budget,' or – in the terminology of the CBO – 'the standardized budget' surplus or deficit. These are variously defined for given levels of employment or economic activity.

Finally, conventional measures do not take any account of the impact of inflation on the deficit. They include as outlays nominal rather than real interest payments, thus ignoring what may be called an inflation tax on the value of federal debt held by the public. A standardized deficit that comprises only the excess of nominal over real interest payments, brings no real increase in the real value of assets held by the public. Thus, aside from money illusion or possible liquidity effects, it should have no real impact on private spending. I might add that, for those who are concerned that deficits are good because they stimulate the economy and surpluses are bad, having now had this huge move of deficit into surplus, why is the economy booming? Of course, the deficits we have discussed are not that huge all of the time. Particularly, relevant to the last several years, a great bulk of the deficit reduction has been not a reduction in the inflation-adjusted cyclical deficit – as I put it, cyclically adjusted and inflation-adjusted – but a reduction in the deficit due to the improvement of the economy itself. This reflects the impact of the economy on the deficit, and only a minor portion of the deficit reduction can be related to the tax increases of the years 1990, 1993 or 1994.

Though I was an early devotee of the permanent income hypothesis, it is important to not go overboard. An increase in taxes on capital gains for the very rich (that is what is contributing largely to a reduction of the deficit) is not going to affect consumption that much. We must go a little bit beyond the crude measures that I keep using – of impact on the economy, the overall deficit – to get into what spending is for and where tax cuts, or tax increases and the like, have their effect.

Having noted all that, we can examine the impact of deficits on the macro economy. I have therefore constructed a 'price-adjusted high employment deficit' (PAHED) and related that to subsequent changes in GDP, unemployment and saving and investment. I may present here just a few of my findings from earlier work.

First, in Figure 6.1, it is apparent that bigger deficits thus properly measured were associated with bigger reductions or lesser increases in unemployment. Since changes in unemployment are associated with changes in output, it is hardly surprising that similar results for growth in GDP may be seen in Figure

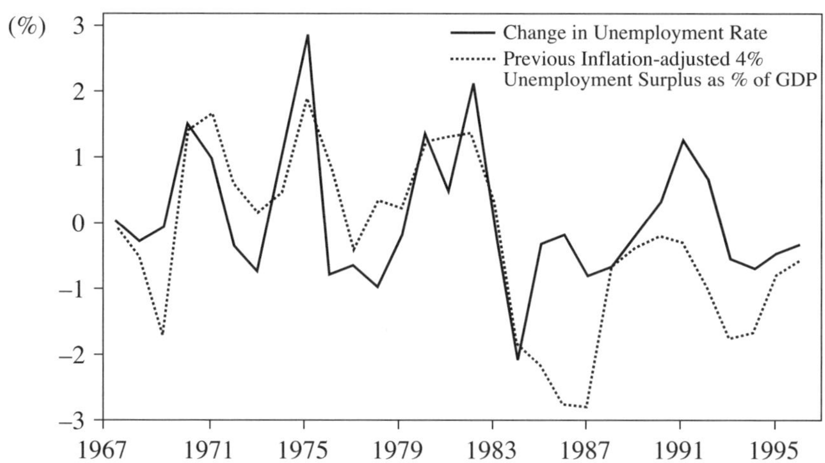

Note: Figure depicts change in unemployment and previous year's inflation-adjusted 4 per cent unemployment surplus or deficit. Unemployment rates are from the Economic Report of the President (Washington, D.C.: Government Printing Office, 1997, Table B-33 p. 338).

Figure 6.1 Effects of inflation-adjusted 4 per cent unemployment surplus or deficit (as a percentage of GDP) on unemployment rate, 1967–96

6.2. But now, the big complaint comes from all the deficit hawks, and even our liberal friends in Brookings, like Charlie Schultze, to the effect that – well, the deficits are crowding out saving and investment. And our national saving – badly measured as it is – is too low.

There is real irony in the Clinton Administration and Robert Rubin telling the Japanese they have to run bigger deficits. How many times have we heard the story that the Japanese were having such wonderful growth because they had such a high rate of national saving, and we are in such terrible shape because our national saving is so low? And where are we now in regard to Japanese national saving and their growth, and our national saving and our growth? A curious thing is that if we relate these properly measured deficits to various measures of national saving and investment, which we presume has to equal saving, there is the curious result that the deficits stimulate not only employment and GDP, but tend to stimulate investment as shown in Table 6.5.

They are associated with greater national saving, properly measured, as shown in Figure 6.3 and Table 6.6. And in addition, greater budget deficits have been associated with greater public investment, which is very important; state and local, as well as federal, tangible and intangible, as shown in Table 6.7. Monetary policy also has a clear impact on the economy, as indicated in the simple relationships incorporating changes in the real value of the monetary base – a dubious measure I suppose, but one I confess I have found to work. By this I mean the monetary base dropping all the 100-dollar bills held by Russians, drug

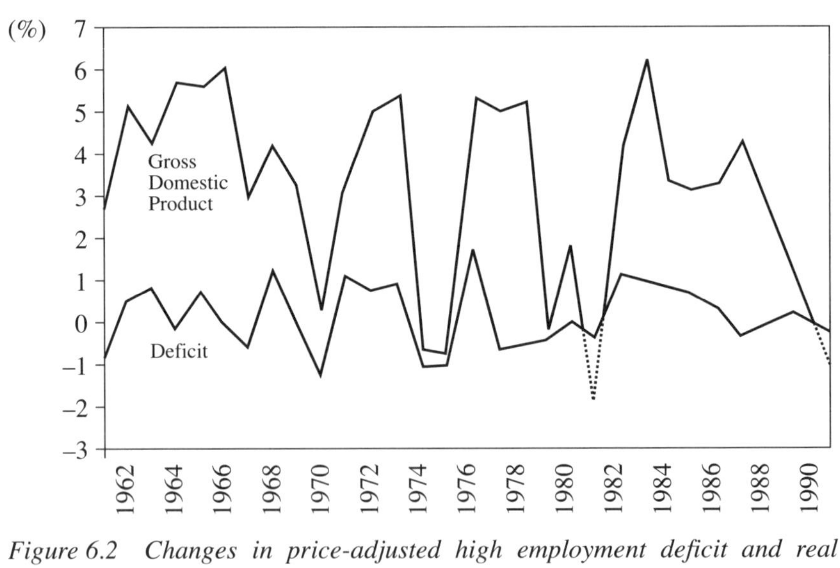

Figure 6.2 Changes in price-adjusted high employment deficit and real gross domestic product as percentages of GDP, 1961–91

Table 6.5 Adjusted deficit and private tangible investment ($I_{j,t} = b_0 + b_1 PAHED6_{t-1}$)

	Regression coefficients*					
	$PAHED6_{t-1}$					
I_1	b_0	b_1	r^2	D-W	rho	n
Gross private domestic	16.488 (0.527)	0.769 (0.297)	0.315	1.63	0.513 (0.181)	34
Net foreign	–0.250 (0.749)	–0.40 (0.086)	0.882	2.05	0.891 (0.088)	34
Gross	16.072 (1.134)	0.473 (0.309)	0.443	1.73	0.762 (0.129)	34
Consumer durables	16.052 (45.080)	0.299 (0.072)	0.931	1.57	0.989 (0.059)	34
Private domestic tangible	24.030 (0.618)	1.335 (0.317)	0.613	1.54	0.539 (0.159)	34
Private tangible	24.064 (0.784)	0.785 (0.355)	0.393	1.600	0.616 (0.159)	34

Notes: *Ordinary least squares with a first-order correction for serial correlation. Standard errors are shown in parentheses. sample period 1957–90.

Variable definitions:

PAHED6 Price-adjusted 6 per cent high employment deficit, as estimated by the BEA for the years 1970–90 and extrapolated backward by the Holloway method on the basis of the BEA middle expansion trend deficit for the earlier years, as a percentage of GNP.

I Real investment of type j-GDPI, NFI, gross, and consumer durables from the BEA – taken as a percentage of GNP. Private domestic tangible is the sum of gross private domestic investment and consumer durables. Private tangible is the sum of gross investment and consumer durables.

dealers, and the like. Perhaps I ought to experiment with others, but it somehow seems to work better than any other variable that I picked up. It seemed to work in terms of the relationship with GDP, growth, unemployment, and savings and investment. You will note that I introduced that into regressions with the properly measured, adjusted measure of the deficit. The change in the real value of the monetary base, DMV, is associated with subsequent decreases of unemployment; increases in GDP and/or savings and investment. And that may be noted in Figure 6.4. Table 6.6 again, and Tables 6.8 and 6.9.

One thing you might have noted is that there is one place where things go wrong – the bigger deficits and the more expansionary monetary policies I have measured contribute to a reduction in net foreign investment. In other words, we find ourselves importing more capital. We begin to run a trade and

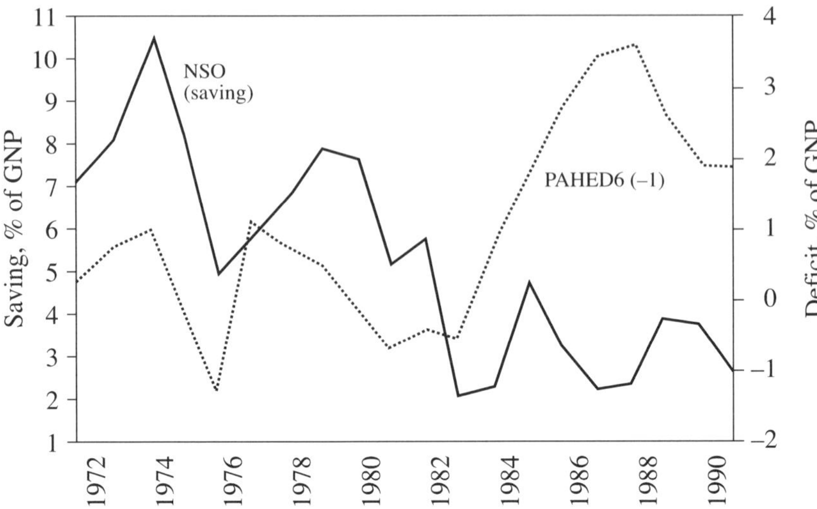

Figure 6.3 Conventional measure of national saving and lagged adjusted deficit

foreign account deficit as well. Not surprisingly the economy is stimulated as a result of the deficits, and we buy more foreign goods, raising our imports and therefore reducing net exports. For those in the broader audience who are terribly worried about our trade deficit and foreign investment, there is a wonderful, simple solution: Award yourself a big recession. You get unemployment up to 12 or 14 per cent, and we get rid of the trade deficit. There is the danger that we drag the rest of the world into 20 per cent unemployment, but that is another matter. So there is most of my story: Budget deficits and easier monetary policy have stimulated the economy in the past. The promotion of lower unemployment or faster growth are demonstrated in order that the hopefully fully discredited NAIRU dogma should not be permitted to stand in the way of their application, now or in the future.

There is still a role for application of the remarkable principles of functional finance, as advanced by Abba Lerner when the old new economics was in its infancy. Budget deficits can be allowed to increase the real value of private assets in the form of government debt until they bring us to full employment. In a paper I did some years ago with Sang-In Hwang, we actually constructed a little model in which we put in the parameters that we thought were correct (but they did not work very well). The idea was that if somehow the stimuli proved too much, a correction was to be found in a resultant decline in real deficits as the inflation tax increases. Inflation reduces the real stimulus of deficits. Deficits can then simply be allowed to proceed and be

Table 6.6 Adjusted budget deficits, changes to monetary base, real exchange rate and alternate measures of national saving, 1972–91

Variable or parameter	Regression coefficients and standard errors	
	NS0	NS1
C	50.478	60.456
	(312.737)	(380.945)
PAHED (–1)	0.757	1.089
	(0.334)	(0.365)
DMB (–1)	5.999	6.858
	(1.935)	(2.109)
DMB (–2)	6.584	7.360
	(1.692)	(1.846)
ERR (–2)	–0.107	–0.099
	(0.035)	(0.038)
AR(1)	1.009	1.010
	(0.082)	(0.083)
R^2	0.798	0.782
D.W.	2.583	2.630
n	20	20

Notes:

C	Constant term.
AR(1)	First-order autoregressive coefficient.
R^2	Adjusted coefficient of determination.
D-W	Durbin–Watson coefficient.
n	Number of observations.
PAHED (–1)	Lagged price-adjusted, BEA 6 per cent high-employment budget deficit as percentage of GNP.
DMB (–1)	Lagged real changes in monetary bass as
DMB (–2)	percentage of GNP.
ERR (–2)	Real exchange rate index, March 1973 = 100, lagged two years.
NS0	Conventional net national saving = gross saving – capital consumption allowances with adjustment, as percentage of GNP.
NS1	Change in total fixed reproducible capital plus change in business inventories and net foreign investment minus statistical discrepancy, as percentage of GNP.

increased at will, relying upon the combination of the increased income after taxes, and the accumulating value of real assets in the form of government debt held by the public to increase their consumption. This would continue on until what is essentially (close to) real full employment is achieved, rather than the so-called NAIRU. At that point, if things were overextended, the

Table 6.7 Adjusted deficit and public investment: $\Delta I_k = b_l \Delta PAHED6$

	JPAHED6*					
ΔI_k	b_0	b_1	R^2	D–W	rho	n
Federal tangible	–0.035 (0.049)	0.102 (0.035)	0.250	1.52	0.336 (0.166)	31
S&L tangible	–0.018 (0.040)	0.006 (0.017)	0.274	1.86	0.566 (0.157)	31
Total government tangible	–0.048 (0.079)	0.110 (0.042)	0.302	1.37	0.473 (0.160)	31
Education	0.052 (0.070)	0.135 (0.035)	0.347	1.73	0.510 (0.158)	31
Government R&D	–0.021 (0.019)	0.011 (0.009)	0.291	2.08	0.525 (0.163)	30
Total government	–0.056 (0.093)	0.228 (0.059)	0.354	1.70	0.390 (0.176)	30

Notes: *Ordinary least squares with a first-order correction for serial correlation. Standard errors are shown in parentheses. Estimated as first differences Sample period is 1961–91 for federal tangible, S&L tangible, and total government tangible, and education and training and 1962–91 for government R&D and total government.

Variable definitions:

APAHED6 Price-adjusted 6 per cent high employment deficit as a percentage of GNP, first difference.

ΔI_k Real investment of type k – federal tangible, S&L tangible, education and training, government R&D and total government – generally from the BEA, taken as a percentage of potential GNP, first differences.

worse consequence would be somewhat more inflation, which would be a reduction to the real deficit because of an increased inflation tax. And this would reduce the stimulus.

This completes my story and I hope you have criticisms, comments, and questions.

NOTES

1. See Eisner (1995, 1996a, 1996b, 1997a, 1997b, 1998a, 1998b).
2. To prevent any bias from the differences between the differences of the means of the high and

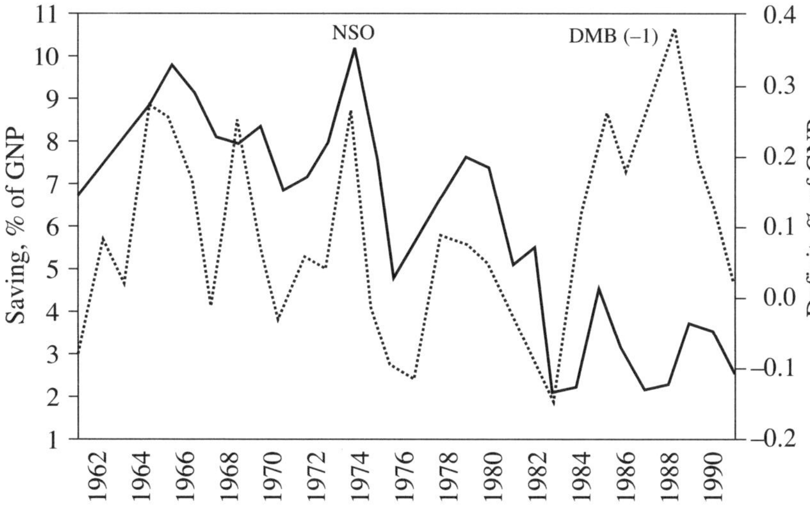

Figure 6.4 Conventional measure of national saving and lagged change in the monetary base, DMB (–1), as percentages of GNP

low unemployment variables and these assigned values of zero, I normalized these variables around zero.

3. It's now more than six years, passing through the peak of an intense boom, into a mild recession and a weak recovery. Still no inflation.

DISCUSSION

AUDIENCE MEMBER: Didn't you deliver a paper recently dealing with Robert Gordon's estimates, and hasn't he changed his mind?

ROBERT EISNER: If Bob has changed his mind, he should let me know. I do have his data, but he won't work with my data or show me what's wrong with it. I argue with him whenever he doesn't run away from me. He's been avoiding me on this subject for a long time now.

But what he does have is quite beautiful. He doesn't admit that anything is wrong with what he did before, but he now has what I call a 'TV-NAIRU,' that is, a time-varying NAIRU. The econometrics and statistics are such that each quarter in which unemployment stays very low and inflation is low, the NAIRU is adjusted down.

So it's not even the proposition that the NAIRU changes with changes in the economy, that is, that you get rid of the minimum wage law, or this or that, and you'll get a different NAIRU. Rather, Gordon's NAIRU just

Table 6.8 *Adjusted deficit, change in monetary base, real exchange rate and private tangible investment (first differences):* $AI_{j,t} = b_0 + b_1 \Delta PAHED6_{t-1} b_2 \Delta DMB_{t-1} + b_3 \Delta DMB_{t-2} + b_4 \Delta ERR_{t-2}$

	Regression coefficients*							
		$\Delta PAHED6_{t-1}$	ΔDMB_{t-1}	ΔDMB_{t-2}	$\Sigma \Delta DMB$	$\Delta ERRt-2$		
ΔI_1	b_0	b_1	b_2	b_3	$b_2 + b_3$	b_4	R^2	D-W
Gross private	–0.097	0.734	6.716	6.207	12.923	–0.071	0.610	2.15
domestic	(0.209)	(0.271)	(1.694)	(1.444)	(2.526)	(0.036)		
Net foreign	–0.059	–0.241	0.016	–0.900	–0.884	–0.032	0.470	2.19
	(0.081)	(0.105)	(0.658)	(0.561)	(0.918)	(0.014)		
Gross	–0.156	0.493	6.732	5.307	12.039	–0.103	0.528	2.40
	(0.204)	(0.264)	(1.652)	(1.408)	(2.462)	(0.035)		
Consumer	0.135	0.257	1.477	0.801	2.278	–0.009	0.525	1.70
durables	(0.063)	(0.082)	(0.513)	(0.437)	(0.765)	(0.011)		
Private domestic	0.039	0.991	8.194	7.007	15.201	–0.080	0.639	1.97
tangible	(0.246)	(0.318)	(1.989)	(1.695)	(2.965)	(0.042)		
Private tangible	–0.20	0.750	8.209	6.108	14.317	–0.113	0.571	2.21
	(0.240)	(0.310)	(1.941)	(1.654)	(2.893)	(0.041)		

Notes: *Ordinary least squares. Standard errors are show in parentheses. Sample period 1962–90; there are 29 observations.

Variable definitions:

PAHED6	Price-adjusted 6 per cent high-employment deficit as a percentage of GNP.
DMB	Change in the real monetary base as a percentage of GNP (December figures divided by 4th quarter GNP implicit price deflator).
ERR	Trade weighted real exchange rate (March 1973 = 100).
I	Real investment of type j-GDPI, NFI, gross, and consumer durables from the BEA – taken as a percentage of potential GNP. Private domestic tangible is the sum of gross private domestic investment and consumer durables. Private tangible is the sum of gross investment and consumer durables.

changes, for whatever reason. God only knows why; it just changes each time.

It's down now to about 5.3 per cent for one of his measures, the CPI; and down to 5.1 per cent for the other. And of course, Gordon's still got his unemployment a little bit below the NAIRU, actual unemployment that is. With time perhaps, if we wait, his NAIRU will finally get down to the level of unemployment.

AUDIENCE MEMBER: So his equations work; he gets a NAIRU?

Table 6.9 Changes in adjusted budget deficits, monetary base, real GDP and unemployment 1962–91: $\Delta Y_t = b_0 + b_1 \Delta PAHED6_{t-1} + b_2 DMB_{t-1}$

Variable or parameter	ΔY_t GDP	ΔY_t Unemployment
C	1.922	0.462
	(0.570)	(0.170)
$\Delta PAHED_{t-1}$	1.227	–0.466
	(0.317)	10.1621
DMB_{t-1},	9.510	–4.414
	(2.493)	11.0321
AR(1)	0.378	–0.010
	(0.208)	(0.233)
R^2	0.481	0.444
D–W	1.713	1.771
n	30	30

Notes:

C Constant term.
AR(1) First-order autoregressive coefficient.
R^2 Adjusted coefficient of determination.
D-W Durbin–Watson coefficient.
n Number of observations.
$APAHED6_{t-1}$ Lagged price-adjusted, BEA 6 per cent high-employment budget deficit as a percentage of GNP.
DMB_{t-1} Lagged real change in monetary base as a percentage of GNP (December figures divided by 4th quarter GNP implicit price deflator).

EISNER: But all the CBO, all the various people that estimate things, they estimate this equation. I can estimate the same equation. And I get their results. They're not faking. You get a NAIRU. The CBO now sets it at about 5.8 per cent. It varies some over time. I've gotten about 5.8 per cent; almost exactly the same figure.

Gordon was insisting it was 6 per cent for God knows how long. Now he has a new system that estimates what he calls a TV NAIRU – a time-varying NAIRU – conceding that the NAIRU is coming down. About three or four years ago I started attacking this problem. We observed the unemployment rate dip below the 6 per cent mark. I asked, 'Where is the accelerating inflation?' Gordon's answer was that there's a lag. So every few months I would ask him again. It's now been three years, and we still don't have accelerating inflation.[3]

MALE SPEAKER: Could you eliminate the trade deficit with a full employment program?

EISNER: I don't know that that would eliminate the trade deficit. I've written a number of papers on that. By the way. I think most of you would agree that the trade deficit, 'ain't no real problem.' If the Japanese want to give us these nice cheap cars (and I have to confess that we drive two Japanese cars in my family), and make them cheaper and cheaper, that's fine in a way.

I would say that there should be a full employment policy to make sure that the trade deficit doesn't contribute to unemployment. Unemployment is a real problem. If we continue to run this current account deficit – a negative net foreign investment – foreign claims on us increase that we eventually have to repay.

There are a few perspectives on that that people have tended to ignore. For one, if the economy is growing, as ours is, and foreign economies are growing, they may well want to hold more of their assets as they grow, and more US securities. And our increasing foreign debt – depending on what deficit you're assuming – will approach an asymptote of a certain ratio of debt to GDP. It's the same relationship for the budget deficit. If, for example, there is a deficit equal to 2.5 per cent of GDP, and the GDP keeps growing at 5 per cent, no matter what the debt/GDP ratio is to begin with, it will end up at 50 per cent of GDP.

If the deficit ratio is raised – let's say to 3 per cent of GDP, and the GDP keeps growing at 5 per cent – then the debt/GDP ratio will grow to 60 per cent of GDP. The same relationship holds then for the current account deficit. The debt relative to the GDP will not be increasing infinitely. It will approach some particular ratio depending upon how large the current account deficit is. This results, for any reasonable figures, with a final debt/GDP ratio that is highly manageable in terms of what percentage of GDP then would have to be paid to service that debt. If it runs into 1 or 2 per cent of GDP, I would say that if you accepted 1 or 2 per cent higher unemployment rate in order to somehow avoid that, you would have a much greater loss in output.

But the other curious angle is that we get a free ride because foreigners apparently have no desire to take this servicing, this income on their debt, and buy our goods and enjoy our automobiles or whatever. They keep piling it on and reinvesting. Maybe they like to owe US assets because they are safe. We are simply getting a free ride with money turned back to us.

AUDIENCE MEMBER: I think that calculations you are making really deal with the impact of the deficit properly measured on the level of private expenditures, and then their impact on unemployment and prices. Why is there a difference between the government making constant payments, or the government owing?

EISNER: You're entirely right. It doesn't make any difference if the government is spending the money to pay for education or to pay for clerks to sit around.

AUDIENCE MEMBER: The deficit is measured in this computation?

EISNER: This computation does not distinguish it. I'm glad you made the point. I somehow wanted to make a comment on capital budgets, but that's sort of a detour from this idea.

AUDIENCE MEMBER: When the economy weakens the budget deficit goes up, which is thought to get the recovery going. Yet, on the other hand, when the deficit shrinks as we grow, presumably there would be a countercyclical effect going the other way where that would weaken the recovery. Is it an asymmetrical situation?

EISNER: No, it's not asymmetrical. With a prosperous economy, the deficit declines, which is just what happened in the last few years. With a slump, the deficit grows. Of course that's one reason why economists, including Charlie Schultze, agree to oppose a balanced budget amendment. As a matter of fact, the balanced budget amendment for this reason would have caused pro-cyclical fiscal policy, and forced a rise in taxes.

AUDIENCE MEMBER: Do you think then that the deficit decline that we're experiencing now will end the cycle?

EISNER: I wouldn't say that. We have an $8 trillion economy, and even though I have spent my research efforts on the deficit, there's much more to the economy than the deficit. If that boom continues unabated in the information revolution – with computers in Silicon Valley and all over the country – we can probably tolerate surpluses for a while, particularly if Alan Greenspan doesn't get in the way, and apparently he won't.

Of course, there's another question regarding whether we should tolerate these surpluses: Should we reduce the debt rather than spend the surpluses to invest in something that would really contribute to the future growth and to taking care of our children and grandchildren?

AUDIENCE MEMBER: Is there a theoretical explanation for why, when the economy gets closer and closer to full employment, prices should not rise. In fact, you seem to claim that they might be rising at full employment.

EISNER: I would concede that there is some level of unemployment below which you cannot push the economy without increasing inflation. That's what I would call full employment, if you wish.

AUDIENCE MEMBER: So your argument revolves around what is full employment?

EISNER: Yes, but that's not the way people have been estimating this NAIRU. And the NAIRU they estimate is far above what most of us would consider to be full employment. Now, as for explanations, I have a few of them in my new-view-of-the-NAIRU paper and in my decline-and-fall-of-the-NAIRU paper.

They relate to things such as the fact that with low unemployment we have higher average productivity and, very possibly, lower marginal cost. We also have a situation where labor unions – perhaps contrary to the usual notion that they're going to be very belligerent when they have low unemployment – do not seem to be pressing unduly. They're happy with the fact that they have jobs and they don't want to jeopardize them. There is another explanation in terms of oligopoly theory, which is, that firms with high profits decide, 'I don't want to invite some other jackass into the industry by keeping my prices abnormally high.'

I mean, you can be convinced or not by all this, but there are these possible theoretical explanations as to why inflation may not be set off by lower unemployment, up to a point. I should add something. I took the old Phillips

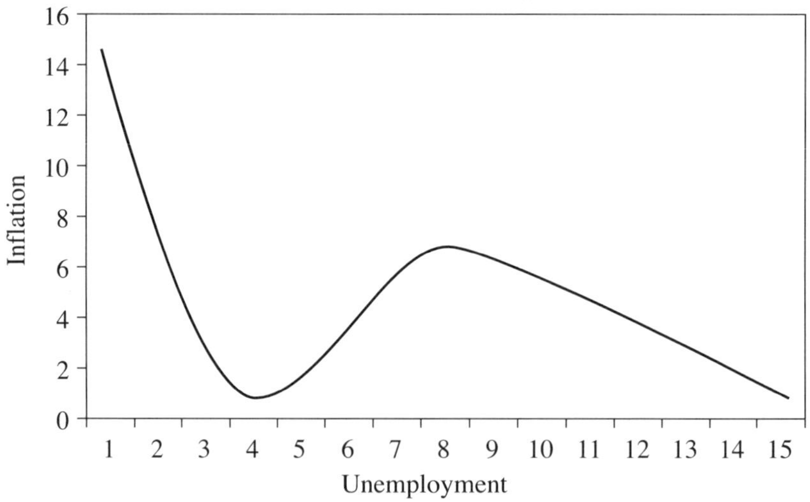

Note: The Cubic Phillips Curve presented here is in general form only. It is drawn from detailed notes of Robert Eisner's conference presentation and replicates his hand-drawn sketch during the discussion period.

Figure 6.5 The Cubic Phillips Curve

Curve, and set it out the way it goes, inflation on the vertical, unemployment on the horizontal access, and the Phillips Curve sloping down, so that inflation gets lower and lower as unemployment gets higher and higher. And then I took the data and I estimated a cubic. I said – inflation is a function not only of unemployment, but of unemployment squared and unemployment cubed. And what do you think I got for my new 'Phillips Curve'?

Inflation was high and did come down starting at very low unemployment, unemployment of 1 per cent. This was a projection but the usual relation suggested that you would have very high inflation. Take unemployment from 1 per cent, then let it keep going up from there. It gets up to about 4.5 per cent, and inflation is very low.

And then, as unemployment begins to go up to above around 4.5 per cent or 4.9 per cent, inflation begins to go up again. If you have an estimated Phillips Curve, you can try out these data sometimes yourself. The normal Phillips Curve falls from left to right.

My Phillips Curve falls and then rises and then falls again. And that gives me 4.9 per cent, about where we are now. That's where you get the lowest inflation. It's true, if you're trying to push the economy up, as Bill Vickrey wants, to 1 per cent unemployment, there will be high inflation.

But again, if you go up to here, you get a peak actually around 8 per cent unemployment. And then when you get above 8 per cent, inflation falls again and becomes low. And that of course is consistent with the other data I have presented.

MODERATOR: Any further questions, on deficits and functional finance?

AUDIENCE MEMBER: Yesterday, Bob, you said we should re-educate the public to understand that deficits are borrowing. And today you've been talking about projections on debt ratios. Why are we talking like this? Why are we accepting government budget constraints? Everything that you have equated to borrowing is just an acceptance of the basic idea of government budget constraints. I don't accept that at all. Why are we accepting that?

EISNER: I'm not accepting that. I quite agree with the principle of functional finance and that our bottom line should be the state of the economy as measured by employment, growth or GDP, and the like. Maybe there's a little bit of semantics involved. It's one thing to say that we should not let the budget deficits stand in the way of what we want to do. I entirely agree with that. But it's another to shy away from the facts.You do want to analyze the impact of the budget so that you know what you're getting. In fact, if you want to get to full employment, this suggests that you should have a bigger deficit.

Take, for example, the simple relationship between the deficit and unemployment. You know what you're going to find? Bigger deficits are associated with higher unemployment. The response is to reduce the deficit. Of course, we have to ask, 'Why are bigger deficits associated with higher unemployment?'

If you take any regression, you're going to find that. When you had high unemployment, you had low national income, low tax payments and a bigger deficit. I think this analysis is really useful to you and all the rest of us who want to damn the deficit. Take whatever deficit necessary in order to get to the state of full employment.

AUDIENCE MEMBER: Some have argued that there are structural changes in the economy that might account for the NAIRU change. To what extent do you agree with that? To what extent do you see this as a permanent change?

EISNER: I think my explanation is better because I've been working at these estimates for three or four years. I was finding the NAIRU suspect on the basis of data well before the so-called change in the economy. I'm now getting huge positive coefficients for low unemployment, indicating that when you drive unemployment further and further below this NAIRU – which I guess came out to be about 5.8 per cent – that is, lower than the CBO NAIRU, you are reducing inflation all the more.

AUDIENCE MEMBER: If we think of functional finance as an integration of a monetary instrument and a fiscal instrument, what is your personal rule by which you would adjust policy? What's the effect going to be on labor?

EISNER: I may offend some people, but I'm an old Keynesian and I always argued, as Keynes did – or anyway as I understood him to do – that interest rates matter and monetary policy matters, but to a limited extent.

I have never taken the position that money doesn't matter, but I have disputed Uncle Milton when he said money is all that matters. I do tend to place greater weight on fiscal policy. I much regret the attitude that monetary policy has become the only game in town in Washington. This I think is a self-imposed restriction of a political nature.

Obviously, I share the concern that you can't expect fine tuning to shift every wrinkle. I also have argued for some time that you have to be careful and note the distinction between short-run and long-run effects. You can't expect a cut in taxes for one quarter or one year to turn the economy around. People will simply save more of it.

I argued during the Vietnam War that the increase in taxes – the temporary surcharge – could not be expected to slow the economy and slow the inflation; and they didn't. I would say that the economy should be stimulated right now in a counter cyclical fashion. The thing to do is to have government expenditures for goods and services, and the kind of tax changes that involve substitution. A federal sales tax would be a better method to encourage people to buy now rather than later. If you simply cut income taxes, people spread out their spending and there isn't much of a counter cyclical effect.

REFERENCES

Eisner, Robert (1995), 'On NAIRU limit, the governing myth of economic policy', *The American Prospect*, Spring, pp. 58–63.

Eisner, Robert (1996a), 'The retreat from full employment', in Arestis, Philip (ed.) *Employment, Economic Growth and the Tyranny of the Market: Essays in Honor of Paul Davidson*, Vol. 2, Cheltenham, UK and Brookfield, US: Edward Elgar, pp. 106–130.

Eisner, Robert (1996b), 'Deficits and unemployment', in Todd Schafer and Jeff Faux (eds) *Reclaiming Prosperity: A Blueprint for Progressive Economic Reform*, Economic Policy Institute, Armonk, NY: M.E. Sharpe Inc., Publishers, pp. 27–38.

Eisner, Robert (1997a), 'A new view of the NAIRU', in P. Davidson and J. Kregel (eds) *Improving the Global Economy: Keynesianism and the Growth in Output and Employment*, Cheltenham, UK and Brookfield, US: Edward Elgar, pp. 196–230.

Eisner, Robert (1997b), 'Une autre interpretation du NAIRU (French Translation of 1997a), in *Cahiers de l'Espace Europe*, March 1997, pp. 9–37.

Eisner, Robert (1998a), 'Damn the NAIRU – and full speed ahead', in Jerry J. Jasinowski (ed.), *The Rising Tide*, New York: Wiley, pp. 61–69.

Eisner, Robert (1998b), *The Keynesian Revolution, Then and Now*, Cheltenham, UK and Northampton, MA: Edward Elgar.

Eisner, Robert and Sang-In Hwang (1993), 'Self-correcting real deficits: a new lesson in functional finance', in Harrie A.A. Verbon and Frans A.A.M. van Winden (eds), *The Political Economy of Government Debt*, Amsterdam and New York: North-Holland, pp. 225–94.

7. The history of Abba Lerner's supply-side inflation

Lynn Turgeon*

Abba Lerner's 'functional finance' arose out of the unusual conditions associated with fighting World War II: full employment, effective price and wage controls and interest rates with a lid of approximately 2 per cent. Nevertheless Lerner came up with an important conclusion applicable to the postwar economy: taxes should be collected only to prevent or reduce inflation, never for revenue purposes; and a government can function without imposing any taxes as long as there is no threat of inflation.[1]

Unfortunately, after the Treasury Accord of March 1951, it was assumed by all and sundry, including the Federal Reserve Board, that there was some threat of inflation, presumably of a demand-pull nature. Thus tax increases were imposed or attempted on several occasions, in particular throughout most of the Korean War. When price controls were eliminated by Eisenhower at the end of that war, the price level, as an indication of false inflationary expectations, actually fell a little. If we can assume (along with Alan Greenspan) an upward bias in our measures of inflation, we might claim that there was insignificant inflation in the 1950s and until the latter part of the decade of the 1960s.

It is the purpose of this chapter to examine Lerner's interpretation of economic policy, in comparison to other Keynesians, looking at the second Eisenhower recession; the 'New Economics' of Kennedy–Johnson; the Nixon 'New Economic Policy'; and the two rounds of hefty OPEC hikes in the price of oil.

At the time of his death, according to D.E. Moggridge, Keynes 'prophesied that in the future, inflation was more likely to be caused by changes in costs than by excess demand.'[2] In contemporary terminology, he thought we had learned how to manage demand-pull inflation but not supply-side inflation. The term 'supply-side inflation' – instead of his usual terms 'sellers' or 'administered inflation' – was first used by Lerner in a short letter written to *The New York Times* toward the end of his life.

* The author would like to express his gratitude to professors Mary Melkonian and Morty Greenhouse for suggested improvements to this chapter.

Lerner was one of the early economists to worry about inflation, speaking of 'sellers' inflation and inflationary depresssion' in a talk to the Political Economy Seminar at Johns Hopkins on November 6, 1957.[3] In a footnote, Lerner mentions that in an 'outstanding article which concentrated on showing the inadequacy and superficiality of proposals to prevent inflation by monetary and fiscal policies and declarations, Professor Sumner H. Slichter seemed to suggest that the distinction between buyers' and sellers' inflation is a futile fantasy.'[4]

According to Slichter 'much time has been wasted in recent years in discussing whether inflation is demand-inspired or cost-inspired.' (Lerner points out that the very next sentence shows that 'it makes sense to distinguish between the blades.') Slichter states, 'changes in the price level may originate either with shifts in the demand schedules or with shifts in the supply schedules.' In another article Slichter definitely aligned himself with the 'sellers' inflation blade' in declaring that 'there is no evidence that prices are rising ahead of costs and are pulling costs up. The evidence is all the other way: that prices are being sluggishly adjusted to slowly rising costs.'

Slichter, who taught at the Harvard Business School, had shocked the business community earlier that decade by claiming that a gently rising price level – a 'natural rate of inflation' – was needed to make capitalism work properly. The above observation was inspired by Eisenhower's second recession in 1957–58 when the federal deficit grew by 13 billion dollars representing greater deficit-financing than had taken place at full employment during the Korean conflict earlier that decade.

It may be significant that the title of Slichter's article in the *Harvard Business Review* (July–August 1957) was 'Government Spending Can Reduce Taxes.'[5] Slichter had apparently discovered the 'passive' or cyclical deficit in a recession that was labeled by Walter Heller in the 1970s as a poor substitute for the 'active' or structural deficits at full employment. If Eisenhower had increased government spending rather than just appearing on television to plead with his audience to go out and buy cars, the deficit would have been smaller and the need for taxes reduced. Eisenhower was also reluctant to follow the recommendation of his long-time adviser Arthur Burns to cut tax rates in order to stimulate the economy before the 1960 election, thereby forcing Richard Nixon to wait eight more years to be elected President.[6] In 1962 President Kennedy, on the other hand, introduced his 'New Economic Policy' that involved the stepping up of military and space expenditures while at the same time introducing the investment tax credit, a supply-side stimulus. Lerner referred to the Kennedy–Johnson policy as an application of his brainchild 'functional finance.'

There are a number of reasons why the New Economics failed by the end of the Johnson Administration. The Johnson Administration made the withholding taxes progressive in 1966 (and eliminated the investment tax credit for four months), thereby producing the first mini-recession (1966–67) in the middle of a war. Incidentally this coincided with the increase in the Social Security taxes that was followed by an upward blip in the CPI. At that time I labeled it as 'legislated inflation.' Finally Johnson got his 10 per cent income tax surcharge on July 1, 1968, which was instrumental in producing a budget surplus the following fiscal year, the last surplus until the recent Clinton 'success.' This surplus, together with Nixon's reduction in real Vietnam War expenditures and his impounding of other expenditures, produced the first regular recession during a war in 1969–70.

The Kennedy and Nixon incomes policies (1962 to 1966 and 1971 to 1974) were counterproductive in that they both assumed that it was possible for labor to share proportionately with capital the gains in labor productivity. The problem with both guidelines was that the share of increased labor productivity going to labor fell behind the proportionate increase provided by the guidelines. By the time labor recognized that profits were growing faster than wages, workers broke out from the planned increase in wages and the respective incomes policies came apart in both 1966 and 1974.

At this juncture some old-time Keynesian economists, particularly Roy Harrod and Abba Lerner, began to deal with a new term – 'stagflation' – that gave a green light to the non-Keynesians to carry out the Keynesian counter-revolution under the leading influence of Milton Friedman and 'monetarism,' a policy approach that received a label only in 1968. Friedman wrote a secret letter to the new President in 1968 urging him to abandon the Bretton Woods fixed rate of exchange and to restore the prewar system of floating exchange rates.

The Volcker group, working under the new Secretary of the Treasury, John Connally, came up with Nixon's 'New Economic Policy' that was introduced on August 15, 1971 at a top-level meeting of Nixon's advisers. All of the economists present opposed the devaluation and floating of the dollar and the 'closing of the gold window.' But Nixon and Connally prevailed. As a result of the expected foreign trade export stimulus, the economy 'took off' and guaranteed Nixon's landslide re-election in November, 1972.[7]

In letters to *The New York Times* and the London *Economist*, Sir Roy Harrod wrote that the 'cure' for demand-pull inflation was supply-side inflation, and vice versa. Any thought of zero inflation was furthest from his mind. In the letter to the London *Economist* (July 29, 1969), Harrod wrote:

> For some weeks now I have been uneasy about the economics in our public policy: a few weeks ago I had a *conceptual breakthrough* [emphasis added]. A sharp distinction should be drawn between the effect on the general price level of a decline in aggregate demand, including its reduction by monetary and fiscal policies, when initially it is running above the supply potential of the economy, and the

> effect of a decline of aggregate demand when it is below the supply potential. . . . When aggregate demand is below the supply potential, a reduction of demand will raise real unit costs . . . and therefore have a price-inflationary tendency. . . . If restrictive policy raises interest rates, this will tend to raise money costs of production. So will an increase of indirect taxes and probably, also to some extent in direct taxes. . . . Most textbooks . . . are in need of revision.

At about the same time, Lerner wrote a little book, *Flation*, dealing with the dilemmas of the Nixon Administration. According to Lerner:

> [M]uch of the failure of traditional economics to explain current problems, or to indicate how to deal with them, stems from the neglect of these (sociological) phenomena, because they cannot easily be translated into statistics or fed into computers as numerical data. They are, nevertheless, well recognized in all descriptions of what happens during inflationary periods when it is clear that there is some excess demand.
>
> In the inflation of 1970–71, all these symptoms were absent. Prices were rising, but the sellers, who were getting the higher prices, were not making unusually high profits. Indeed, they were making unusually low profits. Producers were not trying hard to produce more to sell at the higher prices. They were having great difficulty in selling their current output. . . . In all sorts of ways, they showed that this inflation was different from the usual kind of inflation. In the usual inflation, the sellers find it easy to sell and buyers find it hard to buy. . . . In this inflation, it was the other way around. Buyers found it very easy to buy and sellers found it very difficult to sell. There was a *deficiency* of demand.

It was obvious to anyone who had gone through World War II that the Vietnam War represented an 'underheated' economy compared to the 'overheated' economy of the previous war. The Korean conflict represented the 'goldilocks' or 'just right' economy. All of this was recognized by Arthur Burns in his Pepperdine College speech in 1970. Capacity utilization rates were falling and profits were squeezed despite the lack of an excess profits tax, as in World War II and the Korean conflict.

To add to Nixon's economic problems, OPEC finally got their cartel together and administered a huge deflationary excise tax on the United States economy (in the interpretation of Charles Schultze), just as the Great Recession (1973–75) got going. Instead of the domestic tax reduction proposed by Schultze, Lerner proposed an 'extortion' import tax on oil that he labeled an 'oil purchase tax plan' that might ultimately destroy OPEC's powers of extortion.

Oil – which had been priced in US dollars following Nixon's devaluation of the dollar in 1971 and the further weakening of the dollar in the float that followed the temporary patching up of fixed rates of exchange at the Smithsonian in December 1971 – was now being sold at lower real prices. Lerner felt that the temporary return to fixed exchange rates at the Smithsonian was a second lost opportunity: the failure to continue floating the dollar indefinitely. In my view, Keynes and Harry Dexter White must have been rolling over in their graves at the substitution of floating rates after 1973, as recognized by the Bretton Woods Commission headed by Paul Volcker in 1994. On the basis of twenty years of experience with floating exchange rates, Volcker in effect, rejected the results of his group's work under Connally due to the slower and erratic growth of foreign trade in the floating exchange rate era.

At the Summit meeting of economists called by Alan Greenspan in September 1974, the new Ford Administration hoped to prepare the United States public for a tax increase to 'Whip Inflation Now.' Fortunately the House, led by Representative Al Ullman of Oregon, refused to follow Greenspan's advice and instead came up with a tax cut signed by President Ford in March 1975.

This was followed by a great deal of counterproductive economic thinking: Carter's re-election promise not to cut taxes until he had balanced the budget; Alan Greenspan's committee's recommendation in 1983 for a huge increase in payroll taxes to 'save' social security; Walter Mondale's promise to raise taxes in the years after 1984; and the notorious Bush tax increase in 1990 (aided and abetted by Democratic Representative Tom Foley). About the only hope for Keynesian economics in the 1980s was Ronald Reagan's Military and Commercial Keynesianism that was approved by Walter Heller, as in 1985 he finally recognized that he had been the first practicing supply-sider on the basis of his tax cuts in 1962 and 1964.

Lerner spent the last years of his life working on ingenious plans with Henry Wallich and David Colander to control wage increases if we ever got back to demand-pull inflation. Despite Lerner's clever renaming of 'administered' inflation, he never realized the multi-causal factors producing supply-side inflation: oil price hikes; higher unit overhead costs in an increasingly underheated economy; rising real interest rates in the Reagan years and even, thereafter, disinflation's production of high real interest rates in the Clinton years; increased environmental clean-up costs; growing sales expenditures, such as advertising, affecting particularly the medical component of the CPI; and consumer credit costs.

The steady treatment of supply-side inflation with prescriptions more suitable for demand-pull inflation has led to stagnationist tendencies and deflation in the prices of raw materials and durable consumer goods. Were it not for the growth of services where prices are firmer due to a comparative lack of international competition, we would have serious deflation that would not turn around simply by telling the Federal Reserve to increase the money supply, as recommended by Milton Friedman and Paul Krugman (*Fortune*, February 2, 1998). It is still true, as it was in Keynes's time, that 'we can't push on a string.' Easy monetary policy does not work in a deflationary situation.

What lessons should we learn from our long experience with stagflation?

1. Tax increases, including import duties, are counterproductive until we get back to demand-pull inflation. Tax reductions are called for.
2. Likewise reductions in government spending are counterproductive until we return to demand-pull inflation. The Clinton Administration pared Federal spending, but there have been significant increases in local and state spending made possible by the growth in surpluses at the state and local level.
3. We should revise our ideas on Federal deficits, particularly those that serve as a basis for the requirements of the European Monetary Union. We have a lot of evidence since Slichter noticed the passive deficit during Eisenhower's second recession in 1957–58. All record deficits since then have been run up by Republican Administrations that failed to increase government spending. All attempts to reduce the size of the welfare state, either by US Republicans or Western European states since the end of the Cold War are therefore counterproductive. To take a goal of deficits no larger than 3 per cent of GDP is to ignore the difference between active and passive deficits. All Western European countries covered by the Maastricht Treaty are decidedly underheated and should be allowed larger passive or cyclical deficits, as a percentage of GDP, to get their economies growing again.
4. There is another lesson to be learned from our experience with large passive deficits, particularly those run up by the Reagan and Bush Administrations. While active deficits were associated with demand-pull inflation in the early postwar years, passive deficits were associated with supply-side disinflation, based partly on declining oil prices.
5. Lerner's functional finance and its playing down of the need for taxes should be 'must reading' for contemporary Russian policy-makers. Russia has licked domestic inflation and its economy is poised on the brink of deflation, as reflected on farmers' markets.

NOTES

1. See my ' "Monetary Cranks" and Functional Finance,' *Economic Reform*, April, 1997.
2. Donald E. Moggridge (1992), *Maynard Keynes: An Economist's Biography*, London: Routledge, p. 835.
3. David Colander (1983), *Selected Economic Writings of Abba P. Lerner*, New York: New York University Press, p. 469.
4. Ibid., p. 475.
5. Sumner Slichter (July–August 1957), 'Government Spending Can Reduce Taxes,' *Harvard Business Review*.
6. It seems safe to say that Eisenhower did not have a Keynesian bone in his body, contrary to a recent article by Robert Skidelsky in *Prospect*, wherein he abandons Thatcherism for 'Eisenhower Keynesianism.'
7. The export surplus did not show up until the second half of 1973.

REFERENCES

Acheson, A.L.K. et al (eds) (1972), *Bretton Woods Revisted*, Toronto: University of Toronto Press. (In his contribution, 'Problems perceived in the international finance system', Sir Roy Harrod recognizes that raising taxes, high interest rate and 'damping demand' are all inflationary.)

Lerner, Abba (1972), *Flation*, New York: Quadrangle Books.

Schultze, Charles (1975), *Higher Oil Prices and the World Economy: The Adjustment Problem*, Washington: Brookings Institution.

Scitovsky, Tibor (1984), 'Lerner's Contribution to Economics,' *Journal of Economic Literature*, December: 1547–71.

Turgeon, Lynn (1971), 'The Crisis in Post-Keynesian Economics: A Revisionist Interpretation of Recent Economic History,' *Quarterly Review of Economics and Business*, Vol. 11, No. 4 (Winter) pp. 61–8 (based on lectures given in Prague and Budapest, summer, 1970.)

Turgeon, Lynn (1997), *Bastard Keynesianism*, New York: Praeger.

8. Functional finance and fiscal functions

Richard A. Musgrave

While I have no paper to present, I have been asked to contribute some comments, and I am happy to do so. I will first review Abba Lerner's model of Functional Finance with its focus on budget policy as an instrument of stabilization, and then consider its relation to my three-branch model.

FUNCTIONAL FINANCE AND THE ROLE OF BUDGET POLICY AS AN INSTRUMENT OF STABILIZATION

The Functional Finance model, when presented six decades ago, proposed to lay bare the logic of fiscal stabilization in stark terms, acting as a shock therapy intended to correct popular misunderstandings, specifically those regarding the role of taxation and the nature of public debt.

THE STRUCTURE OF FUNCTIONAL FINANCE

The structure of Functional Finance (Lerner, *The Economics of Control*, 1944, Ch. 24) can be summarized as follows: The function of public expenditures is to render public services at the level required for efficient resource use at full employment. By contrast, the function of taxation does not provide such necessary finance. The state can always print money for that purpose. Taxation, rather, serves to hold down aggregate demand – public and private – to its full employment level. The same is true for borrowing and debt finance. Both taxing and borrowing (debt issue), while thus serving to depress demand, differ in their impacts. Taxation primarily checks consumption by curtailing disposable income, while debt-issue primarily restrains investment by raising the rate of interest. Stabilization policy may thus assure full employment along with maintaining price level stability, and does so at the efficient level of public services. That level, the strength of the economy and the desired distribution of output between consumption and capital formation determine whether a budget deficit or surplus is necessary to raise or lower the level of public debt. That level in itself, however, is of little importance. Debt, when owed by private households or firms, reduces the debtor's net worth, but domestically held public debt does not reduce the nation's wealth. Where there is a debtor, there is also a creditor, debt service merely shifting income from one part of the economy to another.

Comments

The logic of this model, when it was offered almost six decades ago (a time span that is, in my view, not all that long), anticipated the neoclassical synthesis of the 1960s. While retaining a Keynesian spirit, it no longer postulated the lasting liquidity trap or stagnation prognosis prominent in the 1930s vision of Keynesian stabilization policy. Depending on conditions, investment may respond more or less readily to changes in the rate of interest, and money supply matters and stabilization policy may have to redress excessive as well as deficient demand.

In thus offering a flexible framework for macro policy, the basic thesis of the Functional Finance model – that budgetary finance be viewed as part of total (private and public) expenditure control – still stands. Such is the case, even though some amendments are in order, especially regarding the Functional Finance claim that outstanding debt is of no consequence. Interest payments, if tax-financed, are not a mere transfer. The additional taxation incurs a deadweight loss that must be accounted for. Debates in the 1950s concluded that this would not pose a serious problem as long as the increase in debt was matched by rising income; but the experience of the 1980s showed otherwise. Moreover, as debt service claims an increasing budget share, willingness to accept further taxation declines and other expenditures tend to be driven out, a concern that has generated support for budget balancing from traditionally Keynesian quarters. Debt finance of interest payments, in turn, changes the output mix and further constrains the available policy choices.

Other amendments, such as time lags in the effectiveness of various policy tools, may also be added to the central message of Functional Finance, but they only qualify and do not change Functional Finance's central message: The economy, left to its own devices, does not ensure stability. In principle, at least, there are sufficient policy instruments with which stability can be secured. The relationship between income- and expenditure-flows and their determinants remains the proper focus of stabilization policy.

More recently macro theory and the role it assigns to fiscal policy have shifted away from this framework. Based on postulates of perfect markets and rational choice, taxation no longer restrains consumer demand. Taxpayers, well aware of Ricardian equivalence theorem, are now seen to account for the present value of future taxes needed to sustain debt service. As a result, the impact of tax and loan finance consumption is the same. Deficit finance no longer raises aggregate demand via increased consumption, thereby voiding the key instrument of Keynesian stabilization. As I see it, the assumption of perfect foresight, however appropriate to an idealized model of perfect markets, is unrealistic. Consumers are not that perceptive, and cannot know how and when future taxation needed for debt service will be imposed. The consumption multiplier has proven to be smaller than was earlier thought, but an expansionary consumption effect of debt, and restrictive effect of surplus finance, surely remains. Turning to the impact of debt finance on investment, such effects will vary in strength relevant to economic conditions, but fiscal policy still matters. Along with changing theory, the applied policy debate has in fact remained closer to that framework.

Nevertheless, there has been a change in perspective. The stronger economy of the 1990s permitted a shift in the stabilization mix from borrowing, high interest rates and deficit budgets, to increased reliance on tax finance along with low interest rates and surplus budgets. By stressing investment, this shift also accommodated an increasing concern for the long-run effects of budget policy based on demographic change and the need to sustain the social security system. As built-in revenue growth and expenditure restraint generated a budget surplus, its use for debt retirement combined with eased monetary policy supported that goal. Capital formation, by raising productivity and income, eased the burden to be borne by future generations. Choosing the correct mix of expenditure/tax constraint gained key importance. Most recently, fear of recession once more shifted the perspective. Ricardian equivalence notwithstanding, swift tax reduction is once more called for to strengthen consumption, and unlimited effectiveness of monetary policy is no longer taken for granted.

FUNCTIONAL FINANCE AND THE THREE-BRANCH MODEL

Functional Finance, as Lerner saw it, was to focus on stabilization only and said little about the other functions of budget policy, functions that have been central to the traditional economics of public finance. Allowance for these must also be made, and in turn, the simple structure of the Functional Finance model – especially the role assigned to taxation – has to be reconsidered.

Paying for Public Services

Like Pigou, Lerner called for public services to be provided in a manner equating their benefits and their marginal social costs. This can set an unexceptional norm, but there remains the problem of how the norm is to be accomplished.

In a democratic society, what and how much should be provided is not decided by the budget chief but derived from the preferences of voters. These preferences, however, are not known to the chief. When asked, consumers who expect to be taxed accordingly will respond as free riders. A mechanism to secure preference revelation is thus needed. As Wicksell (1896) first noted, this is to be provided by a voting process, involving a combined vote on both the tax and expenditure sides of the budget. Knowing that they must submit to the outcome, voters will be induced to reveal their own preferences. A unanimous vote implies a pure system of benefit taxation. As this is impracticable, a second-best outcome based on plurality voting must suffice. Numerous imperfections arise and much depends on voting procedures, but this, nevertheless, is the best method available.

Taxation, therefore, is not only a tool of macro policy. It is also an inherent part of securing an efficient provision of public goods and is required even if there is no need for stabilization. In my three-branch model, the budget's 'Allocation Branch' performs this allocative function (Musgrave, 1959). In allowing for the role of taxation in choosing public services, the two considerations may conflict. For preference revelation to occur, voters must be confronted with their share in costs as well as in benefits. This is made explicit by tax but not by loan finance. Short of reintroducing Ricardian foresight (rejected above in the macro context), deficit finance thus tends to induce excess budgets, just as surplus finance tends to encourage deficient levels of public services. This, at least, holds for the case of current expenditures, with fiscal discipline calling for loan finance of public investment.

Equity in Distribution

It remains to note the role of distribution, the third part of my three-branch model. As noted before, Wicksell was primarily concerned with taxation's role as a tool of preference revelation. Tax/expenditure voting would approximate an efficient provision of public services. But this is only part of Wicksell's position. Largely overlooked by supporters of his balanced budget discipline was Wicksell's conviction that for the outcome to be just as well as efficient, the underlying distribution of income must also be just. To meet that condition, redistribution via progressive taxation is needed. Although detrimental effects of redistribution limit what can be done, taxation is given a further function. This is again allowed for in my three-branch model, where a distribution branch is added to the allocation and stabilization branches. Here a tax-transfer process provides for the needed adjustments. Though this leaves open the question of how the underlying social welfare function should be determined in a democratic society, the function of taxation is expanded once more.

Lerner himself (1944, Ch. 3), far from overlooking equity, offered brilliant and then novel analyses of optimal distribution. He argues that maximizing aggregate utility is desirable, but questions how it can be accomplished. He notes that, given the assumption of declining marginal utility of income and equal capacities to derive benefits, aggregate welfare would be maximized by distributing a given total income equally. But there is no way to determine whether capacities are equal or how they differ. A simplistic utilitarian formulation will not do. A case for equalization follows, however, if based on maximizing the probable, not-actually-to-be-realized, level of aggregate welfare. A departure from equality, as income is shifted from A to B, improves B's position and worsens that of A. But given declining marginal utility for both, B's gain will be less than A's loss. Inequality in the distribution of a given income total, therefore, will reduce the probable level of aggregate welfare. A case for equalizing policy is made, even though it is qualified by allowing for the effects of redistribution on total income. Lerner was thus the first (along with Vickrey, 1945) to posit the role of uncertainty and impartial choice in the theory of just distribution (Rawls, 1974). He added that, as an alternative to the model of welfare maximization, distributive justice may also be viewed as a matter of fairness. On both counts, Lerner thus anticipated the lively debate that was to follow in the 1970s.

Following that insightful discussion, Lerner's Functional Finance model itself paid little attention to distribution. The level of taxation needed for stabilization will depend on its distribution across taxpayers, so he noted, but beyond this nothing is said about how the taxes needed to restrain demand are to be distributed. Brief reference is made to distributional concerns on the expenditure side of the budget, but this does not suffice. Transfer payments will serve to raise lower-end incomes, but for redistribution to be effective, finance by progressive taxation is needed to reach the upper end. Equitable taxation – equitable in both its vertical and horizontal dimensions – has an essential role in distribution policy, so that taxation once more cannot be viewed only as an instrument of macro policy.

CONCLUSION

The concept of Functional Finance is a good framework in which to view budget policy, and the stark outline of Lerner's Functional Finance model did so brilliantly for its macro role. But the model needs to be extended to allow also for its other functions. Controlling aggregate demand, establishing which services should be provided and equity in their distribution must all be addressed, each of these having its own rationale and requiring implementation. The interaction between these elements calls for mutual accommodation, a difficult task even if each function could draw on its own expenditure and tax instruments, approaches too cumbersome in practice. Instead, the same tax and expenditure tools are used to meet the various needs, thereby adding to the complexity of a comprehensive functional design. Functional Finance as a design of stabilization policy remains a classic of macroeconomics, but it is only one part of budget policy.

REFERENCES

Lerner, Abba P. (1944), *The Economics of Control*, New York: Macmillan.
Musgrave, Richard A. (1959), *The Theory of Public Finance*, New York: McGraw-Hill.
Rawls, John (1974), *The Theory of Justice*, Cambridge, MA: Harvard University Press.
William Vickrey (1945), 'The effect of averaging on the cyclical sensitivity of the yield of the income tax', *Journal of Political Economy*, Vol. 53, No. 3. pp. 275–7.
Wicksell, Knut (1896), *Finanztheoretische Untersuchungen und das Steuerwesen Schweden's*, Jena: Fischer. See also R.A. Musgrave and A. Peacock (eds) (1958), *Classics in the Theory of Public Finance*, New York: St. Martin's Press.

9. Are these trade-offs necessary?

James S. Duesenberry

For over 50 years, monetary and fiscal policy have been guided by the twin objectives of full employment and price stability. The painful memories of the Great Depression made full employment a top priority for many people, but the long tradition of sound money and the inflation of World War II were enough to force a compromise, weakening the full employment commitment of the Employment Act of 1946. Inflation fears were reinforced by the Korean War and even more by relatively mild inflation of the late 1950s. The rapid inflation set off by the Vietnam War and oil and commodity shocks made further resistance to inflation a political priority, so much so that the Federal Reserve was able to take the drastic measures required to start the disinflation process in the recession of 1979 to 1981, action that would have probably been impossible after the first oil shock five years earlier.

I want to begin this chapter with a review of postwar inflation experience and the evolution of theory as a way of evaluating the concept of non-accelerating inflation rate of unemployment (NAIRU). This will hopefully provide a background for a discussion of the problems of managing monetary and fiscal policy. In the second part of the chapter, I shall outline the evolution of attitudes leading to the primacy of monetary policy and the current neglect of any concern for a rational fiscal policy, that is, for any form of 'functional finance.' I will conclude with some observations on current macroeconomic policy problems.

EVOLUTION OF INFLATION THEORY

It may be useful to begin with a review of the inflation theories that led up to the NAIRU concept. In the 1950s, there was a good deal of debate over the relative importance of 'demand pull' and 'cost push' as causes of inflation. The Phillips Curve, imported from the UK, provided a conceptual basis for a more unified approach. Changes in demand caused movements along the Phillips Curve, while changes in the strength of trade unions or in product market competition caused shifts in the curve. The empirical estimates of the Phillips Curve for the US did not show as tight a relationship as the one found by

Phillips in the UK, but the idea was so conceptually neat and provided so many opportunities for economic games that it was quickly enshrined in textbooks. The Kennedy Council of Economic Advisers (CEA) proposed to shift the curve downward by measures designed to reduce 'cost–push' pressures so that expansionist demand policies could be safely pursued. The Phillips Curve idea also offered an opportunity to calibrate compromises between the goals of full employment and price stability. The Curve determined the available opportunities to trade an increase in the inflation rate for a reduction in the unemployment rate. The compromise notion was not new. Sumner Schlicter, in 1953, was roundly condemned by business leaders for asserting that 'creeping inflation' did little harm. The Phillips Curve seemed to give 'scientific' support for his view.

The counter to that view was the assertion that a creeping inflation would induce more wage demands leading to more rapid price increases. Creeping inflation would soon become galloping inflation. Of course, wage–price spirals had long been recognized, usually in connection with instances of massive excess demand during and after wars. In the early 1960s, when the Brookings econometric model was put together, the wage equations included a feedback from prices to wages as well as from wages to prices. The feedback from prices to wages proved to be significant but not large enough to lead to a continuing acceleration of inflation. An initial 2 per cent inflation might ultimately converge to 5 or 6 per cent if there were no change in conditions.

Others disagreed. Milton Friedman in particular argued that an effort to push employment down to a level that produced some inflation and keep it there would lead to an indefinite acceleration of inflation. He termed the point at which wage inflation exceeds productivity growth the 'natural rate of unemployment.' The NAIRU seems to be the same thing, but avoids the suggestion that because it is natural it is a good thing.

The model underlying the NAIRU concept is a drastically simplified version of real world labor and product markets. It assumes a homogeneous labor force hired in a competitive labor market, ignoring the division of real labor markets by area, industry, and occupation. It also ignores trade unions and personnel management practices as well as differences in the intensity and nature of competition among product markets.

The central message of the NAIRU model is that a policy aimed at reducing unemployment to a level below the natural rate and attempting to keep it there will inevitably lead to a continuous acceleration of inflation. The argument goes as follows: Start with a labor market in equilibrium. Because there are frictional problems in any labor market – that is, workers in the wrong place or searching for jobs with imperfect information – there must always be some employment as well as some vacant jobs. To keep the level of vacancies low enough to prevent a rise in wages it is necessary to have some unemployment. The rate of unemployment required to avert wage inflation is the 'natural rate of unemployment.'

If a central bank management, not having read Milton Friedman, acts to increase nominal demand in the interest of reducing unemployment to a level below the natural rate, they will succeed for a time. Then wages will rise with prices to follow, reducing real demand and employment to its previous level. If they do not mind a little inflation, the central bank's managers can raise nominal demand as needed again and again, and for a time there will be a continuing inflation and a reduced level of unemployment. That's the Phillips curve part of the story. We move to the NAIRU by taking account of expectations.

In equation form, $P'_t = F(UE^*{-}UE)$, where P'_t is the rate of inflation, UE is the unemployment rate, and UE^* is the 'natural rate of unemployment.'

In time, however, all participants will come to expect inflation to continue. Prices and wages will rise without any demand pressure. The equation for inflation now becomes $P'_t = P_t^{\prime e} + F\ (UE^*{-}UE)$. But if the expected rate of inflation equals the rate experienced in the recent past, the equation becomes $P'_t = P'_{t-1} + F\ (UE^*{-}UE)$ or $P' - P'_{t-1} = F\ (UE^* - UE)$. If the feedback from lagged inflation is 1, inflation accelerates at a rate determined by the reduction of unemployment below the 'natural rate.'

The adjustment of expectations plays a central role in determining the rate of inflation. In the real world, expectations formed from inflation experience depend on the level of the inflation rate, its duration and the variance about the mean. Cyclical fluctuations dampen the process. But perceptions of the causes and of the policies that may affect inflation are also important. I will argue presently that the process will be much affected by the speed and distribution of changes in demand. A gradual expansion that slowly reduces unemployment will produce very different results from a rapid expansion concentrated in a few sectors.

Even a drastically oversimplified model can yield useful insights into the operation of some of the factors influencing wages and prices, but strong, simple generalizations drawn from that kind of model cannot be used to draw policy conclusions without a lot of further testing. Moreover, in using models as a guide to empirical studies, it is important to remember that the characteristics of labor and product markets change over time. Indeed we have witnessed in the last 30 years a number of important changes affecting wage-making processes. Increased foreign competition in product markets has weakened trade unions, while managements are now less willing to use wages to compete for quality labor or to raise morale. Just when economists discovered efficiency wages, they began to disappear.

In evaluating empirical evidence on the NAIRU concept, it may be useful to examine briefly three episodes of price–wage history. First, the period from the early 1960s to about 1973 looks like an example of the NAIRU approach. In that period, during which unemployment fell to its lowest level since the Korean War, there was a wage–price spiral. Other factors played a role, but the events of the period were as close to the model as you can get in the real world. That might be expected, since the model was inspired by the events of the period.

The next period – from about 1973 to 1980 – was quite a different affair. Unemployment was 6 per cent most of the time, but prices were driven upward by rising oil and commodity prices. Wages rose in response. Union contracts with COLAs negotiated in the 1960s strengthened the feedback, but all large employers, and most smaller ones, followed the patterns established in the 1960s. Moreover, most people expected inflation to continue. Disinflation began only when sharp increases in interest rates, in 1979–81, caused the deepest recession since the Second World War. Even then, the strength and continuity of the price–wage feedback was such that it took two years to bring the inflation rate down to 4 per cent. I think that the special features of this period go a long way to explaining the results obtained by Robert Eisner when he separated periods of high and low employment in his inflation regressions.

The third episode, from 1983 until 2000, contrasts with the others. During this period, except for a mild recession in 1991, output grew steadily at modest levels. Defying all notions of a cycle, the economy picked up speed in the late 1990s. The unemployment rate drifted downward with mild fluctuations, reaching 5.5 per cent by 1988, rising briefly to 7.5 per cent during a short recession, and then moving down again to 4 per cent. The inflation rate, with very mild fluctuations, also drifted down. As long as there was obvious slack in the economy, no one was surprised by the behavior of those prices, but the last few years have created severe problems for inflation theorists. When the unemployment rate fell below 6 per cent, and continued to fall, and nothing happened to wage rates or inflation, some explanation seemed to be required. One might first argue that the 6 per cent figure was not derived from direct observation but from a rather complex processing of econometric relationships with the outcome sensitive to small changes in the parameters. As I noted above, much of the information in those equations came from a rather special experience of the 1970s. A second point, emphasized by Robert Gordon, is that, until recently, oil and commodity prices have caused little trouble. In my opinion, the changes in personnel management, the increasing role of foreign competition and the weakening of trade union bargaining power noted earlier have played an important role in limiting inflation.

Finally, as John Dunlop has argued, the current expansion proceeding at a steady pace with relatively even growth in different sectors has had correspondingly gradual employment growth in many sectors. That gradual growth has given employers time to fill vacancies without raising wages. Personnel managers faced with a dearth of applications for jobs do not rush to raise wages to attract workers. Instead, they do everything they can think to do to avoid wage increases. They intensify the search process; they advertise more; send more interviewers to schools; offer bonuses to employees who bring in recruits. Some retain employees for promotion and take in unskilled workers at the bottom of the ladder. Managements outsource, sometimes using imports, not only because the new source is cheaper, but because they can avoid disrupting the wage structure by raising wages in one shortage sector. Other alternatives include overtime and investment automation. All those devices take time and would not be feasible in a rapid expansion. But in a gradual expansion, like the one we have been having, there is time for employers to make needed adjustments without large increases in wages. Together with the changes in foreign competition and the strength of unions, the Phillips Curve has been much flatter so that unemployment could be reduced without a rapid increase in wages. These observations suggest that our understanding of wage inflation problems would be improved if we thought about labor market conditions in terms of vacancies as well as, or instead of, unemployment. We do not have good global measures of vacancies. Too much attention to the headline unemployment number is often misleading.

Since there has been relatively little rise in prices lately, the expectational aspects of the NAIRU doctrine have not had a recent test. It would be foolish, however, to suppose that inflation is gone for good. The expectational response to a higher inflation will depend on factors noted above. The financial press might lead one to believe that a rate of unemployment below the NAIRU, whatever it may be, will cause an explosion of inflation. In fact, of course, the response will depend on the initial cause, that is, something like an oil shock or, at the opposite end of the spectrum, a continued rate of growth above the economy's potential output. In the one case, there will be expectations of a repeat of the 1970s that will contribute to further acceleration of price increases. In the other, the expectational response should be much weaker. In either case, the responses of fiscal and monetary policy will influence expectations.

The NAIRU concept has been oversimplified, presented with false precision and over-hyped. The popular NAIRU literature suggests that reducing unemployment below some critical point will create an explosion of inflation; there is, nonetheless, a real inflation problem. Governments have all too often pushed demand too far and endured costly inflations and even more costly disinflations. Moreover, they have been reluctant to take the painful restrictive actions needed to bring inflation episodes to an end. In the 1960s, there was widespread agreement that a tax increase was needed to contain the effects of expenditures for the Vietnam War as well as for the 'Great Society' programs.

The President was reluctant and Congress was not helpful. The burden of restraint fell on the always politically vulnerable Federal Reserve that took action that proved to be inadequate. Fiscal and monetary restraint finally slowed demand growth but not until inflation had gained momentum.

There is an upper limit to capacity utilization, one that varies as the structure of the economy varies. When we pass that limit, inflation will start to accelerate. The extent of acceleration depends on the rate of growth of demand and many other factors. What it will take to reverse the process will depend on how long we wait to start; delay will be costly.

MONETARY AND FISCAL POLICY

The goal for monetary and fiscal policy is easy to state and difficult to achieve. We want the fullest utilization of resources consistent with reasonable price stability. We can accept an inflation rate of 2 to 3 per cent. If it gets any higher, policy must change in a way that will bring the rate down. Long delay in acting to disinflate will be costly as will an unwillingness to complete a disinflationary process.

Now I want to turn to the evolution of attitudes toward monetary and fiscal policy. In the early 1950s, there was a widespread agreement – outside of Chicago – that monetary policy was a pretty feeble instrument. Monetary policy was supposed to affect aggregate demand by influencing investment expenditures. Interviews and case studies seemed to indicate that changes in interest rates had little effect on investment expenditures. On the other hand, fiscal policy was supposed to be an effective instrument of stabilization policy capable of stimulating demand and slowing growth as required.

Both of these judgments have been reversed. The public and many economists have acquired great faith in the power of monetary policy and in the skill of Chairman Greenspan in using that power. The Fed is given much credit for the continued growth of the economy, and it is generally assumed that monetary policy can do what is needed to maintain steady growth in all circumstances. Fiscal policy has not only been devalued; it has been forgotten. Debates about budget surpluses pay little attention to the macroeconomic effects of government expenditures and taxes. With 50 years of experience we ought to have learned something about the power of monetary and fiscal policy and how they should be used for reading the message of experience has not been easy.

In the 1950s, monetary policy was first evaluated in terms of simple Keynesian models and found wanting. The limited amount of available evidence indicated that changes in interest rates had little effect on business investment. But in the 1960s and 1970s, restrictive monetary policy worked to check inflationary pressures. In doing so, it caused several recessions, with recoveries following renewed monetary expansion. The severe recession of 1979–81 removed any remaining doubts about the Fed's power to limit the growth of demand. Recessions did not, however, show clearly what the Fed could do to make demand grow.

I will return to that point after a look at the most recent experience. Many evaluations of the Fed's performance in the 1960s and 1970s asserted that it waited too long to take restrictive action when inflation threatened, and then, as the problem became serious, had to raise interest rates sharply, bringing on a recession. This criticism is legitimate with the advantage of hindsight, but it does not do justice to the difficulty of making policy with instruments that operate with a long time lag. Timely action requires good forecasts, and anyone who has followed the forecasts of the last few years knows that good forecasts are hard to come by. Monetary managers have to steer between the risk of doing too little too late in fighting inflation and the opposite risk of unnecessarily slowing the economy. They also must be prepared to quickly reverse policy once disinflation is under way.

For more than a decade, the Fed has followed a rule of taking small actions in the direction indicated by forecasts guided by the maxim, 'If you are not sure where you are going, don't go very fast.' That cautious policy has worked out very well: it certainly has not done any harm, but it is hard to say how much good it has done. It is unfortunate that the experience has fostered the notion that the Fed can control demand at will. This is a dangerous notion. We still lack a reliable basis for judging the effects of monetary policy. Indeed we do not have agreement on the channels through which monetary policy has worked. In the 1960s and the 1970s, sharply rising market interest rates drew funds away from thrift institutions that were then forced to ration mortgage credit. The resulting cuts in home building were important causes of the recessions of those years. While changes in credit markets have largely eliminated rationing in mortgage markets, variations in mortgage interest rates remain important.

Interest rate variations influence international capital flows and exchange rates affecting net exports. However, the reliability of this linkage is reduced by many factors that influence capital flows. The same thing is true of the connections between interest rates and the stock market as well as the links between that market and expenditures for consumption and investment. Finally, interest rates do influence business investment, but our measurement of that relationship is not very satisfactory. In econometric models, the effect of interest rates on business investment is usually measured indirectly; investment expenditures are related to a 'cost of capital' variable. While interest rates are one component in the cost of capital, the most important component is the set of tax rates affecting net investment costs.

Interest rates do affect demand through a number of channels but, because the strength of the different channels varies with a variety of other circumstances, it is difficult to obtain a reliable measure of the strength of interest rate effects. The most recent edition of the Federal Reserve System's macroeconomic model indicates that a one-percentage point reduction in the federal funds rate could generate a 1.5 per cent rise in real GDP. According to Congressional Budget Office estimates, the unified budget surplus might rise to as much as 5 per cent of GDP. That estimate assumes that discretionary expenditures now subject to caps will rise at the inflation rate. It also assumes that we have another ten years of steady growth with no recessions. Allowing for a multiplier, a policy of using the whole surplus for debt repayment would require a drop of the Fed funds rate by 1 per cent or so. Proponents of such a policy seem to be saying 'Not to worry. The Fed will take care of it.' The model indicates that changes in interest rates can have a substantial influence on aggregate demand. Given the forecasting record of econometric models in the last few years, however, we cannot rely on any model to guide monetary policy. Nor can we use monetary policy as our sole instrument for economic stabilization.

That brings us back to fiscal policy. Despite its power, fiscal policy has not worked well as an instrument for short-run stabilization of fiscal policy. Variations in government expenditures take too long to start and to reverse. Temporary changes in tax rates have had limited effect. We can use active fiscal policy to adjust to persisting changes in the balance between private saving and private investment, but not for adjustment of transient changes.

Certainly fiscal policy is a powerful expansive instrument. In the 1960s, the combination of a permanent tax cut, Great Society and Vietnam War expenditures launched a boom that taxed our productive resources and set off an inflation. The Reagan tax cuts also generated a rapid growth in demand that was more than enough to utilize the slack created by the 1979–81 recession. Demand pressures were also absorbed by the growth of the trade deficit. Though a good deal was written about the significance of the deficits stemming from the Reagan policy, popular and political discussion of its macroeconomic significance was muted. As Eisner has argued, because the inflation component of interest costs was offset as inflation reduced the real value of the debt, the deficit in real terms was much exaggerated. From a 'functional finance' point of view, the real issue was whether a reduction in expenditures was necessary to avert inflation or to close the balance-of-payments gap. After years of foot-dragging responses to fiscal commitments, the budget was balanced at last. Because the gap between private investment and private saving reflected in the trade deficit kept growing, expenditure caps and the final 1993 tax increase were consistent with growing demand. Though no one said so, the budget caps and tax increases were the right thing from a functional finance point of view. (The allocation of the budget changes is another matter.)

Continued income growth together with increasing capital gains has swelled federal revenues, while expenditure growth has been limited by the caps that are still in effect and partially enforced. Currently investment remains strong while private saving has nearly disappeared. A private sector deficit is offset by public saving and a growing trade deficit.

Pundits and politicians act as though that situation will continue indefinitely but it can in fact change in a variety of ways. Private saving may rise while investment falls, perhaps in response to a less exuberant stock market. In that case, revenue will fall and higher expenditures will be needed. Fiscal and monetary policy must respond to those changes. Our fiscal concern then should be for the welfare of the economy, not for preservation of the surplus or even for a balanced budget. The basic policy rule should be to aim for a budget surplus (deficit), which balances the excess of private investment over the sum of private saving, and an inflow of foreign capital (balance of payments deficit), with all the elements of that equation evaluated at full employment.

$(I^*–S^*)$–BOP deficit = Govt surplus*, where the stars indicate full employment values for investment saving and government surplus. Private sector investment can be influenced by monetary policy, which also affects the balance of payments through its effect on capital flows, while private saving is affected by the stock market. Monetary policy should provide a first line of defense against variations in the investment–savings balance.

Another effective instrument for that purpose has been the 'automatic stabilizers.' We used to think that automatic stabilizers could be an effective first line of defense against fluctuations in demand whatever their source. Declining tax revenues and increased transfer payments shield private incomes from part of the impact of any reduction in private expenditures. They are especially valuable because they operate without the delay involved in any legislative decision for changes in expenditures or taxes. While they are still important, there has been some erosion of automatic stabilizers. For any given rate of unemployment, fewer people now draw unemployment compensation than in the past. While state funds are currently in good shape, there are continuing efforts to reduce the unemployment compensation tax rates or to divert compensation funds into other uses. In recessions, it has always been possible to make federal loans to state funds in difficulties and to extend benefits to longer-term unemployed. To my knowledge, no one in Congress is thinking of what might happen if another recession should occur. Given the vulnerability of the economy to shocks from the stock market and the balance of payments, they should be not only hoping for the best but planning for the worst. In view of the limitations of monetary policy and automatic stabilizers, it is a dangerous game to make commitments for expenditures or tax cuts on the basis of a hypothetical surplus. It is also dangerous to promise to use a hypothetical surplus to pay off debt. There should be opportunities for some increases in federal expenditures and for some tax rate reductions, but how much room there is will depend on the growth of productivity, and on private sector saving and investment behavior as well as on the inflow of foreign capital.

PART IV

FISCAL AND MONETARY LINKAGES

Conventional thinking separates monetary and fiscal policy; the first is the domain of the Central Bank's management of the money supply, the second arises from the Treasury's balancing of revenue from taxes with expenditures directed by Congress and the Executive. The chief connection between these is said to come from fiscal policy absorbing or releasing savings, so that the interest rate will be driven up or allowed to decline.

Conventional understanding of the money supply is inadequate, partly because it does not recognize the role of the state, partly because it treats money as exogenous. Textbooks present the impact of tax collections and spending incorrectly. Randall Wray shows that government spends by creating money, and that taxes reduce the money supply. Bonds are essentially devices for maintaining the interest rate as pegged. Forstater demonstrates that monetary and fiscal relationships described by Lerner fit into the larger perspective of the role and powers of government in a modern state and their interaction with the private market economy. Lerner's approach, when pulled together, provides a more or less complete political economy. My chapter provides historical background, showing that the conventional way of thinking about the monetary system is not without meaning; on the contrary, it describes relationships that once were true. The development of the economy, however, has led to fundamental changes that have not been matched by the evolution of our theories.

John Smithin carries this forward in an account of an endogenous money system in the context of a growing economy. Interest rates, he shows, can be considered 'competitive' with wage and profit rates; that is, the more that goes to interest, the less is left to divide between wages and profits. Thus cheap money could lead to an increase in both wages and profits, but Smithin also examines why this might not happen.

10. Functional finance and US government budget surpluses in the new millennium

L. Randall Wray

This chapter explores the nature of 'government finance.' The approach presented here is properly called a 'functional finance' approach to government finance – an antidote to conventional principles of 'sound finance.' Readers will recognize the debt owed to Abba Lerner; indeed some functional finance principles were incorporated into Keynesian economics – bastard and otherwise – but I believe the full import of Lerner's principles of functional finance has not been recognized even by followers of Keynes. An understanding of the nature of government finance not only sheds light on 'fiscal policy,' but also on the true nature of what is normally called 'monetary policy.' We will then move on to an analysis of US government budget surpluses at the beginning of the new millennium and the projections that these will continue into the twenty-first century as the government retires its outstanding debt stock.

BRIEF OVERVIEW OF CONVENTIONAL VIEWS ON GOVERNMENT FINANCE

According to the conventional view, tax revenue provides the income needed by the government to finance its spending. A government might be able to spend in excess of its revenue, at least temporarily, if it is able to issue debt that the public will hold. That is the government might be able to borrow from the public to finance deficit spending. One method that is almost universally scorned is for the government to issue non-interest-bearing debt – currency – to finance deficits, whether directly, by the Treasury, or indirectly through the central bank. Because government deficits financed in this manner would be a direct cause of the expansion of the money supply, many economists claim this would be a direct cause of inflation.

If, instead, the government sold interest-earning bonds to finance (or 'fund')[1] its deficit, the money supply would increase – according to most economists – only if the central bank 'accommodated' by increasing bank reserves. So long as the central bank did not accommodate, there should be no direct impact on inflation.[2] However government borrowing is likely, according to a common view, to 'crowd out' private borrowing because government borrowing adds to the demand for loanable funds, driving up interest rates, and displacing interest-sensitive private spending (presumably, investment, housing and consumer durables). Crowding out can be partial, complete or even more than complete, depending on assumptions.[3] Over the longer run if crowding out does occur, this will depress aggregate supply and could thereby induce cost-push inflation.

Finally while most economists recognize that at least under some situations government deficits are desirable (and that, at times, benefits outweigh costs), most would argue that persistent deficits must be avoided. Even Keynesian[4] economists generally argue that structural deficits should be avoided; that is, while a government should run deficits in recessions, these should be offset by surpluses during expansions. It is believed that permanent deficits must be avoided because no government can operate in such a manner as to generate the expectation that it will never be able to retire its debt, that is, the expectation that debt can only be 'rolled over.' While there may not be a specific debt-to-GDP or deficit-to-GDP ratio at which markets lose trust in the government, it is not doubted that such thresholds exist.[5] Governments are thus believed to be subject to market forces that determine the quantity of debt the government can issue as well as the price (interest rate) of the debt. If the domestic population will not take up all the debt, the government is forced to sell bonds in international markets. International markets might even force the government to borrow in a foreign currency (issue foreign currency denominated debt) if the country's finances are questionable. Indeed the government may be forced to impose austerity on its population in order to placate international markets before it will be able to sell bonds internationally.

The principles of 'sound finance' can also be applied to portions of the government's budget, representing individual programs such as the Social Security program. Since 1983, 'sound finance' has meant running large and rising OASDI (Old-Age, Survivors, and Disability Insurance) surpluses in order to 'advance fund' baby-boomer retirements. The reasoning behind this will be familiar to all readers: the number of retirees per worker will rise rapidly early this century, making it impossible to cover (rising) OASDI benefit payments from payroll taxes (without raising them to exorbitant levels) (Papadimitriou and Wray, 1999). Thus surpluses are necessary today in order to 'save' and thereby reduce the burden on future workers. Many analysts have (belatedly) recognized some of the peculiarities of trying to keep separate accounts for a portion of the government's budget. For example, some controversies have centered around the practice of 'accumulating' Social Security surpluses in the form of Treasury debt. Those holding up the troglodyte end of the debate argue that when it comes time for baby-boomer retirements, the Treasury might just default on the debt; they thus favor investing Social Security surpluses in a broader range of – presumably more creditworthy – private assets. The more astute argue that when the time comes, the Treasury will either have to raise other (non-payroll) taxes, borrow or 'print money' to retire the IOUs held by the Social Security Trust Fund. Thus some (including Friedman, 1999) have argued that the Trust Fund is nothing more than an 'accounting gimmick' that allows the government to 'owe itself.'

'Keynesians' (Blinder, 1999; Summers and Yellen, 1999) have defended current practice, arguing that to the extent that Social Security can run large surpluses, this can offset deficits in the rest of the government's budget. Indeed because of the extraordinary turnaround achieved during the Clinton boom, the overall budget has moved to surplus allowing retirement of some publicly held debt. So far (as of 2000) the surplus is entirely attributable to the Social Security program, but on current projections the rest of the budget will move to surplus soon. Indeed surpluses are now projected as far as the eye can see, which leads 'Keynesians' to argue that the government's budget is contributing to national saving and thereby lowering interest rates and stimulating private investment (Blinder, 1999). This will then generate faster economic growth and thereby lessen the 'real burden' on future workers of providing for the elderly. Thus running Social Security surpluses is 'sound finance' that adds to expected surpluses on the rest of the budget. While the normal 'Keynesian' position would be that there is nothing necessarily wrong with running cyclical budget deficits so long as budgets are structurally balanced, the 'excesses' of the Reagan–Bush deficits justify structural surpluses over the intermediate term. This is buttressed by the new-found faith in the ability of Saint Greenspan's Federal Reserve to offset the depressionary impact of budget surpluses (in spite of the oft-repeated warning that one cannot 'push on a string,' as well as the glaring example of the Japanese quagmire), which has led Blinder and Summers to support structural budget surpluses – at least through the first two decades of the new millennium.

BUDGETS AND ACCOUNTING CONVENTION

Let us turn to a more fundamental question: Why is it important to balance budgets? If an economic unit cannot 'spend' by issuing its own IOUs, its spending is limited by its stock of readily accepted medium of exchange and flow of income received in the form of the medium of exchange. We might call this a liquidity constraint. Clearly most economic units are not strictly limited by liquidity constraints because they are able to incur liabilities as they spend.

Sometimes this takes the simple form of postponed payment – for example, allowing 'payment' 30 days after delivery of a good or service – which is the implicit acceptance by the seller of a short-term liability. In other instances a financial intermediary is involved, allowing a seller to receive immediate payment in the form of the medium of exchange while a buyer is committed to deferred payment of principal and interest to the intermediary. Of course variations on these themes lead to complex financial instruments and financial commitments. Minsky (1986) created a tripartite division to describe financial positions: 'hedge' to denote an economic unit whose income flows meet committed outflows in every period; 'speculative' to identify a unit that could meet only interest payments out of income flows over at least some of the contract period; and 'Ponzi' to indicate a unit that would have to 'capitalize' interest – that is, increase liabilities just to make interest payments.

Note that there is no 'deep' economic constraint on ability to spend by incurring liabilities – if one can 'borrow' to pay interest (Ponzi finance), there is no strict limit to the amount of debt that one can service – even if one had no income at all. Recognition of this simple point has long bothered economists, leading to Smith's admonition that banks must require repayment of loans by delivery of bank notes rather than 'fictitious' bills of exchange,[6] as well as to the 'real bills doctrine' (which would limit expansion of bank lending to 'self-liquidating' debts).

Modern economists have tended to resolve this issue by looking at long-run sustainability, often defined as a situation in which the debt-to-income ratio is not permitted to rise beyond some limit. However it should be clear that such a constraint is of necessity arbitrary – rules of thumb, accounting rules or regulatory limits that establish constraints on the ability of an economic unit to issue debt – and because these limits are a human invention, they can be finessed and changed. This is not to argue that such rules are not reasonable. For example, one might reasonably argue that an economic unit with a finite lifespan should be expected to retire liabilities before or at the time of death, unless liabilities can be forced onto heirs. However, there is no 'deep' reason why even the dead could not continue to service debt through Ponzi finance. However, economic units with potentially unlimited lifetimes, such as governments or corporations, do not face this problem. In any case, one could pick from among a number of reasonable constraints that might be imposed – such as a limit to the portion of income flows that ought to be devoted to debt service. Let us emphasize that such a constraint, while reasonable, would be chosen arbitrarily.

When we turn to the case of a sovereign nation, which has the right to issue currency, it is not so easy to determine what is an income flow. Most would identify tax revenues as the appropriate accounting equivalent to a nongovernmental income flow. However, it has long been recognized that governments obtain seigniorage income if they can issue currency whose nominal value exceeds its cost of production. Even in the case of a gold standard, it is supposed that government typically obtained seigniorage either by charging for minting precious metals brought to the mint or by debasing coin. Clearly in the modern economy with a 'fiat' money, the cost of issuing currency falls close to zero. This means that 'printing money' is an alternative to 'tax revenue' as an income source and, because the direct costs to government are nearly zero, 'seigniorage' generates an unlimited income so long as the fiat money is accepted.

Orthodoxy posits a limit to the public's acceptance of government currency – 'money demand' is not infinite except under special circumstances (the liquidity trap). Beyond some point, it is argued, the government might have to issue interest-paying bonds, 'borrowing' money rather than issuing it. This commits government to paying interest. Thus bond issuance could lead to a Ponzi finance situation if tax revenues plus money emission become insufficient to pay interest on the outstanding debt stock (requiring government to issue bonds just to raise the 'money' required to pay interest). As discussed above, this does not in itself lead to a necessary constraint on government spending. Rather most analysts would argue that it is the economic effect on the economy that places a limit on the prudent level of deficits, or growth of deficits, or level of debt or debt ratio.[7] Such impacts could include effects on prices or interest rates.

In the next section, we turn to an alternative view of 'government accounting,' before returning to current debates about the government surplus.

GOVERNMENT BUDGETS AND FIAT MONEY

Abba Lerner presented a functional finance approach as an alternative to the doctrine of sound finance. He argued:

> Functional Finance rejects completely the traditional doctrines of 'sound finance' and the principle of trying to balance the budget over a solar year or any other arbitrary period. In their place it prescribes: first, the adjustment of total spending (by everybody in the economy, including the government) in order to eliminate both unemployment and inflation, using government spending when total spending is too low and taxation when total spending is too high; second, the adjustment of public holdings of money and of government bonds, by government borrowing or debt repayment, in order to achieve the rate of interest which results in the most desirable level of investment; and third, the printing, hoarding or destruction of money as needed for carrying out the first two parts of the program. (Lerner, 1943 p. 41)

I argue that his approach can be applied to all modern economies in which the government provides the domestic currency. The discussion that follows cannot, however, be applied to any country that adopts an external currency – for example, one that operates a currency board. Governments of such economies are not able to issue a fiat money.

Virtually all modern capitalist economies operate on the basis of a high-powered money (HPM) system.[8] The HPM is issued directly by the Treasury (as in the US, where the Treasury issues coins or checks) or through the central bank (as in the US, where the Fed issues paper notes and issues reserves whenever banks present Treasury liabilities for payment) as a non-convertible government (Treasury) or quasi-government (central bank) liability. This HPM generally functions as legal tender, that is, it is sanctioned by the courts as the money that fulfills 'all debts, public and private.' It is the only money that is ultimately accepted in payment of taxes.[9] It is also the money into which bank liabilities are convertible (either on demand or after some specified waiting period), and which is used for ultimate (or net) clearing among banks and between private banks and the central bank. It is the money used as the link between the public and private pay communities.[10] It is the money that sits at the top of the debt pyramid (or hierarchy), or the 'definitive' and 'valuta' money.[11] It is the most liquid liability used domestically – except in rare circumstances where a foreign currency is used domestically (as is the case in some of the formerly socialist countries today). The most important thing to understand is that in a normally functioning modern economy, the domestic HPM is always accepted in exchange for domestic production; anything that is for sale with a dollar price can be had by delivering US currency (coins or notes).[12]

When a modern government spends, it issues a check drawn on the Treasury. Its liabilities increase by the amount of the expenditure, and its assets increase (in the case of a purchase), or some other liabilities are reduced (in the case of a social transfer, for example, Social Security benefit liabilities are reduced by the amount of Social Security checks issued). The recipient of the Treasury check will almost certainly 'cash' the check at a bank; either the recipient will withdraw currency or, more commonly, the recipient's bank account will be credited. In the latter case bank reserves are credited by the Fed in the amount of the increase of the deposit account. For our purposes, it is not important to distinguish between the Fed's and the Treasury's balance sheet. The bank reserves carried on books as the bank's asset and as the Fed's liability are nothing less than a claim on HPM – at any time the bank can convert these to coins or paper notes, or use them in payments to the government. When the recipient 'cashes' a Treasury check, a bank will convert reserves to currency – which is always supplied on demand by the Federal Reserve. The Fed acts as the Treasury's 'bank,' converting one kind of Treasury liability (a check written to the public) to another kind (coins or an IOU to the Fed, offset by Fed issuance of paper notes).

The important thing to notice is that the Treasury spends before, and without regard to, either previous receipt of taxes or prior bond sales. In the US, taxes are received throughout the year (although not uniformly, as receipts are concentrated around certain quarterly dates as well as the 15 April deadline), mainly into special tax accounts held at private commercial banks. It is true that the Treasury transfers funds from the private banks to its account at the Fed when it wishes to 'spend,' but this is really a reserve maintenance operation. When the Treasury spends, bank reserves increase by the same amount (unless cash is withdrawn from banks) so that the transfer from tax accounts is used to stabilize bank reserves. If the Treasury did not make this transfer, its spending would lead to an increase of bank excess reserves, which would have to be drained by the Fed. Thus if the Treasury attempts to transfer funds more or less in step with its spending, this reduces the size of interventions required of the Fed. These additions to and subtractions from reserves need to be carefully monitored, with a central bank injection of reserves used to make up any shortfall (for example, if transfers from tax accounts exceed deposits of Treasury checks), or a reserve drain used to remove excess reserves.

These central bank actions are taken to offset the daily fluctuations that destabilize the overnight interest rate (called operating factors). By consolidating the Fed and Treasury balance sheets one sees that, in reality, the Treasury cannot withdraw taxes from the economy before spending – any transfer of tax accounts from the private economy to the government's balance sheet would have to be exactly offset by government provision of an equivalent amount of HPM through use of the Fed's balance sheet. In practice, a tax payment to the Treasury leads to debit of a commercial bank reserve account. If that bank has insufficient reserve balances at the Fed, it incurs an overdraft that is booked as a loan of reserves from the Fed to the bank. Thus, HPM is restored automatically whenever the Treasury accepts tax payments that lead to insufficient reserve positions. Indeed this is necessitated by 'par clearing': if bank checks always clear at par in payments made to the Treasury, then HPM must be provided as needed to the banking system to ensure there is HPM available for clearing purposes.

In any case, as government is the only supplier of HPM, it cannot receive in taxes HPM that it has not provided to private markets. The original source of all HPM must be the (consolidated, Fed-plus-Treasury) government, and the coordination between the Treasury and central bank is required to maintain reserves. If it were not for the effect of government spending on bank reserves, there would be no need to tie spending to transfers from tax accounts. The coincident timing of tax 'receipts' and government spending (or central bank open market operations) is not an indication of a 'financing' operation but rather is required to maintain stability in the market for reserves. The implication is that tax payments do not 'finance' government spending but that they must serve another purpose. (See Bell, 1998; Mosler, 1997–98; Wray, 1998; and Chapter 5 for further exposition.)

In principle, then, the government first spends HPM (to purchase goods, services and assets or to provide 'transfer payments,' which retires a government liability). Once the government has spent, then that HPM is available to be transferred to the government to meet tax liabilities. As a matter of logic, the public cannot pay HPM to the government to meet tax liabilities until the government has paid out HPM to the public. In a modern capitalist economy, it may appear more complex than this because most taxes are paid using checks drawn on bank deposits, rather than currency. However, this amounts to the same thing since every payment of taxes generates a reserve clearing drain, or a loss of reserves.[13] Thus taxes cannot be paid until actual coins or notes are injected into the economy, or bank reserves have been created. Government expenditure will generate coins, notes or bank reserves that are needed to 'pay taxes.' It is also true that central bank 'lending' (purchases of bank IOUs or discounts against bank assets), as well as central bank purchases of gold or foreign currencies, injects HPM and can thus substitute for government spending more narrowly defined. In practice, in most nations, this is done only on a temporary basis (properly categorized as passive interventions).

Given these considerations, a balanced budget is the theoretical minimum that a government can run continuously – again, with the caveat that if a central bank were willing to continually intervene to lend to banks or to buy gold and foreign currencies, the treasury could run a persistently balanced budget, or even a surplus. Normally if the government were to attempt to run a surplus, the public would find that its 'net money' receipts of HPM would be less than its tax liability, requiring households to dip into hoards of HPM (accumulated from past government deficit spending and purchases of assets) to pay taxes. (Again, an exception must be noted for the case in which the central bank continually lends to banks or buys gold and foreign currencies.) Eventually, of course, the hoards would be depleted. Finally the public could present maturing government bonds for payment to obtain HPM with which to pay taxes but, again, this is limited to the portion of the outstanding debt stock that is maturing (itself a function of previous government deficits and the maturity structure of the debt). (It should also be noted that much of the outstanding debt stock is 'locked away' in tax advantaged accounts, unavailable to a public trying to liquidate claims on government in order to make tax payments.) After the public has run down its holding, the only sources of HPM to pay taxes are new government (deficit) spending or government purchases of assets (including purchases by the central bank). However, for reasons discussed below, it is highly unlikely that an economy can withstand the deflationary impacts of government surpluses for long – thus we would expect surpluses to be short-lived, the normal case being a deficit position, and rising government debt over time.

We have hinted that taxes do not finance government spending. Then what is their purpose? If the government spent HPM but did not impose an HPM tax, it is difficult to see why anyone would trade goods and services to the government in exchange for HPM. Certainly one could not explain the 'origins' of government purchases on the basis of emission of HPM unless there were already in place a demand for the HPM. This original demand must have come from imposition of an HPM tax. Of course once the public has become accustomed to use of HPM in market exchanges, it might be possible to conceive of an inertial demand for HPM that could persist for some time even after abolition of HPM taxes. However without the tax system to underlie demand, it is difficult to imagine that the public would continue to use HPM in private exchanges and even more difficult to imagine that the public would sell things to the government in exchange for HPM if HPM were not needed to make payments to the government. The tax burden must be sufficiently great to create a general demand for HPM in order to pay taxes. Beyond that, taxes are used – as Lerner said – to remove excess HPM income that might generate spending so great as to generate inflationary pressures. Thus taxes can be thought of as one of the spokes of the steering wheel, used to adjust aggregate demand by reducing disposable income when it becomes too high.

MONETARY POLICY: BONDS AND INTEREST RATE POLICY

If government spending is 'financed' through emission of HPM, and if tax revenues – rather than to 'finance' government spending – are adjusted only to ensure aggregate disposable income is at the desired level, then why does the government sell bonds? Of course, governments believe that they must sell bonds to borrow the funds necessary to finance spending. However this is an illusion, as the spending must come first. As we will argue, bond sales (whether by the treasury or by the central bank) function to drain excess reserves; they cannot finance or fund deficit spending. This view builds upon Lerner's second law of functional finance: '[T]he government should borrow money only if it is desirable that the public should have less money and more government bonds' (Lerner, 1943: 40). More specifically, bond sales are designed to substitute an interest-earning government liability for non-interest-earning government HPM, and are properly considered a monetary policy operation rather than a fiscal policy operation.

As discussed above, all government spending is initially financed through issuance of HPM. This normally takes the form of a Treasury check deposited at a private bank, increasing bank reserves by the amount of government spending. To avoid a situation of excess reserves, a simultaneous transfer is made from bank tax and loan accounts to the central bank. In the case of a government deficit, however, the amount of HPM created exceeds the amount of bank reserves removed through tax payments. In a fractional reserve system this normally creates an excess reserve position of the banking system. Some reserves will be withdrawn by the non-bank public, which holds some HPM in the form of currency. However most will remain as excess reserves.

Individual banks will offer excess reserves in wholesale markets – namely the Fed funds market at the Fed funds rate – which can shift reserves around but cannot eliminate the excess. The excess reserves will force a 'market break,' with offered Fed funds finding no takers. While it is true that in the longer run, banks can adjust to a position of excess reserves through normal growth of their loan and deposit portfolio (which, all else equal, increases required or desired reserves), in the short run the adjustment can only be to the Fed funds rate. Since all modern central banks operate with an overnight interest rate target, excess reserves automatically trigger bond sales (typically, reverse repos or matched sale-purchase transactions) by the central bank to drain excess reserves. Note that prevention of a market break requires that this operation is nearly simultaneous with the creation of excess reserve positions.

In the US, primary sales of bonds to drain reserves are undertaken by the Treasury, while the Fed uses repos and reverse repos to 'fine-tune' as it adds/drains reserves to offset daily operating factors. Primary bond sales permanently 'mop up' excess reserves created by government deficits, providing interest-earning alternatives to non-interest-earning excess reserves held by banks and cash held by the public. If a government were to decide to avoid sales of bonds in primary markets, the central bank would eventually drain all the reserves it could through sales of bonds and foreign currency as it would eventually run out of bonds and foreign currency to sell. At that point it would be up to the Treasury to sell bonds to drain any remaining excess reserves. This reinforces the view that bond sales are part of monetary policy and not a financing operation to allow the government to run deficits. It also points out that rather than deficit spending raising interest rates, it actually places downward pressure on interest rates. If the government did not drain the excess reserves, the overnight (Fed funds) interest rate would tend to fall toward zero. If a government leaves some undesired excess reserves in the system, the overnight rate will hover around zero – as it has for a number of years in Japan.

Government spending is never constrained by the quantity of bonds that markets are willing to purchase; rather, bond sales are undertaken to provide an interest-earning alternative to cash and excess reserves. Government spending is constrained only by private sector willingness to provide goods, services or assets to government in exchange for HPM. Anything that is for purchase in terms of the domestic currency can be had through government creation of HPM. If excess reserves result, the government will have to drain them if it wishes to hit a positive interest rate target.

Governments sometimes believe that they must sell bonds in international markets because domestic markets are already saturated with bonds and any further domestic sales would require higher interest rates. While this can be true, it has reversed the causation: the government does not 'need' to sell bonds at all; bond sales are by design an 'interest rate maintenance' operation. Thus, while it might be true that at a higher interest rate government might induce the public and banks to give up some HPM (although this effect is probably quite small because the demand for HPM is highly interest-inelastic), this is not an indication that the government is 'forced' to pay higher rates to 'finance' its deficit. It can always incur more deficits and then drain resulting excess reserves at any interest rate above zero that it desires.

Since bond sales are really nothing more than an interest rate maintenance operation, the government can decide the interest rate it will pay – or alternatively, the price of government bonds – in its monetary policy. Thus government deficit spending is never subject to 'market discipline' regarding either the quantity of bonds sold or the price at which they will be sold as long as the bonds are issued in the domestic currency. When there are excess reserves, the market will 'demand' bonds at any interest rate above zero as the alternative is non-earning excess reserves. There may be very good reasons for maintaining a significantly positive interest rate on government bonds, but it is never necessary to do so merely because the market would like a high interest rate. A high government-borrowing rate is evidence that the government (treasury plus central bank) has chosen a high interest rate – it tells us nothing about 'market forces' of supply and demand. The government can always have a lower interest rate merely by reducing the interest rate target. Interest rates are determined by monetary policy and cannot be affected by fiscal policy.

Note that both bond sales and payment of taxes drain HPM from the economy. However each serves a different purpose. Taxes are used to drain excessive disposable income and to reduce private sector net (or 'outside') wealth to prevent aggregate demand from becoming too high. This is a legitimate function of fiscal policy. However, bond sales – whether conducted by the Treasury or by the Fed are a function of monetary policy. Furthermore, bond sales merely change the form of outside wealth – from holdings of HPM to holdings of interest-bearing debt – but leave wealth intact. Thus while orthodoxy frequently sees bond sales and taxes as 'alternative' means of 'financing' government spending, they actually serve quite different functions and have quite different impacts on the economy.

FUNCTIONAL FINANCE APPLIED TO NEW MILLENNIUM BUDGET SURPLUSES

According to President Clinton's 1999 and 2000 State of the Union addresses, we are on a course to run federal government budget surpluses for the next 15 to 25 years. On current projections these surpluses are so large that all the publicly held debt of the US government would be completely eliminated by 2015. The President actually proposed that some portion of the surplus be 'set aside' to be held in Social Security trust funds. For example, if a budget surplus of $100 billion were to accrue in one particular year, $100 billion worth of government bonds held by the public would be retired, while perhaps $60 billion worth of new government debt would be created to be held in the trust fund. This would be described as 'saving' 60 per cent of the budget surplus to be used later when baby-boomers retire.

The President's analyses have been well received. A number of prominent economists, including at least six Nobel winners circulated an open letter after the 1999 State of the Union address dubbing the President's plan 'good economics' and stating that, 'Although no one can predict how large the budget surpluses will turn out to be, we can be sure that saving them by reducing outstanding government debt is an excellent way to ease the burden on future workers of supporting an aging population.' Lawrence Summers, later appointed Secretary of the Treasury, and Janet Yellen, chair of President Clinton's Council of Economic Advisers, assured us that the President's proposal to 'lock away' most of the projected budget surpluses in the Social Security Trust Fund is based on 'sound accounting' and that it will extend Social Security's solvency through 2055. David Broder's *Washington Post* article (February 7, 1999) proclaimed the plan to be 'the greatest gift to our children' because it will 'help grow the economy' by 'raising national savings.' Unfortunately, the accounting is not sound, and a policy that would preserve surpluses in an attempt to retire Treasury debt held by the public is anything but a gift to our children.

With one brief exception, the federal government has been in debt every year since 1776. In January 1835, for the first and only time in US history, the public debt was retired, and a budget surplus was maintained for the next two years in order to accumulate what Treasury Secretary Levi Woodbury called 'a fund to meet future deficits' (See Wray, 1998: 63; Stabile and Cantor, 1991). In 1837 the economy collapsed into a deep depression that drove the budget into deficit, and the federal government has been in debt ever since. Since 1776 there have been six periods of substantial budget surpluses and significant reduction of the debt. From 1817 to 1821, the national debt fell by 29 per cent; from 1823 to 1836, national debt was eliminated (Jackson's efforts); from 1852 to 1857, it fell by 59 per cent, from 1867 to 1873 by 27 per cent, from 1880 to

1893 by more than 50 per cent, and from 1920 to 1930 by about a third (Thayer, 1996). The United States has also experienced six periods of depression. The depressions began in 1819, 1837, 1857, 1873, 1893, and 1929. Every significant reduction of the outstanding debt has been followed by a depression, and every depression has been preceded by significant debt reduction. Further every budget surplus has been followed, usually sooner rather than later, by renewed deficits. However, correlation – even where perfect – never proves causation. Is there any reason to suspect that government surpluses are harmful?

At the macroeconomic level, government expenditures generate private sector income; taxes reduce disposable income. When government spending exceeds tax revenue (a budget deficit), there is a net addition to private sector disposable income. This addition may well have secondary, tertiary, and even further effects (for example, households may spend on goods produced domestically or abroad, thereby raising consumption or imports as measured in national GDP accounts). Some of that extra disposable income is devoted to saving, first accumulated in the form of HPM which is then exchanged for interest-earning government debt when the Treasury sells bonds. Even if the Treasury did not sell the bonds, however, the private sector would be (nominally) wealthier by an amount equal to the government's deficit, but this would be held in the form of non-interest-earning cash (and bank reserves) for the simple reason that the total value of checks issued by the Treasury to finance expenditures would exceed the total value of checks written by the private sector to pay taxes.

On the other hand, when tax revenues exceed government spending (a budget surplus), private sector disposable income is reduced. Again there may be further effects – consumers may cut back spending, for example. Because checks received by the Treasury exceed the value of checks issued by the Treasury whenever there is a surplus, outstanding cash and bank reserves will be reduced. To restore cash and reserves the private sector sells Treasury bonds. The bonds are purchased by the Fed and the Treasury; the purchase restores reserves and cash. (Sales of bonds between private sector entities cannot add reserves or cash; they simply shift reserves and cash from one 'pocket' to another.) Note that if the Treasury refused to buy the bonds (that is, refused to retire outstanding debt), then only the Fed would be left to buy them. This is why any sustained surpluses must be met by Treasury retirement of the debt, for otherwise the Fed would accumulate vast holdings of Treasury debt (on which the Treasury pays interest) while the Treasury would hold huge deposits in its checking account at the Fed. (In practice, the Treasury tries to end each day with a deposit of $5 billion.) For this reason, it is quite silly to argue about 'what to do with the surplus' and to debate about whether some of the surplus ought to be used to retire outstanding debt. In truth, simple accounting ensures that if the government taxes more than it spends it has reduced the private sector's holdings of claims on government.

Movements of the budget position are largely automatic. Rapid economic growth, such as that experienced in the United States since 1992 or in Japan previous to 1988, tends to cause tax revenues to rise faster than government spending, resulting in surpluses. Recessions and depressions tend to cause tax revenues to fall as spending rises, resulting in deficits. Many economists focus on the secondary or tertiary effects of government deficits and surpluses. While they might agree that deficits increase disposable income and private sector wealth, they argue that deficits also increase interest rates and thus depress investment or that households reduce consumption on the expectation that tax rates will be increased in the future. They argue that while surpluses might reduce disposable income and private sector wealth, they also lower interest rates and thus spur private capital formation. While I believe most of these arguments are based on faulty reasoning (the belief that deficits push up interest rates, for example, is based on the flawed notion that interest rates on government bonds are competitively set; and the 'Ricardian Equivalents' argument is based on the flawed view that bond sales and taxes 'finance' government spending), it is possible that under some conditions the secondary effects might outweigh the primary effects so that, at least for a while, deficits might depress the private sector and surpluses might stimulate it. However history and theory suggest that over the longer run, deficits can allow the economy to grow while surpluses can inhibit growth.

If as projected the federal government continues to run surpluses (resulting in Treasury debt retirement), this must as a matter of course remove $4.5 trillion of private sector income and wealth over the next 15 years. Can an economy withstand such a bloodletting? Our own history suggests not, and we can also look to the recent experience of Japan.

Since World War II, we have had the longest depression-free period in the nation's history. However, we have had nine recessions, each of which was preceded by a reduction of deficits relative to GDP. Preceding the deepest recession since the Great Depression, the deficit fell rapidly toward the end of the Carter presidency. In spite of President Reagan's pledge to balance the budget, he presided over the largest deficits we had seen since World War II. To some extent the deficits grew because of the economic slowdown; however tax cuts and spending increases (primarily for defense) caused a discretionary increase of the deficit. The 'Reagan boom' lasted from November 1982 to July 1990, the longest expansion in the postwar period (until it was surpassed by the Clinton expansion). Predictably this reduced the deficit relative to GDP and preceded the Bush recession. In the early years of the Clinton presidency the deficit grew again and was projected to continue. However, as a result of the long expansion and budget agreements, the deficit was entirely eliminated, and we experienced our first budget surplus in a generation.

Indeed as Godley (1999) has demonstrated, the turnaround of the budget from deficit to surplus was the sharpest in the postwar period. The budget now seems to be so biased toward restraint that economic growth will generate continued surpluses. Given a US trade account deficit, and a government budget surplus, economic growth is made possible only by a domestic private sector deficit, that is, by private expenditures exceeding private income.[14] Godley has demonstrated that the gap between private income and spending had reached entirely unprecedented levels by 1998. That gap continues to increase each year in which GDP grows. Continued private sector deficits also mean growing private sector indebtedness, which by 1999 had also reached record levels. While it is impossible to say with certainty when the private sector will finally decide to retrench, it is simply not conceivable that private sector deficits and debts will grow without limit. Returning to our discussion above, there is no 'deep' accounting necessity that sets a strict limit to the private sector's ability to spend more than its income. By the same token, neither theory nor evidence would suggest that households and firms would deficit spend at an increasing rate forever. It is curious that those who would deny that the government can deficit spend in perpetuity would argue that the private sector will deficit spend for the next two decades in order to allow the government to retire all its debt.

Americans know that Japan's growth rate in the 1980s was the envy of the world, but they are generally unaware that the government deficits as a percentage of GDP rivaled those in the United States. The enormous growth of the 1980s caused government tax revenue to rise faster than spending so that by the late 1980s the budget moved to surplus. The Japanese economy moved into a recession-cum-depression from which it has not been able to recover. Government deficits have been restored, but as a result of the sluggish economy, not as a result of discretionary, expansive, fiscal policy. While there have been some small initiatives to cut taxes and increase government spending, Japan has primarily relied on monetary policy to get it out of recession. Indeed Japan held interest rates essentially at zero in an attempt to stimulate the economy. To this point, the most expansive monetary policy the world has seen since World War II still has not succeeded in jump-starting Japan's economy. This might serve as a cautionary tale for those who believe that Chairman Greenspan can keep the US expansion going in spite of budget surpluses that are expected to rise well above 2 per cent of GDP early this millennium.

It is difficult to take seriously any analysis that begins with the projection that our government will run surpluses for the next 15 or 25 years. Part of our skepticism comes from the inherent difficulty in making projections. Even more important, our economy cannot continue to grow robustly as the government sucks disposable income and wealth from the private sector by running surpluses. When the economy slows, the surpluses will disappear automatically – because the private sector will eventually demand that the government stop draining income from the economy. Tax cuts will be rushed through Congress and the president will put forward spending initiatives.

Finally surpluses, even if realized, cannot be 'locked away' for future use – for example, to be used by retiring baby boomers. In every period that government spending falls short of tax revenues, outstanding government debt is retired. Equivalently, the private sector's stock of wealth is reduced (since a budget surplus reduces disposable income, and this shows up as a reduction of government debt in private portfolios). There is simply no 'surplus' that can be 'spent' or even 'saved.' A government decision to spend more would simply increase spending relative to taxes, resulting in a smaller budget surplus. When total federal government tax revenue falls short of expenditures (including those associated with Social Security), this first takes the form of net injections of HPM. In order to allow the central bank to hit its overnight interest rate targets, the Treasury will issue new debt to the public to drain excess HPM. But it must do this whether or not there is a Trust Fund. Neither budget surpluses over the next 15 years nor accounting fictions can change that simple fact. There may be good (non-economic) reasons for keeping Social Security accounts separate from the rest of the budget, but this should never lead one to believe that a projected 'revenue shortfall' can be cured by having the government issue IOUs to itself.

CONCLUSIONS

All modern governments spend by emitting HPM, normally by having the Treasury issue a check. Taxes are never necessary to 'finance' spending, nor indeed is it possible for them to do so. The government must first provide the HPM before it can receive HPM in tax payment. Thus taxes serve a different purpose. The primary function of taxes is to create a demand for HPM. Why would the private sector provide goods and services to government in return for HPM unless it needed HPM for taxes? Of course we recognize that HPM can be used for many things other than tax payment, but these other uses must be derivative. Taxes also serve another useful purpose, as Lerner emphasized: they remove disposable income and destroy private sector net wealth.

Far from recommending perpetual deficits come what may, the functional finance approach recognizes that the private sector can become overheated, which is remedied through rising taxes to drain HPM and disposable income. Deficits can be too large but also too small. We normally expect that a deficit will be required, however, for the simple reason that the private sector prefers to accumulate some net wealth in the form of HPM and Treasury bonds. For this reason the government will usually be required to run a deficit, which means that its outstanding debt stock will grow over time. This is nothing to be feared. The government never faces a 'financial constraint,' so long as its offers of HPM for goods and services are taken. Because bond sales come after government spending, like taxes, they cannot possibly be required to 'finance' spending. Rather, bond sales are used to drain excess HPM to maintain a positive overnight interest rate. Whether that interest rate target is high or low, it must be set discretionarily by the central bank and then maintained by ensuring that banks have the desired level of reserves. While taxes and bond sales both remove HPM from the economy, taxes drain income and wealth while bond sales merely offer an interest-earning alternative to non-interest-earning HPM.

The functional finance approach concludes that there is no magic deficit-to-GDP ratio or debt-to-GDP ratio that ought to be maintained or avoided. It also demonstrates that there is no sense in which budget surpluses in one year can be 'locked away and saved' for spending in future years. And it leaves one perplexed when faced with the argument advanced by Nobel winners that running surpluses today – hence destroying private sector income and wealth – is the best way to encourage investment in order to enhance living standards into the future.

NOTES

1. Economists often use the term 'finance' to indicate use of money to purchase a good, service or asset. This usually means the money was borrowed short term. The term 'fund' is used to indicate long-term borrowing. Thus one might borrow short term temporarily to 'finance' a purchase, then use long-term borrowing to retire the short-term debt and 'fund' the purchase long term.
2. The deficits still might be inflationary either due to 'bottlenecks' that lead to supply constraints and cost-push inflation, or due to excessive aggregate demand (causing demand-pull inflation) if the economy operates beyond full capacity.
3. It is even conceivable that 'crowding in' might occur – the government's borrowing actually increases the demand for private bonds – although most economists do not pay much attention to this theoretical possibility. Some economists recognize that some government spending (for example, that on public infrastructure investment) is likely to increase private sector productivity and reduce private sector costs, which might encourage private investment. See Aschauer (1998).
4. Both Post-Keynesians and Bastard Keynesians have adopted such positions. For example, Hyman Minsky (1986) argued that Reagan's deficits were too large and in danger of generating the belief that the government would never be able to repay them – which, he thought, might lead to a situation in which the government would not be able to issue new debt.
5. It is common to assert that the debt-to-GDP ratio must eventually converge to some value, for a perpetually rising ratio would be 'unsustainable.' An important determinant of 'sustainability' would be the relation between the economy's growth rate and the interest rate paid on government debt; if the interest rate exceeds the growth rate, then debt would explode even if the 'primary budget' (excluding interest spending) were in balance.
6. See Wray 1998: 21.

7. Although some simply assert that Ponzi finance is unsustainable because it implies debt ratios that increase without limit. In this case, the constraint is simply a mathematical constraint.
8. We prefer to describe government-issued money as HPM rather than fiat money. We include bank reserves as HPM, while many would not include bank reserves in the definition of fiat money.
9. We sometimes say that HPM is a government liability. For what is the government liable? To accept its money in payment of taxes.
10. These terms were used by Knapp to describe transactions in the 'private' economy (private pay community) and transactions between the private sector and the government (public pay community). See Knapp (1924) and Wray (1998).
11. These terms were used by Knapp to describe the 'ultimate' money created and accepted by government. See Knapp (1924) and Wray (1998).
12. In the case of some extremely large transactions, it is conceivable that due to obvious problems arising from dealing with large sums of currency, intermediaries must be used so that no actual currency changes hands. The sale thus leads to credits and debits on computerized balance sheets of intermediaries – which leads to reserve-clearing transfers on the balance sheet of the central bank – but this changes nothing of principle, and these credits could be exchanged for fiat money both in theory and in practice.
13. Unless the tax payment is offset by the Fed's injection of reserves as it purchases assets.
14. As Godley (1999) shows, the private sector's deficit is identically equal to the government's surplus plus the trade deficit.

REFERENCES

Aschauer, David A. (1998), 'How should the surpluses be spent?' Policy Note 2, Jerome Levy Economics Institute.

Bell, Stephanie (1998), 'Can Taxes and Bonds Finance Government Spending: Reserve Accounting and Government Finance,' *The Third Annual Post Graduate Economics Conference: Conference Papers*, Leeds University Business School.

Bell, Stephanie (2001), 'The Role of the State and the Hierarchy of Money', *Cambridge Journal of Economics*, 25 (May), 149–63.

Blinder, Alan S. (1999), 'Strange but True Economics,' editorial in *The New York Times*, March 9.

Friedman, Milton (1999), 'Social Security Chimeras,' *New York Times*, 11 January, A–17.

Godley, Wynne (1999), 'Seven Unsustainable Processes: Medium-term Prospects and Policies for the United States and the World,' *Special Report*, Jerome Levy Economics Institute.

Knapp, George Friedrich (1924), *The State Theory of Money*, Clifton, NY: Augustus M. Kelley.

Lerner, Abba (1943), 'Functional Finance and the Federal Debt,' *Social Research*, 10, 38–51.

Minsky, Hyman P. (1986), *Stabilizing an Unstable Economy*, New Haven, CT: Yale University Press.

Mosler, Warren (1997–98), 'Full Employment and Price Stability,' *Journal of Post Keynesian Economics*, 20 (2), 167–182.

Papadimitriou, Dimitri and L. Randall Wray (1999), 'Does Social Security Need Saving? Providing for retirees throughout the twenty-first century,' *Public Policy Brief*, No. 55, Jerome Levy Economics Institute.

Stabile, Donald R. and Jeffrey A. Cantor (1991), *The Public Debt of the United States: An Historical Perspective 1775–1990*, New York: Praeger.

Summers, Lawrence and Janet Yellen (1999), 'Saving the Surplus will Protect Retirees,' *Wall Street Journal*, 18 February.

Thayer, Frederick C. (1996), 'Balanced Budgets and Depressions,' *American Journal of Economics and Sociology*, 55, April.

Wray, L. Randall (1998), *Understanding Modern Money: The Key to Full Employment and Price Stability*, Cheltenham, UK and Lyme, US: Edward Elgar.

Wray, L. Randall (1999), 'Surplus Mania: A Reality Check,' Policy Note 3, Jerome Levy Economics Institute.

11. Functional finance and full employment: lessons from Lerner for today

Mathew Forstater

The United States economy was already headed for recession when the September 11, 2001 terrorist attacks occurred, worsening conditions in an already troubled global economy. The Asian financial crisis, with fallout in Latin America and the transition economies; the Russian default; continuing troubles in Japan; weaknesses in the structure of the new European EMU; volatility on Wall Street; deflationary pressures in the global economy – recent economic developments invite reconsideration of some of our most deeply held beliefs concerning economic theory and public policy. Even within the hallowed halls of mainstream economics, voices of dissent can be heard. Paul Krugman, Joseph Stiglitz and Jeffrey Sachs are among those whose recent proclamations mark our entry into a period in which orthodox views are openly questioned, creating an atmosphere characterized by a crisis of confidence.

Such periods of impending crisis, and open expressions of self-doubt, question our most deeply held beliefs about the way the world works and create a climate in which the ideas of the great unorthodox thinkers of the past may be revisited. The work of those who in the past dedicated their lives to formulating solutions to the challenges of modern capitalist economies may contain lessons applicable to contemporary conditions. In this spirit, this chapter revisits the early works of Abba Lerner, outlining 15 such lessons regarding macroeconomic theory and policy that are as fresh in the context of the current scene as they were some five decades ago when first formulated.

> Lesson #1: Full employment, price stability and a decent standard of living for all are fundamental macroeconomic goals, and it is the responsibility of the state to promote their attainment.

Lerner rejected the positive/normative dichotomy in economics. His distinction between 'objective' and 'normative' was based not on whether one considers macroeconomic goals as part and parcel of their analysis, but whether one does so openly and honestly:

> Objectivity turns out to be not the avoidance of concern with what is *desired* in a pure concentration on what *is*, but merely the avoidance of smuggling in an

> advocacy of desired objectives without making it clear that this is being done or making it clear whose are the desires being considered. (1969: 131)

Lerner (1941) likened *laissez-faire* to a refusal to take hold of the 'economic steering wheel.' Government must use its powers to 'fill its two great responsibilities, the prevention of depression, and the maintenance of the value of money' (1947: 314).

Lerner's arguments for full employment are worth reviewing. First, 'the economic gains from full employment are enormous' (1951: 31–32). The costs of unemployment are staggering. They include not only the permanent loss of output in goods and services, but also the social costs resulting from increased crime, illness and other social problems.

Full employment increases efficiency. Removing the threat imposed on workers by the existence of a reserve army of unemployed, workers will feel more confident to move out of one job and into another. This often means a movement from a lower productivity job to a higher productivity job (1951: 32).

Individual economic security is an even more important benefit than the increase in goods and services (1951: 33). Though the foremost gain is individual economic security for workers, government commitment to full employment has an important stabilizing impact on business confidence derived from the awareness that the state is committed to maintaining aggregate demand (1951: 33).

A full-employment policy weakens racial and other hiring discriminations (1951: 36). There are incentives in an economic system characterized by general unemployment for workers to seek ways of 'tying up the jobs they have so they cannot be easily fired' (1951: 34). 'The economic interest of a group of workers in protecting their scarce jobs against competition from outside,' so often conducted through racial and other discrimination, would be significantly decreased with the elimination of job scarcity (1951: 36–37). In addition, employers, who have the opportunity to indulge their own racial and other prejudices in hiring when there is widespread unemployment, would no longer be able to do so in a full-employment economy (1951: 36). Full employment also helps to remove wage differentials, acknowledged to be highly related to race and gender (1951: 37).

Full employment is key to social stability (1951: 37ff.). Without employment and income security, citizens are vulnerable to dangerous ideologies, to scapegoating and to anti-democratic political movements.

Full employment and the maintenance of the value of currency are the key initial prerequisites for a decent standard of living for all. To leave such matters to the market would be like driving a car without using the steering wheel. Fortunately, people do not drive their cars without using their steering wheels:

> But are they as reasonable about other things as they are about the desirability of steering their automobiles? . . . Do they not allow their *economic* automobiles to bounce from depression to inflation in wide and uncontrolled arcs? Through their failure to steer away from unemployment and idle factories are they not just as guilty of public injury and insecurity as the mad motorists . . .? (Lerner, 1951: 4–5)

> Lesson #2: Policies should be judged on their ability to achieve the goals for which they are designed and not on any notion of whether they are 'sound' or otherwise comply with the dogmas of traditional economics.

This, of course, is Lerner's functional finance (1943). The state has the ability to promote full employment and price stability and should use its powers to do so:

> The central idea is that government fiscal policy, its spending and taxing, its borrowing and repayment of loans, its issue of new money and its withdrawal of money, shall all be undertaken with an eye only to the *results* of these actions on the economy and not to any established traditional doctrine about what is sound and what is unsound. This principle of judging only by *effects* has been applied in many other fields of human activity, where it is known as the method of science opposed to scholasticism. The principle of judging fiscal measures by the way they work or function in the economy we may call *Functional Finance*. . . . Government should adjust its rates of expenditure and taxation such that total spending in the economy is neither more nor less than that which is sufficient to purchase the full employment level of output at current prices. If this means there is a deficit, greater borrowing, 'printing money,' etc., then these things in themselves are neither good nor bad, they are simply the means to the desired ends of full employment and price stability. (1943: 354)

This principle is so simple, yet apparently so difficult to understand. Support of balancing the budget as the proper means for achieving some economic goal is entirely consistent with the *principle* of functional finance. The balanced budget, however, is not 'sacred,' but simply a means to the desired ends. Those who support a balanced budget should thus agree, in principle, that if some other relation between government expenditure and tax receipts were the best means to attaining those ends, the balanced budget should be abandoned and those other means instituted. But if one promotes a balanced budget as an end in itself – as the 'right' thing to do – it becomes 'irresponsible' to do otherwise, despite potential effects and the sacrifice of macro goals. This is not consistent with the principle of functional finance. It is best referred to as *dysfunctional finance*.

Opposition to government borrowing, lending, taxing, spending, buying or selling should be based on evidence that such actions cause unemployment, inflation, deflation or some other undesirable macroeconomic outcome, or because they hinder the abolition of these undesirable macroeconomic problems.

But if any of those means promotes the desired macro goals or prevents undesirable macro problems, then they should be utilized for that purpose. There is nothing inherently 'good' or 'bad' about any particular relation between government expenditure and tax receipts. Rather, effects derive from the specific economic circumstances and on the results that such a relation will promote under those circumstances. If the amount of taxing, spending, borrowing, lending, buying or selling 'should conflict with the principles of "sound finance" or of balancing the budget or of limiting the national debt, so much the worse for those principles' (1951: 11).

> Lesson #3: Without a full employment policy, society cannot benefit from labor-saving technological advance, that is, efficiency becomes inefficient. With a full employment policy, labor-saving technical advance becomes truly beneficial to society.

Under conditions of continuous full employment, resources are scarce. Thus instituting technical or organizational innovations to free up labor for other uses constitutes a welcome economizing of resources. But in an economy with persistent unemployment, what is efficient becomes inefficient:

> When there is unemployment . . . it is not important or even useful to use less resources in any task. . . . There is no point, for instance, in managing to carry out some task with less labor if there are unemployed workers available, because the workers set free would not be utilized for other tasks any more than the workers who are already unemployed. They would merely be added to the unemployed. Where there is unemployment, an increase in efficiency in any particular productive process does not result in any increase in the efficiency in the economy as a whole. (1951: 143).

Lerner does consider the possibility that, rather than producing the same amount of output with fewer workers, society could produce more output while maintaining the same number of workers. Yet as he rightly points out, though increased saving results from increased income accompanying higher output levels – absent an exactly offsetting higher level of investment or government expenditure – the new higher level of output will not be sustainable, as all production will not be sold, and firms will cut back their production and lay off workers. In the absence of a full employment policy:

> Economizing resources by the use of more efficient methods is like pouring water into a broken vessel with a large hole in it that is already holding as much as it can hold. No matter how much more is poured into it there will remain no more than at the beginning. The savings due to greater technical efficiency merely go to waste in further unemployment just as any additional water merely goes to waste through the hole. (1951: 144)

Nor is it the case that such technical advances are merely neutral. They may also be harmful. First, rather than making more leisure possible with labor-displacing technical advance 'what we get is not the tranquillity of refraining from effort but the frustration of failing to find work. In every socially significant sense the increase in efficiency brings not greater happiness but greater misery' (1951: 144). Second, labor-displacing technical advance may result in lower aggregate output and income. This can occur if technical change leads to redistribution of income from wages to profits, or from those with a higher marginal propensity to consume to those with a lower marginal propensity to consume. In such a case, aggregate spending will decline, reducing effective demand, and thus aggregate output and income (1951: 144–45). With a true full employment policy in place however, labor-displacing technical change is truly efficient, since the increased efficiency will not result in unemployment. Thus, technical advance can be welcomed by society, as it is truly beneficial.

> Lesson #4: Without a full employment policy, a country must suffer over its trade balance. With a full employment policy, there is no need to worry about importing 'too much' relative to exports.

In the absence of full employment guaranteed by functional finance, a country must worry about rising unemployment stemming from an increase in the value of imports over the value of exports. Thus an excess of imports over exports is considered an 'unfavorable balance of trade' and the reverse is considered a 'favorable balance of trade.' But Lerner looks at foreign trade as 'the means by which we obtain for our own use goods that are manufactured abroad' (1951: 321): 'The *input* of the foreign-trade industry consists of the effort involved in the manufacture of our exports. . . . The *output* of the foreign-trade industry consists of the imports which it yields to us for our use' (1951: 321, original emphasis). In other words, exports are a cost and imports a benefit. Thus with a real commitment to full employment, an increase in a country's imports relative to its exports is an increase in its benefits. It is only without a full employment policy that this is undermined, as such a development will have a negative impact on aggregate demand, output, income and employment. Countries therefore attempt to increase employment through promoting exports and restricting imports, that is, by promoting costs and restricting benefits.

The idea that a country can cure unemployment only by developing an export surplus is completely baseless unless the society has developed a taboo against every other way of increasing the level of spending. Functional Finance dissolves any 'imported unemployment' (1951: 327, 332).

> Lesson #5: To achieve full employment, government spending may have to include direct job creation.

Traditional fiscal and monetary policies may be ineffective in achieving full employment. Direct job creation in the form of public works may be necessary in order to attain and maintain full employment and price stability (1944: 315ff). Even public employment that produces no visible good or service is beneficial, in that it still creates jobs for the unemployed and increases aggregate output and income, with all their associated benefits. However, since there are so many public and social services that benefit the economy and society in numerous ways and are not normally undertaken by the private sector, there is no reason that public employment should ever have to be unproductive (see 1951: 90ff).

Public works can increase the productivity of the private sector. In addition, public employment is key to accommodating the reluctance of individuals to disrupt family and community by relocating to find employment.

Lesson #6: Functional Finance is not a policy; it is a framework within which all sorts of policies may be conducted.

There may be misconceptions that functional finance is equated with a particular policy, for example, running a big deficit. Functional finance is rather a general approach within which a whole series of policies may be conducted. The actual policies implemented will depend on economic circumstances that exist at a particular time. In the functional finance outlook what matters are the effects of policies and not the policies themselves, which are mere means. Thus functional finance does not advocate big deficits under any and all circumstances. Nor does it view a balanced budget as inherently 'good' in and of itself, independently of its impact on the economy.

What functional finance advocates first and foremost is that policy be based on an understanding of the monetary and financial system in which we live, and not some idealized vision of some other system, or some system that may have existed at some other time. For example, if fiscal and monetary policy is formulated as if we we're on a gold standard, we not only will sacrifice tremendous potential benefits, we may subject ourselves to grave danger. A fiat currency system should not be run by the logic of a metallic standard system.

Lesson #7: 'Money is a creature of the state.'

The ability of the government to conduct fiscal and monetary policy according to the principles of functional finance is made possible by the fact that 'money is a creature of the state' (1947). The state has the power not only to tax, but to designate what will suffice to retire tax (and other) obligations, that is, what it will accept at its pay offices. By determining public receivability, the state can create a demand for otherwise worthless pieces of paper, leading to general acceptability. The state can issue this currency and use it to purchase goods and services from the private sector:

> The modern state can make anything it chooses generally acceptable as money and thus establish its value quite apart from any connection, even of the most formal kind, with gold or backing of any kind. It is true that a simple declaration that such and such is money will not do, even if backed by the most convincing constitutional evidence of the state's absolute sovereignty. But if the state is willing to accept the proposed money in the payment of taxes and other obligations to itself the trick is done. Everyone who has obligations to the state will be willing to accept the pieces of paper with which he can settle the obligations, and all other people will be willing to accept those pieces of paper because they know that taxpayers, etc., will accept them in turn. On the other hand if the state should decline to accept some kind of money in payment of obligations to itself, it is difficult to believe that it would retain much of its general acceptability. . . . What this means is that whatever may have been the history of gold, at the present time, in a normally well-working economy, money is a creature of the state. Its general acceptability, which is its all-important attribute, stands or falls by its acceptability by the state. (1947: 313)

Thus, a variety of state powers – such as government's ability to tax, declare public receivability, create and destroy money, buy and sell bonds and administer the prices it pays for goods and services purchased from the private sector – constitutes a menu of instruments with which full employment and stability of the value of the currency may be promoted.

> Lesson #8: Taxing is not a funding operation.

Since money is a creature of the state and the government budget should be judged purely on its macroeconomic effects, decisions concerning taxation should be made only with regard to the economic effects in terms of the promotion of full employment, price stability or other economic goals, and not ever 'because the government needs to make money payments' (1943: 354): '[T]axes should *never* be imposed for the sake of the tax revenues' (1951: 131, original emphasis).

> Lesson #9: Government borrowing is not a funding operation.

Similarly, for the same reasons as taxation, Lerner argued that 'borrowing' is not a funding operation. Since it is not a funding operation, it is questionable whether we should even use the term 'borrowing.' Perhaps it would be best to simply refer to bond sales. Thus Lerner argued that 'the government should borrow only if . . . the effects' of borrowing are desired (1943: 355).

> Lesson #10: The primary purpose of taxation is to influence the behavior of the public.

If taxation is not a funding operation, then what is its purpose? The purpose of taxation, according to Lerner, is 'its effect on the *public* of influencing their economic behavior' (1951: 131, original emphasis). First, through its power to determine public receivability, the government can create sellers who will offer goods and services for sale in exchange for the government currency. Thus taxation, as mentioned above, endows otherwise worthless bits of paper with value. Another important way in which taxation affects the public's behavior is through its impact on spending. In the days when Lerner was much concerned with excess demand inflation, this was a major focus. But taxation can affect behavior in many other ways (e.g., taxes on 'bads' are implemented to discourage certain behaviors). For Lerner, this reality, and not funding of government spending, is its primary function.

> Lesson #11: The primary purpose of government bond sales is to regulate the overnight interest rate.

As we have seen, for Lerner, neither taxation nor government bond sales are funding operations. Taxation creates a demand for State money, and also can be used to fine-tune spending and affect other public behavior. What is the purpose of government bond sales if not to fund government spending? For Lerner, the primary purpose of bond sales is to manage reserves and thus the overnight rate of interest (inter-bank lending rate) in the face of government fiscal operations. The government should sell bonds, writes Lerner, 'if otherwise the rate of interest would be too low' (1943: 355).

> Lesson #12: Bond sales logically follow from, rather than precede, government spending.

Since government need not 'borrow' to finance its expenditure, relying instead on bond sales to manage bank reserves and hit some target rate of interest, logically speaking, bond sales follow from rather than precede government spending:

> [T]he spending of money . . . out of deficits keeps on increasing the stock of money (and bank reserves) and this keeps on pushing down the rate of interest. Somehow the government must *prevent* the rate of interest from being pushed down by the additions to the stock of money coming from its own expenditures. . . . There is an obvious way of doing this. The government can *borrow back* the money it is spending. (1951: 10–11, original emphasis)

By selling bonds, government can drain the banking system of excess reserves created by its own deficit spending, and thus prevent the rate of interest from falling to zero bid. Such a process clearly supports the view that, far from selling bonds in order to finance expenditure, bond sales logically follow from spending by the government.

> Lesson #13: 'Printing money' in and of itself has no impact on the economy whatsoever.

For Lerner, there are six (or three pairs of) fiscal instruments of government: taxing and spending, buying and selling, borrowing and lending. 'Printing money' is not independent of these. Therefore, printing money, in and of itself, has no impact on the economy whatsoever. Suppose the government prints money and puts it in a rocket ship and blasts it to the moon. Will the printing of money have had any effect on the economy? Of course not.

> [T]he creation of money has no effects on the economy as long as the printed money remains in the print shop. It is only when the money gets out into the economy that any effects come about. Money which is newly created and kept locked up might as well never have been created. (1951: 132)

Only if the money printed is spent on goods and services or lent through issuing bonds or otherwise given away will there be some economic impact, but these impacts are already covered through the consideration of the six fiscal instruments: 'The printing of money is not an instrument of policy. It is only a servant of these policies, just like printing stationery used in the various government departments' (1944: 312–14):

> All the decisions of any importance are made when it is decided to apply the fiscal instruments. . . . If any of the instruments involves the paying out of money . . . , the effects are just the same whether the money paid out was previously resting in the treasury or whether it had to be printed because there was not enough available in the treasury to permit them to be carried out on the scale that was considered necessary to prevent deflation. The use of the instrument should never be hampered just because there may not be enough money stock in the treasury at the moment. To sacrifice the prevention of deflation because of shortage of money which could be printed is no more sensible than to refrain from carrying out any other important government action because the necessary paper forms or stationery would have to be printed. (1951: 133)

> Lesson #14: When there is unemployment, jobs and money, not resources and goods, are scarce.

In a full employment economy, resources are scarce. Economizing is important, as resources can only be allocated to any use if they are removed from some other productive activity. In an economic system with unemployment, however, goods are not scarce, as more can be produced by employing the unemployed resources. But there are further scarcities in an economy suffering from unemployment:

> What is scarce is *money*. The lack of money to spend on the goods is what keeps the unemployed resources from producing more goods. Work, moreover, instead of being a curse, is desired more than anything else because the alternative is not the enjoyment of leisure but the suffering of unemployment and deprivation. Of course, if people could get income without having to work they would not object too much (although their self-respect in feeling they are useful members of society who are earning their income is too easily underestimated). But it is only by finding work that they can obtain the necessary income they need. (1951: 147–48)

> Lesson #15: Attempts to argue that the deficit and debt are not really as big as they look, or that if we measure them differently or keep a capital account, they are not really that bad, are counterproductive.

For Lerner, 'deficit doves,' by trying to placate concerns about government budget deficits and the national debt, actually do harm to their own position as 'proponents of organized prosperity' (1951: 15):

> A kind of timidity makes them shrink from saying anything that might shock the respectable upholders of traditional doctrine and tempts them to disguise the new doctrine so that it might be easily mistaken for the old. This does not help much, for they are soon found out, and it hinders them because, in endeavoring to make the new doctrine appear harmless in the eyes of the upholders of tradition, they often damage their case. Thus instead of saying that the size of the national debt is of no great concern . . . [and] . . . that the budget may have to be unbalanced and that this is insignificant when compared with the attainment of prosperity, it is proposed to disguise an unbalanced budget (and therefore the size of the national debt) by having an elaborate system of annual, cyclical, capital, and other special budgets. (1951: 15)

For Lerner, even more dubious are those who declare their agreement with the principles of functional finance but waffle in their support because they believe the public will not understand; or those who claim that functional finance seems reasonable but believe there must be something wrong with it they are unable to uncover (1951: 16). The former tend to be 'intellectuals' who underestimate the public's capacities, while the latter tend to be members of the public who hold intellectual adherents of sound finance in unwarranted high esteem. Both tendencies result in stalling policies for prosperity. Lerner compares the situation to the fable of the emperor with no clothes, in which the people are too timid or fearful to speak out. When it comes to functional finance:

> The scholars who understand it hesitate to speak out boldly for fear that the people will not understand. The people, who understand it quite easily, also fear to speak out while they wait for the scholars to speak out first. The difference between our present situation and that of the story is that it is not an emperor but the *people* who are periodically made to go naked and hungry and insecure and discontented – a

ready prey to less timid organizers of discontent for the destruction of civilization. (1951: 16, original emphasis)

CONCLUSION

Abba Lerner's work on functional finance and full employment contains lessons as relevant today as when they were put forward some five decades ago. At a time when orthodox theory and policy offer little to explain either causes or cures in the form of effective policy approaches, we could do well to revisit these ideas and the ideas of other great economics thinkers of the past. Of more than antiquarian interest, their work contains valuable lessons that can inform current analysis and formulation of approaches to macroeconomic policy.

The global economy is troubled by deflationary pressures, excess capacity, and growing unemployment. Lerner's principles of functional finance, complemented by his state theory of money, serve as a guide to macroeconomic policies appropriate for the contemporary political economy that can increase aggregate demand and promote full employment and economic growth with stable prices. A public service employment program can be used to operate the economy based on the lessons learned from Lerner. Any nation can define its currency by the public service employment wage-benefits package, and the deficit can adjust to the private sector's desire to net save. The economy can move directly to full employment, and socially beneficial community services will have all the labor power they need. There is no excuse for involuntary unemployment in today's world: joblessness means only that we have not learned our lessons well.

REFERENCES

Lerner, Abba (1941), 'The Economic Steering Wheel', *University of Kansas City Review* (June).

Lerner, Abba (1943), 'Functional Finance and the Federal Debt', *Social Research*, 10: 38–51.

Lerner, Abba (1944), *The Economics of Control*, New York: Macmillan.

Lerner, Abba (1947), 'Money as a Creature of the State'. *American Economic Review* 37(2) (May) 312–17.

Lerner, Abba (1951), *The Economics of Employment*, New York: McGraw-Hill.

Lerner, Abba (1969), 'On Instrumental Analysis,' in R.L. Heilbroner (ed.), *Economic Means and Social Ends: Essays in Political Economics*, Englewood Cliffs, NJ: Prentice-Hall, pp. 131–6.

12. Anchors aweigh: from real to nominal money and from market to government stabilization

Edward J. Nell

The traditional monetary system was ‘anchored’ in precious metal. In the earlier forms of the system, the metal was mined and minted into coins until sufficient coins were in circulation for exchange against current goods and services. This proved to be expensive, so paper came to be substituted. But the value of the paper depended on that of the coins. That is, the value of the monetary unit was tied to the value of metal through the fact that the circulating medium could be converted into metal. This prevented ‘overissue’ of the paper currency, the correct issue being the amount needed to replace metal where that amount is determined by the needs of circulation.

Since prices were subject to a constraint, it was difficult for inflation to take root. But because the money supply depended on reserves, which had to be earned or obtained in the market, the system tended to be inflexible. For instance, it could not easily adapt to changing levels of activity. It also faced problems in raising the large sums of money needed for the construction of networks necessary for collective goods and services – classically, railroads, but later, telephones, radio, and television, not to mention highways. To reap the advantages of scale, these had to be built ahead of demand, amortized over long periods. Nor could the state issue money without backing, thus making it difficult for government to fulfill its new roles.

In the interest of flexibility, the anchor has been weighed; modern money is no longer convertible into anything else. We have a different kind of monetary system, one without a supply function for the article that serves as money. This has important consequences. First, the value of money must now be set exogenously (essentially inherited from history), but secondly, the rate of interest is no longer determined by the market. It cannot be determined by supply and demand, because there is no longer any supply function. Instead it is pegged by the central bank.

These changes have taken place in the context of a shift in technology in which generalized diminishing returns have been replaced by almost universal constant or increasing returns. This has largely eliminated the stabilizing price mechanism (Freeman, 1994; Nell, 1998a, 1998b). Further, related technological advances have led to a greatly expanded role of the state; its budget now provides the only automatic stabilizer (Stein, 1990).

I. MONEY AND VALUE

Money is all the more complex because it has public and private aspects of equal significance. Privately, the supply of the money article and provision of credit are profitable and prominent businesses. Publicly, money provides large-scale externalities that are positive when the system is operating smoothly, and negative, even catastrophic, when it breaks down. Therefore, in virtually every case, the state or some public authority has been called upon to manage or supervise the operation of the monetary system.

By 'monetary system' we mean that the economy possesses a universal medium of circulation that also serves as a unit of account and as a store of value. To elucidate, by 'the economy' we mean a self-sufficient capitalist production system (usually forming the basis of a unified social system in a given territory). If there is more than one medium, the relation between them must be 'universally' recognized and fixed throughout the economy.[1] All transactions in the economy must be monetized.[2] That is, all output must be sold for money, all income paid in money, all costs covered by monetary payments, and so on. The medium must have a determinate value, and there must be a definite quantity required for its circulation. Finally, the system should be stable.

In one sense money is always a token; it has very little use in itself.[3] And the unit of account, the basis for an accounting system, is always 'imaginary.'But the unit of account may be attached to valuable metal in a process that results in a coin with an 'intrinsic value.'[4] The unit of account may also be stamped on paper, or recorded in depository records that have no value in themselves, resulting in money with a mere conventional value. In the first case, there are market adjustment processes that tend to maintain the value of the circulating medium; in the second, there are no such processes.

The Circulation

To see how this works, it is necessary first to determine how much money is needed, that is, how much *value* embodied in a medium of exchange will be needed to circulate the goods and services making up the total product. 'Circulate' means that the sum of value will exchange in successive transactions, following a definite path, for all the goods and services in the economy, and end up where it began ready for the next period. (Of course, some funds will be withdrawn from circulation and held in hoards; money is also an asset.)[5]

In order to understand exactly how the amount of money in circulation is determined, we must understand the circuit. This, in turn, explains the amount of convertible paper that can be issued. From the circulation we can determine the amount of the money article needed, and thus determine the cost of the monetary system; with the shift to bank credit money, the circulation enables us to determine the cost of the banking services required for full monetization. (Banking services in excess of this must be doing something else, possibly something that is important and valuable, but possibly just supporting stock market 'churning' or real estate speculation.)

An account of the circuit will reveal the means of determining the precise amount of money needed for circulation. It will show that this amount is precisely determined, that it is a unique quantity and, finally, that the amount so determined is stable, that is, small changes in the system do not lead to large fluctuations in monetary requirements. As a result there is a well-defined demand for money for circulation so that, given a supply function, the value of money will be determined by market processes. As we shall see, this will hold even when coins have largely been supplanted by convertible paper.

A further extension allows for paper to be largely displaced by bank deposits, so that its circulation takes place through the clearing of checks. For example, today bank money normally originates in loans made by banks. When a bank makes a loan, it creates funds – credits – that go into a checking account. Typically the borrower uses the money to buy goods or services. The funds are transferred to someone else's checking account, and are spent again.

We can illustrate the circuit by tracing the flow of funds (Nell, 1996, 1998a; Lavoie, 1992). They begin with banks advancing funds for 'working capital,' that is, wage payments, in heavy industry, the capital goods sector. (The wage bill of the capital goods sector, W_k, turns out to be sufficient to 'circulate' the entire output; the ratio W_k/Y, can be termed the 'circulation coefficient', Nell, 1996; 1998a, 2002, 2003a, 2003b) Workers in the capital goods sector are paid, and spend the funds on consumer goods. Firms in the consumer goods sector apply their sales receipts to a new round of production and payment of wages. The wages they pay out return to them immediately, as workers in the consumer sector buy consumer goods. This is a 'short circuit' in which firms pay their workers and wages return as receipts.

We assume that production timing is coordinated, so that the sectors begin and finish in tandem. (If the timing were not coordinated, there would be costs that coordination could eliminate.) Then when production in both sectors is complete, the funds initially advanced as working capital to firms in heavy industry will now have accumulated in the hands of firms in the consumer sector. These firms, in preparation for the next round of production, will now spend funds on replacements of equipment and new investment. Firms in capital goods that specialize in producing equipment for the consumer sector will sell capital goods for the accumulated funds. With the receipts, they will repay the banks and buy their own replacements and equipment from the rest of the capital goods sector, who will then repay the banks, and, in turn, buy their replacements and new equipment, preparing themselves for the next round.[6] Through this repeated process, funds will return to firms in the capital goods sector, who, in repaying the banks, complete the circuit (see Figure 12.1). Loans have been paid off, so funds have returned to the starting point, while all outputs have been sold for money and all incomes have been paid in money.

This account gives us the step-by-step process by which money passes from 'hand to hand,' that is, from one sector, or category, of agents to another. These critical junctures are the points at which bottlenecks may arise, leading to inflationary pressures. The diagram of the circuit gives us a quick overview, and also makes it clear that there are *separate* critical junctures for wages and for prices. Pressures may trigger wage inflation, or price inflation, and either may, or may not, be passed along, depending on the state of the markets. Price and wage inflation can proceed at different rates, with important implications for macroeconomic adjustment.

To summarize, the circuit runs as follows. Banks loan to heavy industry firms; heavy industry pays workers' wages; workers spend their wages returning them to consumer firms as sales receipts out of which the consumer industry pays wages to its workers; workers promptly return the funds as they buy consumer goods. The consumer sector then buys replacement equipment and makes new investments, returning funds back to heavy industry as sales receipts; heavy industry then, in the final step, repays the loans to the banks. The money making the rounds is bank deposit money, and, as we shall see, may consist entirely of *bank deposits that were created by the making of loans*.

Indeed, in the modern world, the loans are automatic. The bank gives the firm a line of credit, analogous to a credit card or a home equity loan, and the firm draws on it when it needs to pay its labor force. When the loan is paid off, the funds disappear from individuals'checking accounts and the money is gone (at least until the bank makes another loan). If the banks have done their job well, choosing creditworthy borrowers, they will be in a position to enact the process all over again.

An earlier version of the circuit features merchants instead of banks, but follows the same route as the later version. In the earlier version, merchants might purchase the net output of the consumer sector for coins. Having sold their net output, firms in the consumer sector could purchase replacements and new capital goods. This would then set off the 'secondary circulation' in the

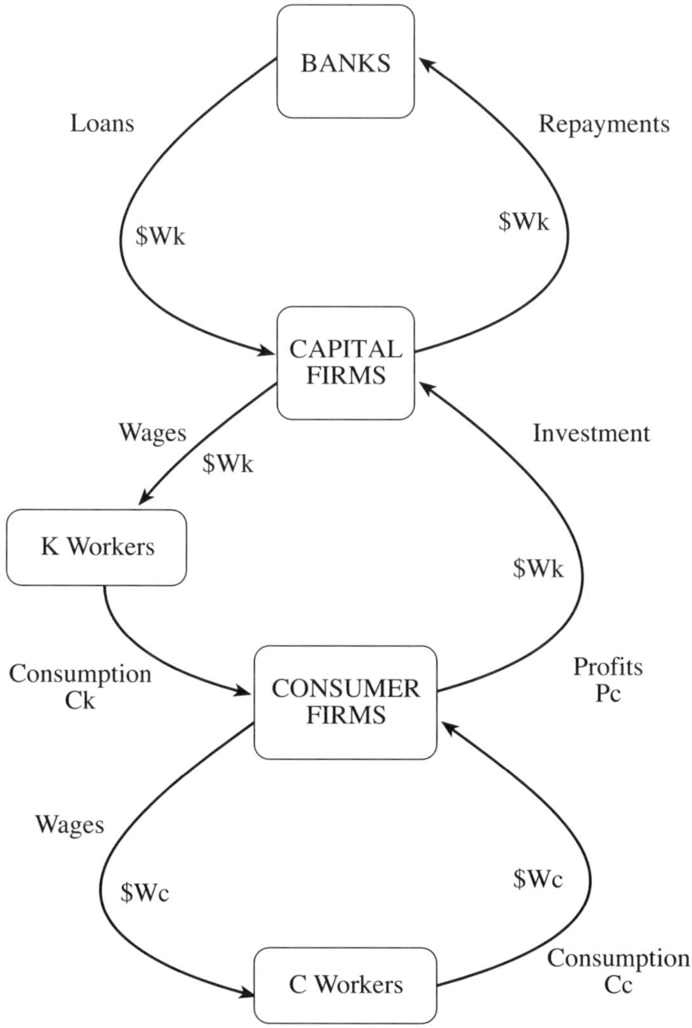

Figure 12.1 The circulation of output by money

capital goods sector. That sector would then purchase its replacements and net new equipment, and begin production, paying out wages. As its workers spend, they buy consumer goods from the merchants; as the funds return to the merchants, they buy further goods from the consumer sector, which in turn pays its workers, who return the funds to merchants as they buy the goods. When production is complete, the consumer sector has a new set of goods, the funds are all back in the hands of merchants, and the system is ready for another round. The merchants will have made their profit, in the form of an inventory of goods from the difference between buyers' prices and sellers' prices. Some of this they may consume; another portion can be sold abroad or to mining for the additional coins or bullion needed for the larger output of the next round (Nell, 1998a, 2002, 2003a, 2003b).

In this case we can see how the 'value of money' can be established through the interaction of demand and supply, where the former takes a form reminiscent of the quantity equation, and the latter is governed by cost of production. For this, however, money must be expressed in a standard. Assuming that it is supplied appropriately, in order for money to have a stable value in circulation, it has traditionally been thought enough to express it in a stable standard.[7] But the study of the circuit shows that expressing money in terms of something stable is not the issue. It must be put into circulation in a manner that will enable it to complete a stable, closed, complete *circuit*. Then, but only then, can we say that it has a stable value in circulation. So it is not a single transaction, for example, with a 'standard,' that defines the value of money, but a stable *sequence* of transactions, determinate in value and following a definite order.

Different Kinds of Money

We might explore further on what a monetary system might be based. What might be used as money and why? What principle might define the article or articles serving as money? Will the principle define a private or a state form of money? Such a principle must enable the system to solve two problems: it must establish the value of the money article, and it must give the public the confidence to accept and use the article as money. (Note that most actual monetary systems might involve more than one principle.) In general, we can distinguish two kinds of monetary systems – 'real' and 'nominal' – and each may be established as a public monopoly or as a decentralized private system. Finally, each could be a simple issue, for example, of coins or paper bills, or 'leveraged.' That is, the basic supply could be augmented by subsidiary issues of tokens convertible on demand into the original. Let's examine these in turn.

In the economy of early capitalism money was 'real,' that is, based on the value of metal, usually gold or silver. In the early stages, publicly minted coin was the principal medium of circulation, assisted by trade credit. Later, paper money and bank deposits, leveraged on coin and bullion, took over the bulk of circulation.[8] Paper money and bank deposits, however, were initially understood to be tokens; they stood in for 'real' money, which is metal. They were therefore convertible on demand into a medium possessing intrinsic value.

This meant that the quantity of money flowing through the system adjusted through the price mechanism. First, consider metal coin. When prices change, the value of money in circulation must change inversely, that is, when prices rise, money is worth less than before; when prices fall, money is worth more. The money in circulation may be considered money demanded for use. But money (metal) has a real value deriving from production; this may be considered its supply price. If the value in circulation is out of line with this real value, then money must be withdrawn from, or added to, the circulation. Supply and demand, through the price mechanism, determine the amount of money in circulation. This process brings about adjustments in the quantity of money in circulation, and, much less reliably, in the amount of credit offered. In short, in a real money system, whether simple or leveraged, market processes determine the value of money and also, as we shall see, the rate of interest.

Paper money was supposed to be backed by coin or bullion. It was issued in proportion to the reserves of the state or the banking system, the ratio being determined by the probability of conversion. An overissue would lead paper to fall in relation to metal, setting off a 'reflux' as the public turned in the excess paper for the more valuable coin. Too large an overissue could lead to a drain of reserves, leaving members of the public holding effectively inconvertible paper.

By contrast in *nominal* money systems (whether simple or leveraged), where money is a token given value by fiat, both of these must be determined outside of or apart from the market. In a closed economy with a system of fiat and balance-sheet money, the command over goods and services of the nominal unit of account – the dollar, or the pound, or the peso – and, as we shall see, the basic rate of interest on money (in the modern economy the rate that banks have to pay to the central bank), must both be 'exogenous.'[9] The first is a convention that ties the accounting system of the economy in question to its world of goods and services; in practice, of course, this will always be given by history. The unit of account at any time will be worth so much in goods and services, because this is what has been established in practice, historically deriving from the metallic system. But once the tie to precious metal has been broken, there is no market, no organized system of pressures, to keep the level of this unit stable at the given initial value. It is what it is because of the arbitrary facts of history. No market forces, however, will keep it that way. This opens the door to inflation.

The second 'exogenous price' in nominal money systems is the supply price of reserves or clearing balances, that is, the basic interest rate. In the old metal-based system, as we will explain later, this was determined by supply and demand, and (with certain exceptions) tended to move in a stabilizing manner; in a boom, it would tend to rise, in a slump, to fall. But in a modern system it is arbitrary, although within limits, of course, including the need to keep the banking system prosperous as well as orderly. This rate is stabilized by the central bank that has the necessary market power to accomplish this.

So we can arrange our cases: real money and nominal money, both of which can be public or private, simple or leveraged. Public coinage and public fiat money are based on the state's power to declare a monopoly. 'Leveraging' signifies that the initial money is augmented by a secondary issue based on some kind of promissory support. We can classify well-known examples accordingly, making use of a simple table (see Table 12.1).

Here we can make some observations on nominal money. The difference between public and private nominal money is demonstrated dramatically by considering what happens to each in the case of a 'run.' A run on state fiat paper – Confederate dollars or French assignats – leads to escalating inflation. No one will hold the money; it is spent as quickly as possible. A run on private bank money, however, means withdrawing funds from the system, and this leads to reduced deposits and a constriction of credit. The result is not inflation, but recession. But there is also an important similarity. Both rest on the powers of the state, fiat money directly, but bank-created money indirectly through deposit insurance, regulation, and guarantees provided by the lender of last resort.

A consideration of the underlying determinants on which money is issued reveals two basic principles by which money acquires value, through 'intrinsic' value yielded by production and minting, or through 'conventional' value bestowed through some official process. Either can be augmented by 'fiduciary' issues. Let's examine these.

Production and minting, giving rise to 'intrinsic value'

Real value, unleveraged – coins, bullion, plate The use of precious metals developed spontaneously in trade, and in settlement of debts and other obligations. Such metals obtained their value from the process of production. In early systems, this would be labor value. But in addition to mining and

Table 12.1 Classifying real and nominal money

	Simple	Leveraged
Real Public	State coinage	Bank-issued paper
Real Private	Bullion Private minting	Bank-issued paper
Nominal Public	State fiat paper	Bank deposits, backed by paper
Nominal Private	Deposit creation, with organized clearing	Deposit insurance, bank capital backing

processing, coins must be minted. The mint stamp guarantees that a lightweight coin can be exchanged for one of full weight, bringing in the fiduciary principle. Mining and minting provide the supply; early minting was often conducted by private interests as well as the state. The value of such money was determined by supply and demand, as we shall see.

The fiduciary principle

Convertible paper, bills of exchange, coins of wood, tin, leather Bills of exchange and token coins arise spontaneously in private transactions. Bills and tokens have value because they have a presumed use that the market believes will be honored. Token coins are believed to be exchangeable for goods; they normally circulate only in limited regions in which their issuers are known. These are almost pure fiduciary cases, but there is also present an element of the fiat principle, namely, that the promises are enforceable in courts. But the principle example draws on the intrinsic value principle: Private banks issue banknotes and these are accepted because the promise of convertibility into precious metal is believed. Metal coins have intrinsic value, but, as noted, also rest to some extent on the fiduciary principle; worn and underweight coins are accepted because it is believed that they are exchangeable for coins of full weight, and this, in turn, may be enforceable in court, bringing in the fiat principle.

Conventional value I: fiat of the state

Inconvertible paper money – Civil War greenbacks, assignats Inconvertible paper money is issued in denominations that accord with a conventional unit of account in which prices are already established. Paper money will be accepted because it can, or must, be used to pay taxes or to settle debts in the state courts. This is the Chartalist principle: Money is whatever the state decrees to be money. There is a slight touch of the fiduciary element here as well. The government's decrees have to be believable, and the government must be judged capable and willing to enforce them. Fiat money can be issued at will by the state, in response to its own needs, but there is no necessary relation of that amount to the needs of the economic system as a whole.

Conventional value II: double-entry bookkeeping

Modern bank deposits Bank deposits are generated privately, in response to market demand, and denominated in conventional accounting systems. Thus, the issuance of money will respond to the needs of the economy as defined in the prices and values expressed in the reigning money of account. But while the banks are private, a banking *system* can hardly be conceived without a 'lender of last resort,' or some form of state backing. The deposits of a given bank will first be accepted as a medium of exchange because of the belief that the bank has assets equal to its liabilities (with risk covered by the bank's capital). (Here the Chartalists have a point: bank deposits will be more readily accepted if they can be used to pay taxes.) But secondly, bank deposits circulate because the public believes the bank *can manage the liquidity of its liabilities*. And for this any given bank depends on all the rest, that is, depends on the banking system.

Banks can create money by lending. The loan is an asset secured by the collateral or good name of the borrower; the deposit is a liability. Liabilities circulate in the process of production, income creation and expenditure, and return to repay loans. (They are accepted because of the reputation of the bank, which, in turn, depends on the quality of its assets.) So assets and liabilities exactly match; what the bank must do to make the process work is manage its liquidity problems.[10] But, to repeat, for this it must rely on the banking system, which must ensure enough liquidity to enable liabilities to be created, circulate, and be extinguished.

Taking these principles in order: intrinsic value has no necessary direct relation to the state, although coinage has been chiefly state-managed. A fiduciary medium can arise privately, but it almost certainly could not become, and remain, universal without state backing. A fiat medium must rest on credible state power. Conventional value has an important but indirect relationship to the state: a bank deposit system needs state support to ensure the universal acceptability of bank money. Bank money must be acceptable in paying taxes. In this sense, the modern banking system 'leverages' fiat money. Moreover the banking system needs state support to ensure liquidity and to provide stability.[11] In 'manias' (the tulip craze, stock market booms), the collateral for loans will be increasing in value, justifying the loans that provide the fuel driving the boom. There is no anchor unless the state provides one.

Giving Value to Money

Notice that to each of these monetary principles there corresponds a system of *monetary valuation*, that is, a process by which money acquires and maintains value. In the cases of intrinsic value and fiduciary money, money acquires value through market processes, although these may be mediated or managed by the state. But market valuation processes are not involved in the valuation of either fiat money or bookkeeping money. They cannot be. An economic process involves balancing supply and demand at the margin, and imputing the value so determined to intramarginal units; but neither of these forms of money is *supplied* by an economic process that generates a marginal cost function.

Money of intrinsic value acquires its value in production, and this is maintained and stabilized through the working of the Mint. The supply function related the value of a marginal unit of money to the amount mined and minted in the current period. This curve will tend to be flat or possibly rising. The demand function showed the number of units at various levels of unit value required for the circulation of the currently produced volume of goods and services. Such a curve would be falling from left to right.[12]

A glance at Figure 12.2 tells us that the adjustment process is stable. If $M < M^*$, money demanded or required will be greater than that in circulation; the shortage will constrict prices, and the value of money will rise. Money will command more in circulation than warranted by its value based on its cost of production, leading more to be thrown into circulation. Conversely, if $M > M^*$.

Unfortunately, the relation is not that simple. There is an important potential for instability here, which also recurs in the other cases. Suppose instead of reacting to the current level of the value of money (price level), the market reacted to its *changes*. Thus when the value of money in circulation is higher than the 'normal' value, instead of throwing money into circulation, market agents will note that the value is rising, and so will hold back, anticipating further increases. When prices are rising – and the value of money falling – market agents will anticipate further price increases, and will spend as quickly as possible. In each case, the reaction is self-fulfilling, and the system is unstable.

To prevent or contain such instability, Governments control the Mints and establish mint prices, for example, 'gold points,' at which the Mint will buy or

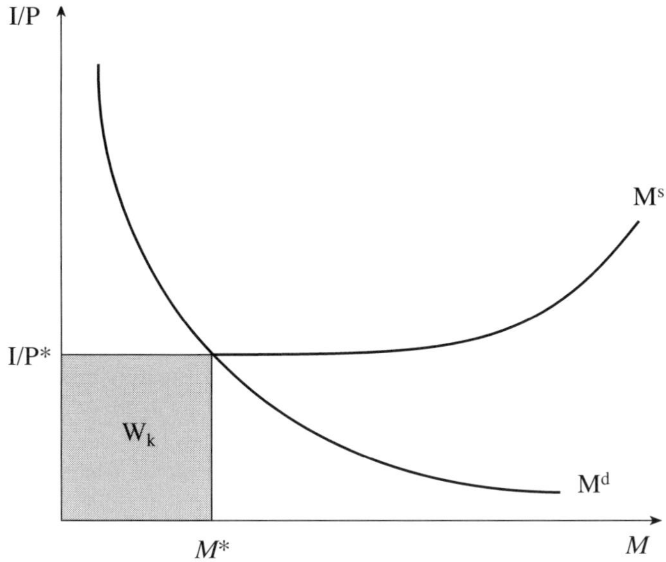

Figure 12.2 Determination of price level and quantity of money

sell bullion or plate in order to keep the movement of the value of money within limits.

Fiduciary money acquires value because it is 'backed' by a stock of goods, for which it can always be exchanged at a stable price. It also has intrinsic value though it acquires such value 'second-hand.' (For example, the lord of the manor issues tokens – in pay for labor or for goods – which can be turned in for grain at his warehouse; a merchant issues a bill which can be redeemed for goods. The value is guaranteed by the promise of redemption at a fixed rate.) Bank notes will apparently be stabilized automatically. If too many are issued, they will fall in relation to their backing and so, according to the 'reflux' principle, will be turned in. But here again the same kind of potential instability can be seen. For if the notes are *falling*, it will pay to wait before turning them in. In that case, the overissue will not be corrected, and the notes will continue to fall. Again, government policy has sought to prevent overissue. Money needs to be managed.

A more advanced fiduciary system establishes money of some kind backed by a 'buffer stock' of goods, whose prices are stabilized by the managers of the stock, who buy when prices are falling and sell when they are rising. This permits control of the instability, but it may lead to overproduction of the goods held in the buffer stock.

Fiat money is just paper or some other token that becomes generally accepted because it may be used or even required in payment of taxes. The tokens have no value in themselves; they are given value by fiat, and the particular rate at which they exchange is arbitrary. Rate of exchange will be chosen for convenience and accepted – if it is accepted – by convention.[13] So we are calling this *conventional value*.

However, even if paper can be given a value arbitrarily, that value must be maintained, and here supply and demand again come into play. When government is small, and the banking system is privately managed, the *conventional value* of money in exchange for privately produced goods depends on the quantity that has been issued in relation to those goods, and must be supported by limiting that quantity. Limiting the issue, however, may be undermined by the ability of markets to leverage the money issued, creating credit and near-monies. Moreover, if the government issues fiat money to cover its purchases, requiring that money back in taxes, a deficit will create an excess supply. Once this supply has become greater than the amount the public wishes to hold for precautionary reasons, the excess will tend to drive down value.

When government is large and manages or oversees the banking system, however, it may be able to set or at least influence prices through its budget.[14] It may have enough market power to force businesses to sell to it at prices of its choosing. Or it may use its own production to set 'yardstick' prices, as TVA did, for example (Nell, 1988).

Modern bank money is created on the basis of a given unit of account and a given set of prices that are expressed in that unit. Banks create deposits by making loans, generally as the result of firms activating pre-negotiated lines of credit analogous to the credit cards that households use. These advances are paid to workers, who spend them on consumer goods; they reappear as receipts, and are used as profits to fund investment spending, and so on. In other words, bank advances for working capital circulate in the same way that real money did, and such circulation effectively monetizes all the transactions of the economy (Deleplace and Nell, 1996; Nell, 1998a, Ch. 5; Nell, 2002, 2003a, 2003b).[15]

Bank money is created *ex nihilo*, but the circumstances have to provide appropriate institutional support. Like inconvertible paper, this kind of money will also have value only by convention. That is, it has no intrinsic value and it is not backed by anything. It cannot be converted into gold, for example. Why then should anyone accept it, if, say, they could obtain gold-backed money? Suppose some banks offered convertible money, and others offered inconvertible money. The inconvertible money, but not the gold-based money, can be used to pay taxes (as in the US after 1933). If the level of taxation is low, and especially if the government inspires little confidence, the public will continue to use the gold-backed money, and buy the inconvertible money at tax time. But this strategy will pose the risk that there may be a shortage of tax-paying money at tax time, driving up its price. If the level of taxation is high, this could impose a serious, unexpected loss. If this loss, adjusted for its probability, is larger than the carrying costs of the inconvertible money, the public will accept and use that money.

Once the public decides to accept and use the inconvertible money, however, Gresham's Law comes into play. The weaker currency will be accepted, but it will also be passed along as fast as possible, building up holdings only for tax-paying. The gold-based money will also be accepted, but being judged sounder, it will tend to be held as an asset, so it will gradually drop out of circulation. But these problems will disappear when governments are strong and stable.

A system based on bank money has no 'anchor.' Since banks are in business for profits, they will create loans to meet any creditworthy demands, so bank money cannot easily be constrained in quantity. To maintain the value of such money, however, prices and wages must remain steady in terms of the unit of account. To keep money wages and prices steady, therefore, it has seemed that demand must be kept weak, creating an overhang of unemployed labor and excess productive capacity. It is clear that this is wasteful; to argue that it is unnecessary, however, we must show how the value of bank money could be anchored some other way. Such a proposal will be suggested in the last section of this chapter.

The absence of an anchor also leaves the interest rate floating free. There is no supply function tying the quantity of money to reserves and reserves to the interest rate. Reserves are the balances banks hold with the central bank; these will fluctuate with the state of trade and with the government's tax and spending activities. Excess or deficiencies in the reserve balances will lead to sharp fluctuations in overnight rates. The central bank therefore has to smooth this out. Whatever rate the central bank sets in the market for its loans will automatically become the minimum rate. In short, the central bank has no choice but to *peg* the basic interest rate. Once the system ties money only to conventional value, the connecting links must be protected and managed by the state.

II. TRANSFORMATIONAL GROWTH AND THE EVOLUTION OF THE MONETARY SYSTEM

A 'transformational growth' perspective (Nell, 1998a, Ch. 6) would suggest that these principles are connected in an evolutionary pattern: as technology developed, production and employment took on new forms, and came to require different kinds of financing (Nell, 1998b). To keep pace, the monetary system also had to adapt and develop in new ways.[16]

This took place in several stages. In the first instance, as transactions became more complex, metallic money proved inconvenient. Paper claims to gold could be used more easily, and came to replace gold. But bankers noticed very early that a given supply of gold could support a larger amount of circulating paper, since only a fraction would be presented for conversion at any given time. Convertible paper based on a fractional reserve, however, is fiduciary money. It is based on the trust the public has in the banks.

But governments famously had difficulty raising money. Taxes were not only hard to collect at the best of times, but too much effort put into tax-collection could lead to revolt. An alternative was to print money. But how to give it value? The answer, as Chartalists remind us, was to require it back in taxes. However, when governments most needed to print money, it was hardest to give it value, precisely because of the difficulties in the first place of collecting taxes (Davies, 1996). Fiat money required the consolidation of state power, in particular, the ability to impose and collect taxes.

A further possibility for governments was to borrow. Indeed, the Bank of England arose precisely for the purpose of financing the Crown.[17] But the Bank was thereby made into an intermediary between the public, other banks, and the Crown. It was in a position to guide, even to dominate, the financial scene. And bank deposit money required some form of state-backed support for the banking system. It obviously required universal clearing, but it needed more. It needed guarantees.

As information became more reliable, more easily verified and transmitted, creditworthiness could be checked more efficiently, so credit could be extended more widely until selected credit instruments became acceptable in settlement of debts (Hicks, 1989). With improved communications, funds could be moved more rapidly, and, although this was at first rare, after the telegraph, instantaneously. As production became more sophisticated, new and more flexible forms of financing developed for its service. Metal and convertible paper, however, adjust through changes in the value of the circulating medium – which is to say, prices and money wages must vary.[18]

This works well in a craft economy with stable output and employment and flexible wages and prices. But it will not do in a mass production economy with volatile employment and output and in which prices and wages are inflexible, or only rise. Monetary arrangements capable of adjusting more quickly are necessary.

So the system shifted to bank deposits, that is, pure accounting money. Banks can issue lines of credit so that they advance loans and create deposits on demand. But pure accounting money has no value; it can only measure and record value. The crucial implication is that the system moved from money of intrinsic value, which adjusted through flexible prices in the conditions of the craft economy, to accounting money provided on demand in mass production. As we shall see, the state, either actively or by default, must fix and maintain the value of this money.

In short, while we tend to think that monetary theory has developed, becoming deeper and more complex, this is only half the story. Taken by itself it is misleading. It is certainly true that early monetary writers seem to hold to an unsophisticated quantity theory, while later writers have a deeper appreciation of liquidity, and still later writers see the role that liquidity plays in portfolio composition. Yet most of these writers may be faulted for failing to understand the endogenous flexibility of the money supply, a fact that has only come to the forefront of understanding fairly recently.

What is misleading is the failure to see *that monetary relationships themselves have developed historically*. The development of monetary theory is largely a reflection of the historical development of the monetary system. Specifically, the monetary system developed from one that adjusted through the same price mechanism that (weakly) stabilized commodity production and labor markets, to a system that had no adjustment mechanism at all, leaving it inflation-prone. In the first system, some versions of the quantity theory make good sense, and, in the short-run, money is exogenous in some respects. As the system develops, however, credit becomes increasingly important and more and more 'money-like,' more liquid. So liquidity becomes more significant in practice, and therefore takes on a greater importance in theory. Still later, with the replacement of price-adjustment by multiplier-accelerator systems, money becomes significantly endogenous.

In the first system, covering the greater part of US history, unbalanced government budgets did pose some sorts of problems, problems particularly important in the nineteenth century. In the second system that came to maturity during World War II, unbalanced budgets posed few, if any, problems. In the first system, the value of money was fixed by tying it to commodities (gold and silver, for example), and stabilized by the price mechanism (supplemented by Mint or bank policies). In the second, the value of money *has no anchor, and there are no stabilizing market forces*. In the first, government is small and tends to be neutral; in the second, government is large – it *must* be large in order to do the job of stabilizing – and is a major force in the markets.

Another important change follows from the changes in the determination of the value of money. Before 1933 the value of both kinds of money was anchored and regulated by a connection to gold. As a result, the rate of interest was also determined in the market. But today the value of money is a matter of historical accident, that is, it is *exogenous* to the market. And – as we shall see – this implies that the same is true of the rate of interest. This does not mean that market forces are irrelevant to either. Quite the contrary, a variety of market forces bear on them; yet neither is set by market forces in any particular market.

The connection between the market determination of the value of money and the market determination of the rate of interest is important, not least because the demise of the former brings an end to the latter. We can review this more closely.

Forms of Money I: The Gold Standard

In its earliest and simplest forms, the gold standard meant that the money in circulation, including the money the government minted, consisted of gold coins.[19] When the US officially joined the gold standard in 1879, the value of the dollar was set as equal to the value of 23.22 fine grains of gold, where 480 fine grains made a fine troy ounce. This was equivalent to \$20.67 per ounce.[20]

Under the gold standard, the constraint on the creation of bank money posed by reserves is critical. Bank money consists of notes issued as claims to *real* money, that is, to gold or silver coins, money with intrinsic value. But at any time, most of the public would prefer to use the more convenient paper money, provided they are confident that they can convert the (intrinsically worthless) paper to gold at a moment's notice. For this purpose, reserves are kept in proportion to the note issue. Initially these were reserves of gold coins, later they were held in treasury money. But the treasury could not issue notes without itself having reserves of gold (coins and bullion), and these could not easily or quickly be expanded or contracted.[21]

To see how this works, suppose banks had to keep 50 per cent reserves. But in a booming economy, in which business is good, a bank wants to issue more notes in order to make more loans. So the bank prints two dollars and spends one of them buying gold. The note issue rises; indeed, any individual bank can do this. So the reserve requirement does not seem a burdensome constraint. But if any significant number of banks increase their issue in this way, then the dollar price of gold will rise, which is to say, the value of paper dollars, in terms of gold, will fall. So the public will immediately turn in the paper for gold, and the additional notes will be cancelled! Any individual bank, at any time, can increase its issue, or make additional loans and shop for reserves. But taken together, the price mechanism ensures that the quantity of reserves will be an effective constraint.

The same is true for treasury money. To create more, the government must first obtain more gold, for example, from excise taxes, or from foreign exchange earnings. Or it could borrow the metal, although gold was not always readily available and sometimes had to be imported from Europe. In the nineteenth century, this could take several weeks. In the meantime, banks short of treasury money would try to borrow from other banks and to encourage members of the public holding treasury money to deposit it in their bank. To this end, banks would raise interest rates. It often took large and rapid rises in rates to attract relatively small amounts of extra reserves. When treasury money was readily available, however, interest rates tended to fall. These conditions created frequent fluctuations in short-term interest rates associated with changing needs of banks for reserves and the changing availability of gold and other reserve assets. And these interest rate fluctuations sometimes led to other sorts of financial instability.

When short of reserves, banks will raise interest rates to attract additional reserves; they will also restrict their lending. All but the best customers will be refused new loans. As loans are paid off, the amount of bank deposits will shrink, which implies, of course, that the volume of bank money declines. With fewer deposits, banks will eventually come to find their reserves sufficient for their needs. On the other hand, if banks had excess reserves, they would tend to expand their loans, creating more deposits and thus increasing the amount of bank money. In short, the amount of bank money will tend to adjust itself to the amount of reserves. This should be familiar as the traditional money multiplier story.[22]

So in a gold standard world, without a central bank, reserves do limit lending. However, this may require the system to face severe strains.[23] In a boom, banks will lend more and will seek to create deposits or issue notes. To do this, they will have to attract additional reserves, requiring that they raise interest rates. In a slump, they will issue less and lend less, and will seek to shed reserves, lowering interest rates. In other words, interest rates are market-determined, and at least weakly stabilizing. However, they cause banks to become over-extended in booms and to be burdened with non-earning assets in slumps. Let's look more closely at the way supply and demand work in the case of reserves and the interest rate.

The endogenous determination of the interest rate

In a boom, banks will lend more and will seek to create new deposits or issue additional notes. To support these activities, they will have to attract additional reserves. This will lead them to bid up interest rates, as they seek to attract idle reserves from one another and from hoards. In a slump, they will issue less and lend less, and will seek to shed reserves, lowering interest rates. In other words, while long-term average rates are determined by costs and competition, current interest rates reflect the balance of supply and demand in the market. They move pro-cyclically.

This is illustrated by a simple model. On the one hand, the rate of interest (in relation to the rate of profit), is likely to affect investment inversely, and investment, in turn, will have an impact on prices and employment. Changes in prices and employment will call for changes in reserves. (Even in the conditions of the craft economy, the monetary system and the real economy cannot be separated – the classical dichotomy does not hold). On the other hand, shortages or surpluses of reserves will lead to market pressures driving interest rates up or down. Monetary adjustments do complement and reinforce the stabilizing effects of the price mechanism.

Interest rates, investment, and the demand for reserves

To see these relationships clearly, we can plot them on a diagram (see Figure 12.3). The origin will represent the normal position, assumed to be the average over the cycle. Here the rate of profit will be at its normal level, and the rate of interest will be just sufficient to cover the expenses of the banking system, allowing just enough profit for it to grow at the same rate as the rest of the economy. The vertical axis will represent increases of the interest rate above and below the normal level. The horizontal axis will show the level of reserves, similarly above and below the normal level.

First we have the relationship between above or below normal interest rates and investment, which translates into demand for reserves.

> Investment depends inversely on the interest rate. The more expensive it is to borrow in relation to normal profits, the lower will be investment spending; and the less expensive, the higher investment spending will be.

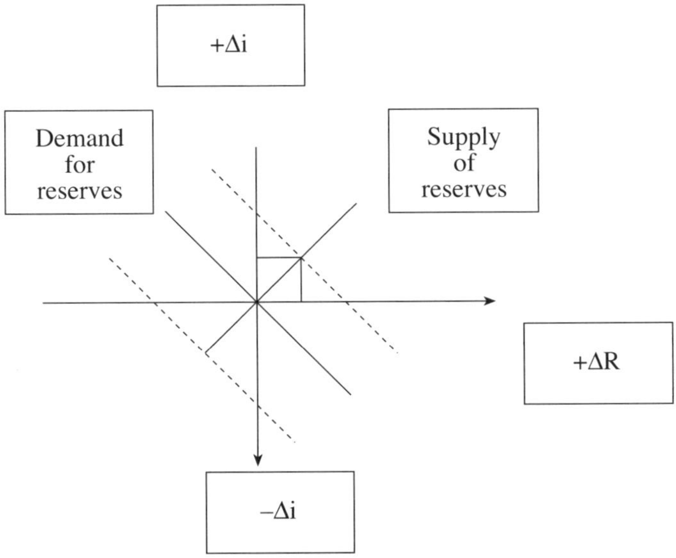

Figure 12.3 Demand and supply for real reserves set the interest rate

> Savings depends positively on prices (in relation to wages) and on employment. When prices are bid up, profits increase and are saved.
>
> Prices in relation to wages, and to employment and output, all depend positively on investment.
>
> For equilibrium, savings has to equal investment.

Taken together, these propositions tell us that if interest is low, for example, investment will be high. The resulting demand pressure will drive up prices in relation to money wages, lowering the real wage and increasing employment (and output), raising profits, and thus, savings; this will go on until savings has risen to match the high level of investment. The process works in reverse: If interest rates are high, investment will be low, and prices will fall relative to money wages. So with real wages high employment will fall, and profits and savings will be down. So savings *adapts* to investment, in a Keynesian fashion. But savings depends on profitability and employment, and not on the interest rate, so the latter cannot be determined here.[24]

The preceding implies that the required level of reserves depends on the money value of output, therefore on prices and employment. Thus, required reserves will be large when interest rates are low, and small when they are high. Banks start out with a 'normal' level of reserves; this will have to be adjusted as the interest rate changes. So the curve passes through the origin, falling from the left to the origin and continuing through it. Higher than normal interest rates mean low investment, output and employment, and consequently, lower than normal demand for reserves. Lower than normal interest means higher activity and higher required reserves.

Interest rates and the supply of reserves

To complete the simple diagram, we must show that reserves will be increased when interest rates are raised and that, when interest rates are lowered, reserves will be reduced. That is, the supply of reserves varies positively with interest rates. This needs careful explanation.

Since g has risen, it might seem that gold output would rise *pari passu*. If so, things would be simple. Gold producers would expand mining and processing, and so increase their purchases of capital inputs by an amount necessary to raise gold output to the higher level necessary to ensure that new gold/existing gold stock will equal the new higher growth rate, g_1. But the increased purchase of capital inputs would mean an increase in the supply of gold; reserves would therefore increase. The increased purchase of capital inputs/normal purchase of capital inputs would equal the new growth rate, assuming equilibrium ratios. Hence gold reserves would expand in the necessary ratio. But what *incentives* would lead gold producers to this?

Consider this: The pressure of the boom will tend to bid up prices (relative to money wages), which would seem to *reduce* the value of money, whereas a *rise* in the value of money is needed to induce mining. That is, there should be a shortage of money relative to goods, as would be expected with a rise in employment and output in a boom; this would call for more output from the mines. But the rise in prices suggests an increase in money relative to goods!

This would mean a lower value of money (monetary gold), which would hardly be an inducement to produce/supply gold. However, gold producers do not necessarily have to sell gold. They could hold it and deposit it with the banks in return for interest. In equilibrium, the rate of interest should equal the rate of profit. So gold producers should be indifferent as to whether they are *investing* new gold – (for example, plowing it back into the business, that is, selling gold to buy capital inputs to earn the rate of profit) – or *lending* it to earn the rate of interest. They will sell enough to keep the supply of gold in circulation at the level required, and will lend enough to keep the rate of interest at the equilibrium level.

So when a boom develops, the growth rate will rise, and prices will be driven up relative to money wages, raising profits. That is, goods prices measured in the actual circulating medium – paper and credit – will rise, relative to wages in that medium. By itself, this would appear to lower profits in gold, since gold's command over goods would be less; but the boom is fueled by an *excessive* issue of paper and credit. So paper and credit will fall in relation to gold. Thus new gold can be exchanged for more paper than the invested gold commanded earlier. In current terms the rate of profit will be unchanged.

The banking system will be pressed to find reserves to back the new issues of paper and credit. Its efforts will drive up the interest rate. When the growth rate rises, a boom develops. As new paper and credit are issued, existing reserves come to be inadequate; so, in order to back their issues, banks will compete to borrow reserves from one another. (There will always, normally, be periods in which a given bank's reserves will temporarily be excessive, making them willing to lend.) This will engender a widespread increase in borrowing pressure, driving up interest rates. This may somewhat increase reserves, as it will attract 'hoarded' gold from inventories. But why would a rise in interest rates lead directly to a rise in mining?

Mining will increase because the higher rate provides gold producers an opportunity to increase earnings. Their normal output will continue to be sold as before. But if they increase their output, they can deposit the additional gold with the banks, and collect interest at the higher rate. (This is equivalent to selling the gold for goods. That is, the interest rate must mirror the relation between the spot price of gold and its price for delivery at a later date. A rise in the interest rate must be reflected in a rise in the discount applied to the delivery price of gold.)

Thus adjustments in the interest rate will tend to attract or release reserves so that the actual level on hand will be brought into line with that required by the level of activity. Higher prices and output call for higher reserves; to attract more reserves, a higher interest rate will be needed, but this will also tend to reduce investment and so bring about lower levels of output and employment. A lower interest rate, in turn, would tend to release reserves, but it would also tend to stimulate investment, increasing activity and thus raising the demand for reserves. At some intermediate level of the interest rate, the level of reserves attracted should just match the level required. This will be the temporary equilibrium level, as determined by market forces.[25]

Putting the two functions together, with the normal equilibrium at the origin, we see that a shift upward in investment – due, perhaps, to boom psychology – will raise the demand for reserves (upper dotted line). This will now intersect with the supply at a higher rate of interest and a higher-than-normal level of reserves. A slump would lead to just the reverse (see lower dotted line).

As in the case of supply and demand for circulating funds, by the conventional account, this should be a stable market. If actual reserves are inadequate, those demanding reserves will be willing to pay higher interest charges, and the higher interest will attract more reserves. But note that if there are delays or time lags, the reactions could take the form of a 'cobweb.' With a steep demand function and a moderate supply function, the cobweb might well be divergent. In that case, government would be needed to maintain stability by adjusting the interest rate. The policy of the central bank would be 'to lean against the wind' in order to move the interest rate in the right direction. But the bank can also ensure that the changes will be large enough to have the desired impact.[26]

In a modern system, however, the rate of interest is not determined by demand and supply for reserves. Reserves are arbitrary and can be manipulated, reserve ratios can be evaded, and above all, reserves are not a special kind of money, like gold. They are just accounts at the central bank – accounts that can be created by the central bank. As a result, there is no independent supply function.[27]

The chief reason for the shift from gold and convertible paper to modern bank money was that gold and real reserves could not be quickly adjusted. The quantity in circulation adjusted through the price mechanism; but as the economy shifted to mass production, employment became highly variable; the wage bill would fluctuate with layoffs and re-hiring. The wage bill, however, (together with spending on investment) provided the chief market for bank lending, which would now have to adjust quickly to changing demand. But a gold-based system could not expand without first increasing reserves, which had to be attracted by higher interest rates. In a slump leading to extensive layoffs and reduced demand for loans, reduced lending would leave banks with excess reserves – an unnecessary expense – leading to reductions in rates and efforts to shed reserves. The counter-cyclical movement of the interest rate certainly helped to stabilize the economy, but it put a great strain on the banking system.

Forms of Money II: Modern Money – Asset and Liability

Now let us look at modern money, which is not anchored in gold or precious metals, and consider how money that is purely a matter of convention or fiat obtains and keeps its value. In the older economy, money was anchored to metal that had 'intrinsic value.' Such money is an asset to its possessor, but it is no one's liability.[28] This connection is broken in modern systems in which money has no intrinsic value. It is an asset to its possessor, and a liability to its issuer. Between these, we have a system in which paper money and bank deposits are *loosely tied* to intrinsic value by being *convertible* into bullion, plate or coins. Such money is also a liability to its issuer. The implications of the change from money of intrinsic value to modern money are striking.

The value of money is now a matter of 'exogenous pricing.' There is *no supply function*. Nothing is supplied in the sense of being produced and having a unit cost, except a service. But the service does not have a unit cost, nor is the cost of the service in any way tied to the number of units of money issued. This service is one that the banks provide, and for which they are compensated by the rate of interest. But that does nothing to determine the value of money. There are no market processes to determine money's value; it is set by history – in particular, the history of money wages – and by accident.

Deposits, loans and bank capital

A modern bank is generally a corporation owned by a group of stockholders.[29] Their initial investment is the basis of the bank's capital. Over time, this capital grows if the bank makes a profit and retains a portion of that profit in the business rather than turning it over to stockholders. The capital shrinks when the bank makes a loss. The capital is what the bank is worth to its owners.

Banks are in the business of making loans and in the process of doing so they create deposits. The role of bank capital is to make depositors comfortable with leaving their funds in the bank. The capital represents the difference between the bank's assets and what it owes to depositors. As long as the bank has capital, any losses from bad loans will be borne by stockholders rather than the depositors.[30] When a bank's capital becomes too low relative to its assets, either because it has over-expanded or made bad loans, it must forgo making any additional loans. In this way, the amount of bank capital becomes a constraint on banks' lending and the amount of deposits they create.[31]

The central bank

A banking system needs to have a way that checks can clear, a way that funds can be transferred from one bank to another. There are several avenues for this. The most important of these is for all banks to keep deposits at a central bank. In the US, that bank is the Federal Reserve. As checks pass from one bank to another, these deposits change hands. Since the Fed is the government bank, these deposits are a kind of Treasury money.

Banks can create currency in the same way they create deposits. When making a loan, instead of giving the borrower a checking account, they can give her a piece of paper good for that sum. Like the deposit, this is an IOU of the bank. The borrower, instead of writing checks for goods she wishes to buy, could simply give the seller this piece of paper. United States banks issued their own currency until the creation of the Fed in 1911. Since then, currency has come from the Federal Reserve and is a form of treasury money.

This means that banks now have a new problem. In order to do business, they need to have a supply of currency sufficient to meet their customers' demand and a balance at the Fed sufficient to clear their checks. Banks can make loans and create deposits, but they cannot create balances for themselves at the Federal Reserve; they must make deposits, or have them advanced against their capital. This could be an important constraint on the ability of banks to make loans. Such a constraint is enhanced by laws in the US and other countries by requiring that banks keep a percentage of funds, beyond what is needed for clearing of their deposits, on deposit at the central bank.

But before we say this, we have to examine the point of origin of these reserves. They are not *real* reserves, not money of intrinsic value. Rather, they are deposits created by a special bank, the Federal Reserve. In this regard, the Fed operates like any other bank; that is, it makes loans and creates deposits. However, it only makes loans to banks and only accepts deposits from banks and the Federal government. There are other important differences. The bulk of the Federal Reserve's assets are not loans, but government bonds. The Fed sometimes buys these bonds from the public, paying for them by creating deposits, much as an ordinary bank creates a deposit when it makes a loan. If the Fed sells some of these bonds to the public, deposits are destroyed. As long as the public is willing to buy and sell bonds, the Fed is able to create deposits and currency at will. Like banks of the nineteenth century, the Fed can create currency as well as deposits.

Reserves

The deposits and currency created by the Federal Reserve are the reserves of the modern system. It would seem that if the Fed could control the amount of these reserves, it could thereby limit the ability of banks to lend, and thus control their ability to create deposits. By controlling reserves, the Fed could control the total quantity of money. As we saw earlier, real reserves did constrain banks. It has seemed plausible, and monetarists everywhere have believed, that modern, nominal reserves could provide a similar constraint. But central banks all around the world, including the Federal Reserve, have tried to exercise such control, most recently in the late 1970s and early 1980s, and, in virtually every case, their attempts have failed.

The reasons behind this failure are complex (Goodhart, 1984). At a minimum, a central bank is responsible for orderly markets, for efficient clearing, and for regulation that ensures the safety and solvency of the system. Maintaining orderly markets requires the smoothing out of basic interest rates, seeing that seasonal factors and tax collections, for example, do not unduly affect financial markets. Clearing of all valid checks is necessary if bank deposits are to serve as part of the currency. Safety and solvency mean that sound banks must not be allowed to fail because of liquidity shortages. These points add up to the fact that the Fed cannot refuse to provide reserves if they are needed. First, a reserve deficiency or excess will have a strong and immediate impact on the Federal funds rate. (Because reserves earn zero interest, an excess will drive the rate down strongly, while a shortfall puts a bank in violation of the laws, causing it to bid urgently for funds.) Second, checks written against valid deposits cannot fail to clear because the bank is short of reserves;

if this were likely to happen it would inhibit the use of bank deposits as currency. So the Fed must provide reserves. Finally, to safeguard the system and ensure its orderly working, reserves must be available to protect sound banks against temporary liquidity shortages.

Let's consider this more closely. The Fed's calculation of the amount of reserves that a bank requires is based on the average amount of deposits and reserves available over roughly the preceding six-week period.[32] If a bank is short of reserves, it has two days to make them up. It cannot change the amount of reserves that it needs, for that amount is dependent upon the reserves it had in the past. Instead, the bank in question must get more reserves. If an individual bank is short of reserves, it can always borrow from another bank that has more reserves than it needs. This is called 'borrowing Federal funds.' But if all banks are short of reserves, reserves can only be obtained from the Fed. If banks are forced to scramble for reserves, problems will develop and check clearing may be disrupted, driving interest rates up sharply. This is exactly what the Fed is supposed to prevent. To meet its responsibilities, the central bank has little choice but to provide the necessary funds.

Too large a supply of reserves can also be a problem. For banks, reserves are assets, but they are assets that earn the bank nothing.[33] Deposits at the Federal Reserve earn no interest and, of course, currency earns nothing. Having currency and deposits at the Fed is necessary and useful, but no bank will want to keep more than it needs. A bank with more than it needs will seek to lend reserves to banks that are short of reserves. As long as there are banks wishing to borrow, this is fine. But if all banks taken together have an excess, the interest rate on these funds (called 'the Federal Funds rate') will fall. Yet this may not eliminate the excess, at least not in the short term. Lower interest rates may eventually increase the need for reserves, but only after banks have lowered their own rates and increased the amount of loans. So in the short run, an excess of reserves could drive the Federal Funds rate to zero. To avoid this, the Fed steps in to sell some of its assets to the public, which are paid for out of banks' reserves. Managed properly, such sales will reduce the amount of reserves to what is needed by the banking system.

This does not mean that the Federal Reserve has no ability to influence the process. But its influence is indirect. The Fed chooses an interest rate at which it will buy or sell certain types of short-term assets. This is its target interest rate. Because of its ability to buy as much as it pleases (or sell vast amounts), it can effectively set this interest rate. If it raises this rate, other rates, including those changed by banks on loans, will also rise. The higher interest rates will discourage borrowing and will reduce the amount of reserves that banks require. If the Fed lowers this rate, borrowing will increase and so will the amount of reserves that banks need.

The Fed also has other tools at its disposal. It regulates the banking system, and it can apply pressure to banks by strict enforcement of regulations. It also serves as an information conduit and as a coordinator; it can use these positions to exercise behind-the-scenes influence.

Thus, effectively, banks are not constrained by their need for reserves. The Federal Reserve and other central banks influence the amount of deposits indirectly through their ability to influence interest rates. The overall constraint on a modern banking system in a mass production economy is the availability of bank capital.

Now for the 'punch line.' This means that expansion and contraction of lending is not tied to levels of reserves, indicating that the previous equations for interest rates do not hold. The supply of money does not depend on reserves. It is constrained only by bank capital; but banks need not economize on capital, the way they had to economize on reserves. Therefore, interest rates are no longer determined by a market process.

The interest rate must now be pegged, since the central bank is required to maintain orderly markets, and has to intervene to prevent seasonal and regional fluctuations. The central bank has to smooth out interest rates. It cannot allow volatility, particularly when fluctuations could lead to unstable patterns of movement. With no supply constraint, financial markets are liable to extreme movements. In short, the central bank has to exercise control over financial markets, so it had better ensure that the level of the interest rate is appropriate.

III. THE MONETARY SYSTEM AND THE GOVERNMENT

In the older economy, the monetary system did provide a constraint, and this constraint helped stabilize the economy; changes in the value of reserves worked in conjunction with the price mechanism. By contrast, the modern monetary system offers no constraint, and, in fact, inflations and asset price booms are self-financing, since price rises increase the value of collateral, on the one hand, and raise the value of bank capital on the other. The modern monetary system also allows for a creative use of the central government's budget. The shift in money from real to nominal, following the changes in technology, has brought a new role for the government. The government budget is both much larger and plays a stabilizing role in the way it affects the economy.[34]

The Old System and the New[35]

The money supply in a craft system – convertible paper and metal, with bank deposits convertible into either on demand – denotes a set of activities that are quite distinct from the demand for money. That is, to supply money, metal has to be coined or paper printed; worn out coins and paper are replaced. New coinage or new printing will be done in response to price incentives; if the value of money in circulation lies above or below the intrinsic value of the monetary standard, then money will be supplied or withdrawn. By contrast, in a mass production monetary system, bank deposits have no backing other than the power of the state, money is only supplied when demanded, and it is always supplied when effectively demanded (when there is adequate collateral). In the modern economy supply and demand for money are indistinguishable. Money is independently supplied and demanded in the monetary system of a craft economy; it is created and cancelled in the process of circulating the total of goods and services produced in a modern economy.

In the craft economy, neither the central bank nor the government had much control over either the money supply or the interest rate. Rather, both were largely determined by market forces and the price mechanism. The money supply adjusted automatically to keep the value of money in circulation equal to the intrinsic value of the monetary standard. The rate of interest adjusted to keep the volume of credit advanced in line with the banking system's reserves. Even if the central bank had some ability to influence interest rates, it still had to 'lean against the wind,' which meant moving more or less in step with the market. By contrast, in a mass production system, the money supply accommodates almost instantaneously to the demand for money, and the nominal (short-term) rate of interest can be set by the central bank; in some circumstances, it can also set the nominal long-term rate.

Reserves in a craft system act as backing for money of an inferior grade. Metal backs paper, paper backs bank deposits. In each case, the reserves are fractional, since withdrawals will not be likely to require the full amount, except in the case of a run. The reason is simple: the inferior money is more easily handled and used. It is more efficient, but it lacks intrinsic value. Fractional reserves imply a money multiplier; that is, if the amount of metal in the system increases, the total amount of money will increase by a multiple of that original increase. By contrast, the reserves in a mass production monetary system provide no backing – they have no intrinsic value. Government guarantees (for example, deposit insurance, lender of last resort), provide for the safety of the currency. Holdings of gold and silver are historical relics; paper and deposits are backed by the state's power to tax. Reserves are nothing but clearing balances, and once electronic funds are in place, they are hardly needed at all. There is no money multiplier.

The rate of interest in a craft economy is set by supply and demand. That is, when aggregate demand is exceptionally high, more funds will be needed for circulation. This will require attracting additional reserves away from private hoards. Banks will have to bid for reserves by raising interest rates. By contrast, in a modern monetary system, reserves do not provide a constraint, and banks do not have to bid for them. The central bank cannot fail to provide them; it has to accommodate, although it may choose to impose penalties. These, however, are a matter of policy; they are not the result of a market process. But the central bank has to keep order in financial markets, which requires smoothing out of interest rates. It cannot allow volatility, so it must peg the rate of interest.

The Government Budget in a Modern Economy

To understand just what a government budget imbalance means, consider a world of three parts: the domestic private sector, the government sector, and the 'foreign' rest of the world. In this scheme, the government deficit is the domestic private sector's surplus with the government; the government's surplus is the domestic private sector's deficit. The current account surplus is its surplus with the rest of the world. Now compare the country's current account surplus with a private sector surplus (the government deficit). The two surpluses are exactly the same in nature and have the same effects. The current account surplus is generally considered a 'good thing,' since it represents an excess of sales over purchases; by the same token, the government deficit should be regarded as a 'good thing' for the private sector.

The government budget tends to move counter-cyclically. In a slump, incomes will be reduced and spending curtailed, so tax collections will fall, but welfare and related spending to support the unemployed will tend to rise. Other government budget items are likely to be unaffected. Hence, the overall effect will be to throw the budget into deficit. By contrast, in a boom, tax collections will rise and welfare spending will tend to decline, so a surplus will tend to emerge. In short, in an economy with demand-based cyclical fluctuations, the central government budget will tend to move in a counter-cyclical fashion.

Now consider the monetary implications of deficits and surpluses. A deficit arises when the government spends more than it receives in taxes; this means a net increase in money in the system. Such money will appear as excess reserves in the banking system. If allowed to remain, it will drive down interest rates. Looked at another way, it will drive up security prices. A surplus is just the opposite; it arises when the government spends less than it takes in, and it creates a reserve deficiency, tending to force interest rates up.

In order to maintain its desired level of interest rates, the treasury must issue bonds to absorb funds, or buy bonds to provide funds. Government borrowing, in other words, serves the purpose of keeping interest rates at the level the central bank and/or the Treasury think appropriate.

In short, when a modern government spends, it always creates the money to do so; the central bank creates a balance for the government, which gives the central bank bonds in exchange.[36] That is, money is created when the government spends, drawing on its balances with the Fed, and its spending appears as receipts in the accounts of businesses and households, who, in turn, re-spend these funds. The money will remain in the banking system until it is drained out by taxes. Note that the government does not 'raise money' through taxation. Taxation ensures that the government's money will be accepted. When taxes are paid, the government's balance with the central bank is reduced; that is, the money is destroyed. A check in payment of taxes, when cleared, reduces the government's balance at the central bank; it therefore reduces the money supply.

The Government Budget, Contrasting the Old and New

Taxes in a craft economy raise money. The state cannot issue new paper without adequate backing. Given a reserve ratio, its ability to issue is limited by its reserves. So to spend, it must have money on hand; either it spends out of its reserves, which requires calling in paper or getting away with a lower reserve ratio, or it must raise the money by collecting taxes. By contrast, in a mass production system, taxes are not needed to raise money. The government creates money as it spends; when it collects taxes, it reduces the amount of money in circulation. Money collected in taxes is destroyed – paper money is burned, and checks that pay taxes reduce the government's liabilities, which are part of the money supply.

Financial markets in a craft economy serve the purpose of raising money for investment, but that is not their chief purpose in the modern era. In the earlier system, bonds were issued to mop up savings and assemble funds for large-scale long-term investment. Savings – supply of funds – were a function of the rate of interest; higher interest rates tended to call forth more savings. Investment – demand for funds – would be greater the lower the rate of interest, and would be smaller the higher the rate. Hence supply and demand for loanable funds tended to determine the bond rate of interest. By contrast in modern financial markets, stocks do not tend to raise money; buy-backs tend to equal or outweigh new issues. Bonds are often issued to finance takeovers and mergers. And this is the chief function of financial markets under mass production – they become the markets for corporate control.

Government spending in a craft economy requires having money on hand. The Government is constrained. It cannot create money; it must raise funds by collecting taxes or by borrowing. (Obviously, all through history, governments have sought – with a good deal of success – to evade or loosen this constraint. Debasing the coinage and issuing non-convertible paper are perhaps the best-known methods.) But borrowing means issuing bonds; it is, or may be, interpreted as a tacit admission that the government cannot effectively collect the money it needs in taxes. If that is so, how will it be able to service and eventually repay the bonds? By contrast, in a mass production system, the government creates the money it needs for its spending. Taxes are collected to ensure that the money is acceptable. Bonds are rolled over, and may be perpetual; they never have to be repaid. The government is constrained in its spending not by the monetary system, nor by the ability to collect taxes, but by the real capacities of the economy. If the economy is operating at less than full capacity, then the constraint is not binding. However, another constraint, internal to the government itself, may be important: What the government can do at any one time depends on its capacity to effectively plan and supervise its activities, and this ability – dependent on the available managerial skills – will normally be limited. Moreover, expanding this ability will itself be an activity requiring planning and supervision, and so can only be carried out by drawing on the very set of skills that are in short supply.

Deficits, then, have a very different meaning in the two systems. In the craft economy, deficits are a burden. They are likely to drive prices up, they will certainly tend to drive up interest rates, and they may damage the credit of the government. By contrast, in a mass production economy, deficits are merely a residual, albeit when they have emerged 'automatically,' they are a residual with an important function: to stimulate the economy in a time of recession. Deficits do imply an increase in so-called 'high-powered' money that will have to be offset if interest rates are not driven down. And they may over the long term lead to undesirable effects on income distribution and on the division of output between consumption and investment, although this depends as much on interest rates, and especially on the i/g relationship, as it does on the deficit itself.[37] Table 12.2 summarizes these points.

The new monetary system is without an anchor. So nothing supports the value of money, which is to say prices are not subject to any constraint. Money has only conventional value, so if the conventions on pricing change, there is nothing to prevent inflation. Pressures of demand might lead to inflation and, on the other hand, inflation might be controlled by reducing demand. But at the same time, the size of government has risen dramatically, and the government budget tends to move counter-cyclically. This provides an automatic stabilizer for output and employment. But if the Phillips Curve exists, it would tend to exacerbate inflationary pressures.

And that is the way it has been seen: the government's stimulus to the economy is believed to promote inflation. Unemployment and inflation are thought to move inversely; the higher unemployment (the weaker is aggregate demand), the weaker will be the inflationary pressures. On the other hand, the lower unemployment, that is, the stronger demand, the more dangerous the tendencies to inflation. This is the central implication of the Phillips Curve, the much disputed basis for the anti-inflationary policies of the last half-century.

Table 12.2 Contrasting the craft economy and mass production

	Craft	Mass production
Monetary system		
Money	Supply and demand	Creation and cancellation
Control	Little or none	Nominal interest rates
Reserves	Act as backing	Clearing balances
Rate of interest	Set by market	Pegged
Government budget		
Taxes	Raise money	Destroy money
Financial markets	Raise money	Corporate control
Government spending	Needs money on hand	Creates money
Deficits	Burden	Residual

IV. THE PHILLIPS CURVE: THE LINK BETWEEN INFLATION AND UNEMPLOYMENT

The idea behind the Phillips Curve is that higher inflation is associated with lower unemployment, and vice versa. Intuitively, this seems plausible enough. The stronger the economy, the more business is booming, the more jobs there will be. So we can expect the rate of unemployment to be lower. Indeed, it may fall to a point where shortages of various labor skills begin to emerge. In general, the more the economy is booming, the more likely there are to be shortages and inflationary pressures. By the same token, in a slump, excess labor and excess capacity will reduce inflationary pressures, and may even lead in some areas to price cutting.

So much is common sense; but making it theoretically precise has not been easy. The early Keynesian approach, drawing on institutional studies (Duesenberry, 1958), clarified the intuition but left it very loose. Everything depends on where shortages emerge and what policies there are for dealing with them – the inverse relation between unemployment and inflation was by no means necessary. But the link came to be seen as the way to tie up loose ends and close the model. Rather than leave money wages exogenous, they would be determined by the dynamics of inflation.

Then it became important to have a theory that explained the linkage. The Phelps–Friedman Monetarist approach grounded the unemployment–inflation connection on ad hoc asymmetric expectations, which New Keynesians have tried to bolster and fit better with a framework of rational choice. But the success of this enterprise has been limited. For one thing, it is not clear why the relevant expectations and information should be asymmetric. For another, the argument concerns the labor market; corporate pricing decisions are not examined. Finally, even if passive pricing is accepted, the framework is the labor-market model of marginal productivity, and this is itself seriously questionable, both theoretically and practically.

The evidence for the Phillips Curve is not very strong (Michie, 1987). It is well known that yearly data on the inflation and unemployment rates for the US from 1961–69 trace out a pattern that might reasonably be construed as a Phillips Curve. But after 1969, running on through the end of the 1990s, the points are all over the place. In the 1970s, unemployment and inflation rise together, at times quite strongly; they fall together through the 1990s, again markedly. At other times they appear to have no relationship. Indeed, it has been observed that, by today's standards, the original econometrics on which the Curve was based, using British data, would not be acceptable (Wulwick, 1989). For one thing, the 'identification problems' are too serious and too difficult. (That is, if a new point is not 'on' the Curve, does it mean that the previous construction was faulty or incorrect, or has the previous curve, correctly identified, shifted, presumably in response to other variables?) Finally, over the larger part of the second half of the postwar period, there is virtually no evidence of anything resembling a Phillips Curve. If it did exist, where has it gone? What has changed?

An important school of thought holds that the Phillips Curve shows only short-run relationships. An attempt by policy to reduce the level of unemployment will generate an increase in the rate of inflation. But it will only have a temporary effect on unemployment. In the long run, the level of unemployment will move to its 'natural' level.

The Friedman–Phelps critique holds that unemployment depends on real forces, and that output cannot rise for long above its 'natural' level; policy may raise it temporarily above the natural level, but it will return there as business and workers adjust their behavior to offset the effects of policy.[38] Further, despite policy, inflation will continue. Inflation at any time depends on past inflation through expectations. Hence any given level of inflation will tend to persist, since expectation will generate demands for money and the monetary system will normally accommodate.

The idea of a 'natural rate' rests on the twin foundations of a 'natural' level of output and unemployment, together with the suggestion that inflation is driven by expectations in the environment of an accommodating monetary system. On an intuitive level, the idea underlying the 'natural rate of unemployment' is not that plausible. Supposedly the 'general equilibrium' of the economy will generate a certain level of frictional unemployment; supplies and demands will be matched as well as they can be given the practical realities. This will be the 'natural rate of unemployment.' At this rate, inflation will be steady; there are no new inflationary pressures, since the labor market will be in equilibrium.

However, if there are expectations of inflation, the monetary system will accommodate them. Agents today will expect prices to behave as they did yesterday, based on the logic that if they rose yesterday, they will do so again today. On this basis they will formulate their plans and make their demands on the banking system. Money will be created accordingly, and credit advanced, so prices will rise today as they did yesterday. (The expectations generate the demand for money; the demand for money is accommodated, and the new money creation causes the price increases. The expectations are self-fulfilling, even though money creation is the ultimate cause of the inflation.) But there will be no additional pressure from the economy. Hence there will be no tendency for inflation to *accelerate*. So this natural rate will be the 'NAIRU,' the 'non-accelerating inflation rate of unemployment.'

This rate has to be the target for which policy makers aim. If they try to reduce unemployment below this rate, they may temporarily succeed, but inflation will ultimately take off. If they raise unemployment above this rate, inflation will decline, but it will not stay lower, or even continue to fall, unless inflationary expectations are lowered. For this to happen, unemployment must stay high, but unnaturally high unemployment, coupled with lower than normal inflation, will lead employers to believe that real wages are exceptionally low. So they will begin to hire labor, and unemployment will move back to its natural level. Inflationary expectations are therefore unlikely to be lowered.

There are two immediate and quite decisive theoretical objections to this theorization. First, conventional theory cannot show that the 'general equilibrium' is either unique or stable. There may be any number of possible equilibria, and any or even all of them may be unstable. The system could switch from one equilibrium to another, or it could set off on an unstable path of movement. So the natural rate might not be unique, but could be changing, or even unstable. Secondly, the argument depends on the 'Classical Dichotomy.' The general equilibrium is supposed to be independent of what the monetary authority is doing, and, more generally, of what is happening in financial markets.

As a practical or empirical matter, the 'natural rate' presents serious difficulties. The NAIRU is that rate of unemployment at which inflation *holds steady*; that is, at higher levels of unemployment inflation will fall, at lower levels it will supposedly rise. But surely it matters whether the natural rate is associated with a low or a high steady rate of inflation? Whichever it is, such apparently steady inflation rates have been associated with a large number of very *different* levels of unemployment in the last few decades. Even if a plausible definition can be given of the natural rate, it clearly has been moving in irregular and unpredictable ways.

In any case, Robert Eisner has shown that the econometric studies estimating the natural rate are seriously flawed. A very simple procedure demonstrates this. Take all the levels of unemployment above the 'natural' rate; these are, in fact, associated with reduced inflation, and higher levels of unemployment are associated with lower rates of inflation. But then consider levels of unemployment below the natural rate. These are *not* associated with higher rates of inflation. Sometimes lower unemployment goes with lower inflation, sometimes it does not. The relationships are all over the place. In general the conclusion has to be that raising unemployment is likely to lower inflation, but lowering it need not, and very likely will not, increase inflation.

It has been shown that the alleged linkage between inflation and unemployment is actually quite weak. What is true is that inflation can be slowed down or stopped by creating enough unemployment. It is not at all clear that inflation is necessarily set off by high demand, and moreover, it is obvious that many other things can trigger inflation, for example, exchange rate changes, primary price increases (oil shocks), etc. But stopping inflation by creating unemployment is extremely expensive in terms of forgone output, especially forgone growth. So the question arises whether inflation could be controlled in some other way.

After all, with the development of the postwar modern economy, we have seen a change in the size of government relative to the rest of the economy, and the government has taken on many new functions. Moreover, the way the government interacts with the economy has changed, in particular the way the government budget relates to the monetary system. The government budget tends to be counter-cyclical, and government borrowing is an important component of interest rate policy.

V. REINVENTING AUTOMATIC STABILIZERS FOR THE MODERN SYSTEM

In the modern economy, government spending is largely defined by various needs of the economy, so it tends to be independent of the cycle. The exception to this is welfare spending, which tends to rise in a slump and fall in a boom. Tax collections, on the other hand, will increase in a boom, and decline in the slump. So the government's budget in the modern economy will tend to run into deficit in the slump, and is likely to exhibit surpluses in a boom. This, of course, tends to have a stabilizing effect on aggregate demand. The question is, can this be extended to providing a stabilizing effect on wages and prices?

Consider a stabilization program that will help to maintain the value of money – a program that sets a pool of labor to work for a fixed money wage, where that wage is stabilized by operating the pool as a buffer stock. The government sets up a set of public works programs – an employer of last resort

(ELR) system – that will hire anyone wanting a job for what effectively becomes the minimum wage (Harvey, 1989). Many of these jobs will involve training and education or re-education; others will provide goods and services that have public value in the form of externalities, but are not profitable on a private basis. Whenever the private sector expands, it can hire from the ELR, attracting workers by offering a wage marked up above the ELR wage; whenever it contracts, its laid-off workers can take jobs in the ELR.

On this proposal, ELR spending will substitute, largely or in part, for welfare and unemployment compensation. Tax collections will fall in a slump, though not so sharply, since ELR wages are less than private sector wages. Hence the Government's budget will continue to be counter-cyclical. But now it will also act to stabilize the lower end of the wage scale. It provides an anchor. Of course, this will not tie prices down perfectly. Like all anchors, it could be dragged by strong enough forces. For example, varying sectoral demands could lead relative wage scales to change, or the markup over some kinds of wage costs could vary. But even so, the stabilization of the lower end of the wage scale would provide a dampening effect. In short, the modern monetary system permits, though it does not cause, inflation; but today's counter-cyclical government budgets can be extended and adapted so as to counteract inflationary pressures.

NOTES

1. The old English system illustrates the point: a pound, for example, was always 20 shillings; a shilling, 12 pence; a dollar, 20 nickels, and so on. A dollar issued by one bank is equal to a dollar issued by another.
2. In early economies – Feudal Europe, the US Western frontier – not all productive and distributive activity was monetized. Many exchanges were carried out by barter and were often done partly for non-economic motives, for example, charity, reciprocity, or in response to community needs. By contrast, in the modern economy, all activities are monetized and production is carried out with goods and services purchased for money, the producer's aim being to sell the output for more money than the amount advanced for production. That is, designed to earn a profit in money, production begins with money and ends with more money (Deleplace and Nell, 1996).
3. As Berkeley pointed out (Johnston, 1970), a country rich in gold and silver but poor in industry is not truly wealthy. It cannot consume the gold and silver any more than Midas could; it will soon spend its metal reserves on imports from industrious nations, and then it will have nothing.
4. The importance of clearly distinguishing between the unit of account and its embodiment in coins can be illustrated by reference to the disastrous British Recoinage of 1695. Following Locke's advocacy, the worn and underweight – and so undervalued – old coinage was more or less completely replaced by new coins of full weight. Money was more valuable, so prices fell. But *debts* were reckoned in the unit of account; hence the burden of debt was increased throughout the kingdom, with unfortunate effects on commerce and trade, the exact opposite effect of what had been intended. Locke may fairly be accused of not understanding the difference between the coinage and the unit of account (Johnston, 1970, VIII).
5. Keynesian and Post-Keynesian writers have extensively studied the question why money, an

asset without an obvious yield, should be held in portfolios. In the process, however, the equally important questions of how money circulates, and how much money is required to carry out circulation, have been lost to sight.

6. The whole circulating fund, a 'wage fund,' but only equal to the wages of the workers in the capital goods sector, will be spent on replacements and new capital goods purchased from the subsector of capital goods industries that specializes in supplying the consumer goods industries. There will therefore be a sequence of transactions within the capital goods sector as that first subsector buys its replacements and new equipment from the 'second' subsector that supplies it, and then that second subsector buys from a third group of firms supplying it, and so on. (Nell, 1986, 1998a, 2003a, 2003b; Deleplace and Nell, 1996. Also see Lowe, 1976; Hagemann, 1992 for studies of models that partition in this way.)
7. Suppose a good is chosen as standard which does not change in value when the economy changes from growing on a Golden Rule path to a condition of extreme divergence from the Golden Rule. As shown in Nell (2002, 2003a, 2003b), $W_k = P_c$ along the Golden Rule path, and in general not otherwise. So money would be expressed in terms of a stable standard, but would not have a stable value in circulation. (If divergences are small, however, they will not matter for industrial economies, Nell, 1998a, ch. 7).
8. Minting introduces a fiduciary element; it must be believed that the Mint will exchange worn coins for new ones. Most minting has been a state monopoly, not only for the profit from 'seigniorage,' but because mint prices were an important regulatory tool, as we shall see. However, private coining was common in different periods during the Middle Ages.
9. A closed economy need not be taken to mean an economy without foreign trade or factor – capital or labor – flows. Rather, it is one in which trade and factor flows are prevented from exercising any influence over economic magnitudes – prices, quantities, and income flows.
10. That banks create deposits (liabilities) on the basis of promises to repay with interest (assets), and then manage the resulting liquidity problem, has been understood for a long time, see Keynes (1930: 23–5). For a recent statement, see Hicks (1989, Ch. 6). But the fullest analysis is to be found in the French 'circuitiste' literature, for example, Cencini (1995), where bank money is defined as 'simultaneously an asset *and* a liability,' Also see Deleplace and Nell (1996, p. 13).
11. Prior to the Civil War, New Orleans bank dollars were discounted by as much as 7 per cent in New York. It took Federal legislation and regulation to establish a universal dollar.
12. If, as is likely, the value – or supply price – from mining and minting reflects constant costs over the relevant range, then a characteristic classical result holds. Value is governed from the supply side and quantity from the demand (Garegnani, 1970).
13. Historically, fiat money has usually been introduced as a temporary expedient in wartime, sometimes with reasonable success, as with 'greenbacks' in the US Civil War, sometimes disastrously, as in the case of the 'assignats' of the French Revolution.
14. Government can be large or small; banking can be privately managed or state-managed.
15. The account of circulation makes it possible to identify a specific sum of money, or credit-money, and show that this amount, appropriately advanced, will 'monetize' all transactions in the economy, including the realization of profits. Given assumptions about technology and institutions, this sum of money, and the sequence in which it moves, can be shown to be unique. It provides a precise definition of 'velocity' (Nell, 2003).
16. The original adoption of money did not necessarily take place because money is more efficient, or lowers transaction costs, as is often argued. Indeed, the use of money may increase both the complexity and the costs of transactions. But monetary calculation allows the determination of the relative profitability of different activities, and monetary competition ensures that the most profitable ones will flourish and the least profitable will be dropped.
17. As Hicks has pointed out, this put the Bank in the enviable position of being too valuable to the Crown for the latter to take action against it, or fail to meet obligations to it.
18. In a craft economy, when aggregate demand is below normal, prices and, to a lesser extent, money wages will fall so that real wage tends to rise. With employment fairly stable (and assuming a classical savings function), consumption demand is raised, tending to stabilize the system. With prices and wages falling, the value of circulating money rises, which will tend to draw money into circulation from hoards, tending to raise demand in a stabilizing

move. Adjustment will work in the opposite way for above normal aggregate demand. (However, were the market to react not to the levels of change, but to the rates, the movements would tend to be *destabilizing*, Nell, 1998a, Ch. 6).

19. Silver was also used. Indeed, for most of the nineteenth century, the US used both gold and silver, or bi-metallism. In practice, one metal or the other dominated depending on their relative price.
20. This did not mean that a dollar coin contained that much gold. Minting a coin from gold cost something, and governments and monarchs traditionally took a profit on coining called 'seigniorage.' The Mint covered its costs and earned a profit by reducing the gold content of the coin so that it was less than the value that the coin represented. The coin would be accepted at face value, however, because it could be used to pay taxes and was legal tender and would settle debts at that value. So long as the government was strong enough to impose and collect sufficient taxes, it could proclaim that a coin weighing less than so many units of gold would have a value equal to the value of that number of units of gold. The value of raw gold, of course, was determined by the cost of mining and refining the gold. The Mint markup was fixed, and any variations between the value of the coin and the value of the gold it contained (plus the markup) would tend to be self-correcting through the price mechanism.
21. We are simplifying here. Under national banking, there were many kinds of treasury money, among them, gold coins, silver coins, paper money, for which the treasury held amounts of gold, and silver-backed paper money. There also were greenbacks. This paper money was issued during the Civil War, had no connection with gold or silver, and could be used as bank reserves.
22. Shortages of reserves at times also brought about what were known as 'partial suspensions' of payments. Banks would refuse to convert notes to gold; or more commonly, in later periods, they would refuse to pay out treasury money to depositors. When this happened, banks would try to maintain their reserves, keeping them within the banking system by refusing or limiting withdrawals of cash. Checks, especially from the stronger banks, would usually still clear, but someone wanting currency would most likely have to pay extra for it. For example, a check of $104 might bring only $100 in currency (Taussig, 1939: 421).
23. Leaving aside disruptions due to loss of confidence and panic.
24. Supporters of the loanable funds approach may object, but there is little evidence that saving has ever been very responsive to interest. More importantly, there is a theoretical objection. When interest increases, wealth-holding households find their income higher, but by the same token, business firms find that their profit income net of interest is down. When everyone has adjusted to the change, wealth-holding households may save more, but businesses will be saving less. Focusing on the private sector and assuming that all capital income is saved, these changes will cancel each other. If wealth-holding households consume a portion of capital income, but businesses, in the light of competitive pressures, save it all, then a rise in interest would *reduce* saving.
25. This provides an explanation for what Keynes called 'Gibson's Paradox,' namely the strong and centuries-long correlation between the level of prices and the interest rate (Keynes, 1930).
26. Note that fiscal policy cannot be very effective here. A deficit does provide a stimulus, but at the same time it will shift the demand for reserves up, raising interest rates; a surplus provides a drag, but will lower interest rates.
27. Wicksell (1898, 1911), developed this idea. If the 'money rate of interest' lay below the 'natural rate of return,' then the economy would have a tendency to inflate. If the money rate were above the natural rate, the economy would deflate. If there are no real reserves to constrain the system, the inflation and deflation will tend to continue indefinitely.
28. In fact, the Mint had a small liability; it had to issue new, full-weight coins to replace any worn or underweight coins presented to it.
29. This is true of all commercial banks and most savings banks in the US Mutual savings banks and credit unions are cooperatives owned by their depositors.
30. Deposit insurance has changed this, but only to a degree. Should a bank's losses exceed its capital, small depositors are protected by the Federal Deposit Insurance Corporation. Large depositors are not so protected. Small depositors need not concern themselves with the state

of a bank's capital. In theory Federal regulators do that for them. These regulators are supposed to step in whenever a bank's capital falls below a minimum amount. As we saw in the Savings and Loan crisis, regulators are often unwilling or unable to do so. So large depositors still must concern themselves with the state of a bank's capital.

31. In the traditional treatment of the creation of loans and deposits – the money multiplier story – a bank starts off with an amount of currency and funds on deposit at the Federal Reserve. These are its reserves. It can make loans and create deposits only as long as it has sufficient reserves to support those deposits. Suppose that a bank has capital sufficient to allow it to loan $19 million and to create deposits of $19 million. In addition, it has $1 million in reserves consisting of deposits at the Fed and currency. If, to meet legal requirements and to have sufficient funds to clear checks and provide customers with currency, the bank had to keep reserves equal to 10 per cent of deposits, then this bank could only loan $10 million and create $10 million in deposits. But as we shall see, when reserves are nominal, the reserve requirement is no longer binding.
32. The actual procedure is more complex than this. Required reserves on time deposits are based on the average of time deposits over a two-week period ending a month previously. Reserves on demand deposits (checking accounts) are based on average deposits over the previous two weeks. A bank's cash reserves are counted during the same period as time deposits are counted, while its deposits at the Fed are counted for a period of two subsequent weeks. At the end of all of this, the amount a bank needs and has is calculated and the bank is given two days to make up any shortage (Meulendyke, 1998).
33. Banks today keep very little in the way of reserves beyond their vault cash.
34. The increase in the size of government in relation to GNP, from 3–5 per cent in 1900 to 30–50 per cent by 1960, is one of the defining features of the modern economy, one that is not at all well understood. It clearly interacts significantly with the shift from craft to mass production, and with the changes in the economic roles of the household. (For a discussion, see Nell and Majewski, forthcoming, Ch. 4.)
35. A word of caution: We have presented the monetary and financial systems of the craft economy in simplified terms, showing the working of a money market based on precious metals. But in actual fact, at all times, the circulation of incomes and goods depends heavily on credit, and on the *fiat* of the state. As a consequence, even in a craft system, with money based on precious metal, deficits were no threat to the financial standing of the government, provided it was powerful and well-organized enough to be able to levy and collect taxes. To put it simply, as we shall see, if a government can tax, it can issue fiat money.
36. 'Monetizing the deficit' has not been allowed, of course, since the Treasury–Fed Accord of the early 1950s. But this simply means that the Treasury issues bonds on the bond market when it writes checks in excess of its tax revenues, and deposits the receipts from the bond sales in its account. These bonds will always be accepted because they replace non-interest-bearing excess reserves, exactly equal to the amount of the deficit.
37. In the short run, deficits provide a stimulus, but their size does not matter. However, in the long run, the size of the government debt in relation to productive capital (public and private) can matter, though exactly how it matters depends on the desired financial regime, on whether the interest on the public debt is saved or invested, and on the minimum acceptable level of the interest rate. Consider a simple model: Suppose the desired financial regime is one in which $g \geq i$. Suppose further that all earnings from private wealth are saved and invested, while all earnings from holdings of public debt are consumed. (Much of this may be socially desirable consumption, including formation of human capital, or maintenance of the social fabric, as when interest on public bonds goes to support hospitals, universities, and foundations. But it does not directly increase productive capital.) Assume that all wages are consumed, and that all taxes fall on wages, and that all government spending is collective consumption (again, this may be useful and indirectly productive). Under these conditions, the surplus of output over consumption of all kinds, Y – C, will be profits, P. By definition, P = rK. Private wealth, $W_{p,}$ will earn interest and dividends, and, by assumption, equity and debt will earn at the same rate. These earnings are all saved and invested, so $iW_p = I = gK$. We assume now that g = i; so $W_p = K$. Government debt will be D_g. Then total profits,

$$P = i(W_p + D_g), \text{ so, re-arranging,}$$
$$D_g = P/i - W_p = P/i - K = (r/i - 1)K.$$

That is, given that the rate of interest is to equal the rate of growth, the size of the government debt cannot be greater than the difference between the present value of the stream of profits, capitalized at the rate of interest, and the replacement cost of the capital stock. By lowering the rate of interest, the acceptable size of public debt can be increased; but the *minimum* rate of interest will be that which provides earnings to the financial system just sufficient to cover the costs of providing financial services (Nell, 2002, 2003a, 2003b). (If there is consumption out of earnings from private wealth, then $gK = s_p iW_p$, where s_p is the propensity to save out of private wealth income. If g = i, then $W_p = K/s_p$. Private financial wealth will be greater than the replacement cost of capital. If there is saving for investment out of earnings from public debt, then D_g can be correspondingly higher.)

38. The argument has been extraordinarily influential, yet from a critical perspective its strength is hard to see. For one thing, it rests on a factually incorrect account of the labor market – institutionally wrong, but also econometrically unsound. (Neither employers nor workers make 'marginal' decisions, nor do they act 'as if' they did; the real wage is not inversely related to levels of employment.) For another, the capital theoretic foundations of marginal productivity theory are unsound (Harcourt, 1972; Garegnani, 1970; Laibman and Nell, 1977; Nell, 1992, Chs. 5, 6, 7). And finally, the assumed asymmetric behavior is *ad hoc* and not very plausible.

REFERENCES

Cencini, Alvaro (1995), *Monetary Theory: National and International*, London and New York: Routledge.

Davies, Glyn (1996), *A History of Money: From Ancient Times to the Present Day*, Cardiff: University of Wales Press.

Deleplace, Ghislain and E.J. Nell (1995), *Money In Motion*, London: Macmillan.

Duesenberry, James (1958), *Business Cycles and Economic Growth*, New York: McGraw-Hill.

Freeman, C. (1994), 'Economics of Technical Change', *Cambridge Journal of Economics*, 18: 463–514.

Garegnani, Piero (1970), 'Heterogeneous capital, the production function and the theory of distribution', *Review of Economic Studies*, 37, 407–36.

Goodhart, Charles (1984), *Monetary Theory and Practice,* London: Macmillan.

Hagemann, Harald (1992), 'Traverse analysis in a post-classical model', in D. Halevi, D. Laibman and E.J. Nell, *Beyond the Steady State*, London: Macmillan.

Harcourt, G.C. (1972), *Cambridge Controversies in Capital Theory*, New York: Cambridge University Press.

Harvey, Philip (1989), *Securing the Right to Employment*, Princeton, NJ: Princeton University Press.

Hicks, Sir John (1989), *A Market Theory of Money*, London: Macmillan.

Johnston, Joseph (1970), *Bishop Berkeley's QUERIST in Historcial Perspective*, Dundalk: Dundalgan Press.

Keynes, John Maynard (1930), *Treatise on Money*, London: Macmillan.

Laibman, David and E.J. Nell (1977), 'Reswitching, Wicksell effects and the neo-classical production function,' *American Economic Review*, 63, 100–13.

Lavoie, Marc (1992), *Foundations of Post Keynesian Analysis*, Aldershot: Edward Elgar.

Lowe, Adolph (1976), *The Path of Economic Growth*, Cambridge: Cambridge University Press.
Meulendyke, Ann-Marie (1998), *U.S. Monetary Policy and Financial Markets*, New York: Federal Reserve Bank of New York.
Michie, Jonathan (1987), *Wages in the Business Cycle*, London: Frances Pinter.
Nell, Edward (1988), *Prosperity and Public Spending*, London and New York: Unwin Hyman.
Nell, E.J. (1992), *Tranformational Growth and Effective Demand*, New York: New York University Press.
Nell, E.J. (1996), 'The circuit of money in a production economy', in G. Deleplace and E.J. Nell (eds), *Money in Motion*, London: Macmillan, pp. 246–303.
Nell, Edward (1998a), *The General Theory of Transformational Growth*, Cambridge: Cambridge University Press.
Nell, Edward (ed.) (1998b), *Transformational Growth and the Business Cycle*, New York and London: Routledge.
Nell, E.J. (2002), 'On realizing profits in money', *Review of Political Economy*, 14(4), 519–530.
Nell, E.J. (forthcoming 2003a), 'Monetizing the classical equations', in *The Cambridge Journal of Economics*.
Nell, E.J. (forthcoming 2003b), 'The quantity equation and the classical theory of production and distribution', in G. Mongiovi and F. Petri (eds), *Proceedings of the Sraffa Conference*.
Nell, Edward J. and Reymond Majewski (forthcoming), *Leviathan's Wallet*.
Patinkin, Don (1965), *Money, Interest and Prices*, New York: Harper and Row.
Stein, Herbert (1990), *The Fiscal Revolution in America*, Washington, DC: AEI Press.
Taussig, F.W. (1939), *Principles of Economics, 2 vols, 4th edn revised*, New York: Macmillan.
Wicksell, K. (1962 [1898]), *Interest and Prices*, translation by R.F. Kahn, New York: Augustus Kelley.
Wicksell, K. (1934 [1911]), *Lectures on Political Economy, Vol. II 'Money'*, translation by E. Classen, London: George Allen and Unwin.
Wray, Randall (1998), *Understanding Modern Money*, Cheltenham, UK and Lyme, US: Edward Elgar.
Wulwick, Nancy (1989), 'Phillips' approximate regression', in *Oxford Economic Papers*.

13. Interest rates, profits and economic growth

John Smithin

INTRODUCTION

The purpose of this chapter is to present a simple macroeconomic model that emphasizes the interaction of the (real) interest rate, the 'rate of profit',[1] autonomous demand, and the rate of growth of real GDP. The significance of similar interrelationships for economic performance under capitalism has been stressed, in particular, by Edward J. Nell (1998) in the context of the theory of transformational growth. The analysis here shares this general perspective, while offering different hypotheses about some of the causal relationships.

The model developed here is a revised and up-dated version of earlier constructs put forward in Smithin (1994, 1997). The revision deals specifically with the role of expected aggregate demand, and the functional distribution of income, in the growth process. As in traditional Keynesian models, demand growth is an important determinant of economic growth. Also, interest rates (the return to financial capital) and profits (the return to industrial capital) impact on growth rates in various ways. The results are intended to provide insight into certain aspects of the political economy of a capitalist-type economic system.

PRODUCTION, THE SUPPLY OF OUTPUT, AND THE FUNCTIONAL DISTRIBUTION OF INCOME

Let the relationship between aggregate output, $Y(t)$, and aggregate labor input, $N(t)$, be as follows:

$$Y(t) = A(t)N(t) \tag{13.1}$$

where $A(t)$ is average labor productivity. However the basic premise is to be a model of capitalist 'monetary production,' and hence it is important to recognize the inevitable lapse of time between the planning and execution of the production project, including acquiring the necessary finance (via endogenous credit money), and ultimate sales in the marketplace. This is the essential 'gamble' or 'bet' entailed in making the production decision (Parguez 1996; Rochon 1999). In this simple model a time dimension can therefore be introduced by assuming that output produced in the current period (t) will not actually be available for sale until the next period (t+1). It is not suggested, obviously, that this uniform one-period marketing lag is literally realistically descriptive. It is simply the minimal specification required to introduce the notion that the overall production/sales process takes time. This latter general idea *is* asserted to be both realistic and fundamental. An important implication is that interest charges become an integral part of final production prices.

Given the above assumptions, the income-based breakdown of nominal GDP in the current period (that is calculated from sales in the current period) will be as follows:[2]

$$P(t)Y(t-1) = [1 + k(t-1)][1 + i(t-1)]W(t-1)N(t-1) \tag{13.2}$$

In this expression, $P(t)$ is the aggregate price level, $W(t-1)$ is the nominal wage level prevailing in the last period, $i(t-1)$ is the nominal interest rate prevailing last period, and $k(t-1)$ is the profit share or mark-up (actually realized in the current period) on last period's production.

Now take logarithms of Equation (13.2), and use the convention that a lower case letter represents the logarithm of the corresponding upper case variable ($\ln N = n$, etc.). Also recall that (e.g.) the expression $\ln(1 + k)$ can be approximated by k. After some re-arrangement, this will yield:

$$a(t-1) = k(t-1) + r(t-1) + [w(t) - p(t)] \tag{13.3}$$

where $r(t-1)$ is the real rate of interest prevailing in time $t-1$, defined as $r(t-1) = i(t-1) - [p(t) - p(t-1)]$.[3] There must also be a forward-looking version of Equation (13.3) as seen from the point of view of those planning current production. This will be:

$$a(t) = k(t) + r(t) + [w(t) - p(t)] \tag{13.4}$$

This expression can be described as the 'interest–wage–profit frontier,' and is arguably the fundamental relationship on the supply side in a money-using capitalist economy (Smithin 2001). The average product of labor must resolve itself into three shares in the functional distribution, that is profit, the real rate of interest, and real wages. This notion is clearly reminiscent of the concept of the 'wage–profit frontier' that is a prominent feature of the literature on capital theory deriving originally from Sraffa (1960). The present treatment, however, introduces rentier incomes (or the cost of finance) as a separate charge on the total product.

In fact, it is important to note that the rate of interest is here consistently regarded as a different concept from profit and, in terms of income distribution, is competitive with it. The distinction made is that between the return to lending money or financial resources as such, and the return to entrepreneurial or productive activity. These ideas clearly differ from the neoclassical conception in which the rate of interest is literally identified with the rate of profit on 'capital' (somehow defined). Nell (1998), in contrast, makes clear the distinction between interest and profit, but does argue, nonetheless, that there must be long-run forces in the capitalist economy tending to equalize interest rates, the rate of profit, and the rate of growth, via the process of 'capital arbitrage' (Nell 1998: 162). See also Nell (1988, 1999). In other words, capital funds will be allocated to growth in real assets, or growth in financial assets, depending on the highest rate of return.[4] Another feature of the present treatment, however, is that these forces are held to be weak as between financial investments of various kinds and the activity of actually organizing production, the latter being treated as a sociologically distinct category. Equity investment from this point of view is seen simply as another version of rentier activity.[5] There should, therefore, be arbitrage between (e.g.) the returns on fixed income assets and shares, but *profits* are seen as simply the surplus over and above both wage costs and all 'financing' costs including dividend payments.

AGGREGATE DEMAND CONSIDERATIONS

On the demand side of the model, the starting point is a version of the simple expenditure-based GDP breakdown, $Y = C + I$, where C normally stands for 'consumption' and I for 'investment.' If the current framework is to be interpreted as a pure circulating capital model, however (see note 1), such that the only 'investment' actually going on is that in the wage bill one period in advance, it is better simply to define C as 'expenditure on goods and services by households,' and I as 'expenditure on goods and services by firms,' rather than thinking of the latter as necessarily 'productive' in any way. Expected future nominal aggregate demand, as viewed from the perspective of those making production decisions in the current period, is therefore:

$$P(t+1)Y(t) = P(t+1)C(t+1) + P(t+1)I(t+1) \qquad (13.5)$$

As far as household expenditure is concerned we postulate a straightforward Keynesian-type consumption function:

$$P(t+1)C(t+1) = P(t+1)X(t+1) + cP(t+1)Y(t) \quad (13.6)$$

or, in real terms:

$$C(t+1) = X(t+1) + cY(t) \quad (13.7)$$

where $X(t+1)$ is real expected 'autonomous expenditure,' and c is the traditional marginal propensity to consume (MPC). In other words (recalling the underlying assumption of endogenous money, or a monetary circuit), it is assumed that a certain proportion c of the income created by current production will in future actually be spent on that production, and that there is also a component of household expenditure that is autonomous or exogenous, and about which producers must form an expectation. The assumption of a uniform MPC clearly does draw attention away from the possible impact of differential savings propensities on demand, as occurs, for example, in the 'Cambridge' growth models of Kaldor (1955/56) and Pasinetti (1961/62).[6] The influence of income distribution in the present model comes primarily from the supply side. However, the importance of the impact of profitability on demand as well as on supply is also insisted on. A simple assumption to be made about this is that firms' expenditure should be some function of expected profitability. Using the traditional symbol Π to stand for real profits, a possible specification is:

$$I(t+1) = e\Pi(t+1) \quad (13.8)$$

where e is some positive fraction. Even if firms do choose to designate this expenditure as 'investment,' at this stage in the exposition, as mentioned, we do not need to inquire how far it is actually productive, in the sense of impacting on present or future values of $a(t)$. This may be the intention of some of the individual firms or entrepreneurs making the expenditures (whether they succeed or not), but, equally, the firms may well simply absorb goods and services for their own sake. For example, they may redecorate the boardroom, buy a fancier limousine or executive jet for the use of top management, schedule a sales conference at a golf resort, etc. (Smithin 2001). Therefore, all that equation (13.8) states, in principle, is that firms are willing to devote a certain proportion of their profits to expenditures of one kind or another. In what might be described as the Keynesian tradition, the exposition focuses on the demand-creating aspects of firm expenditures, with any further discussion of an impact on productivity left to the section on technical progress below. We can therefore sum up the aggregate demand side of the model as follows:

$$Y(t) = X(t+1) + cY(t) + e\Pi(t+1) \quad (13.9)$$

This incorporates the basic ingredients of a standard Keynesian-type construct, noting, however, that an *increase* in profits tends to increase demand, via the impact on firms' expenditure, rather than reducing it, as might occur in a framework where only the effect of profitability on consumption is considered.[7]

A SIMPLE MACROECONOMIC MODEL

To derive a complete macroeconomic model from the framework set out above we make the following assumptions: (a) that expected profits will be conditioned by the current realization of profits, and hence that expectations are 'adaptive' in that sense; (b) that we can think of the level of real interest rates as being determined essentially by the monetary policy of the central bank; and (c) that real wages will tend to increase with growth, because of the increased bargaining power of labor.

Obviously the first of these assumptions would have been anathema to the 'rational expectations' theorists of the 1970s, but is defensible on grounds of the reasonableness or plausibility of the assumed behavior. More importantly, the issue of short-run expectations formation loses its strategic significance in the present context. The discussion of these issues in the 1970s took place in the context of simple 'natural rate' models, in which the possibility of any permanent demand-side impact on output, employment or growth was ruled out by assumption. In that context, the only possibility for any non-neutrality result would depend on the ubiquitous nominal rigidities or misperceptions, and apply only in the short run. So-called 'rational expectations' were simply a device to rule out the misperceptions route and hence reduce the short run to the long run in accordance with contemporary ideological preferences. However this kind of logic does not apply in the current model, where, regardless of the assumptions made about expectations, there would *still* be permanent or long-run effects of any demand-side changes. Changing the assumptions about expectations formation in the present framework might cause disagreements about the likely cyclical behavior of the particular economy under consideration, but would not change any of the more fundamental results.

The second assumption implies that the underlying monetary theory is essentially that of the Post-Keynesian 'horizontalist' school (Moore 1988; Lavoie 1992; Rochon 1999). It is important to note, however, that as in Smithin (1994), the central bank is assumed to have substantial influence, not just over nominal rates, but also over the real rate. There is a 'monetary theory of the real rate of interest,' as opposed to a 'real theory of the real rate of interest,' in the terms used (disapprovingly) by Burstein (1995).[8]

The third assumption – that real wages rise with growth – is a hypothesis about macroeconomics and the determinants of real wages at the systemic level, rather than a labor-supply function derived from the theory of labor/leisure choice. It suggests simply that the bargaining power of labor is likely to be enhanced in a fast-growing economy. It is not argued, however, that the parameters of the relationship are derived from microeconomic labor-supply elasticities, or that the level of employment or unemployment that emerges from the system is a chosen position on the part of labor, or is in any sense optimal. Suppose, therefore, that real wage behavior is given by:

$$[w(t) - p(t)] = w_0 + hg(t) \tag{13.10}$$

where w_0 is some base level of real wages (perhaps determined by sociological and institutional considerations), h is a positive coefficient, and $g(t)$ is the current growth rate.

Then, assuming that real interest rates are kept steady at r by monetary policy, equations (13.3) and (13.4) become respectively:

$$a(t-1) = k(t-1) + r + w_0 + hg(t-1) \tag{13.11}$$

$$a(t) = k(t) + r + w_0 + hg(t) \tag{13.12}$$

Now use assumption (a) in equation (13.9), and divide through by $Y(t-1)$:

$$Y(t)/Y(t-1) = X(t+1)/Y(t-1) + c[Y(t)/Y(t-1)] + e[\Pi(t)/Y(t-1)] \tag{13.13}$$

By definition $Y(t)/Y(t-1) = 1 + g(t)$, where $g(t)$ is the growth rate. Also, introduce the notation that $x(t) = X(t+1)/Y(t-1)$, defined as expected autonomous demand for the next period relative to output produced in the previous period. This represents the expected growth of autonomous demand, which for the purposes of the present modeling exercise will henceforth be treated as a parameter, $x(t) = x$. Equation (13.13) can then be rewritten as:

$$g(t) = [1/(1-c)][c + x - 1] + [e/(1-c)][\Pi(t)/Y(t-1)] \tag{13.14}$$

To simplify the notation, allow the expression $\Pi(t)/Y(t-1)$ to be proxied by $k(t-1)$.[9] Using equation (13.11), a simple two-equation macro model is then given by:

$$g(t) = [1/(1-c)][c + x - 1] + [e/(1-c)]k(t-1) \tag{13.15}$$

$$k(t-1) = a(t-1) - r - w_0 - hg(t-1) \tag{13.16}$$

Finally, treating labor productivity also as a parameter a, for the time being, the growth cycle or business cycle in this model will boil down to:

$$g(t) = [1/(1-c)](c + x - 1) - [eh/(1-c)]g(t-1) + [e/(1-c)](a - r - w_0) \quad (13.17)$$

It is interesting to note that the coefficient on lagged growth is negative, which, from the basic theory of difference equations, will lead to oscillating behavior, either damped or explosive depending on the absolute value of the coefficient. If $|eh/(1-c)| < 1$, the system will converge and there will be a steady-state growth rate given by:

$$g = [1/(1-c+eh)][c + x - 1] + [e/(1-c+eh)](a - r - w_0) \quad (13.18)$$

Similarly, a steady-state profit share:

$$k = [h/(1-c + eh)](1 - c - x) + [(1-c)/(1-c+eh)](a - r - w_0) \quad (13.19)$$

Equations (13.18) and (13.19) therefore summarize the long-run determinants of the rate of growth and profit respectively.

A GRAPHICAL INTERPRETATION OF THE RESULTS

The above results can be visualized in a simple graphical framework by constructing the following equilibrium loci:

$$k = a - r - w_0 - hg \quad (13.20)$$

$$k = (1/e)(1 - c - x) + [(1-c)/e]g \quad (13.21)$$

These are summarized in Figure 13.1.

This diagram has a number of precedents, or near-precedents, in the literature. For example, Robinson (1962: 129), as is well-known, draws a bow-shaped figure in a graph with the 'rate of profit' on the vertical axis and the 'rate of accumulation' on the horizontal axis. Both schedules in Robinson's diagram are positively sloped, however, so they do not really correspond to the situation in Figure 13.1 above, where real wage growth tends to cut into profits. Lavoie (1992: 287) also presents a linear version of Robinson's diagram illustrating the 'double-sided nature' of the growth process. There is a more direct analogy between Gordon's (1995) 'social structuralist' model and that in Figure 13.1 Gordon also presents a bow-shaped figure (Gordon 1995: 343),

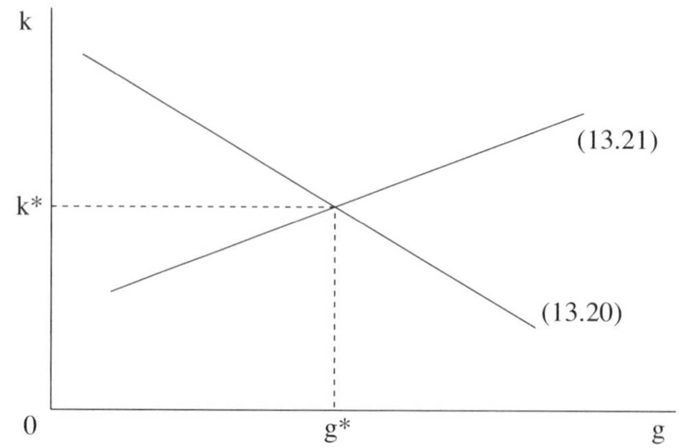

Figure 13.1

though not graphing the profit share or profit rate against the growth rate but against the level of capacity utilization. Interestingly, however, the curvilinear relationship presented by the author is on the supply side of the model, unlike that of Robinson. Gordon's demand side is an upward-sloping straight line, much as in Figure 13.1 In the world depicted by Gordon, an increase in capacity utilization first increases profits (via the spreading of overheads, etc.), but then reduces profit as the bargaining power of labor increases. Figure 13.1 above, therefore, corresponds roughly to the downward-sloping (more pessimistic) section of Gordon's diagrammatic treatment.

As can be seen in Figure 13.1, on the assumptions set out above, there will be a definite relationship between real interest rates, economic growth and the profit share. A lower real rate of interest (a cheap money policy) will increase both the rate of growth and profitability – vice-versa for a fall in interest rates. The rate of interest does therefore determine, or help to determine, profits as in the famous conjecture on this topic by Sraffa (1960: 33).[10] Note, however, the specific way in which interest and profit are related in this context. As mentioned, there is no tendency for the two to be equal; profit and interest are two different concepts. Also, on the definitions used here, a fall in the rate of interest tends to *increase* the profit markup. This seems to accord with commonsense notions of the likely impact on industry of monetary tightening, although it differs from what has sometimes been suggested in theoretical discussion.[11] It should be recalled, of course, that according to the current definitions, the profit share is a residual after both wage and financing costs have been taken into account. If we think, alternatively, of the share of profit as encompassing *both* the return to rentiers and industrial capital, then opposite movements of interest and profit as defined here obviously would at least be compatible with an increase in the total markup over wage costs.

Another Keynesian-style result that seems to follow from the above analysis is that an increase in the (growth of) autonomous demand increases the growth rate. It should be stressed immediately that this is a permanent or 'long-run' effect, as was the interest rate result discussed above. Neither is an artifact of ephemeral short-run rigidities or misperceptions. It is interesting, however, that in the case of a demand expansion, the increased growth and employment is actually accompanied by a fall in profitability. In terms of political economy, this may go some way towards explaining that hostility of business to Keynesian economics sometimes expressed by its leading spokespersons, and which has puzzled some observers (Smithin 1996).[12] The mechanism by which the fall in profit occurs is fairly easy to understand. It is simply a question of the increased growth improving the bargaining power of labor and hence real wages, thereby cutting into profit.[13] This need not occur in the case of lower interest rates, as in that case there is space for an increase in both wages and profits.

Finally note that an exogenous increase in productivity via technical progress will increase both profitability and the rate of growth. In a more realistic scenario, in which productivity was not treated parametrically, this (that is, the increase in profit) would clearly be what provides the incentive for technical progress under capitalism. The next section, therefore, goes on to address this issue, and relaxes the assumption that the productivity of the system is a parameter.

GROWTH WITH ENDOGENOUS TECHNICAL PROGRESS

The possibility to be considered in the current section is that growth itself endogenously improves productivity, in the spirit of 'Verdoorn's law' (Hagemann and Seiter 1999). In this case, the growth/profit relationship in equation (13.20) may be sufficiently altered to become something like:

$$k = a_0 - r - w_0 + (v - h)g \tag{13.22}$$

where a_0 is a positive constant, and v is a coefficient representing the responsiveness or sensitivity of productivity to economic growth. As v is assumed to be positive, the slope of the growth/profit relation on the supply side is now ambiguous. It may continue to be negative, in which case the analysis in Figure 13.1 would go through, but it could also switch round to become positive. The reason for this is that growth now has two effects: It will still improve the bargaining power of labor and hence increase real wages, but there is now also the possibility that technical progress will occur. This may partially or wholly offset the impact on profits. The case of the upward-sloping growth/profit relationship is depicted in Figure 13.2.

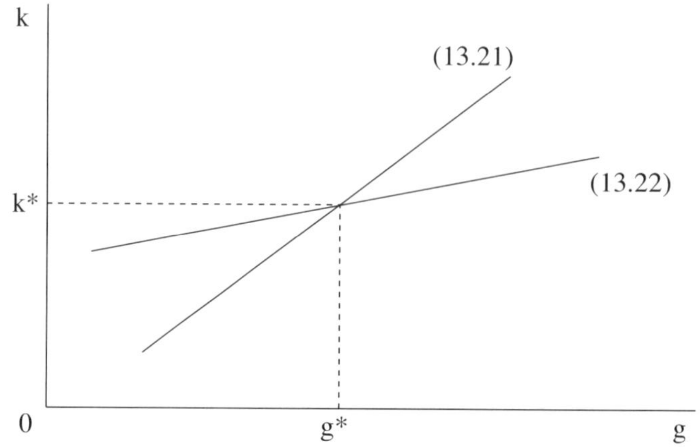

Figure 13.2

If the supply-side growth/profit relationship is upward-sloping, there will likely be a more harmonious relationship between industrial capital and labor. Now a demand-led expansion can increase both profits and real wages. The rate of increase in productivity is more than enough to offset increases in real wages caused by the increased bargaining power of labor. The nature of the business cycle will be altered also, as the negative coefficient in equation (13.17) will now turn positive. One interpretation of this, presumably, is that convergence will be smoother. Under these circumstances of higher growth and a smoother cycle, it is plausible that 'business support' for Keynesian economics might well come around. But, note also that this outcome is dependent on the continued upward rate of productivity growth. If this begins to slacken or fail, the situation can change once again, and we may have a period of breakdown or crisis accompanied by a sharp change in political attitudes.

CONCLUSIONS

This chapter has presented a simple macroeconomic model of economic growth, emphasizing the interaction of the real interest rate, profit, and the rate of growth of autonomous demand. The basic premise is a capitalist monetary production economy with endogenous money, in which the overall production/sales process takes time and requires finance. The real rate of interest on money enters primarily as a component of the cost of production, and it is argued that this concept should be sharply distinguished from profit. The key relationship in the model is an interest–profit–wage frontier, the characteristics of which depend on such things as the bargaining power of labor and the technical progressivity of the system.

One main result of the model is that a cheap money policy (lower real rates of interest) will tend to increase *both* the growth rate and profitability (that is, increase the return earned by industry as opposed to that of the financial sector). However, if the endogenous rate of increase in technical progress is not strong, an increase in the rate of growth of autonomous demand, while it also increases the growth rate, tends rather to reduce profitability. This may help to explain the otherwise puzzling phenomenon, in some circumstances, of business hostility to so-called 'Keynesian economics.' An exogenous improvement in technical progress, as might be expected, increases both the growth rate and profits. Hence the incentive for innovation under capitalism.

If growth itself tends to improve productivity via a technical progress function of some kind, the growth/profit relationship illustrated above *may* be sufficiently altered to become upward-sloping. In this case the rate of increase in productivity is more than enough to offset improvements in the real wage caused by the improved bargaining power of labor. This would imply a more harmonious relationship between labor and industrial capital, as both profits and real wages can increase with demand-led growth. However, it may also perhaps explain periods of breakdown or crisis, in situations where the rate of increase in productivity does not keep pace.

ACKNOWLEDGMENTS

The author would like to thank Hassan Bougrine, Marc Lavoie, Markus Marterbauer, Ed Nell, Mario Seccareccia and Hana Smithin for helpful comments and suggestions that have improved this chapter. The usual disclaimer should apply.

NOTES

1. Strictly speaking the variable defined as $k(t)$ below can only be interpreted as a 'rate of profit' in a pure circulating capital model with no fixed capital. Otherwise it would have to be described as a 'profit share' or 'markup,' and a profit rate *per se* could only be calculated if we possess some method of valuation of existing capital. For these reasons the present framework is, in fact, set up essentially as a circulating capital construct, and the various terms are used interchangeably. I am grateful to Marc Lavoie for discussion of this point.
2. It does not make any difference for present purposes whether all the goods produced last period are actually sold or not. Unintended inventory accumulation at current prices can be counted as part of GDP.

3. The term $p(t)$ is, of course, an expected variable as seen from the vantage point of time $(t–1)$.
4. See also Lavoie et al. (2000) who provide a detailed discussion of the theoretical issues and present empirical evidence on the interest/growth relation using Canadian and US data.
5. *Cf.* Robinson (1956: 8) who writes that: '[T]he institution of limited liability . . . has brought about a divorce between ownership and control, which makes many shareholders, in effect, more like lenders than entrepreneurs.'
6. Slattery and Slattery (1998) have provided an interesting extension to the Kaldor/Pasinetti model that includes rentier incomes as a separate category.
7. On this point see the discussion by Gordon (1995: 244–5).
8. Choosing the real rate as an independent variable does have the advantage of enabling the discussion to focus only on the so-called 'real' variables of the model rather than on inflation. A number of different inflation theories would be compatible with the growth theory developed here.
9. Strictly, $\Pi(t)/Y(t–1) = k(t–1)//[1 + k(t–1)]$, so this represents an approximation of roughly the same order of magnitude as in equations (13.3) and (13.4) above.
10. According to Sraffa (1960: 33): '[T]he rate of profit . . . is . . . susceptible of being determined from outside the system of production, in particular by the level of the money rates of interest.'
11. *Cf.* the discussion by Mongiovi (1996: 114–15) of the model suggested by Pivetti (1985). In that framework, the overall rate of profit, r^*, is defined by the sum of the money rate of interest and the 'normal' rate of profit, that is, $r^* = i + r^n$. If r^n is taken as given, an increase in i must increase overall r^*. In the argument here, industrial profits are variable rather than fixed, and it is changes in the latter that are at issue rather than the total markup. See also Davidson (1996).
12. It may seem obvious why rentiers would oppose expansion and full employment; they would prefer a high interest rate – and hence, high unemployment – regime. If, however, it is assumed that profits usually increase with growth, it would be less easy to explain why industry might be opposed to expansion. The point is that profits may *not* increase with growth in all circumstances.
13. Interestingly enough, some of the recent neoclassical literature has stressed this mechanism (as a cause for complaint). Balls (2000) reviewing some of the literature circulated by the NBER in the USA states that some recent studies have been making 'crowding out' arguments relating to the impact of government spending on growth; that is, high government spending leads to higher wages (in both the public and private sectors), which leads to lower profits, and hence to lower private sector investment. Note, however, that in the present model the lower profits are still associated with higher (demand-led) growth, not lower growth, so it becomes a question of political economy as to whether or not this is a good thing.

REFERENCES

Balls, A. (2000), 'How government spending slows growth,' *NBER Digest*, January.

Burstein, M.L. (1995), *Classical Macroeconomics for the Next Century*, Toronto: York University.

Davidson, P. (1996), 'In defence of post Keynesian economics: a response to Mongiovi,' in S. Pressman (ed.), *Interactions in Political Economy: Malvern after Ten Years*, London: Routledge, 120–32.

Gordon, D.M. (1995), 'Growth, distribution and the rules of the game: social structuralist macro foundations for a democratic economic policy,' in G.A. Epstein and H.M. Gintis (eds), *Macroeconomic Policy After the Conservative Era*, Cambridge: Cambridge University Press, 335–83.

Hagemann, H. and S. Seiter (1999), 'Verdoorn's law,' in P.A. O'Hara (ed.), *Encyclopedia of Political Economy*, London: Routledge, 1228–31.

Kaldor, N. (1955/56), 'Alternative theories of distribution,' *Review of Economic Studies*, 23: 94–100. As reprinted in Sen (1970: 81–91).
Keynes, J.M. (1936), *The General Theory of Employment Interest and Money*, London: Macmillan.
Lavoie, M. (1992), *Foundations of Post-Keynesian Economics Analysis*, Aldershot, UK and Brookfield, US: Edward Elgar.
Lavoie, M., G. Rodriguez and M. Seccareccia (2000), 'Transformational growth, interest rates and the golden rule', Paper presented at the annual meetings of the Canadian Economics Association, Vancouver, May.
Mongiovi, G. (1996), 'Some critical observations on Post Keynesian macroeconomics,' in S. Pressman (ed.), *Interactions in Political Economy: Malvern after Ten Years*, London: Routledge, 110–19.
Moore, B.J. (1988), *Horizontalists and Verticalists: The Macroeconomics of Credit Money,* Cambridge: Cambridge University Press.
Nell, E.J. (1988), 'Does the rate of interest determine the rate of profit,' *Political Economy: Studies in the Surplus Approach* 4, (2): 263–67.
Nell, E.J. (1998), *The General Theory of Transformational Growth: Keynes After Sraffa*, Cambridge: Cambridge University Press.
Nell, E.J. (1999), 'Wicksell after Sraffa: capital arbitrage and normal rates of growth, interest and profits,' in G. Mongiovi and F. Petri (eds.), *Value, Distribution and Capital: Essays in Honor of Pierangelo Garegnani*, London: Routledge, 266–93.
Parguez, A.(1996), 'Beyond scarcity: a reappraisal of the theory of the monetary circuit,' in G. Deleplace and E.J. Nell (eds), *Money in Motion: The Post Keynesian and Circulation Approaches,* London: Macmillan.
Pasinetti, L. (1961/62), 'Rate of profit and income distribution in relation to the rate of economic growth,' *Review of Economic Studies* 29: 267–79. As reprinted in Sen (1970: 92–111).
Pivetti, M. (1985), 'On the monetary explanation of distribution,' *Political Economy: Studies in the Surplus Approach*, 1: 73–103.
Robinson, J. (1956), *The Accumulation of Capital*, London: Macmillan.
Robinson, J. (1962), 'A model of accumulation,' in *Essays in the Theory of Economic Growth*, London: Macmillan, 34–59. As reprinted in Sen (1970: 115–40).
Rochon, L-P. (1999), *Credit, Money and Production*, Cheltenham, UK and Northampton, US: Edward Elgar.
Sen, A. (ed.) (1970), *Growth Economics*, Harmondsworth: Penguin Education.
Slattery, E. and S.P. Slattery (1998), 'The rentier in a Post Keynesian/Kaleckian macro economic model,' Paper presented at the annual meeting of the Academy of Economics and Finance, Montgomery, Alabama, February.
Smithin, J. (1994), *Controversies in Monetary Economics: Ideas, Issues and Policy*, Aldershot, UK and Brookfield, US: Edward Elgar.
Smithin, J. (1996), *Macroeconomic Policy and the Future of Capitalism: The Revenge of the Rentiers and the Threat to Prosperity*, Cheltenham, UK and Brookfield, US: Edward Elgar.
Smithin, J. (1997), 'An alternative monetary model of inflation and growth,' *Review of Political Economy*, 9 (4), October: 395–409.
Smithin, J. (2001), 'Profit, the rate of interest, and "entrepreneurship" in contemporary capitalism,' *Kurswechsel*, 2/01, July: 89–100.
Sraffa, P. (1960), *Production of Commodities by Means of Commodities: Prelude to a Critique of Economic Theory*, Cambridge: Cambridge University Press.

Interlude II

ROUNDTABLE DISCUSSION

FORSTATER: This afternoon I'm pleased to moderate a panel of distinguished visitors and local scholars. Since they all are familiar to you, I'm not going to run through their many publications and accomplishments. Please join me in welcoming our panel. First, from Middlebury College, we have David Colander. Next is the graduate faculty's Robert Heilbroner. Then James Duesenberry from Harvard University, Robert Eisner from Northwestern University, Edward Nell, also from the graduate faculty of the New School, and finally, Richard Musgrave from Harvard University.

Proposing, as we do, to revive the Functional Finance approach to macroeconomic policy and develop it for today's world, we are brought face to face with a number of problems. How can we respond to the current (1998) enthusiasm in the US, for balanced budgets, even for running surpluses to pay down the national debt? In Europe, where it is proposed that national powers to run independent fiscal policy be forfeited to a common currency managed by an independent central bank, will there be any room for Functional Finance? On the other hand, recent crises seem to indicate that the international financial system is pretty fragile. Let's consider each of these situations in turn.

PART I

Presently, in the United States and in other countries, there is strong support across the political spectrum for balanced budgets and even for running a surplus in order to begin to pay down national debts. What are the possible economic impacts of this trend and how will it affect national economic policy in the near future? I would like to ask Professor Musgrave to begin.

RICHARD MUSGRAVE: Political pressure supports debt repayment as a way to reduce interest payments and save Social Security. However, debt repayment also serves to check spending. If the US economy continues to be as strong as it has been, it will generate potential surpluses. But the possibility of setting them aside for Social Security reserves may well be outweighed by pressure for tax reduction.

The public is really not concerned about public debt. Their real concern is tax reduction and reduction in the size of the public sector. On the other hand, once the economy slackens and it is not a certainty that debt reduction will have significant effects on interest rates, attitudes toward debt reduction will change very quickly. The recent attitude of the IMF toward Japan reveals that policy is still very much directed by the neoclassical synthesis, that is, the Keynesian model. If the economy slackens, bigger deficits will be drawn. So I don't think surpluses will be applied toward paying down the debt.

ROBERT EISNER: The impact of this kind of thinking is quite unfavorable. There is a widespread misunderstanding as to the nature of the balanced budget and the surplus we are now having. They are only to a minor extent due to the reduction in the inflation- and cyclically-adjusted deficit.

Interestingly, most of this deficit reduction has resulted from the surge in the economy. There may well be very substantial surpluses. We've been underestimating the strength of the economy as well as the impact of this strength on taxes because the distribution of income has turned out to be so heavily weighted toward the rich and those in higher tax brackets. Looking at the capital gains that are being cashed in, we may well continue to have substantial surpluses. My concern is first that, if we continue running surpluses, the macro pressures will at some point slow the economy, limit our growth and increase unemployment.

Second, there is a great need in both the short run and the long run for public investment, particularly in education, research, infrastructure and health. All of these are jeopardized by the commitment to run a surplus and pay off the debt. Think how much we could do to meet these needs beyond paying off a relatively minuscule amount of debt. We could do much more than Clinton has proposed. Ultimately, paying off the debt is a terrible menace.

I'm alarmed at some of the current proposals for Social Security reform. The real danger to Social Security comes from its alleged saviors. Some of the proposals that use the surplus to shore up Social Security – beyond accounting – would do no such thing. In reality the surplus would be used to pay down the debt.

JAMES DUESENBERRY: I agree with much of that, but let me note the temporary bulge in tax revenue because of the capital gains boom. That will continue for a couple of years even if the market suddenly goes soft. But it won't last indefinitely; it's a one-shot thing.

There is another concern. Sooner or later, we are going to have a slump of some sort. I'm not necessarily predicting a recession, but I think we would like to be prepared if there were one. We need automatic stabilizers beyond the ones we now have that, incidentally, we don't respect. If we have any kind of slowdown, we automatically go into some kind of deficit. There is such ideological force behind balancing the budget that even in a situation in which the desirability of a deficit should be obvious to everyone, even in a downswing, a big push develops to cut expenditures in order to balance the budget.

ROBERT HEILBRONER: I think there are two quite separate, but somehow overlapping questions in this important concern with government spending. One has to do with how most economists understand the 'deficit' problem; the other with how almost all non-economists – including many congressmen, government officials and, I dare say, all voters – see it. I shall dramatize the difference with what will appear to be a dangerous assertion: Very few, if indeed any, economists think that 'deficits' in themselves are a problem. This is because economists know something that non-economists have yet to learn – namely, that the word 'deficit' means only one thing: borrowing. The word does not mean or imply squandering, committing fiscal sins, or incurring dangerous burdens.

To understand 'deficit' as 'borrowing' sheds a powerful light. Of course, one can borrow money and regret it, as every householder and businessman knows; but one can also borrow money and gain from it, as many a family that has taken out a much needed home mortgage, or business that has borrowed to increase its profitability, can testify.

'Ah,' the skeptic will reply, 'but that only applies to financially sound households and profitable businesses.' True. But is government less financially sound than households or businesses? Does not every national government have the power to create money, which no householder or business can do? And are not US Treasury bonds always ranked first and foremost in terms of creditworthiness?

So why do non-economists consider deficits – that is, government borrowing – to be so wicked and/or dangerous? The only answer is that the word 'deficit' suggests a shortage of something. Of what? Not creditworthiness. Can it be legality? Unlike individual borrowings, government borrowings – deficits – are established by legislative action. Is it, then, the purposes to which government borrowings are put that are considered wicked compared with private borrowings?

The answer is that, of course, deficit money can be used for bad purposes – for example, building a highway where it isn't needed. But private borrowing can also be used for ill, as when a firm borrows to improve its profitability by flooding the airwaves with television advertising for a defective product.

How then, can we separate good borrowing, both public and private, from bad? The only answer is by careful follow-ups and fearless reporting of both public and private expenditure, not to mention a strong sense of social responsibility for both. Is that asking a lot? It is. But it asks it equally of private and public undertakings, and the questions apply whether the projects are financed by income or by borrowing.

EISNER: I have a suggestion. For the government, the deficit is defined as borrowing aside from the creation of money. For businesses, borrowing is not a deficit because they have capital purchases. Suppose we take balance to be defined as a situation in which the debt grows in proportion to national income. Suppose it is established, as a rule of thumb, that the current operating budget being balanced, the government will then borrow for investment purposes. Properly accounted for, an amount of borrowing equal to that investment will keep the debt growing at a constant rate.

Let's turn to your question regarding the amount of government investment and borrowing. To begin, the government wants to keep public capital stock in a constant ratio to GDP. This could be amended to say that we've decided the government side could be less or more. But having chosen a ratio, sticking to that ratio would be the first rule of thumb.

HEILBRONER: All I ask is that the budget problem, to be resolved, have an explanation that can be understood by the public. Whether that is the maintenance of constant ratios or the targeting of a deficit amount, makes no difference to me at all.

MUSGRAVE: What, according to you, is the budget problem that needs to be resolved?

HEILBRONER: I mean only that the government be allowed by law to have a capital budget with some expenditures – not called 'deficits' – that are part of a capital account budget, so that they can be regarded as legitimate and taken off the agenda of wickedness. It's the aura of wickedness that makes things difficult.

MUSGRAVE: The question is that, if you have such a rate, will it be at all times the correct rate? Keeping public capital in a constant ratio to GDP really takes fiscal policy out of stabilization.

HEILBRONER: Not necessarily, because it is not that large. If you could run externalities on each and every bill that is brought up, fine. But that cannot be done. A way must be found to allow the government to borrow an amount sufficient to fulfill necessary capital requirements. That's all I'm asking.

DUESENBERRY: Maybe we're spending too much time on the capital question. Looking at federal capital expenditures, we've got $50 or $60 billion total; all of the federal, state and local gross spending, without any depreciation, is around $200 or $250 billion. In talk about government deficits, the rhetoric may be about infrastructure, but the practice is programs like Medicare. In the Reagan budget, the tax reduction component had two expenditure components: a big defense component and, while it was not part of Reagan's policy, a big, built-in expansion of Medicare.

NELL: I wouldn't criticize Medicare.

DUESENBERRY: No, but you don't solve the problem of deciding the level of deficits by establishing a capital budget.

ALL: How do you do it?

MUSGRAVE: I don't know whether we are discussing appropriate policy or how to calm an uncomprehending public. If you assume an economy that calibrates full employment, then, in such a setting, a budgetary rule that buffers the capital budget and stabilizes the current budget is desirable. Also, as it supports intergenerational equity, it really makes sense. But do we want a capital budget rule on those grounds? Or do we want it because, given the stupidity of the public, the capital budget will allow us to get away with a bigger deficit?

HEILBRONER: We are trying to do two things at once. The idea is to try to find a politically acceptable way of doing what economists know should be done. If everybody were an economist and thought like Bob Eisner, there would be no problem.

MUSGRAVE: But what if the economy is such that it does not equilibrate at full employment, and suppose it turns out that we need a deficit bigger than the capital budget?

DAVID COLANDER: I have two brief points. First, using a capital budget confuses the issue because it is unclear what the capital budget is. Second, it is important to remember that we are talking about an $8 trillion economy. Quite honestly, I believe that the politically acceptable surpluses or deficits of $100 billion dollars or so are too small to make much of a difference at all in such a huge economy. The political debate is usually about such small amounts that it doesn't make a damn bit of difference what the government does.

EISNER: David has a point. As much as Heilbroner would like to have his deficits to keep the economy going, I think we lose sight of the fact that we are talking about very small amounts in an $8 trillion economy. Of course, this leads to arguments with those who differ, those who claim deficits haven't done any good just because they're too small. Remember what happened during the New Deal days and World War II. We got out of a depression by spending.

COLANDER: What you are talking about is enough spending to matter, a deficit that's going to operate outside the corridor of normal operations. Only at that point can we start talking about functional finance. It certainly is not one little pebble that's being dropped. The deficit has to be large enough to make a sizeable wave – three or four percentage points of GDP.

AUDIENCE MEMBER: If you are about talking three or four percentage points, then think politically, and take a look at what Clinton was pushing as an approach to running a deficit. With amounts of $3 billion to $15 billion, they were having an enormous argument about a minuscule percentage that wouldn't have made a bit of difference one way or the other.

DUESENBERRY: If we're going to talk about such a small amount, then there's no problem: it doesn't matter one way or the other. But we do not want to take the attitude that there is no problem in public debt. If we look at the current budget, we see that there is something like $250 billion of interest. Now, you might say that half of that is reducing principal through the crisis bank. There are people who are screaming about not wanting to pay more taxes and yet we have built up, through the policies of the early 1980s, a charge on the budget that goes on for a long time. As Bob Eisner just mentioned, if we want to have at any given time a fixed target for the ratio of government debt to the GDP, then what happens if the target ratio is raised and taxes are reduced, or if there are some current expenditures? Taking the tax reduction first (because it's the worst case), we can then go backwards from that. If taxes are reduced then, over time, the interest burden will gradually build until we wind up with the same taxes with which we began.

It amounts to the classic case of borrowing to spend now, and ending up with greater expenditures later. The only difference is that if the cycle takes a long time, there is an inter-generational transfer. How far that kind of transfer should be pushed must be compared with what is gained.

It depends upon which way the bids go, but people seem to be worried more about their children than about what they are getting out of the spending currently. That's the ultimate question to be rationalized: What you get now versus what you're going to give up in the future. I don't think we can play the game of saying, 'You're never going to give up anything in the future,' unless you say that, periodically, we're going to have an inflationary period that will wipe out the burden of the debt.

EISNER: That must be related to a growing economy.

DUESENBERRY: The target ratio can be raised.

EISNER: That would, of course, raise the interest burden. I insist that it is a political problem rather than an economic problem. The word 'transfer' is correct. Interest payments are not even counted in the federal debt, nor in the national income. Two or three per cent of GDP is not a big amount. It is a political rather than an economic issue. I don't know that the transfer affects the distribution of income very much. I am often told that the rich own the government debt and they are getting the interest and us poor people are paying the taxes. I suspect it is rather the other way around. The rich are not dumb enough to own taxable interest in government bonds. And the rich are paying much more of the taxes than the poor. (I don't mind that they're paying them.) I don't see that there is even a distributional problem. But it *is* a political problem.

DUESENBERRY: It is a political problem in the sense that we have people who make a big fuss over very small tax reductions, reductions even smaller than the deficit considerations earlier. Suppose we ask . . ., how much? What kind of taxes are implied by the interest burden of these deficits? A few bucks apiece. So that if they're that fussy about their taxes then what about the tax burden that results when you talk about deficits of 3 or 4 per cent of GDP? But the total federal revenue is only 20 per cent of the GDP. So it ain't hay. We should not just forget about deficits. The deficit is a real subject.

NELL: I'd like to make two points about the deficit that need to be borne in mind. Even many of the economists' concepts of the deficit probably need some better adjustment. For example, a number of taxes fall on savings. To compute the stimulative effect of a deficit we should not calculate 'expenditure minus taxes.' It is expenditure minus taxes that fall on income that will be used to fund expenditure. In so far as, for example, the recent expansion of tax collections comes from taxes on capital gains, on corporate profits, and on the well-to-do, we might expect a fairly large component of that to be savings, which would have been a withdrawal.

The demand-effect of a deficit comes from the fact that it represents the difference between an injection and a withdrawal. If the taxes fall on a portion of income that is already a withdrawal, it will not be withdrawn twice. So the net stimulative effect has to be properly computed.

Next, some kinds of expenditures may have a larger multiplier-effect than others. Some kinds of expenditures may simply, in effect, go into savings. We need to re-think the stimulative aspect of the deficit.

MUSGRAVE: I might add that that was a big concern in the 1930s, the computation of the impact of deficits, depending on what taxes were cut and what expenditures were made.

NELL: The Conference Board used to compute measures of 'fiscal thrust,' as they called it, which were designed to capture the same idea. It seems that this has definitely passed out of public discussion.

Another obvious point relates to the questions as to why the Reagan deficits didn't have more of a stimulative effect? Obviously, they were offset by a foreign trade deficit. On the other hand, Bob Eisner has quite correctly pointed to the fact that not all foreign trade deficit is in fact a withdrawal. But it is still the case that there is a foreign trade deficit, and that it does represent a diminution of purchasing power. To the extent that this is so, the foreign trade deficit does represent a diversion of purchasing power from internal or domestic to foreign sources. To calculate the overall stimulative impact, this needs to be carefully accounted. A domestic deficit has to be adjusted for the foreign trade deficit.

EISNER: I would like to respond to one of Ed Nell's points concerning the measuring of the impact of the deficit, which I think we frequently miss. I hate to say it, but the counter-cyclical effect may be considerably less than the long-run effect. Keeping in mind some of the income hypotheses – or any of Jim Duesenberry's work on consumption – we will find that if we have a deficit that represents a short-run portion of purchasing power, it is not likely to have as much effect as something that people can count on as permanent income.

Indeed, as I've often argued, this really is a substantial limitation of counter-cyclical fiscal policy, especially tax policy. There has to be either direct government expenditures for goods and services, which make up a deficit, or tax cuts of an inter-temporal substitution nature, so that, for example, there will be a subsidy to borrow. Or taxes have to be cut if people, for example, buy a car, or make certain expenditures now rather than later. To the extent that there is simply a change in the income tax receipts, the effect is going to be much less than some people might hope.

HEILBRONER: I want to ask one last question. Do you think there will be intelligent voting in the Senate and in the House and from the public, as long as they don't understand what 'the deficit' means?

COLANDER: I think we will get unintelligent voting even if they do understand what the deficit means.

AUDIENCE MEMBER: Perhaps there is a solution in what Clinton and Gingrich discovered – what might be called homeopathic political economy – in which more and more debate is spent on smaller and smaller government measures, thereby satisfying the public's feeling for democratic discussion. The damage politicians can do is minimized by keeping their hands off anything of any size.

HEILBRONER: I would like to reverse that. I would like to remove some of the glaze that the word 'deficit' throws over people's eyes. Then there would certainly be grounds for intelligent, informed disagreement about how it should be used for war purposes and so on.

EISNER: One possibility is to change the way the deficit is described, for example, 'We're running this deficit to finance highways and create jobs for people in the construction industry.'

DUESENBERRY: We can't say we're 'running deficits.' We have to say we're 'making an investment' in highways.

COLANDER: Yes, you change the nature of it. You can call it 'full employment deficit.' The history of deficits and how they have worked bears witness to an inherent public reaction against deficits and against attempts at its redefinition. There has been a series of redefinitions, and other games along those lines. None have made a difference. There's just a built-in reaction against the idea of the deficit.

DUESENBERRY: There's an inherent reaction against expenditure too. Let's remember that Reagan also threw a rock through a jewelry store window. The Democrats all rushed in to join in the looting, and nobody complained.

JOHN SMITHIN: Bill Mitchell argued before the break that anyone who talks in terms of the correct ratio or what the right budget deficit is and so on and so forth is, well – nuts.

NELL: I was going to raise the same question. It seems to me that there is another important thing for us to think about, and I can show it to you, right here. Here is a five-pound note from the Bank of England. [Holding up a five-pound note.] Written on it is 'I promise to pay the bearer on demand, the sum of five pounds,' signed by the Chief Cashier. This note is meant to be convertible. Now, what it is convertible to, I suspect, is five one-pound coins.

DUESENBERRY: That's right. Someone sent a ten-dollar federal reserve note to some bank in Cleveland, and they sent back two fives.

NELL: This is an example, in a certain sense, of backward thinking or cultural lag. This is fiat money, or bank money. It has nothing to do with convertibility into anything of some intrinsic or other kind of value. Nor does it have anything to do with a gold standard or anything of that sort. American money now claims to be legal tender – period. We used to have silver certificates and, until the early 1960s, silver had to be kept at West Point to provide 'backing' for these notes. No longer. The point is that when we are talking in terms of a monetary system that is grounded, in a sense, in government taxes and in the prices that are paid in the government budget, then we do not need to worry about deficits. Deficits are simply a non-issue in this kind of system. The question has as much or as little substance as the 'I promise to pay the bearer' claim.

Think of it this way. We pay taxes with dollar bills that the Internal Revenue Service burns! What are these things that are paid in taxes collected on April 15 and promptly burned? They are burned because they're old and worn, and it's too much trouble to sort the good ones out, and so on. So taxes reduce the money supply! And it's just the same when you pay with a check – the Treasury's account with the Fed is credited, and that account is not part of the money supply. Of course, somewhere along the way, new money is going to be issued. But when? When it is needed. It is not issued to replace what is being canceled.

Louis XIV had problems. He had to collect coins to pay his troops. On several occasions, campaigns were endangered, virtually lost, because he couldn't pay his soldiers. Taxes meant bringing in money, and if you couldn't collect taxes, you couldn't borrow either. If there isn't enough in taxes, why would anyone lend to the King? If you can't collect taxes, how are you going to pay your lenders? So there was a big problem in raising money for military purposes. By contrast, the United States, since World War II, has not had that problem. It can simply issue money.

MUSGRAVE: How much in taxes do you have to collect to make this fiat money valuable? Is it one dollar? Is it one cent? Or is it twenty trillion dollars? What is the amount?

NELL: That's a great question. I've tried to speculate on the answer to that in my chapter. The taxes have to impact directly or indirectly on everyone, and be enough to be noticeable. But beyond that, I must say, I couldn't get very far.

DUESENBERRY: If the acceptability of a certain kind of fiat money is established once, it doesn't have to be done over and over again.

NELL: Let's suppose that the government is trying to establish a certain set of prices in its budget. Its budget has to be large enough that failure to sell to the government is going to create a significant problem. In other words, it has to have a substantial multiplier effect on the economy. It is surely no accident that, historically, fiat money comes into being when government expenditure on goods and services rises into double digits or even up to 20 per cent.

MUSGRAVE: But couldn't legal tender simply be issued to buy for needs at cost?

NELL: Absolute monarchs did that, but it didn't always work. Charlemagne, for example, lost control of the currency and private minting took over.

DUESENBERRY: In the US, we went from the Civil War until the First World War with the government's big problem being what to do with its surpluses. There was the fiat money system, national bank notes and, primarily, private banks. We didn't even have a central bank until 1914. We had a collection of state-chartered banks and national banks with a small base in federal debt. The problem with the fiat money system was that government wasn't doing anything financially; the quantity circulating in the country was negligible.

After the Civil War, inflation stopped, and there was deflation. The last part of the nineteenth century was a deflationary period. Maybe, if the government had done more, it would have been less so. But the fact that it didn't disturb the acceptability of the currency once it had been established – nor the acceptability of the bulk of the money supply, which is after all, not notes but bank deposits – has nothing to do with the government. There was private bank money, without a central bank. So currency remains acceptable once it has been accepted.

HEILBRONER: Do you fellows want to take away the mystique that now obscures the meaning of the word 'deficit,' that separates it from borrowing? I'm sure the answer is yes, of course you want people to know that the word 'deficit' means borrowing. They do not know that.

How can they possibly make a reasonable decision when the word 'deficit' implies wickedness? Ideally, the President would explain all this. I would like a way to allow the government to have a certain amount of spending, which I presume will be done for capital purposes, for which they do not bear an onus.

EISNER: We should tell the public that everybody borrows. Households borrow and businesses borrow.

FORSTATER: I am going to abuse my role as moderator by taking the last word on this issue before going on to the next question. I would like to read a brief quote from Jim Tobin.

For every buyer there is a seller. For every lender, a borrower. One person's expenditure is another's receipt. My debts are your assets. My deficit, your surplus. If the prudent among us insist on running and lending surpluses, some of us are willy-nilly going to have to finance budget deficits. When no one else ends up borrowing the surpluses of the thrifty, the Treasury ends up doing so. The truisms – that borrowing is a counterpart to lending and deficits the counterpart of surpluses – are overlooked in popular and congressional discussions of government budgets and taxes. The moral is inescapable, if startling. If you would like the federal deficit to be smaller, the deficits of business must be bigger. Would you like the federal government to run a surplus and reduce its debt? In business, deficits must be big enough to absorb that surplus, as well as the funds available from households and financial institutions. It's a matter of accounting identities. As long as there is a desire to net save on the part of the public, then the government is going to have to run a budget deficit.

PART II

FORSTATER: Let's move on to our second set of issues: The current trend towards monetary integration – as in the economic and monetary union in Europe – will mean that certain sovereign powers, upon which functional finance is founded, will no longer hold. What are the political and economic implications of these and similar plans? And how will such arrangements affect nations' abilities to conduct coordinated fiscal and monetary policies?

MUSGRAVE: Looking at the European Union, I think there are two issues. The basic question is whether there can be a uniform macro policy within a uniform currency area if there are rigidities and incomplete factor mobility. It's easy to sense the analogy, 'If it can be done in the US, why can it not also be done in Europe?' But Europe is not the US because, in Europe, factor mobility is very incomplete, and there is a different attitude toward labor and labor's rights. I think it's very questionable whether the American experience can be duplicated.

The second question is, of course, what are the arrangements – monetary and fiscal – going to be? There is only a uniform monetary policy, but there is no fiscal policy. There can be no uniform fiscal policy because there is a 3 per cent deficit limitation. On both these grounds, it is very questionable whether this experiment will work. It seems to me that, absent factor mobility, there must be the probability for regional differentiation in policy. It is very difficult to have that with a central monetary policy. I think, in the end, there would have to be some retreat to give flexibility for member-state fiscal policy differentials.

DUESENBERRY: I certainly agree with what you have said, but I am not even sure that budgetary flexibility for national governments solves the problem.

They will be in somewhat the same situation as the American states, which have constitutional budgetary flexibility as far as the federal constitution is concerned, but do, in fact, have limitations on their capacity to borrow. Let's say that they would have no limitations on their capacity to run deficits, but limitations on capacity to borrow because of their status as essentially private borrowers who are unable to increase the money supply to pay off debts. On top of whatever European Union restrictions there may be, there's a financial market restriction on local fiscal policy. I don't know that either one of them has to be totally changed, but together they clearly can cause lots of trouble.

In addition to the movement of populations and expenditures between regions, there is also the whole system of fiscal interchange that we have in the US between the federal government and the states. In Europe, that kind of fiscal interchange is mostly concentrated on transfer to the low-income countries and on common agricultural policy. That tends to chew up the Brussels budget, leaving not very much to push around to deal with any national problem. I agree with the thrust of what has been said, although I think conditions are even worse.

EISNER: On this financial matter, though, there is something to be considered. EU countries are not going to be in the situation of a sovereign government that grows its own money. Perhaps that shouldn't be that severe a problem. After all, businesses borrow in this country all the time and they can't create money. And households borrow. At least, a reasonably strong government, as in France, can borrow. People would be happy to buy their debt and they can run a deficit that way.

There is another problem that bothers me very much and of which you are all aware, and that is the 3 per cent budget deficit limit. Maybe I'm overly optimistic, but it seems to be turning out that, with Europe again recovering, their deficit will get down below 3 per cent. They will have some flexibility there as well.

NELL: I'm worried about the creation of a money monetary unit that has no fiscal policy behind it. The ability of the central European government to conduct a fiscal policy was virtually non-existent. Yes, there are some expenditures and some revenue sources that are open to it, but only to a very small degree.

If this does not expand, the European monetary unit has no fiscal policy backing it. We've just said that taxation is a source of backing for this. Of course there is taxation, and taxes by member states will be paid in the European currency. But this still differs from full-scale fiscal policy, and I'm not sure how to examine it. I'm not sure what the implications are, but I suspect that it's very important that the Maastrich rules are being enforced because they will prevent a collapse of the value of this money. That is to say, the European Union is tying itself into a situation of slow growth and permanent unemployment.

In thinking about the issue, we should be careful about discussing 'capital flows,' particularly short-term capital flows. These are not really flows of capital. They are flows of *money*. No act of saving created them, nor are they destined for investment. They represent money created by banks, uncontrolled money.

EISNER: I think we ought to be sure we understand the issues concerning financial flows. Billions of dollars flow but, thinking of Tobin, we need to remember that for every flow, if dollars move out, somebody else is holding them. It is really a churning rather than a flow.

People somehow have the image that we're exporting capital. We're not exporting capital. The Russians may be exporting capital when their new millionaires buy castles in Switzerland and move into them. That's really taking capital out. But this currency is going back and forth. Somebody else owns the security. It may change prices and that may have some impact.

DUESENBERRY: First, we are not exporting capital. The US as a whole has been importing capital for the last ten years. On the other hand it is also true that, in terms of growth, we have had very big outflows and inflows, a mass of planes on both sides of the waters that, in the sense of the net debt position of the nation, cancel each other out. However, they do not cancel each other in terms of the troubles they create. In Asia, the basic problem was a great deal of bad banking abetted, and encouraged, by a lot of corruption.

What is really amazing, of course, is that the European banks were lending on apparently very little information. They were greatly surprised when things went wrong. By and large, macro policy was not the issue, though it was somewhat of a problem. It seems to me that serious international standards of banking supervision would have done a lot of good.

FORSTATER: As has been noted, a country like Turkey does not seem to have any problems continuing to borrow quadrillion billion lira a week, whereas Orange County, California has gone bankrupt. Are the nations of Europe, by signing on to the Maastrich Treaty and the EMU, placing themselves in the position of US state and local governments? The difference between Orange County and Turkey is that Orange County cannot print its own currency.

EISNER: I have an answer to that question: The governments of France and Germany are not Orange County. I don't know how stupidly Orange County is run, but they put all manner of restrictions on their abilities to raise taxes and the like. And there is no reason for a major country's government to do that.

HEILBRONER: What about Indonesia?

EISNER: Indonesia is bigger than Orange County.

PART III

FORSTATER: From the Euro, we've moved to discussing instability. So let's take up the third question, the recent financial crisis in Asia that has made apparent the fragility of the present international economic and financial organization. How might functional finance help inform policies to address global economic instability?

COLANDER: I think functional finance is already playing an important role in global stability. There is a belief, as I said in my chapter, that if things get bad enough, governments will enter in and do something. That is quite a change. When a recession gets serious enough, I still believe that the underlying regime is one of functional finance. That's really the only time I see it necessary to talk about functional finance at all.

AUDIENCE MEMBER: Doesn't the credit of the US rest on its standing as the lender of last resort? It's not a matter of backing up international, multi-lateral systems, but of the credit of the United States government.

EISNER: I remember that Alan Greenspan, in the 1987 financial crash, immediately made money available. I haven't followed Korea that closely, but I gather they have quickly been able to get international, private financing. There may sometimes be the need for a lender of last resort for credit to get over a momentary difficulty, but it doesn't necessarily have to be used continually.

MUSGRAVE: That is part of the problem. But, of course, the other part of the problem is that the pushing around of capital on a short-term basis will create instability in these crisis situations. What is needed, in principle, to create stability in international capital flow is some kind of a penalty tax on early withdrawal. Capital flows in and, if it is withdrawn within a year, there is a 10 per cent tax; if within two years, less tax; and if it stays five years, no tax.

COLANDER: The reality of these markets is such that money flows in for five or ten minutes. To a currency trader, 'long run' means two minutes. These markets are driven by expectations. They have extremely small spreads. The key element is the belief that someone is going to be the market maker of last resort, to make sure the system operates and survives.

NELL: Once again I want to underline the point that 'short-term capital' movements between countries are not really movements of capital. They are movements of money. Capital is created by saving and investment; an act of saving that is not offset by a corresponding investment must lead to an adjustment in the level of income. There is nothing like that in these flows of credit and money created by banks. There is very little regulation or supervision, and no overall control. It is hardly surprising that uncontrolled money creation has led to problems.

DUESENBERRY: I think that we have a lot of short-term debt. There is no reason that bank supervisors should allow banks to get into that position. The withdrawal penalty is one way to prevent that. Another way is to require banks to hold differential reserves against short-term foreign liability. A further approach is to limit Korean or Thai banks in their lending. When dollar-denominated debt is lent to firms that earn their income in local currency, if anything happens to bring down the value of the local currency, the debt is bound to go bad.

It doesn't make any sense, from the point of view of bank supervision, for banks to have unmatched positions in foreign exchanges. A great deal of the problems of international banking would be knocked out without any fancy taxes if there were reasonable bank supervision. About 35 years ago, the Swiss had a big capital inflow boom because they were so safe, and goodly, and so on. They were charging negative interest rates on foreign deposits in Swiss banks, to keep foreign currency out and to keep from bidding up the value of the currency.

NELL: I have a couple of observations. One is that corruption and bad banking practices are nothing new in Southeast Asia or, for that matter, anywhere. These countries have received a great deal of blame for their terrible banking practices and terrible corruption and so on, but it is evident that the situation goes back at least a decade, perhaps two. At that time, these same countries were hailed as great success stories. I am very suspicious of any explanation that raises these particular issues as a cause of crisis, or of the severity of a crisis. Once something begins to unravel, corruption and bad practices will be uncovered. Many practices may not actually be corrupt, but just bad business. Though they may partly account for the severity of a crisis, they are unlikely to be its trigger.

It's worth remembering that shortly before the crisis in Asia, most of these countries were receiving very good reports. The crisis coincided with the successful reduction of the US budget deficit, and with the simultaneous lowering of inflation and expansion of the US economy. It is possible that part of the story is not so much that Asia went down, but, rather, that the United

States – in reducing its deficit – went up. A capital movement to the US might be considered against the background of the US becoming more attractive, just as the asset bubbles in Asia began to weaken. These things happened together. It might be that the movement of short-term capital from Asia to the US – to New York – was triggered partly by the perception that New York was a very good, non-inflationary climate that looked as though it would remain that way for a while.

Once short-term capital movement begins, it will have an effect on exchange rates, and this in turn will imply inflation in the Asian economy. So the process becomes self-feeding. Once the exchange rates begin to go, the implication is that within a few months there will be inflation, so it's time to move. That could be at least part of the story.

COLANDER: I want to add another piece of the story. In one of my assignments for my students, they follow *The Wall Street Journal* fairly closely. About nine months before the Asian crisis, we started to see a lot of articles about excess capacity in the automobile industry. The report was, 'Look at these Korean firms. They are suddenly adding one to two million in additional capacity for cars; this does not make any logical sense; it's going to absolutely destroy the automobile market.' That started my students thinking about the Korean banking system where firms can get the capital to do something that clearly is not going to be carried out with appropriate market stability. Then suddenly, there was a financial crisis, and one of the causes was the banking sector in Korea.

DUESENBERRY: The same is true in Thailand. Thailand also has a real estate boom, plus an auto boom, plus a fuel boom.

FORSTATER: So first, the international financial economy encourages a boom, then it pulls out, bringing a crash. That would seem to call for a Functional Finance approach. On that note, then, I think it is time to retire to the cocktail reception in the green room. Please join us. And join me in offering thanks to our panel.

PART V

FUNCTIONAL FINANCE AND FULL EMPLOYMENT

Suppose we accept the general outlook of Functional Finance: We can and should actively intervene to promote and maintain prosperity. Just how is this to be done? What specific policies might we propose, and how would they be different from those of the more conventional but activist Keynesian?

Per Gunnar Berglund explores the significance of the 'Functional Finance' contention that taxes should never be collected for revenue but, rather, are levied for their economic impact. (Nell previously showed that in the past, when the monetary system was based on real reserves, taxes were, and had to be, collected for revenue. As Wray also demonstrated, by contrast in modern monetary systems tax revenue is not a precondition of government spending.) Ingrid Rima proposes that the distinction between micro and macro approaches to employment be replaced by a 'systems' approach, one which is a better fit with Functional Finance. She then assesses different policy proposals: tax cutting, development of foreign trade and wage subsidies, focusing most attention on public service employment. William Mitchell shows that, when inflationary pressures have developed in the labor market, the ELR (employer of last resort) can be combined with traditional fiscal and monetary policy to reduce aggregate demand.

14. Equality and enterprise: can functional finance offer a new historical compromise?

Per Gunnar Berglund*

'Look after Employment, and the Budget will look after itself.'

John Maynard Keynes

INTRODUCTION

The first draft of this chapter, which I presented at the New School conference on Functional Finance in April 1998, was cast as a tribute to William Vickrey who died in 1996 soon after he had been awarded the Nobel Prize in economics. Sad to say, in the past two years, two more eminent Functional Financiers have passed away: Robert Eisner and Lynn Turgeon, both of whom appeared at the New School conference and died shortly thereafter. I am deeply indebted, intellectually as well as personally, to these great and amiable men. The following pages should be viewed as my humble tribute to this distinguished trio that represents the very finest of American economics.

FUNCTIONAL FINANCE AND THE ROLE OF TAXATION

This chapter addresses a fundamental question in the theory of Functional Finance, a question put succinctly by Lynn Turgeon: 'Why should we tax people when there is Functional Finance?' The core message of the doctrine of Functional Finance is that the government budget should be regarded as a *means* to attain real-economy goals like maximum output and employment. The size of the budget deficit and government debt does not matter per se; the budget should be assessed only in the light of its impact on the real economy (Lerner 1943: 39)

* I am indebted to Ray Majewski for comments on an earlier draft.

Government expenditures – both the *spending* that furnishes public services and the *transfers* that redistribute income – form an indispensable part of any modern democratic welfare state. But they come at a cost, and the name of that cost is *taxation*. Taxes can be levied in innumerable ways, some of which might create big problems while others may be rather less disruptive. There are many more or less elaborate theories of optimal taxation, most of which attempt to minimize the negative consequences of levying taxes at a certain level, the level sufficient to 'fully finance' all government expenditures, that is, to balance the budget.

Functional Finance does not deny the importance of allocating expenditures for the greatest benefit to society and designing taxes so as to minimize their negative impact. What the doctrine of Functional Finance does deny, however, is the need for a balanced budget. Three interrelated lines of argumentation can be identified as supporting Functional Finance's rejection of balanced budgets.

First, there is the question of the time perspective, that is to say the period over which the budget is to be balanced. In Abba Lerner's words, 'Functional Finance rejects completely the traditional doctrines of "sound finance" and the principle of trying to balance the budget over a solar year or any other arbitrary period' (Lerner 1943: 41). This critique applies equally to the widespread idea that the budget must be balanced 'over a full business cycle,' a notion that is all the more arbitrary in view of the fact that it is by no means clear how the notion of a business cycle should be defined.

Secondly, there is William Vickrey's (1986a, 1992a) question of the exact sense of the ordinary concept of a government budget deficit. What precisely is to be balanced? As Robert Eisner's extensive research into the intricacies of accounting conventions and their economic impact has shown,[1] customary conceptions of budget deficits are so riddled with problems that it is doubtful whether they are useful for any purpose whatever. Should capital expenditures be excluded from the deficit? If so, which expenditures are to be classified as 'capital'? Should interest costs on the public debt be reckoned net of inflation? There is also the 'very pertinent question of what constitutes "balance" in a moving economy' (Eisner 1997: 9). If everything else grows, why not the government debt as well?

The third and perhaps most fundamental objection to the idea of budget balancing is the Chartalist view that 'money is a creature of the state' (Knapp 1924: Chapters 1 and 2; Lerner 1947; Wray 1998: Chapter 2). The chief defining criterion for 'money' is its supreme liquidity or general acceptability, which is established 'if the state is willing to accept the proposed money in payment of taxes and other obligations to itself' (Lerner 1947: 313). The money need not be *issued* by the state itself; it is the state acceptance that secures full liquidity. Such acceptance involves *accreditation* of the issuer, which lays bare the Chartalist logic that money comes into existence by means of state credit.

Since the state defines what 'money' is and thus, in a sense, 'lends' it into existence, it can never run out of it. In other words, the state can never default on its debts (when denominated in the home currency) unless it chooses to do so by refusing to pay. The state, therefore, operates under quite different financial conditions than do private agents. While private agents are financially constrained by their ability to raise cash by sales of commodities or by borrowing, the state does not face any such constraints.

There is in principle no limit to the amount of cash that the state can raise for the purpose of its own expenditures. While it is true that the state must raise the funds required for its expenditures by means of taxation or borrowing, it is equally true that those funds emanate from the state itself. Creditworthiness – or the ability to honour financial obligations – is a concept that pertains to debtors, not to creditors. It is meaningless to speak of the creditworthiness of the state, for the state is the ultimate creditor in respect to its own currency.

Thus the Chartalist contention is that the state can borrow as much as it wants in its own currency. So why indeed should it tax people? According to Lerner's 'first law of Functional Finance' (1943: 40), taxes should only be raised in order to prevent excessive inflation. The mechanism he had in mind is straightforward: Increased taxes will reduce disposable incomes, a reduction that will tend to curtail private spending. Lower spending involves generally slacker markets and perhaps more unemployment, thus alleviating inflationary pressures.[2]

This familiar mechanism of inflation reduction, however, is by no means as uncomplicated as it seems at first blush. Tax hikes can easily produce *higher* inflation. For instance, increases in sales taxes are overwhelmingly likely to induce higher prices, and – when the economy operates at (or near) full employment – such price rises are likely to be followed by compensatory wage increases. Lynn Turgeon (1996: 25, 28, 32, 58) called this phenomenon 'supply-side inflation,' and argued that since the mid-1960s, this type of inflation has been predominant. The very medicine prescribed against inflation may not only worsen the disease itself but also bring about unemployment as its highly undesirable by-product.

Thus we must add to the list of unpleasant consequences of taxation the risk of stagflation.[3] The conclusion that follows from this general picture is that taxes should be kept as stable and as low as possible. Aggregate demand reductions to curb inflation ought to be brought about by means of cutbacks in government expenditures. In general, taxation should take a back seat in the policy game of 'tuning' aggregate demand – whether the tuning is 'fine' or not. This rule may be viewed as a first amendment to Lerner's laws of Functional Finance.

The second amendment concerns the general level of taxation. The Turgeon question of why there should be any taxation at all is merely a logical *reductio ad absurdum* of the general principle that taxes should be reduced as far as possible *in relation to a given size of government spending*. It is quite conceivable that bigger government might call for higher taxes. But Functional Finance does not recognize any direct and simple relationship between the two. In order to assess the appropriate level of taxation, the impact on the economy must first be assessed.

The conventional wisdom of the balanced budget involves a dilemma: the boons of high government expenditures must be weighed against the evils of high taxation. Countries with extensive welfare state arrangements – and therefore big government sectors – are also societies of relatively limited economic disparities. Big government is a means to bring about greater equality. On the other hand countries with small government sectors and greater disparities are often viewed as more dynamic and entrepreneurial. Equality comes at the cost of reduced enterprise. The cradle-to-grave medically insured, comfortable life of Euro-sclerosis stands against the stressful but affluent life of the dynamic, successful American job machine. Those who subscribe to the conventional wisdom hold to the inescapable and immutable iron law of the trade-off between Equality and Enterprise: We cannot have more of the one without sacrificing some of the other.[4] The science of the balanced budget is indeed dismal; its basic message is neatly captured by Keynes's ironic aphorism: 'the more the fewer, and the higher the less' (Keynes and Henderson 1929: 91).

Functional Finance promises to surpass the limitations of this conventional wisdom. While it may not be able to dispel the trade-off altogether, it should be able to improve upon it. In other words, with Functional Finance we can break the fetters of this iron law and obtain more Equality at any given level of Enterprise, or more Enterprise at any degree of Equality, than what the conventional doctrine of the balanced budget can offer. This free lunch is made feasible by employing the magic wand of maximum deficit financing.

Functional Finance holds that the level and quality of government services and the level of social security benefits has nothing to do with taxation because these items appear on the *debit* side of government budgets. Tax revenues appear on the *credit* side. The tacit presumption of a balanced budget underlies the perpetuation of the pernicious myth that when the government spends it hands out 'taxpayers' money.' As soon as we transcend the illusory constraint of the balanced budget, the notion of 'taxpayers' money' dissipates. Credit and debit become independent entities.

The independence of debit and credit, however, does not imply that there is no need for the government to worry about the consequences of spending unlimited amounts. The consequences that count, however, are those that impact the real economy – not the financial deficit as such. Functional Finance must stress the fact that government spending and taxation have different effects on aggregate demand. An increase in government spending affects a direct addition to aggregate demand, but also has an indirect effect, partly through increased private-sector income and wealth, partly through higher investment induced by higher capacity utilization. Lowered taxes, on the other hand, will only work indirectly via the private sector wealth position and income flow. The debit and credit sides of the budget are functionally asymmetrical. Expansionary policy measures operating on the debit side (increased government spending) are far more powerful than credit-side interventions like lowered taxes. Thus the government deficit – the difference between spending and taxes – does not work symmetrically. The size of the deficit therefore says very little about the likely impact on output and employment.

Acknowledging this asymmetry, one must wonder why tax cuts are ever suggested as a means to stimulate economic activity. There seems to be no sense in using such a sub-optimal tool when increased spending would do the job both quicker and better. The motives for lowering taxes must be sought elsewhere. There may of course be good political reasons for lowering taxes. People generally do not like paying taxes, a sentiment that may make tax cuts an easier way to go from the political and legislative point of view. But that is no *economic* argument. From the economic point of view, the fact remains that taxes are less efficient than public spending with respect to the goal of stimulating aggregate demand.

The strong arguments for lower taxes lie on the supply side. Whereas increased public spending works almost exclusively on the demand side, tax cuts operate on *both* the demand and the supply side. The demand effect of a tax cut would be relatively weak compared to an increase in government spending, but it would have the advantage of stimulating aggregate supply along with demand. Insofar as the supply-side elasticity with respect to taxation is substantial, lower taxes might prove a powerful tool for expanding potential output and adjusting the growth path which is compatible with any given rate of inflation.

At any rate, as long as there is some supply-side elasticity, there is a preliminary economic case for lowering taxes. But lowering taxes while keeping spending unchanged will widen the deficit, and a bigger deficit will likely stimulate aggregate demand. Tax cuts therefore provide a parallel and simultaneous stimulus of both the demand and the supply side.

Important for Ministers of Finance is which of the two effects is the greater. So long as the supply-side effects outweigh the demand-side effects, there is scope for more public spending to counteract deflationary tendencies. But if the demand-side stimulus should be greater than the supply-side impact, then it might prove necessary to cut back on spending programmes in order to maintain a reasonable degree of price stability. Conversely if public spending is maintained at a certain level or proportion of the domestic product, then taxation must be calibrated so as to avoid inflationary or deflationary imbalances. A Minister of Functional Finance in the limbo of this tax minimization problem should indeed ask himself how low he can go before inflation rears its ugly head.

When this line of reasoning is taken to its logical extreme, the credit side of the budget might be completely cleared and tax revenues (net of subsidies) kept at the zero level.[5] The very notion of a 'tax-free' economy may seem unrealistic, particularly from a political point of view,[6] but that should not deter us from investigating the logic of this *reductio ad absurdum*. For by looking into the extreme, we may learn more about the commonplace.

By divorcing the credit side from the debit side, Functional Finance opens up a Pandora's box. Taxes can no longer be viewed as necessary in order to 'finance' public spending because the state can always find the cash it needs. The role of taxes, as well as public expenditures, must therefore be viewed solely in the light of their real-economy impact, and public spending is no doubt the most effective means to control aggregate demand. Lowered taxes might stimulate aggregate supply and this effect is their prime economic rationale.

While Functional Finance holds that the budget is subject to no financial constraints, it acknowledges that the calibration of spending and taxes is subject to certain macroeconomic balance constraints, namely the prevention of unsound inflation and deflation. The following sections are an attempt at defining and analysing those constraints in terms of a simple macroeconomic model. The aim of the model is to investigate the possibility, as raised by Turgeon, of an entirely 'tax-free' economy where all public expenditures are financed by means of borrowing.

A SIMPLE MACROECONOMIC MODEL FOR THE CLOSED ECONOMY

Let us start our inquiry into the principles of a 'tax-free' economy by setting up a simple model for the demand side of the economy. For simplicity and convenience, we shall restrict our exposition to the closed-economy case. Foreign trade, cross-border income flows, and portfolio transactions will be disregarded.

The first step is to express the private-sector demand D_P as the mathematical product of the private net wealth position V_P and the wealth-to-spending turnover rate u.

$$D_P = u \cdot V_P. \tag{14.1}$$

Our second step is to insert this relation into the definitional relation that the domestic product Y is the sum of private demand D_P and government demand D_G. We obtain

$$Y = D_P + D_G = u \cdot V_P + D_G. \tag{14.2}$$

Next, we note that the national wealth V is made up of private wealth V_P and government net wealth V_G.

$$V = V_P + V_G. \tag{14.3}$$

Solving equation (14.3) for V_P and substituting into (14.2) yields

$$Y = u \cdot V_P + D_G = u \times V - u \cdot V_G + D_G. \tag{14.4}$$

The national wealth in a closed economy is by definition equal to the value of the national capital stock K, making the two substitutable for one another. By invoking a capital–output relation v, linking the value of the capital stock (national wealth) to the domestic product, we complete our model.

$$K = V = v \cdot Y. \tag{14.5}$$

We proceed to substitute $v \cdot Y$ for V in equation (14.4) to obtain

$$Y = u \cdot V_P + D_G = u \cdot v \cdot Y - u \cdot V_G + D_G. \tag{14.6}$$

Subtracting $u \cdot v \cdot Y$ and factoring out Y gives

$$(1 - u \cdot v) \cdot Y = D_G - u \cdot V_G. \tag{14.7}$$

Finally, we divide by $(1 - u \cdot v)$ and obtain

$$Y = \frac{D_G - u \cdot V_G}{1 - u \cdot v}. \tag{14.8}$$

Equation (14.8) is a convenient shorthand expression of the 'multiplier' kind. Note that only two parameters have been used: u and v. Insofar as these parameters remain fairly stable over time, equation (14.8) will provide a useful tool for the Functional Finance analysis. Experience suggests that v may be supposed to be long-term stable at a value somewhere around 4 in most industrialized economies. The value of u, on the contrary, seems to be subject to a gradual, long-term decline, a fact repeatedly pointed out by Vickrey (e.g. 1994a, 1997). Indeed the long-term decline of u in conjunction with the long-term constancy of v makes up the main ingredients of 'stagnationist Keynesianism.'

A Note on Government Deficit and Debt

Government enters into the model through two variables: government spending D_G and government net wealth V_G. Note that the category of government spending excludes transfer payments. Only purchases of goods and services are included. Government net wealth refers to the sum of government-owned real capital assets K_G and government net financial assets NFA_G.

$$V_G = K_G + NFA_G. \tag{14.9}$$

The term *government debt* should be taken to refer to the government's net financial assets with a negative sign, $-NFA_G$. A proper set of government accounts, including capital accounts for the recording of capital formation and revaluation items for holding gains and losses, defines the government *budget surplus B* as the per-period *change* in government net wealth ΔV_G. The budget deficit is of course of the same absolute value, but with a negative sign.[7] We will distinguish between the total budget surplus B, thus defined, and the *financial* budget surplus FB (and the corresponding deficit $-FB$), defined in terms of the per-period change of the government's net financial assets, as ΔNFA_G and $-\Delta NFA_G$, respectively.

The definition of government net wealth in equation (14.9) is applicable also to the private sector. The private sector net wealth V_P is defined as the sum of privately owned real capital assets K_P and the private net financial asset position NFA_P.

$$V_P = K_P + NFA_P. \tag{14.10}$$

Again note that the national wealth is the sum of private and government net wealth (equation (14.3)), that the national capital stock is sum of the private and government capital stocks,

$$K = K_P + K_G, \tag{14.11}$$

and that the national wealth and capital stock are equal in value (equation (14.5)). By combining these propositions, we obtain

$$NFA_P = -NFA_G. \tag{14.12}$$

That is to say: the private sector net financial asset position is equal to the government debt. Government and private-sector net financial asset positions are simply the mirror images of one another: the net debt of the one is the net assets of the other.

Setting the Size of the Public Sector

Let us now assume that economic policy is aimed at keeping the size of the public sector at a particular proportion of the domestic product. The 'size of the public sector' is however a two-dimensional phenomenon: it concerns the size of government production as well as of government spending. There is no necessary relation between the two, although most governments have found it convenient to self-produce a substantial proportion of their absorption (spending). In most modern economies, government absorbs some 20 to 30 per cent of the domestic product, whereas government production usually furnishes only some 10 to 20 per cent.

Government production, like all other production, requires real capital. Let us denote the government-owned proportion of the national capital stock with a, so that

$$K_G = a \cdot K = a \cdot v \cdot Y. \qquad (14.13)$$

Using equation (14.9) and substituting into equation (14.7) yields

$$(1 - u \cdot v) \cdot Y = D_G - a \cdot u \cdot v \cdot Y - u \cdot NFA_G. \qquad (14.14)$$

We now proceed by adding $a \cdot u \cdot v \cdot Y$, and by factoring out $(1 - a)$:

$$[1 - (1 - a) \times u \times v] \times Y = D_G - u \times NFA_G. \qquad (14.15)$$

Finally, we divide by $[1 - (1 - a) \cdot u \cdot v]$:

$$Y = \frac{D_G - u \cdot NFA_G}{1 - (1 - a) \cdot u \cdot v} \qquad (14.16)$$

This result may be compared to equation (8). The difference is that equation (17) expresses the domestic product in terms of government debt $-NFA_G$ instead of government demand and government net wealth V_G as in equation (8). This rewriting required an extra parameter a, which set the relation between NFA_G and V_G. The rest remained the same: government demand D_G as well as the parameters u and v are common for both models.

Now let us turn to setting the proportion of government spending in the domestic product. Suppose this proportion is b, so that:

$$D_G = b \cdot Y. \tag{14.17}$$

Substitution of this equation into (14.16) yields

$$[1 - (1 - a) \cdot u \cdot v] \cdot Y = b \cdot Y - u \cdot NFA_G. \tag{14.18}$$

By subtraction of $b \cdot Y$, factoring, and division by $[1 - (1 - a) \cdot u \cdot v - b]$, we obtain

$$Y = \frac{-u \times NFA_G}{1 - (1 - a) \cdot u \cdot v - b}. \tag{14.19}$$

Comparing this equation with equation (14.17), we find that by introducing the parameter b, we effectively 'traded' the government demand variable for an extra parameter. Equation (14.18) expresses the domestic product Y solely in terms of the government debt $-NFA_G$ and a set of four parameters: a, b, u and v.

A slight rearrangement (cross-multiplication and changing signs on the right-hand side) of equation (14.20) yields an expression for the ratio between government debt and the domestic product, the *debt-to-GDP ratio* θ.[8]

$$\theta = \frac{-NFA_G}{Y} = \frac{1 - (1 - a) \cdot u \cdot v - b}{u}. \tag{14.20}$$

This equation is a convenient tool with which to assess the determinants of the debt-to-GDP ratio. On the right-hand side we have the four parameters (a, b, u and v), which jointly determine θ. The share of government production, as well as absorption, in the domestic product appears to lie within the control of the economic policy makers. The overall capital-output ratio v, however, seems to be very much of a 'technical' parameter, the value of which is determined quite independently of economic policy making. The crucial factor, therefore, must be the private-sector wealth-to-spending turnover rate u.

The Debt-to-GDP Ratio and the Private-sector Wealth-to-spending Turnover Rate

Let us examine how the debt-to-GDP ratio θ depends on the value of the private-sector wealth-to-spending turnover rate u. The partial function $\theta(u, \bullet)$ clearly depends on the setting of the other three parameters (a, b and v). In order to illustrate the relation we will give two reasonable numerical examples depicting 'big government' and 'small government,' respectively.

Both examples have in common the assumption of $v = 4.00$, which is to say that the capital–output ratio is 400 per cent. Experience tells us that the overall capital–output ratios of modern economies usually vary only slightly around this level. It may be added that the results are fairly robust. Minor changes in v will have no major impact on θ.

The examples differ with respect to the values of the parameters a and b. Both have in common, however, that a is two-thirds of b, which means that the government sector production covers two-thirds of its absorption. This ratio may also be regarded as a stylized fact for most modern economies.

The 'big government' example is based on the assumption that $a = 0.20$ and $b = 0.30$. The public sector produces 20 per cent and absorbs 30 per cent of the domestic product. These percentages depict roughly the situation in the industrialized countries with the largest public sector shares, for example, the Scandinavian welfare states Denmark, Norway and Sweden.

In the 'small government' example, we assume that $a = 0.10$ and $b = 0.15$, that is that the government sector furnishes 10 per cent and absorbs 15 per cent of the domestic product. This corresponds, roughly, to the industrialized countries with the smallest government sector shares, for example, Japan and the United States.

The reason why we have chosen these two extremes in setting our parameters is that any reasonable public–private mix should lie somewhere in between these values. We should expect, therefore, that the debt-to-GDP ratio be situated somewhere in the 'corridor' shaped by these limiting assumptions.

As shown in Figure 14.1, the debt-to-GDP ratio θ is an asymptotically declining function of the private wealth-to-spending turnover rate u. This means that the more prone the private sector is to spend – to turn over its net wealth into effective demand – the less need there is for the accumulation of government debt. Those who regard public debt as a problem should therefore seek remedies in augmenting the turnover rate u, that is, should encourage households and firms to 'let the good times roll' and become more spendthrift. But if government debt is viewed as a blessing rather than a curse, the opposite conclusion follows. The more parsimonious the private sector, that is, the lower the turnover rate u, the bigger the scope – not to say the *need* – for government debt accumulation.

A second conclusion to be drawn from Figure 14.1 is that 'big government' will diminish the need for government debt accumulation. This is just another manifestation of the notorious paradox of thrift, and all the more ironic since those who call for reduction of the public sector often do so with

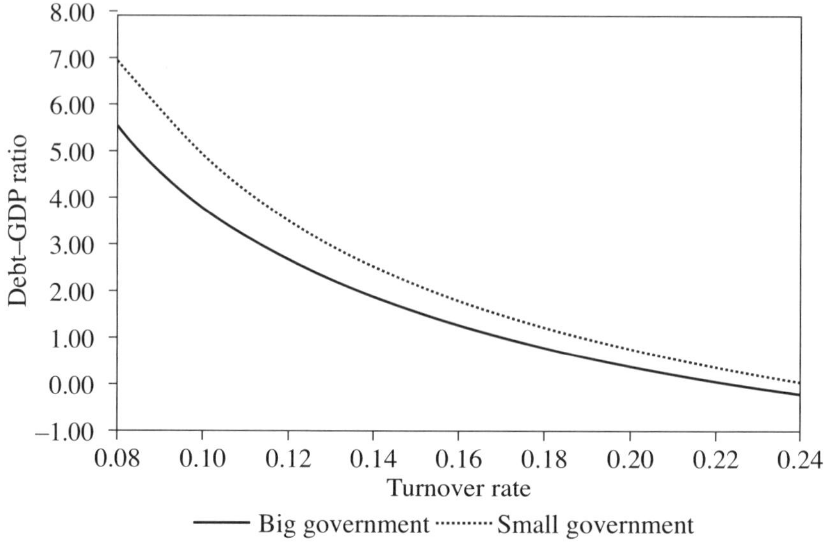

Note: See Appendix for assumptions and data tables.

Figure 14.1 Two arithmetical examples of the relation between the debt-to-GDP ratio and the private wealth-to-spending turnover rate

express reference to the need for reducing the public debt! In the name of economic logic, those who worry about the size of the public debt should advocate bigger government, not smaller. On the other hand, the view that the public debt is beneficial does not square with the advocacy of bigger government. Debt-lovers should rather call for smaller government.

Steady State of the Debt-to-GDP Ratio

By differentiating the definition of the debt-to-GDP ratio (see equation (14.21)), remembering that $FB = \Delta NFA_G$, and defining the *deficit-to-GDP ratio* $\beta = -FB/Y$ and the *GDP growth rate* $\psi = \Delta Y/Y$, we obtain[9]

$$\Delta\theta = \frac{Y \cdot \Delta(-NFA_G) \cdot \Delta Y}{Y^2} = \beta - \theta \cdot \psi. \tag{14.21}$$

We examine the steady-state conditions by setting $\Delta\theta = 0$:

$$\Delta\theta = \beta - \theta \cdot \psi = 0 \Rightarrow \beta - \theta \cdot \psi. \tag{14.22}$$

In order to maintain a stable debt-to-GDP ratio, the deficit-to-GDP ratio β must equal the mathematical product of the debt-to-GDP ratio θ and the GDP growth rate ψ. It should be stressed that the feasible size of the steady-state deficit-to-GDP ratio is proportional to the size of the debt-to-GDP ratio. The larger the debt, the higher the feasible deficit.

The Primary Deficit

Part of the government's financial surplus consists of net interest receipts (an item that is usually negative). We shall denote this *interest net* by R. The remainder of the financial surplus is called the *primary surplus*, PFB. Thus the interest net and the primary surplus add up to the financial surplus, so that

$$R + PFB = FB. \tag{14.23}$$

The size of the interest net depends on two factors: the size of the government's net financial asset position NFA_G, and the average interest rate on government net financial assets r.

$$R = NFA_G \cdot r\cdot. \tag{14.24}$$

Let us now define the (net deficit) *interest-to-GDP ratio* $\rho = -R/Y$. By using the definition of θ we obtain

$$\rho = \theta \times r. \tag{14.25}$$

In analogy with the definition of the deficit-to-GDP ratio β, we shall also define a corresponding *primary* deficit-to-GDP ratio $\beta' = -PFB/Y$. Thus it holds true that

$$\beta = \beta' + \rho. \tag{14.26}$$

Now invoke the steady-state condition for θ (equation (14.23)), as well as equation (14.26), and substitute both of them into (14.27). After solving for β', the equation reads

$$\beta' = \theta \times (\psi - r). \tag{14.27}$$

The steady-state size of the primary deficit-to-GDP ratio is determined by the debt-to-GDP ratio θ and the *difference* between the GDP growth rate ψ and the interest rate r. What this important relation tells us is that in order for the deficit to contribute to the financing of government spending on real goods and services (not merely to the transfer of wealth to creditors!), we must see to it that the GDP growth rate exceeds the rate of interest.[10] The larger the gap between the GDP growth rate and the interest rate, the more powerful the 'leverage' of government debt and primary deficits.

Substituting Debt Growth for Taxation

Suppose, for example, that the GDP growth rate exceeds the interest rate by five percentage points. Then the steady-state deficit-to-GDP ratio will be 5 per cent of the debt-to-GDP ratio. If the debt-to-GDP ratio is at, for example, 60 per cent, then the primary deficit-to-GDP ratio can be permanently maintained at 3 per cent. Incidentally, these figures are the same as those stipulated in the European Union Maastricht Treaty as 'convergence criteria' for debt and deficit. Note that if the GDP growth rate exceeds the interest rate by five percentage points, then no less than one-fifth of the public sector in our 'small government' example, and one-tenth of the 'big government' example, can be *permanently* financed by allowing the government debt to grow continuously. Taxpayers would be relieved accordingly.

Once we acknowledge the feasibility of substituting a permanently growing public debt for taxation, we have opened up a Pandora's box. Whereas the figures in the above example indicate a substantial, albeit limited, contribution to the financing of public spending, other figures will give other results. In principle, there is nothing that prevents us from imagining the full financing of *all* government spending by simply allowing the public debt to grow and thus levying no taxes. We have reached the nexus of Functional Finance where debt dynamics and Chartalism meet to answer Lynn Turgeon's pertinent question: Why should people be taxed at all?

Let us retain the assumption of a five percentage-point excess of the GDP growth rate over the interest rate. Suppose now that the debt-to-GDP ratio could be raised to 300 per cent. The arithmetic then yields a primary deficit-to-GDP ratio of 15 per cent, which is sufficient to finance the whole of the 'small government,' and half of the 'big government.' In order to deficit finance the entire 'big government,' the debt-to-GDP ratio must be boosted to an astronomic 600 per cent.

The key to accomplishing the substitution of debt growth for tax finance lies in keeping interest rates below the GDP growth rate. So long as the interest rates exceed the GDP growth rate, the government debt will work the other way round, as a drag on the private sector and the taxpayers. The required low-interest policy may not be easy to bring about and even more difficult to sustain, particularly in today's institutional setting with internationally open financial markets. At the very least, a unilateral move towards lower interest rates presupposes the maintenance of a flexible exchange rate regime.

The analysis of the practical difficulties of these policies and the possible need for institutional reform, however, fall outside the scope of this chapter. Our purpose here is merely to bring to the reader's attention the core principle of substituting debt growth for taxation, which should be a hobby horse of Functional Finance. The larger the excess of GDP growth over the interest rate, the greater the 'leverage' of government debt increases into primary deficits, and the more taxation can be replaced with deficits and debt growth. The difference of five percentage points chosen in our examples was not picked out of a hat. Modern economies seem to be able to grow, in real terms, by at least 3–4 per cent per annum, and it does not seem unreasonable to assume that real interest rates can be brought down, by appropriate monetary policies, to some 1–2 per cent below zero. The difference implied lies in the region of four-to-six percentage points. Thus the 5 per cent 'lever' suggested in our examples does seem to lie within reach for practical policy.

The Wealth-to-Spending Turnover Rate Revisited

This *reductio ad absurdum* brings us right back to the relations depicted in the graphs of Figure 14.1 that show consistency requirements in terms of the private wealth-to-spending turnover rate in order to finance all government expenditure by debt growth instead of taxation. Full deficit financing of 'big government' does not seem practicable. The graph does not even cover the point of intersection between the 'big government' curve and the required debt-to-GDP ratio of 600 per cent. In order to accomplish such a gigantic debt-to-GDP ratio, the private wealth-to-spending turnover rate would have to be lowered to less than 0.08, meaning that the private sector on average would turn over its wealth into effective demand once every twelfth year. However the idea of deficit financing the 'small government' does appear somewhat less far-fetched. The 'small government' curve crosses the required 300 per cent debt-to-GDP ratio at a private wealth-to-spending turnover rate of about 0.13, corresponding to the private sector revolving their wealth at an average pace of once every eighth year.

These different wealth-to-spending turnover rates may say very little until we get some idea about the actual wealth-to-spending turnover rates in the real economies of today. As in the case of the capital–output ratio, there is some variation, but there nevertheless appears to be a tendency for this rate to hover around the 0.20 level. Which puts in perspective the needed lowering to less than 0.08 in the 'big government' case. It just does not seem realistic to bring down the turnover rate by nearly two-thirds. The turnover rate reduction required in the 'small government' case (by one-third, from roughly 0.20 to 0.13) is also quite large, but much smaller and more manageable than the 'big government' case.

Thus the whole matter of permanent deficit financing of government spending revolves around one particular parameter: the private-sector wealth-to-spending turnover rate u.[11] Unless u can be brought down to a sufficiently low level, there will be no room for the public debt needed to yield the required deficits. This suggests that the future efforts of Functional Financiers might best be directed to the question of how this turnover rate can be affected and regulated by means of policy measures.

TAX REFORM IN ORDER TO LOWER THE TURNOVER RATE

We have already written off the possibility of full deficit financing of the 'big government.' A necessary practical condition is that the government share of GDP be limited, that is – in the case of European welfare states – be cut back. This need not involve any reductions of the volume and quality of services provided by the government sector. If aggregate supply is relatively elastic with respect to the level of taxation, then tax cuts may provide for a great expansion of the private sector. A vigorously growing private sector will tend to reduce the *share* of the public sector in the economy, a reduction that might render unnecessary any actual cutbacks of the real size of government.

Provided that government demand is kept within the 'small government' percentage limit, the stability of the system depends crucially on the ability to bring down the private-sector wealth-to-spending turnover rate u to the required level of roughly 0.13. Since the present-day turnover rate is in the neighborhood of 0.20, spending habits will need some restriction in order for the 0.13 level to obtain. How, then, can we conceive a means with which to accomplish this?

The answer, we believe, lies in tax reform. We must invent a system of taxation that *discourages* the private sector from spending to the necessary extent. The natural solution to this problem, is to invoke a system of *progressive spending taxation*, meaning that private-sector spending, at least on consumption, should be progressively taxed.[12] Such a tax may be established within the framework of the ordinary income tax. All that is needed is to allow deductions for saving. The progressiveness of the income tax itself will then provide disincentives to spending.

If allowances were made for saving, then the level of income taxation would be subject, to some extent, to individual discretion. Frugality and tax-avoidance would go hand in hand, while the spendthrift would suffer from high taxation. The personal rate of income taxation would depend on the level of personal-consumption spending as well as the size of personal income. From the point of view of egalitarian ethics, such a taxation system may seem quite unfair. For high-income earners usually spend a much smaller proportion of their income on personal consumption and may therefore avoid a great deal of taxation. Invoking fairly sharply progressive tax rates may however mitigate this injustice.

It is however questionable whether taxation of income really is an expression of equity. The mere earning of income does not involve any claim on the nation's real production resources. Personal saving means an excess of that person's contribution to the nation's output over her absorption of currently produced goods and services. That excess will enable other people to incur a corresponding deficit, that is, to absorb more than they productively contribute. The very intention of the tax reform suggested here is to make the whole of the private sector a net contributor, or net saver, in order to make room for the public sector's deficits.

Any taxation of the contributions – of factor incomes that is – is likely to reduce the willingness to contribute. This is just another way of expressing the elasticity of supply. One may question what society gains by preventing people from working as much and as well as they desire. Indeed, preventing people from contributing and doing their best may well involve a measure of paternalism and injustice in itself.

From a Functionalist perspective, the earnings and wealth of individuals should be a subordinate problem. What really counts is the extent to which people contribute and how much of their contributions they use up. The 'stagnationist' tendencies of modern economies, as emphasized by William Vickrey, essentially means that there is a general willingness on the part of the private sector to contribute more in terms of output than it uses up in terms of spending. There is a 'savings gap' that calls for an ever-growing public debt in order to balance overall supply and demand.

This stagnation tendency, the growing savings gap, has often been viewed as a problem. But why should one look at it that way? Isn't the gap really a big resource? Should it not be encouraged? For the bigger the gap, the greater the scope for deficit financing of public spending. Indeed, the graver the stagnationist tendencies of the private sector, the lower the taxes can go, and the greater the scope for public borrowing and a growing debt. Instead of encouraging private spending as a remedy for stagnation, should we not promote private saving to widen the savings gap? For by so doing, we could deficit finance all the more, and enjoy the supply-side benefits of reduced taxation.

A progressive personal consumption tax might be calibrated in such a way as to encourage an *average* level of personal consumption that is consistent with the desired *aggregate* volume of consumption. The per-person target level could be calculated by taking an estimate of the economy's overall capacity to supply consumption services and divide by the number of taxpayers. The sharper the progressiveness of the tax penalty for exceeding the target per-head level of spending, the stronger the individual incentives to hold consumption levels near the target. In order to bring the overall level of taxation down to the zero level (in accordance with Turgeon's idea of a 'tax-free' economy), tax revenues collected from spendthrift, over-the-target consumers could be transferred to low-consuming households. This could be accomplished by means of an automatic transfer mechanism along the lines of a 'negative income tax.'

This is not the place to expound a detailed tax reform proposal. Our primary concern is to show the main principles on which such a reform might be based. The purpose of such a tax reform would be twofold: It would discourage private spending and encourage saving in order to make room for big, permanent public deficits. It would maximize aggregate supply by bringing down the overall rate of net taxation – taxes less subsidies – to zero.

FUNCTIONAL FINANCE AND THE NEW HISTORICAL COMPROMISE

Egalitarian ethics versus the right to contribute – those are the elements of the perennial conflict between Equality and Enterprise. It is generally believed that there exists an inescapable trade-off between the two. The more the Equality, the fewer the pennies, and the higher the taxes, the less the Enterprise. Too much Equality will render a fair but slack society riddled with 'Eurosclerosis;' Enterprise can only be bought at the cost of a staggeringly unequal society plagued by an alarming rate of poverty in the midst of plenty.

The political left embraces Equality, while the political right preaches Enterprise. The polarity of political life rests heavily on perceptions of economic necessity. The compromise that Functional Finance can offer involves a mitigation of the polarity. By substituting debt growth for taxation, and by invoking progressive personal consumption taxation, we may indeed combine the best of both worlds. We can have more Enterprise and more Equality at the same time!

True, a tax reform along the suggested lines is likely to involve a considerable degree of *income* inequality. That seems to be the inevitable price for having tax-free Enterprise. In the absence of taxation there will be no economic disincentives that discourage work and productive efforts in general. Progressive taxation of consumption will however provide strong incentives for the leveling out of differences in standards of living. Lifestyles, after all, are based on levels and patterns of consumption, not income. It seems, therefore, that the requirements of remunerative justice (that is, getting paid in proportion to inputs), and of distributive justice (moderate differences in consumption levels), could both be better satisfied by such a reform than the existing case today.

Since remunerative and distributive justice may be considered the bees in the ideologists' bonnets, this tax-reform approach also suggests a new historical compromise to replace the social compact of the high-taxation welfare state. Functional Finance could pave the way for the peaceful cohabitation of the killer-bees of right-wing Enterprise and the bumble-bees of left-wing Equality. There would at any rate be less grumbling in the hive. It would be rash, of course, to propose anything concrete at this premature stage, but the logic of this overall vision of a virtually tax-free economy, still retaining a fair measure of public spending, should be interesting enough to warrant attention and further discussion. It may well prove to be an erroneous and impossible strategy in the end, but even if it does, there are important insights to be had from taking it all the way to that end.

NOTES

1. (Eisner 1984, 1986a, 1986b, 1986c, 1986d, 1986e, 1988, 1989a, 1989b, 1989c, 1991a, 1991b, 1991c, 1992a, 1992b, 1993a, 1993b, 1993c, 1994a: chapter 5, 1994b, 1994c, 1994d, 1994e, 1994f, 1994g, 1997: Chapter 2; Eisner and Hwang 1993; Eisner and Pieper 1986, 1987, 1988a, 1988b, 1989, 1992.)
2. Lerner was concerned that the increased powers of organized labor might cause money wages to accelerate well before full employment was reached, and sought other solutions than slack markets and unemployment to the problem of inflation. Various proposals in this vein have been put forward by Lerner, Colander and Vickrey – for example, Colander's 'tax-based income policy,' Lerner's 'market anti-inflation plan' and Vickrey's 'marketable markup warrants' scheme (Colander 1986, 1992; Lerner 1978, 1980a, 1980b; Lerner and Colander 1982; Vickrey 1986b, 1986c, 1992b.)
3. Another problem with taxes as a tool for aggregate demand management is that temporary changes in the level of taxation may prove relatively ineffective with respect to aggregate demand due to 'inter-temporal substitution' effects.
4. Given that the allocation of resources is optimized subject to the overall tax/expenditure level.
5. It should be noted that this does not necessarily involve the abolishment of taxation. Taxes may still be retained, but counterbalanced by 'negative taxes' or subsidies of the same size. It is the aggregate outcome that matters for our purposes.
6. There may also be economic arguments against the zero-tax economy. A particularly interesting argument has been put forward by Wray (1998), who asserts that taxes secure the value of the currency. Wray also acknowledges, however, that taxation is a sufficient, but not a necessary, condition for the maintenance of the value of the currency (ibid. 4n).
7. In practice, however, governments do not tend to make use of this comprehensive definition of the budget surplus in their actual accounting. Most governments break out the financial-assets part and limit the government deficit to the per-period change in government debt. Governments also generally exclude the holding gains on financial assets, thus limiting the deficit to the transaction changes in government debt. There is also a tendency to mix up the central government debt and deficit with the debt and deficit of government as a whole. Our concepts refer to the consolidated public sector, including central and local government as well as social security trust funds.
8. We will use the standard expression 'debt-to-GDP ratio' despite the fact that the domestic product is best measured as the *net* domestic product, that is, after deduction for capital consumption. Readers may bear in mind this slight violation of terminological stringency.
9. Again GDP is used as convenient shorthand for the domestic product, whether it is measured in 'gross' terms or not.

10. A number of aspects of the relation between interest rates and the growth rate are explored in Nell (1998: Chapter 13).
11. Provided, of course, that the gap between GDP growth and the interest rate can be upheld with appropriate monetary measures.
12. An important contribution along these lines is Lawrence Seidman's volume *The USA Tax: A Progressive Consumption Tax* (1997a; for a brief presentation see Seidman 1997b). While Seidman's proposal is well considered and detailed, it is unfortunately void of the insights of Functional Finance.

REFERENCES

Colander, David (ed.) (1986), *Incentive-based Incomes Policies: Advances in TIP and MAP*, Cambridge, MA: Harper and Row.

Colander, David (1992), 'A Real Theory of Inflation and Incentive Anti-inflation Plans', *American Economic Review*, 82 (2), 335–40.

Eisner, Robert (1984), 'Which Budget Deficit? Some Issues of Measurement and Their Implications', *American Economic Review*, 74 (2), 138–43.

Eisner, Robert (1986a), *How Real is the Federal Deficit?* New York: Free Press.

Eisner, Robert (1986b), 'Will the Real Federal Deficit Stand Up?' *Challenge*, 29 (2), 13–21.

Eisner, Robert (1986c), 'The Revolution Restored: Keynesian Unemployment, Inflation and Budget Deficits', *Eastern Economic Journal*, 12 (3), 217–21.

Eisner, Robert (1986d), 'Real vs. Nominal Debt', *Challenge*, 29 (5), 58.

Eisner, Robert (1986e), 'The Real Federal Deficit: What It Is, How It Matters, and What It Should Be', *Quarterly Review of Economics and Business*, 26 (4), 6–21.

Eisner, Robert (1988), 'Which Budget Deficit?', in E. Brown, (ed.), *Readings, Issues, and Questions in Public Finance*, Homewood, IL: Irwin, pp. 208–14.

Eisner, Robert (1989a), 'Debt and Deficit and Other Illusions,' in G.R. Feiwel (ed.), *The Economics of Imperfect Competition and Employment: Joan Robinson and Beyond*, New York: New York University Press, pp. 709–20.

Eisner, Robert (1989b), 'On Keynesian Underemployment, Prices, and Wealth Effects of Government Debt', in A. Barrere (ed.), *Money, Credit and Prices in Keynesian Perspective*, New York: St. Martin's Press, pp. 162–9.

Eisner, Robert (1989c), 'Budget Deficits: Rhetoric and Reality', *Journal of Economic Perspectives*, 3 (2), 73–93.

Eisner, Robert (1991a), 'Debunking the Conventional Wisdom in Economic Policy', *Challenge*, 33 (3), 4–11.

Eisner, Robert (1991b), 'Deficits and Us and Our Grandchildren', in J.M. Rock (ed.), *Debt and the Twin Deficits Debate*, Mountain View, CA: Mayfield, pp. 81–107.

Eisner, Robert (1991c), 'The Real Rate of U.S. National Saving', *Review of Income and Wealth*, 37 (1), 15–32.

Eisner, Robert (1992a), 'The Twin Deficits', in D.B. Papadimitriou (ed.), *Profits, Deficits and Instability*, London: Macmillan, pp. 255–67.

Eisner, Robert (1992b), 'Deficits: Which, How Much and So What? *American Economic Review*, 82 (2), 295–8.

Eisner, Robert (1993*a*), 'Fiscal and Monetary Policy Reconsidered, Again: Basic Lessons', *Journal of Economic Education*, 24 (3), 245–9.

Eisner, Robert (1993b), 'National Saving and the Twin Deficits: Myth and Reality', in J.H. Gapinski (ed.), *The Economics of Saving*, Norwell, MA: Kluwer Academic, pp. 109–33.

Eisner, Robert (1993c), 'Clinton, Deficits, and the U.S. Economy', *Challenge*, 36 (3), 47–50.

Eisner, Robert (1994a), *The Misunderstood Economy: What Counts and How to Count It*, Boston, MA: Harvard Business School Press.

Eisner, Robert (1994b), 'Real Government Saving and the Future', *Journal of Economic Behavior and Organization*, 23 (2), 111–26.

Eisner, Robert (1994c), 'Real Government Saving and the Future: Reply', *Journal of Economic Behavior and Organization*, 23 (2), 170–71.

Eisner, Robert (1994d), 'Deficits, Saving, and Economic Policy', *American Economist*, 38 (2), 3–11.

Eisner, Robert (1994*e*), 'National Saving and Budget Deficits', *Review of Economics and Statistics*, 76 (1), 181–6.

Eisner, Robert (1994f), 'Challenge to the Natural Rate Doctrine', *Journal of Post Keynesian Economics*, 17 (1), 159–61.

Eisner, Robert (1994*g*), 'Keynes Is Not Dead, Just Drugged and Dormant', *Journal of Post Keynesian Economics*, 17 (2), 211–29.

Eisner, Robert (1997), *The Great Deficit Scares: The Federal Budget, Trade and Social Security*, New York: Century Foundation Press.

Eisner, R. and S.I. Hwang (1993), 'Self-correcting Real Deficits: A New Lesson in Functional Finance', in H.A.A. Verbon et al. (eds), *The Political Economy of Government Debt: Contributions to Economic Analysis*, Amsterdam: North-Holland, v. 219, 255–94.

Eisner, R. and P.J. Pieper (1984), 'A New View of the Federal Debt and Budget Deficits', *American Economic Review*, 74 (1), 11–29.

Eisner, R. and P.J. Pieper (1986), 'A New View of the Federal Debt and Budget Deficits: Reply', *American Economic Review*, 76 (5), 1156–57.

Eisner, R. and P.J. Pieper (1987), 'How to Make Sense of the Deficit', in R.H. Fink and J.C. High (eds), *A Nation in Debt: Economists Debate the Federal Budget Deficit*, Frederick, MD: University Publications of America, pp. 87–101.

Eisner, R. and P.J. Pieper (1988a): 'Deficits, Monetary Policy, and Real Economic Activity', in K.J. Arrow and M.J. Boskin (eds), *The Economics of Public Debt*, New York: St. Martin's Press, pp. 3–38.

Eisner, R. and P.J. Pieper (1988b), 'The Relationship between Real Deficits and Real Growth: A Critique: Rejoinder', *Journal of Post Keynesian Economics*, 11(1), 161–8.

Eisner, R. and P.J. Pieper (1989), 'Inflation-adjusted Government Budget Deficits and Real Economic Activity: Rejoinder', *Annales d'Economie et de Statistique*, 0 (13), January–March, 139–47.

Eisner, R. and P.J. Pieper (1992), 'Real Deficits and Real Growth: A Further View', *Journal of Post Keynesian Economics*, 15 (1), 43–9.

Godley, W. and F. Cripps (1983), *Macroeconomics*, Oxford: Oxford University Press.

Keynes, J.M. and H.D. Henderson (1929 [1972]), 'Can Lloyd George Do It?' in *Essays in Persuasion: The Collected Writings of John Maynard Keynes*, v. 9, Cambridge: Macmillan, 86–125.

Knapp, G.F. (1924), *The State Theory of Money*, London: Macmillan.

Lerner, A.P. (1943), 'Functional Finance and the Federal Debt', *Social Research*, 10 (1), 38–52.

Lerner, A.P. (1947), 'Money as a Creature of the State', *American Economic Review*, 37 (2), 312–17.

Lerner, A.P. (1978), 'A Wage-increase Permit Plan to Stop Inflation', *Brookings Papers on Economic Activity*, (2), 491–505.

Lerner, A.P. (1980a), *MAP: A Market Anti-inflation Plan*, New York: Harcourt Brace Jovanovitch.
Lerner, A.P. (1980b), 'A Non-monetarist View of the Nature of Stagflation and a Plan for Mobilizing the Market Mechanism to Cure It', *Social Research*, 47 (2), 339–51.
Lerner, A.P. and D. Colander (1982), 'Anti-inflation Incentives', *Kyklos*, 35 (1), 39–52.
Nell, E.J. (1998), *The General Theory of Transformational Growth: Keynes After Sraffa*, Cambridge: Cambridge University Press.
Seidman, L.S. (1997a), *The USA Tax: A Progressive Consumption Tax*, Cambridge, MA: MIT Press.
Seidman, L.S. (1997b), 'A Progressive Consumption Tax,' *Challenge*, 40 (6), 63–84.
Turgeon, L. (1996), *Bastard Keynesianism: The Evolution of Economic Thinking and Policymaking since World War II*, Westport, CT: Greenwood Press.
Vickrey, W.S. (1986a): 'Budget-smudget. Why Balance What, How, and When?' *Atlantic Economic Journal*, 14 (3), 6–13.
Vickrey, W.S. (1986b), 'The Need for a Direct Anti-inflation Program', in D.C. Colander (ed.), *Incentive-based Incomes Policies: Advances in TIP and MAP*, Cambridge, MA: Harper and Row, pp. 27–34.
Vickrey, W.S. (1986c), 'Design of a Market Anti-inflation Program', in David Colander (ed.), '*Incentive-based Incomes Policies: Advances in TIP and MAP*', Cambridge, MA: Harper and Row, Ballinger (1986), pp. 149–58.
Vickrey, W.S. (1992a), 'Meaningfully Defining Deficits and Debt,' *American Economic Review*, 82 (2), 305–10.
Vickrey, W.S. (1992b), 'Chock-full Employment without Increased Inflation: A Proposal for Marketable Markup Warrants', '*American Economic Review*, 82 (2), 341–5.
Vickrey, W.S. (1993a), 'Today's Task for Economists', *American Economic Review*, 83 (1), 1–10.
Vickrey, W.S. (1993b), 'The Other Side of the Coin', *American Economist*, 37 (2), 5–16.
Vickrey, W.S. (1994a), 'Necessary and Optimum Government Debt', in *Public Economics: Selected Papers by William Vickrey*, New York: Cambridge University Press, pp. 421–31.
Vickrey, W.S. (1994b), 'Why Not Chock-full Employment?' *Atlantic Economic Journal*, 22 (1), 39–45.
Vickrey, W.S. (1997), 'A Trans-Keynesian Manifesto (Thoughts about an Asset-based Macroeconomics)', *Journal of Post Keynesian Economics*, 19 (4), 495–510.
Wray, L.R. (1998), *Understanding Modern Money: The Key to Full Employment and Price Stability*, Cheltenham, UK and Lyme, US: Edward Elgar.

APPENDIX: DEBT-TO-GDP RATIO BY PRIVATE WEALTH-TO-SPENDING TURNOVER RATE: ASSUMPTIONS AND DATA UNDERLYING FIGURE 14.1

Table 14A.1 Assumptions of the 'big government' and 'small government' examples

Assumptions/Example	'Big government' (%)	'Small government' (%)
Share of government production in the domestic product	20 ($a = 0.20$)	10 ($a = 0.10$)
Share of government spending in the domestic product	30 ($b = 0.30$)	15 ($b = 0.15$)
Overall capital–output ratio	400 ($v = 4.00$)	400 ($v = 4.00$)

Table 14A.2 Calculations of steady-stake debt-to-GDP ratios for different levels of the private wealth-to-spending turnover rate

u	'Big government'	'Small government'
0.08	5.55	7.03
0.09	4.58	5.84
0.10	3.80	4.90
0.11	3.16	4.13
0.12	2.63	3.48
0.13	2.18	2.94
0.14	1.80	2.47
0.15	1.47	2.07
0.16	1.18	1.71
0.17	0.92	1.40
0.18	0.69	1.12
0.19	0.48	0.87
0.20	0.30	0.65
0.21	0.13	0.45
0.22	–0.02	0.26
0.23	–0.16	0.10
0.24	–0.28	–0.06

15. The operational role of functional finance for labor market behavior and outcomes

Ingrid H. Rima

Before World War II, economists who concerned themselves with 'labor issues' often identified themselves with that distinctively American approach known as 'institutionalism.' With the economic malaise of the 1930s, their interests overlapped with those of macroeconomists like J.M. Keynes, Abba Lerner, Alvin Hansen, and Adolph Lowe, all of whom took the position that the functioning of the macroeconomy can and should be managed to protect society from the vagaries of the free market.

After 1945, the postwar economy brought with it relative prosperity and other institutional and societal changes that fundamentally altered labor market behavior and outcomes, and, consequently, the ways in which economists defined the problems they would single out for study. Two societal changes stand out with respect to labor markets: the first is the perception of education as an investment in a future income stream; the second is the perception of labor force participation as an activity that is competitive with other uses of time, not only for males, but also for females. For economists trained in marginal analysis, these institutional developments were interpreted as offering an opportunity to pursue a new research agenda. Unfortunately, they also led most labor economists toward their present predominantly microeconomic orientation in which scant attention is paid to the interdependence of the behavioral decisions of firms and households or to their links to the macro economy. The latter is conventionally presumed to have strong tendencies toward labor markets that equilibrate at employment levels that provide jobs for all who wish to work at prevailing real wages.

From the 1970s to the present the economy has shifted from the 'factory age' to the 'computer age,' which has also been accompanied by a sectoral change in the 'job mix' from goods production to services. While total employment has grown, the changing job mix has compromised employer–employee relationships that enabled workers to progress along 'job ladders' after being hired to fill entry-level jobs. As they progressed, workers tended to be shielded from both wage cuts and job cuts. Indeed, core firms were themselves insulated from market vagaries by their ability to set output prices by marking up average labor costs. Unlike firms in the periphery, they became 'price makers' who could establish a symbiotic relationship with their unions as long as they were able to pass along wage increases to their customers.

Not only has the proportion of jobs in the manufacturing sector declined in the last two decades but, what is even more dramatic, there has been a shift toward fixed production coefficients. Thus the notion that business firms typically rely on 'factor substitution' is increasingly inconsistent with modern technology and, often, with work place rules. The production capacities of increasing plant sizes and multi-plant operations typically operating with excess capacity reduces labor productivity, because the latter is dependent on the proportion of capacity utilized. These structural changes increase the adverse employment effects of future deficiencies in aggregate demand. This is the rationale for the North American Free Trade Agreement (NAFTA) agreement and the 1994 General Agreement on Tariffs and Trade (GATT) accord that signal a US commitment to utilizing trade policy as an engine of economic growth and job creation. Their passage is an institutional fact of life implicitly directed toward alleviating the possibility of long-term involuntary unemployment. Given the premise that contemporary labor market theory has about the tendency of markets to clear, many economists are unable to conceptualize, let alone solve, the problem of unemployment. The critical question, then, is what sort of analytical framework can be developed to replace, or at least supplement, the still-dominant micro/macro compartmentalization of economics, especially as it relates to labor market phenomena and behavior.[1]

THE PERSPECTIVE OF A SYSTEMS APPROACH

I suggest the adoption of a systems perspective that views the economy as comprised of three major subsystems: the production subsystem, the anthropogenic subsystem, and the monetary-financial subsystem. The anthropogenic subsystem is composed of families, schools, unions, religious organizations and other social institutions that contribute toward educating, training, motivating and directing the production of human competencies. Human competencies are 'inputs' employed by the production subsystem that includes for-profit business firms, federal, state and local government agencies, educational and non-profit institutions and the military. Their relationships are readily visualized in terms of a Venn diagram like that displayed in Figure 15.1.

The rectangle that is the universal set represents the economic system. The two inner circles represent the anthropogenic subsystem *A* and the production

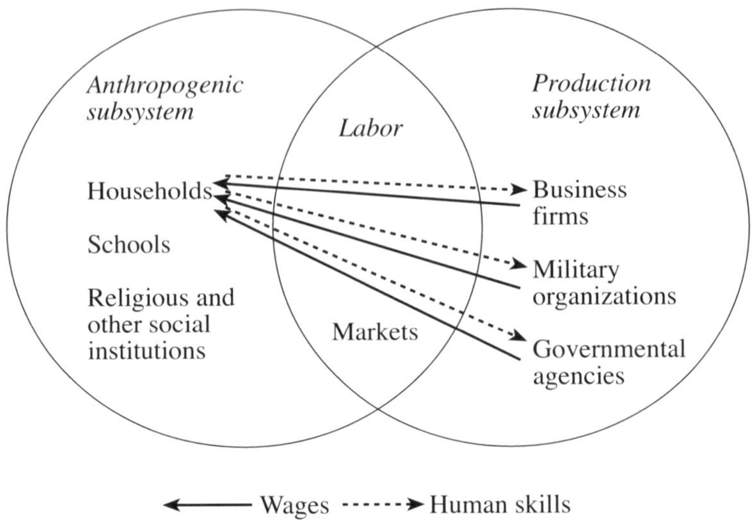

Figure 15.1 The economic system and its subsystems

subsystem *P*. Realistically, employers (including the military) are also subsets of the anthropogenic subsystem, because they provide various kinds of training. However, for simplicity, the *A* set is represented as comprised of only two subsets: households and schools. The anthropogenic subsystem and the production subsystem are linked via the labor market. If *A* is a set and *P* is a set, the labor market is usefully interpreted as the union of subsystems *A* and *P*. Operationally, there is a flow of 'inputs' from the anthropogenic subsystem *A*, and an income flow (that is, wages, salaries and other labor income) that reflects payments by the production subsystem *P* to households for the human competencies they sell to employers. What distinguishes these relationships from those perceived by mainstream theorists is that wages and other worker payments are conceived as being determined by social institutions, rather than by the labor market, while short-run employment is envisioned as being determined by the level of aggregate demand in the market for goods and services.

The monetary subsystem clearly interacts with both *A* and *P* and all three are subsets of the universal set, which is the economy. A systems approach to understanding the functioning of the economy thus leads in the direction of an aggregate or macroeconomic perspective of labor market behaviors and outcomes, which is considerably broader than the microeconomic approach of the contemporary mainstream. A systems approach also clearly incorporates the fiscal and monetary institutions of the economy. It thus offers an approach not only for examining the labor market aspects of the anthropogenic and production subsystems, but also lends itself to recognizing the relevance of functional finance as a tool for managing the aggregate economy. Based on the output–employment function and the premise (*à la* Kalecki, 1971) that the wages earned by the household are spent on consumption, while the profits retained by the production subsystem finances investment, the link between the effective demand for output and employment is thus restored, for it is the level of *C+I* that generates the level of employment. Hence, employment emanates from the demand for output (and not the labor market), while wage rates are institutionally determined. This is the rationale for representing the labor market in Figure 15.1 as a union of subsystems *A* and *P*.

THE COMPLEMENTARITY BETWEEN A SYSTEMS PERSPECTIVE AND FUNCTIONAL FINANCE

Proponents of functional finance are committed to the principle that government's power to tax, spend, borrow and manage its debt can and should be used as an instrument for achieving the goals sanctioned by a democratic voting process for the macroeconomy. The premise of functional finance is quite explicitly that a dynamic capitalistic economy is inherently unstable, so that unemployment and price instabilities periodically impose economic pain on the economy as a whole, which impacts most severely on labor markets. Wages and salaries comprise two-thirds of earned income; both J.M. Keynes, and subsequently Laurence Klein and Richard Kosabud, have shown the ratio of the wage relative to the profit share to be historically constant in national income (Keynes, 1939; Klein and Kosabud, 1961). The implication, as Kenneth Galbraith (1974) put it, is that institutional influences have tended to generate 'countervailing' forces when the historical balance shows tendencies toward disruption. The rationale for functional finance is found, quite simply, in its capacity to rein in the potential for a price-directed economy to 'overshoot' or 'undershoot' rather than steer the economy directly toward its objective of 'full' employment, while avoiding significant upward pressure on prices.

Both objectives were clearly articulated in the US in the Full Employment Act of 1946. This landmark legislation in American economic history required the federal government to assume responsibility for creating and maintaining useful employment opportunities for all who are able and willing to work. It was amended in 1978 by the Full Employment and Balanced Growth Act, which specified a numerical unemployment rate goal not to exceed 3 per cent among individuals aged 20 and over, and 4 per cent among individuals 15 to 20, to be achieved within a period of five years. The 1978 Act also recognized that employment policy is unavoidably intertwined with anti-inflationary policy.

The ongoing legal requirement that policies maintain low rates of unemployment, while restraining inflation and avoiding deflation, speaks to the issue of the means by which these policies may be made operational should the malaise of serious unemployment recur. It is unrealistic to expect that the very low unemployment rate of approximately 4.5 per cent of the 1997–2000 years – the lowest rate to be achieved by a peacetime economy – can be extended indefinitely into the future. When the economy falters, as it has in the US since March 2001, and is less responsive to repeated cuts in interest rates than was generally expected, the central question becomes: What other measures might be put into place? Tax cuts as a fiscal measure came to the fore for the first time in spring 2001 since the famous Kennedy tax cuts of the 1960s. Inexplicably, however, the tax reductions were not presented as part and parcel of a comprehensive program of public finance comprised of tax expenditure and debt management components. Thus it contrasts with functional finance as a multi-pronged policy designed to become operative automatically as needed in order to steer the economy in the event of an identifiable lapse to 'full' employment, however defined, by 'the prevention of depression and the maintenance of the value of money' (Lerner, 1947: 314). It is precisely because 'money is a creature of the state' (Lerner, 1947) that government is able to tax, borrow, manage its debt and make expenditures, including those that encourage the private sector to create jobs and, failing that, to become the employer of last resort (ELR). Simultaneously, government must maintain money's purchasing power by restraining whatever deflationary tendencies might accompany unemployment that triggers automatic countermeasures.

A public service sector was created under Titles II and VI of CETA, the Comprehensive Employment and Training Act of 1973. In excess of 300,000 Public Service Employment slots were funded under all CETA titles between 1975 and 1977 (Rima, 1996: Chapter 18).[2] Public funds were used to provide employment to individuals disadvantaged in terms of skills and therefore especially vulnerable to unemployment. The provision of income via Public Service Employment (or ELR) thus helps to maintain the viability of the anthropogenic (or *A*) sub-system by supporting consumption expenditures and school attendance. The former helps support the production (or *P*) subsystem, while also limiting premature school leaving that crowds the labor market with young, inexperienced job seekers. In principle, a Public Service Employment program should thus be phased out in a counter-cyclical fashion. This means that the jobs created be those that require only very short and non-specific training.

ADDITIONAL ASPECTS OF PSE

One of the chief limitations of the PSE approach is that PSE subsidies may be misdirected when used by state or local governments to pay employees already hired, or workers who would have been hired in the absence of the program. This kind of 'fiscal substitution' appears inherent in a PSE approach because it functions as a disguised form of revenue sharing.

A study prepared under the auspices of the National Planning Association estimated a fiscal substitution effect of 0.46 after one year.[3] Subsequent studies produced conflicting results, but verified that the fiscal-substitution effect can be substantial (Bergman and Bennett, 1977).[4] The greater the substitution of federal funds for state and local funds, the less effectively PSE will operate as an employment program.[5] There is also evidence that the persons who were hired into public service unemployment were predominantly whites with nine or more years of education (Johnson and Tomola, 1978). Their human competencies and experience suggest that they are likely to have a better than average chance of finding jobs in the private sector. However, once placed in public service, these persons presumably have less time and less incentive to search for private sector employment, so their employment in the public sector may discourage their search for private sector employment. Their employment in the public sector may also represent a less productive use of their capabilities than would result from private employment could it be made available.

The fact that a high proportion of persons placed into public service employment are not truly disadvantaged appears to be associated with the tendency for public service employment legislation to create jobs of a type more typically associated with permanent careers. The more career-oriented public service jobs become, the more difficult for the jobs created to be temporary. In principle, a public employment program (ELR) should thus be phased out in a counter-cyclical fashion. This type of timing would mean that the jobs created be those that require only very short and non-specific training and that they lend themselves to being filled by persons of various ages with a wide range of previous training and experience. It is clearly difficult to plan a program that incorporates all these features. It is, however, worth recognizing that, while the fiscal-substitution effect limits the effectiveness of the PSE program as an unemployment-reducing tool, it may nevertheless be effective as an antipoverty program if it alters the composition of employment to favor disadvantaged workers.

THE IMPACT OF A TAX CUT AS AN ALTERNATIVE EMPLOYMENT POLICY

A tax cut can, in principle, be used as an alternative to public service employment. The critical question at issue is the relative efficiency of the two mechanisms for creating increments of employment. The Council of Economic

Advisors addressed itself to this question by estimating the number of jobs created and paid for under a $1 billion Public Service Employment program as compared with an equivalent federal tax cut (Chiswick and O'Neill, 117). It was estimated that a $1 billion PSE program could pay for approximately 110,000 job opportunities at $9,000 per job. However it was also estimated that a portion of these jobs would merely displace jobs normally generated by state and local governments without federal aid. On the basis of past experience, it was estimated that only initially does a PSE program create more jobs than can be achieved by means of a tax reduction. This is the case because, unlike the effect of the PSE program, the performance-effect of a tax cut continues to increase. If the objective of a program is to increase aggregate employment as much and as rapidly as possible, a PSE program can be more effective in the short run (per unit of budget deficit), than any other type of fiscal policy, if the fiscal-substitution effect is small (Bergman and Bennett, 1977). This is important to recognize because time is of the essence when an economy is confronted with a serious unemployment problem. Delay is likely to increase the magnitude of the problem, thereby expanding the magnitude of the effort that is required to halt the contraction of employment. Thus, the *speed* of the impact of the policy must be considered as much as its size in guiding the choice between PSE and tax cuts as employment-policy tools.

WAGE SUBSIDIES TO INCREASE EMPLOYMENT

The application of functional finance to the operation of the labor market in the form of the payment of wage subsidies to employers to encourage the hiring of disadvantaged workers is a means for altering the mix of employment in their favor while also improving the inflation/unemployment trade-off. One proposal, which related specifically to teenage workers, suggested giving all teenagers vouchers that can be used either for schooling or to subsidize employers who hire them (Feldstein, 1973). This proposal has not been translated into policy. However, under the now phased-out Concentrated Employment Program (CEP), employers were reimbursed for the costs of job training to encourage them to hire workers they would otherwise not consider. Reimbursement of training costs incurred by firms that locate plants in or near slum areas is provided for under the Jobs Opportunities in the Business Sector (JOBS) program.

The Revenue Act of 1978 also provided for tax credits of up to 50 per cent of the wages paid to individuals who are members of 'targeted groups.' These groups included persons receiving vocational rehabilitation, economically disadvantaged youths, economically disadvantaged Vietnam veterans, SSI recipients, general-assistance recipients, youths participating in cooperative-education programs and economically disadvantaged ex-convicts. Tax credits are not (and should not) be made available to employers receiving federally funded payments to provide on-the-job training for such persons.

From the standpoint of the employee, a wage-subsidy scheme is intended to have essentially the same effect as direct-job creation. That is, the intent of the subsidy would be to change the relative wage paid by firms for secondary as compared with primary labor. Primary workers become relatively more expensive to employ if, in effect, a subsidy reduces the relative cost of employing secondary workers. Thus, the unemployment rate of secondary workers would tend to decline as this group is substituted for primary workers in the private sector. However, it has been argued that wage subsidies do not promise the same reduction in unemployment as does direct-job creation. While there is an additional incentive to employers to hire disadvantaged workers, their job-search behavior may not be modified, because their relative wage is the same as it would be without the wage subsidy. The actual impact of wage subsidies on employment, as is the case with public-service employment, is an empirical question that requires further investigation in order to test the theoretical conclusions that have been reached about the effectiveness of alternative ways of changing the employment mix so that disadvantaged workers do not continuously bear the dual burden of unemployment and inflation disproportionately.

At present, relatively low rates of unemployment in the private sector have compromised the need for public service employment. Wage subsidies to the private sector have also been scaled back because of limited funding. Yet the ongoing creation of *well-paid* jobs remains a priority issue. Since the economy's best-paid jobs have historically been in the manufacturing sector, manufacturing's revival is being encouraged by a variety of measures, including the stimulus of export demand to create new employment opportunities. These policy measures are examined below.

TRADE POLICY AS AN ASPECT OF FUNCTIONAL FINANCE

Monetary and fiscal policy indirectly affect wage rates and prices by impacting interest rates and debt management as well as tax revenues and expenditures, which in turn impinge on the operation of market forces. The inadequacies of these policies, when the economy is experiencing inflation and/or a large public debt, have encouraged pursuit of a broader free trade policy in the US, stimulating export demand to create new employment opportunities. 'Export-led growth' policies have long been favored by the less developed countries and the newly developed countries which regarded them as the policy measures of choice for propelling their economies rapidly into the twenty-first century. In contrast, the US has been far less active in pursuing trade as a vehicle for long-term growth and job creation. While the US has actively supported tariff reductions, the 1993 NAFTA, as a measure aimed at improving job growth, reflects an important change in the US policy mix. Nevertheless, worldwide productivity growth suggests a potential for a worldwide dearth of aggregate demand and greater competition for goods markets. Since Americans have a high propensity to consume imported goods, a relative decline in household spending bodes ill not only for the US economy, but also for the economies of its trading partners. In principle, therefore, assuming that the political climate would allow it, the introduction of public service employment as part of a functional finance program, while providing a degree of support for the economies of our trading partners – whose export expenditures (along with those of government) are implicit rather than explicit in our simplified systems model of the macroeconomy – would serve as a floor under the level of the American economy.

CONCLUDING THOUGHTS

As substantial as the gains enjoyed by the American economy from the long boom of the closing decades of the twentieth century are, the downside is that much of the 'baby-boom' generation is left with the misleading impression that low unemployment, low inflation and rising stock prices are a normal part of ongoing growth. The historical facts suggest the contrary. Yet there is little contemporary appreciation of the relevance of developing an arsenal of automatic stabilizers that are continuously available to be pressed into service when (and not if) the need arises for stabilizing the economy's level of employment.

While downturns manifest themselves in multiple ways, none are more painful than involuntary unemployment. Keynes identified involuntary unemployment as the pervasiveness of jobless workers who are qualified and willing to work at particular jobs at the current level of real wages but are unable to find employment. Its central importance has been blurred by the very low (that is, 4 to 4.5 per cent) unemployment level of the recent past. This experience has underscored the mainstream belief that the economy has an inherent tendency toward 'full' employment. Even before society's early experiences with technological unemployment during the nineteenth-century factory era, political economists (as they were then called) wrote about the positive role that falling market wages would tend to have in restoring the balance (that is, equilibrium) between labor supply and demand. Labor markets were thought to 'clear' through the mechanism of price changes in essentially the same way as commodity markets became cleared because employers were believed to always stand ready to employ workers who are willing to accept wages that approximate the market value of the product they produce. Thus in the past, and even today, political economists have counseled that a wise government is one whose legal system traditionally prohibits combinations of workers into unions that demand higher wages on the ground that this action leads chiefly to condemning some of their number to joblessness.

Keynes's contrary perspective gave impetus to the tradition of economic thought maintaining that when there is large-scale unemployment, money and real wages are both resistant to downward revision, so that modern economies may find themselves predisposed to experiencing 'involuntary unemployment' because of the insufficiency of aggregate demand. As the belief of economists in the relevance of the concept of involuntary unemployment has been compromised, so too has their appreciation of the inherent link, in a modern economy, between employment and aggregate effective demand. Hence consumption and investment expenditures move in the *same* direction contrary to the mainstream view that the price mechanism causes consumption and investment to move inversely with one another, which also tends to stabilize employment.

If, alternatively, employment is conceived as a function of output (or sales) that reflects the level of real wages, what emerges is a vision of the labor market that links output to expenditure. Output reflects the product-producing capability of the economy, given its production function; thus the expenditure of the wages earned and spent on consumption goods, plus the profits retained by businesses that finance investment, generates the economy's level of employment. Employment is not determined by a wage/price mechanism in the labor market. Rather, the labor market reflects the utilization of workers to harness the stock of capital needed to supply the output of consumer goods that wage recipients buy with the wages they earn. Conceptually the labor market may thus be represented as the union of the anthropogenic subsystem (*A*) and the production subsystem (*P*) in Figure 15.1. This is a representation that makes it quite clear that the labor market is not an independent entity in which the wage/price mechanism can produce a 'clearing' of all workers seeking jobs at current wages. It follows that when the malaise of unemployment manifests itself, to avoid the consequences of unemployment that is 'serious' – both in terms of numbers and duration – a revisit of the concept of functional finance is clearly relevant. The reactivation of the role of government as the employer of last resort by restoring the PSE program (phased out in 1978 when financing of the CETA provisions ended), along with other automatic stabilizers, would then follow. In sum, these policies could impart strong tendencies toward stability to dynamic price-directed economies by circumventing the need for hasty makeshift *ad hoc* measures under emergency conditions.

NOTES

1. Contemporary labor market theory presents a fairly straightforward application of traditional demand and supply analysis that has been transferred from its commodity market origins onto a presumed equivalent: the human resource market. This characteristic was the basis for Ingrid Rima's 'Reinterpretation of the Labor Supply function,' *Journal of Post-Keynesian Economics*, 1983.
2. The program phased out in 1981 because the 1978 Act did not provide ongoing funding.
3. *An Evaluation of the Economic Impact Project of the Public Employment Program*, Manpower Administration, U.S. Department of Labor Control No. 42-2-001-11 Final Report (May 1974).
4. Supplement to the 1976 Report to the Council of Economic Advisors.

REFERENCES

Bergman, Barbara and Robert L. Bennett (1977), 'Macroeconomic Effects of a Humphrey–Hawkins Type Program,' *Papers and Proceedings of the American Economics Association*, February, 265–70.

Chiswick, Barry and June O'Neill (1977) *Human Resources and Income Distribution: Issues and Policies*, New York: W.W. Norton, pp. 117.

Feldstein, Martin S. (1973), 'Lowering the Permanent Rate of Unemployment,' *Joint Economic Committee*, 93 (1), Washington: General Printing Office.

Galbraith, J.K. (1952), *American Capitalism: A Theory of Countervailing Power*, New York: Houghton Mifflin, pp. 515.

Galbraith, John Kenneth (1974) *The New Industrial Estate*, 2nd edn. rev., Harmondsworth: Penguin.

Johnson, George E. (1977), 'The Fiscal Substitution Effect of Alternative Approaches to Public Service Employment Policy,' *Journal of Human Resources*, 12 (1).

Kalecki, M. (1971) 'Class Struggle and the Distribution of National Income', reprinted in *Selected Essays on the Dynamics of the Capitalist Economy 1933–70*, Cambridge: Cambridge University Press.

Keynes, J.M. (1939), 'Relative Movements of Real Wages and Output,' *Economics Journal*, 49, 48.

Klein, L. and R.F. Kosabud (1961), 'Some Econometrics of Growth: Great Ratios of Econometrics,' *Quarterly Journal of Economics* 75, 173–98.

Lerner, Abba (1941), 'The Economic Steering Wheel,' *University Review*, June.

Lerner, Abba (1943), 'Functional Finance and the Federal Debt', *Social Research*, February, 10, 38–51.

Lerner, Abba (1944), *The Economics of Control*, New York: Macmillan.

Lerner, Abba (1947), *American Economic Review* 37 (2), 312–317.

Lerner, Abba and David Colander (1951), *The Economics of Employment*, New York: McGraw-Hill.

Lerner, Abba and David Colander (1983), 'Reinterpreting the Labor Supply Curve,' *Journal of Post-Keynesian Economics*, 5 (2).

Rima, Ingrid H. (1984), 'Involuntary Unemployment and Labor Supply,' *Journal of Post-Keynesian Economics*, 6 (4), 540–550.

Rima, Ingrid H. (1995), *Labor Markets in a Global Economy*, Armonk, NY: M.E. Sharpe.

Rima, Ingrid H. (1996), *Labor Markets in a Global Economy: An Introduction*, Armonk, NY: M.E. Sharpe.

Rima, Ingrid H. (2000), 'Sectoral Changes in Employment: An Eclectic Perspective on "Good" Jobs and "Poor" Jobs,' *Review of Political Economy*, 12 (2).

16. The job guarantee: full employment and price stability in a small open economy

William F. Mitchell

1. INTRODUCTION

High and persistent unemployment has pervaded almost every OECD country since the mid-1970s. The period of rising unemployment began with the rapid inflation of the mid-1970s. The inflation left an indelible impression on policy makers who became captives of the resurgent new labor economics and its macroeconomic counterpart, monetarism. The goal of low inflation led to excessively restrictive fiscal and monetary policy stances by OECD governments driven by a false analogy between the household budgetary constraints and government budgetary constraints (Mitchell, 1996, 1998). This has resulted in rising labor productivity combined with GDP growth in OECD countries that is generally below that necessary to absorb the growth in the labor force.[1]

Ultimately, mass unemployment arises because the government budget deficit, relative to the desires of the private sector to meet its tax obligations, is too small to save and to hold money for transactions purposes. It is thus a macroeconomic phenomenon and can never be a 'real wage' problem as Keynes noted many years ago. The solution to this problem is for government to use deficit spending to introduce a Job Guarantee policy that can simultaneously achieve full employment and price stability (Mitchell 1996, 1998).[2] The Job Guarantee approach to full employment opposes the current policy directions of governments in the OECD economies that emphasize fiscal consolidation and supply-side reforms like deregulation and privatization.

The fallacious analogies that government spending, taxation and debt issue is equivalent to the spending and financing decisions of the household and that governments, like households, should seek financing prior to spending has led to the pursuit of budget surpluses in order to avoid the higher tax and interest rates that would allegedly arise. Reemerging free-market ideology has convinced us wrongly that government involvement in the economy imposes costs, and we have thus supported governments that have significantly reduced their fiscal involvement in economic activity.

Economies that avoided the plunge into high unemployment over this period maintained a 'sector of the economy which effectively functions as an employer of the last resort, which absorbs the shocks which occur from time to time . . .' (Ormerod, 1994: 203). The Job Guarantee policy fulfills this absorption function. In this chapter some features of the Job Guarantee approach to full employment and price stability are developed (see Mitchell, 1996, 1998, 1999a, 1999b, 2000a). Under the Job Guarantee approach, the government continuously absorbs workers displaced from private sector employment. The Job Guarantee workers serve as a 'buffer stock' of labor being paid the minimum wage that sets a wage floor for the economy, thus preventing the occurrence of serious deflation and defining the private sector wage structure. Government employment and spending automatically increases (decreases), as jobs are lost (gained) in the private sector. We will demonstrate that this policy approach generates full employment and price stability. Specifically we contrast the inflation control mechanisms of the Job Guarantee model with those in an economy subject to a NAIRU.[3] The concept of the Non-Accelerating Inflation Buffer Employment Ratio (NAIBER) first developed in Mitchell (1998) is explained further.

There are two broad ways in which government can maintain price stability: first, it can adopt the NAIRU approach by suppressing the budget deficit and generating unemployment; second, it can conduct a Job Guarantee policy whereby the public sector, setting and maintaining a base level wage, absorbs all the current idle workers into paid employment. The relevant price stability concept is the NAIBER.[4] The change in the buffer employment ratio (BER)[5] disciplines the wage–price pressures in the private sector by asserting the buffer stock wage as the numeraire.[6] No rational government with an understanding of the workings of its own currency works and the role of the budget deficit would choose the NAIRU approach with its enormous costs of lost output and social alienation.[7]

This chapter also considers the financial implications of the Job Guarantee model in the context of a small open economy. In addition to the normal arguments that monetarists and others use to justify their case against fiscal activism (crowding out, inefficient resource usage), it is often argued that increased globalization imposes further restrictions on the ability of governments to pursue independent fiscal and monetary policy. In the case of Australia, it is alleged that budget deficits only result in growing current account deficits and rising debt levels. Reacting to this, it is asserted that external funds managers can enforce higher interest rates leading to even lower growth and higher unemployment in the domestic economy. It is shown that all the orthodox arguments against the use of budget deficits are spurious and not founded on any firm empirical evidence.

The outline of the chapter is as follows: Section 2 briefly explains the motivation that led to the development of the Job Guarantee approach to full employment and price stability; Section 3 compares and contrasts the inflation control mechanisms of the NAIRU and the Job Guarantee approaches; Section 4 considers the financial considerations. Concluding remarks follow.

2. THE DEVELOPMENT OF THE JOB GUARANTEE APPROACH

In Australia, despite the paradigm shift in macroeconomics from Keynesian demand management to the monetarist supply-side approach, empirical evidence still supported the use of expansionary fiscal and monetary policy and public sector job creation (for example, Mitchell, 1987a, 1987b, 1994, 1996; Mitchell et al., 1995). The solutions proposed, however, relied heavily on income policy guidelines and were not, in retrospect, comprehensive enough. Further, the stimulus that would be forthcoming was not conceived to be adequately focused to support environmental sustainability, a goal usually ignored in orthodox macroeconomics. In this context, the Job Guarantee reflects work that was conceived when this author was a fourth-year student at the University of Melbourne in the late 1970s.

The logic of the policy was suggested by a series of lectures on the Wool Floor Price Scheme introduced by the Commonwealth Government of Australia in November 1970. The relatively simple scheme worked through government hearing submissions from the Wool Council of Australia and the Australian Wool Corporation (AWC) to establish a floor price for wool. The government then guaranteed that the price would not fall below the level established. There was a lot of lobbying to get the floor price above the implied market price. The price was maintained by the AWC's purchase of stocks of wool in the auction markets. The purchases were financed from a Market Support Fund (MSF) accumulated through small contributions from growers based on the value of its clip. Fund shortages were made up with government-guaranteed loans. For economists, the major controversy was an issue as to whether the 'tinkering with the price mechanism' was price stabilization or price maintenance (Throsby, 1972: 162). This was not unimportant in a time when prices were in sectoral decline and a minimum guaranteed floor price implied ever-increasing AWC stocks. Other problems included the pressure of substitutability from synthetic fibers and the maintenance of production levels, which by themselves would continue to depress prices. The debate over the scheme (adequately summarized by Parish, 1964; and Lloyd, 1965) focused on the price intervention.

By applying reverse logic, one could utilize the concept without encountering the problems of price tinkering. In effect, the Wool Floor Price Scheme generated 'full employment' for wool production. Clearly, in the wool situation, there was an issue as to what constituted a reasonable level of output in a time of declining demand. But the same argument is not relevant when applied to available labor. We define full employment to be the state of no involuntary unemployment ensured by a sufficient number of available jobs in relation to the labor supply at current money wage rates. This amounts to a rejection of the notion that all unemployment is voluntary. It also contradicts the idea that full employment can be defined by market relations, the intersection of the labor demand and supply curves at some 'equilibrium price' (for example, Phelps, 1967; Friedman, 1968). Accordingly mass unemployment is construed as a macroeconomic problem related to deficient demand, which in turn reflects a deficient budget deficit.

The reverse logic noted above implies that we should impose a price guarantee below the 'prevailing market price' and generate a buffer stock of working hours to absorb the excess of working hours at the current market price. This will generate full employment without the problems of price tinkering. That idea was the seed of the Job Guarantee model.[8]

The work of Benjamin Graham (1937) is also instructive. He discusses the idea of stabilizing prices and standards of living by surplus storage. He documents the ways the government might deal with surplus production in the economy. Graham (1937: 18) says, 'The State may deal with actual or threatened surplus in one of four ways: (a) by preventing it; (b) by destroying it; (c) by "dumping" it; or (d) by conserving it.' In the context of an excess supply of labor, governments had adopted a 'dumping' strategy via the NAIRU. It made much better sense to use the conservation approach. Graham (1937: 34) notes:

> The first conclusion is that wherever surplus has been conserved primarily for future *use* the plan has been sensible and successful, unless marred by glaring errors of administration. The second conclusion is that when the surplus has been acquired and held primarily for future *sale* the plan has been vulnerable to adverse developments.

The distinction is important in the development of the Job Guarantee model. The Wool Floor Price Scheme was an example of storage for future sale and was motivated not to help the consumer of wool, but the producer. The Job Guarantee policy is an example of storage for use where the 'reserve is established to meet a future need which experience has taught us is likely to develop' (Graham, 1937: 35). Graham also analysed and proposed a solution to the problem of interfering with the relative price structure when the government built up the surplus. In the context of the Job Guarantee policy, this means setting a buffer stock wage below the private market wage structure, unless strategic policy, in addition to the meager elimination of the surplus, was being pursued. For example, the government may wish to combine the Job Guarantee policy with an industry policy designed to raise productivity. In such a case it may buy surplus labor at a wage above the current private market minimum. In the first instance, the basic Job Guarantee model with a wage floor below the private wage structure shows how full employment and price stability can be attained. While this is an eminently better outcome in terms of resource use and social equity, it is just the beginning of the matter.

Graham (1937: 42) considered that the surplus should 'not be pressed for sale until an effective demand develops for it.' In the context of the Job Guarantee policy, this translates into the provision of a government job for all labor, which is surplus to private demand until such time as private demand increases.

3. THE JOB GUARANTEE AND INFLATION

In this section we focus on inflation control and show that the Job Guarantee, able to simultaneously generate full employment and price stability, is superior to the current NAIRU approach, which uses unemployment to maintain inflation control. Broadly, there are three options available to an economy that desires price stability. First, as in the NAIRU approach, it can use unemployment as a tool to suppress price pressures. Second, it can introduce a Job Guarantee and use movements in the Buffer Employment Ratio (BER) to control inflation. Third, it can introduce the Job Guarantee policy and augment it with an incomes policy. We do not consider this third option.

3.1 The Role of Unemployment in Inflation Control

The OECD experience of the 1990s shows that high and prolonged unemployment eventually results in low inflation (Mitchell, 1996). There are several observationally equivalent theoretical explanations for the inflation–unemployment trade-off. The orthodox explanations center on the role of the NAIRU and the requirement that to lower unemployment the government must run agent expectations ahead of the actual data. Each time the agents are tricked into mistaking a nominal price change for a relative price change, the inflation rate rises. Ultimately the only sustainable non-inflationary unemployment rate occurs when expectations are realized, a condition immutable to aggregate policy manipulation.

Alternatively, Post-Keynesians and others locate the trade-off on a model of conflicting claims among capitalists and workers to real income. Sawyer (1985: 17) argues that unemployment acts as a 'control mechanism, albeit a socially and economically inefficient one.' By disciplining the aspirations of labor to be compatible with the profitability requirements of capital, unemployment can temporarily balance the conflicting demands of labor and capital (Kalecki, 1971). Similarly low product market demand, the analogue of high unemployment, suppresses the ability of firms to pass on prices to protect real margins. The lull in the wage–price spiral, in the sense that inflation is stable, could be termed a macroequilibrium state. The implied unemployment rate under this concept of inflation is termed the macroequilibrium unemployment rate (MRU) by Mitchell (1987a) and has no connotations of the voluntary maximizing individual behavior that underpins the NAIRU concept. Mitchell (1987a) develops this concept into an explanation of hysteresis.[9]

The fact that at some stable inflation rate there is an associated unemployment rate, and that increases in the latter ensure the former, does not provide a theoretical reason for income distribution conflicts between powerful groups in the economy. We might also call this unemployment rate the NAIRU, but in doing so we add nothing to the understanding of the inflation process. Clearly different theoretical underpinnings support this observation, each theoretical structure bringing with it an entirely different comprehension of the role of the NAIRU and its implications for activist government agendas designed to provide full employment.

3.2 Inflation Control – the NAIBER

To demonstrate how the Job Guarantee generates full employment with price stability, let us consider two situations: (a) introducing the Job Guarantee into a NAIRU economy with high unemployment; (b) maintaining the Job Guarantee in the fully employed economy subject to inflationary biases in the private sector. Initially we outline the relationship between falling unemployment and inflationary pressures in a NAIRU economy.

We consider a stylized economy with a dual labor market where the sectors are differentiated by their wage-setting mechanisms. Prices are set according to markups on unit costs in both sectors. Wage-setting in Sector A is contractual and responds in an inverse and lagged fashion to relative wage growth (A/B) and to the wait unemployment level (displaced workers who think they will be re-employed soon in Sector A). Wages are relatively flexible upwards in Sector B and respond immediately. A government stimulus to this economy increases output and employment in both sectors immediately. The compression of the A/B relative wage stimulates wage growth in Sector A after a time. Wait unemployment falls due to the rising employment in A but also rises due to the increased probability of getting a job in A. The net effect is unclear. The total unemployment rate falls after participation effects are absorbed.

The wage growth in both sectors may force firms to increase prices, although this will be attenuated somewhat by rising productivity as utilization increases. A combination of wage–wage and wage–price mechanisms in a soft product market can then drive inflation. This is a Phillips Curve world. To stop inflation, the government has to repress demand. Higher unemployment brings the real income expectations of workers and firms into line with the available real income, and inflation stabilizes. This describes the fundamental mechanisms in a NAIRU economy.

What would happen if the Job Guarantee were introduced to solve the problem of unemployment in this economy? For simplicity of argument, we assume the Job Guarantee wage is set at the bottom of the private sector wage structure although not low enough to enforce poverty on full-time workers. If there were poverty level wages being paid in Sector B, then there would be pressure on Sector B employers to restructure their jobs in order to maintain a workforce. The Job Guarantee wage sets a floor in the economy's cost structure for given productivity levels. The dynamics of the economy change significantly. The elimination of all but wait unemployment in Sector A and frictional unemployment does not distort the relative wage structure so that the wage–wage pressures that were prominent in the upturn in the NAIRU economy are now reduced. But the rising demand softens the product market, and demand for labor rises in Sector A. The Job Guarantee introduces no new problems faced by employers who wish to hire labor to meet higher sales levels. They must pay the going rate, which is still preferable to appropriately skilled workers than the Job Guarantee wage level. The rising demand per se does not invoke inflationary pressures as firms increase capacity utilization to meet higher sales volumes.

What about the behavior of workers in Sector A? Wendell Gordon (1997: 833) said, 'If there is a Job Guarantee program, the employees can simply quit an obnoxious employer with assurance that they can find alternative employment.' With the Job Guarantee policy, wage bargaining is freed from the general threat of unemployment. However it is unclear whether this freedom will lead to higher wage demands than otherwise. In professional occupational markets, it is likely that some wait unemployment will remain. Skilled workers who are laid off are likely to receive payouts that forestall their need to get immediate work. They have a disincentive to immediately take a Job Guarantee job, which is a low-wage and possibly stigmatized option. Wait unemployment disciplines wage demands in Sector A. The demand pressures, however, may eventually exhaust this stock, and wage–price pressures may develop.

At first blush it might appear that the BER would have to be greater than the NAIRU for an equivalent amount of inflation control. This is because the Job Guarantee workers will have higher incomes and so a switch to this policy would see demand levels higher than in a NAIRU world. But the Job

Guarantee provides better inflation proofing than does a NAIRU approach because the Job Guarantee workers represent a more credible threat to the current private sector employees. In other words, the Job Guarantee pool is a more effective excess supply of labor.

The Job Guarantee employees are more attractive than when they were unemployed, not the least because they will have basic work skills, such as punctuality, in place. This reduces hiring costs for firms in tight labor markets who would have lowered hiring standards and provided on-the-job training. They can now pay higher wages to attract workers or accept lower costs that would ease the wage–price pressures. The Job Guarantee policy thus reduces the 'hysteretic inertia' embodied in the long-term unemployed and, with growth bottlenecks reduced, allows for a smoother private sector expansion.

A further source of cost pressure comes via the exchange rate for small trading economies like Australia. Under a fixed exchange rate regime, unless there is a coordinated fiscal policy among countries, it would be difficult for a small open economy to pursue its own full employment strategy. With higher spending on imports arising from domestic expansion, the stimulus would spread throughout the fixed exchange rate bloc and the small country would face a borrowing crisis negating its full employment ambitions. It is easy to see that a Job Guarantee model, to be effective, requires a flexible exchange rate. We can identify two external effects. First, given the higher disposable incomes of Job Guarantee workers compared to wages of the unemployed, imports would likely rise. With a flexible exchange rate, the increase in imports would promote depreciation in the exchange rate. The current account could be expected to improve, net exports increasing their contribution to local employment. Final outcomes would depend on estimates of export and import price elasticities. Recent work by Dwyer and Kent (1993) finds that import elasticities are small (around –0.5). Thus, following depreciation, import spending will actually rise because we are paying disproportionately more for fewer imported goods and services. Improvement in the current account thus depends on the estimate of the export elasticity. *State of Play 8* (Indecs, 1995: 125) says, 'Fortunately, this seems to be the case. . . . [T]he supply responses to higher prices are thought to be strong in both agriculture and mining, and the numbers for manufactures are . . . embarrassingly high. . . . There is little objective reason to be worried by elasticity pessimism' (see also Bullock et al., 1993). Vickrey (1996) said, 'The danger of world speculative gyrations under freely floating conditions would be greatly diminished under a well-established full-employment policy, especially if combined with a third dimension of direct control over the overall domestic price level.'

Direct control to allow the depreciation to be insulated from the wage–price system could be an income policy. If the increased spending led to depreciation through rising imports, a comprehensive incomes policy would be required to reduce inflationary pressures. Workers and firms would have to agree to allow real depreciation to stick, as part of the return to the collective will. For everyone to have jobs, those who are currently employed would have to sacrifice some real income to permit others to increase their claim on it. The scheme itself would not force up labor costs

The Job Guarantee wage provides a floor that prevents serious deflation from occurring and defines the private sector wage structure. However, if the private labor market is tight, the non-buffer stock wage will rise relative to the Job Guarantee wage, draining the buffer stock pool. The smaller this pool, the less influence the Job Guarantee wage has on wage patterning. Unless the government stifles demand, the economy will then enter an inflationary episode, depending on the behavior of labor and capital in the bargaining environment.

In the face of wage–price pressures, the Job Guarantee approach maintains inflation control by choking aggregate demand and inducing slack in the non-buffer stock sector. As the slack does not reveal itself as unemployment, the Job Guarantee may be referred to as a 'loose' full employment. This leads to the definition of a new concept, the NAIBER, which, in the buffer stock economy, replaces the NAIRU/MRU as an inflation control mechanism. The BER is the ratio of buffer stock employment to total employment.

As the BER rises, due to an increase in interest rates and/or a fiscal tightening, resources are transferred from the inflating non-buffer stock sector into the buffer stock sector at the fixed buffer stock wage. This is the vehicle for inflation discipline. A major advantage of the Job Guarantee approach is that the disciplinary role of the NAIRU, which forces the inflation adjustment onto the unemployed, is replaced by the compositional shift in sectoral employment, the major costs of unemployment thus being avoided. The only requirement is that the buffer stock wage be a floor and that the rate of growth in buffer stock wages be equal to or less than the private sector wages growth.

So far we have analysed the effects likely to accompany the introduction of the Job Guarantee and compared the outcomes to a NAIRU economy. However, there are further issues that arise when we consider the *maintenance* of full employment using the Job Guarantee policy. While orthodox economists typically attack the Job Guarantee policy for fiscal reasons, economists on the left also challenge its validity and effectiveness. Mitchell (2000b), analyses the arguments presented by Michal Kalecki in his 'Political aspects of full employment,' published in 1943 in the *Political Quarterly*, which laid out the blueprint for socialist opposition to Keynesian-style employment policy. A summary of Mitchell's conclusions are useful although more complete detail can be obtained from the above-mentioned publication.

Kalecki (1971: 139) lists three reasons why industrial leaders would be opposed to a full employment 'achieved by Government spending': first, that the private sector opposes government employment per se; second, that the private sector does not like public sector infrastructure development or any subsidy of consumption; and third, a more general claim involving a dislike by the private sector 'of the social and political changes resulting from the *maintenance* of full employment' (emphasis in original).

Firstly, Kalecki's argument that business leaders fear public spending that might be in competition with their own investment is erroneous, because the Job Guarantee jobs are most needed in areas that have been neglected or harmed by capitalist growth. The chance of overlap and therefore substitution is minimal. Secondly, Kalecki (1971: 140–41) worries that under a regime of permanent full employment, 'the sack' would cease to play its role as a disciplinary measure. However the Job Guarantee creates loose full employment rather than tight full employment because the buffer stock wage is fixed (growing with national productivity). The issue comes down to whether the Job Guarantee pool is a greater or lesser threat to the employed or unemployed when wage bargaining is under way. This is particularly relevant in relation to the significance of the long-term unemployed in total unemployment. It can be argued that the long-term unemployed, because they are not a credible substitute, exert very little downward pressure on wages growth. The Job Guarantee workers, however, do comprise a credible threat to current private sector employees for reasons noted above. The Job Guarantee pool provides business with a fixed-price stock of skilled labor from which to recruit. In an inflationary episode, business, because it can achieve cost control, is more likely to resist wage demands from its existing workforce. In this way longer-term planning with cost control is achievable. In this sense, inflation restraint exerted via the NAIBER is likely to be more effective than using a NAIRU strategy.

4. THE JOB GUARANTEE AND THE BUDGET DEFICIT

The International Labour Office (1999) argues:

> [A]ny strategy for full employment must be based on a sound macroeconomic framework. To achieve this, unsustainable current account imbalances, or foreign debt accumulation, must be reduced and low rates of inflation achieved. This requires the continuous adjustment of policies, a realistic exchange rate, fiscal discipline and wage moderation (wage increases in line with labor productivity). But in times of global deflation this is not necessarily sufficient as a guide to policy, and a boost to demand may be needed, perhaps going so far as to generate expectations of inflation, in addition to the accepted policy of balancing budgets over the business cycle as a whole (International Labour Office, 1999).

Critics of the Job Guarantee allege that it relies on sustained budget deficits that are untenable. It is true that the government must allow the budget deficit the necessary increases and decreases to maintain full employment for the Job Guarantee to be viable. In this section, we demonstrate that orthodox arguments advising against sustained budget deficits are unfounded. One of the most damaging analogies in economics is the supposed equivalence between the household budget and the government budget. For example, Barro (1993: 367) has written, '[W]e can think of the government's saving and dissaving just as we thought of households' saving and dissaving.'

This analogy is flawed because it ignores the fundamental difference between the household and government. The household cannot spend before it has sources of finance available (income, savings, borrowing), but must spend to survive. The government, however, can spend without prior financing. Government spending is desired by the private sector because it brings with it the resources (fiat money) that the private sector requires to fulfill its legal taxation obligations. The household cannot impose any such obligations. The government has to spend to provide money to the private sector to pay its taxes, to allow the private sector to save and to maintain transaction balances. Taxation is thus more correctly seen as a vehicle by which the government transfers real resources from the private to the public sector rather than a source of financing for government spending. If people want to save and still be able to pay their taxation obligations in the fiat currency, then there should always be a budget deficit.

The logic, according to those who draw the household analogy, states that to finance the deficit debt would have to be issued. Accordingly bond sales, which will accumulate as debt, finance government. As with a household, rising debt cannot be sustained indefinitely and so spending must be curbed and brought in line with financial reality. In the meantime, demands that debt places on available savings pushes interest rates up and crowds out 'more efficient' sources of private spending. These 'household' logicians divide into two camps. In one camp there are the orthodox monetarists who eschew government debt and advocate balanced budgets. Their wrong-minded logic has imposed extremely high macroeconomic costs in terms of lost growth and high unemployment in the western economies since the mid-1970s. The other camp, which includes some Post-Keynesians, while comfortable with using deficit spending to increase economic activity, couches its recommendations in conservative logic bounded by appropriate movements in the debt to GDP ratio. As long as the ratio is stable there is no problem. For example, the Bank of International Settlements (1994) concluded that a deficit is sustainable as long as the government debt to GDP ratio (hereafter the debt ratio) does not increase permanently. A framework for analyzing the relation between deficits and the debt ratio is provided by Bispham (1988) and Glyn (1997).

But when pushed, there is little difference between the two camps. Glyn (1997: 226), an advocate of expansionary fiscal policy to reduce unemployment, however, seems to abandon that logic when he argues, 'financial markets, the ultimate arbiters of such matters, may look simply at the size of the deficit.' The BIS (1995: 88) concur, 'It is difficult to persuade markets that low inflation is sustainable in the presence of large budget deficits.' Glyn (1997: 227) concludes, 'Given the experience of the past 20 years it would be difficult to convince that increased deficits at the beginning of the expansionary program would be rapidly scaled down as the private sector took up the main thrust of expansion. There seems little alternative to financing through taxation most of an expansionary programme.' Further, Glyn (1997: 224) says '[I]t is misleading to treat them (interest rates) as entirely exogenous. It is likely that beyond a certain level, a higher deficit will lead financial markets to exact a higher real-interest rate.'

The two camps however fail to understand the relationship between fiat currency, public debt and taxation in a monetary capitalist economy, a topic examined by Mosler (1997–98) and Wray (1998). They show the priority of spending and argue that debt issue is not essential for governments to spend beyond tax revenue. Mosler (1997–98) shows that bond issues are essential only to support the cash rates set by the central bank. Deficit spending without Treasury bond sales would generate excess reserves in the banking system, so that government debt helps to maintain a positive overnight interest rate for private banks. Deficits add to the net disposable income of households that provide markets for private production. An endogenous credit economy, then, serves to provide the deposits necessary to make payments, which facilitate production. Higher demand stimulates investment that creates capacity as a legacy to the future. The higher current demand, the higher future productive capacity. Thus spending brings forth its own savings. Savings are not required as a prior pool for spending to occur. The point is clear: When fiat money is used, government spending increases reserves in the banking system. Taxation and borrowing drain the reserves. This gives the clue to the function of borrowing. A deficit generates a net build-up in reserves in the banking system. Spending occurs and private firms and individuals deposit proceeds from selling goods and services to the government in commercial banks, which build up reserves. Unless those reserves are drained from the system, they will earn the official discount rate. The role of the government bond issues is to give these returns a way to earn a return in excess of the discount rate.

William Vickrey (1996: 10) argued, 'The "deficit" is not an economic sin but an economic necessity. Its most important function is to be the means whereby purchasing power not spent on consumption, nor recycled into income by the private creation of net capital, is recycled into purchasing power by government borrowing and spending. Purchasing power not so recycled becomes non-purchase, non-sales, non-production and unemployment.' In an endogenous money world, there can be no crowding out unless the monetary authority stops lending.

The recent Asian financial troubles and IMF intervention have once again given credence to the view that increasing levels of debt will eventually lead to lenders refusing to take up further public borrowing. Usually this is cast in terms of countries with low levels of capital that have major private debt denominated in a foreign currency used to finance imports. Crises occur when the export revenue, which services the debt, falls for one reason or another. But none of these countries would have any trouble issuing debt in its own currency.[10]

To fine-tune this point, government spending would still have occurred if there were no bond issues. The excess reserves would be held somewhere in the banking system earning zero return. If the Treasury offers too few or too many bonds relative to the holders of reserve balances at the Central Bank, the Central Bank 'offsets' those operations to balance the system. In any case, the 'money' is in one account or another at the central bank. We then ask the question – 'Why should government care if the holders of the excess balances choose the one that does not pay interest as opposed to the ones that do (buying bonds)?' – the answer is simple: 'They would be indifferent.'

The Job Guarantee policy also requires that the government have the ability to implement a largely independent monetary and fiscal policy. In this section, we examine the effects of budget deficits on interest rates and current account performance and also seek to establish causality within the term structure of interest rates. As noted above, Glyn (1997: 226–27), an advocate of fiscal activism, believes that taxation should be used to 'finance' necessary spending. He accepts the notion that international financial markets will react to higher budget deficits and 'exact a higher real-interest rate' (Glyn, 1997: 224).

Mitchell (2000a) structured this contention into a set of empirically testable hypotheses:

1. Is there evidence of a relationship between budget deficits and short-term and long-term interest rates? If there is no discernible statistical relationship found, it is difficult to argue against fiscal activism based on financial crowding out arguments.
2. Is there evidence of a relationship between long-term interest rates across countries in globalized financial markets? If there is no relationship detected, then the view that financial traders in the large markets like Japan and the United States can render domestic monetary policy ineffective is problematic.

3. Is there any evidence that the relationship between domestic long- and short-term interest rates is unstable? Stability implies that the cash rate, which is set as a policy instrument, and the longer-term interest rates, which are influenced by market considerations, move together in a proportional manner over the long run.
4. Is there any evidence to support the twin-deficits hypothesis that imposes causality from the fiscal deficit changes to changes in the current account deficit? A lack of such a direct relationship also provides further support for the use of budget deficits under the Job Guarantee policy.

Using a range of econometric testing methodologies, Mitchell (2000a) found no evidence to support any of these contentions. First, it appears that the long-term interest rates in the large markets do not 'cause' enduring movements in the long-term rates in Australia. The evidence appears to support the idea that, after the move to freely determined exchange rates, globalization has led to more independence of long-term rates between Australia and the rest of the world. Second, the yield gap appears to be stationary over a range of time periods. In other words, the difference between domestic long-term and short-term interest rates is stable over time. This is contrary to the view, often alleged by antagonists of the use of activist deficit-based government policy, that Australian monetary authorities are at the behest of global funds managers and are thus unable to pursue their policy objectives. Third, the paired relationships between the cash rate and the medium- and long-term rates in Australia are cointegrated, indicating that, over a long period, there are no systematic departures over a long period between the rates of interest. Fourth, the tests fail to support any notion of causality between changes in the Current Account deficit and changes in the Budget Deficit. Neither direction of causality was detected. Finally, no relationship between changes in the deficit/GDP ratio and changes in the real interest rates could be detected at short or long lags. The evolution of real interest rates appears to be independent of changes in the relative size of the deficit. These results are consistent with those found in the literature for other economies (see Kasman and Rodrigues, 1991; Christiansen and Pigott, 1997).

5. OTHER JOB GUARANTEE CONSIDERATIONS

Issues not dealt with in this chapter but central to the development of the Job Guarantee model and addressed elsewhere include:

- Does the Job Guarantee merely convert the unemployed poor into working poor? (Mitchell, 2000b)

- Is the Job Guarantee just a workfare scheme? (Mitchell and Burgess, 1998a; Burgess et al., 1998).
- Do the Job Guarantee workers do anything useful? How does the Job Guarantee model counter the criticisms that the jobs are make-work and a waste of resources? (Mitchell, 1998).
- Should the Job Guarantee policy replace all safety net welfare payments for the unemployed? Should people be entitled to welfare support in the event that they refuse to take a buffer stock job? (Mitchell, Watts and Burgess, 2000)
- Is the Job Guarantee policy essential to preserve human rights given that the current system deliberately denies a large number of its working-age population employment? (Mitchell and Burgess, 1998b, 1998c)

6. CONCLUSION

We conclude that unemployment is an entirely social construct engineered by humans. There is nothing natural about it at all. The renowned ex-Dominican priest, Matthew Fox, has stated that humans are the only species not to have full employment. Instead of being primarily concerned with how much employment we can derive from using raw materials and energy sources, the dominant concern of capitalism is in maximizing the monetary return on privately owned capital. It seems that this focus results in large numbers of human resources being left idle. As Paul Hawken (1997) says, 'We fire people, perfectly capable people, to wring out one more wave of profits. Some of the restructuring is necessary and overdue. But, as physicists Amory Lovins and Ernst von Weizsacker have repeatedly advised, what we should do is fire the unproductive kilowatts, barrels of oil, tons of material, and pulp from old-growth forests – and hire more people to do so.' The restructuring has been exacerbated by the abandonment of the goal of full employment by governments since the mid-1970s.[11]

Unemployment arises because the budget deficit is too low. It is always a macroeconomic problem. The Job Guarantee policy is the only logical way of providing jobs for everyone with guaranteed price stability. Whether it is accompanied by an incomes policy is a matter of refinement rather than substance.

NOTES

1. Mitchell (1996) provides extensive analysis and data to support this contention.
2. Mitchell (1996, 1998, 1999b), Mitchell and Watts (1997), Mitchell and Burgess (1998a, 1998b), and Mitchell, Watts and Burgess (2000) outline a case for the introduction of a full

employment policy based on the Job Guarantee model developed by Mitchell (1998). Mitchell and Burgess (1998b) place the Job Guarantee approach within the context of human rights and argue that the government has to be responsible for the maintenance of rights in this regard.

3. NAIRU refers to the non-accelerating inflation rate of unemployment and is used in this chapter to characterize the approach to inflation control advocated by monetarists, whereby a stock of unemployment is required to discipline the wage–price process.
4. NAIBER refers to the non-accelerating inflation buffer employment ratio and is the ratio of buffer stock employment to total employment that is required to stabilize inflation.
5. The buffer employment ratio (BER) is the ratio of buffer stock employment to total employment and rises (falls) as the private sector contracts (expands).
6. A third approach is a special case of the BSE policy. The government may not wish to let the market drive the BER high enough to equal the NAIBER and can intervene using an income policy to maintain a lower than otherwise BER while still maintaining price stability.
7. Mitchell and Watts (1997) indicate that the daily losses from unemployment in Australia are around $156 million or $3 100 per capita per annum. This is more than twice the alleged microeconomic inefficiencies estimated in the 1991–92 Annual Report of the Australian Industry Commission.
8. At the time, I also considered that the scheme could be financed by a levy on existing incomes, which was analogous to the MSF. As a result of other work, I no longer consider that there is a financing problem (Mitchell, 1996; Mosler, 1997–98; Wray, 1998).
9. Mitchell (1987a) argues that the MRU is cyclically sensitive and rises with the actual rate of unemployment as a result of cyclical changes in behavior of the labor market. He concludes that aggregate demand changes can influence the long-run steady-state unemployment rate subject to there being a minimum irreducible unemployment rate. Wage demands in the private sector are inversely related to the actual number of unemployed who are substitutes for those currently employed. When the economy slows, many workers lose their skills through obsolescence and new entrants are denied relevant skills. So the wedge between effective and actual excess supply rises in a downturn. The effective excess supply is the threat component of unemployment. To some degree, this insulates the wage demands from the cycle. The more rapid the cyclical adjustment, the higher is the unemployment rate associated with price stability. Stimulating jobs growth decreases the wedge because the unemployed develop new and relevant work skills. These upgrading effects provide an opportunity for real growth to occur as the MRU declines.
10. Vickrey (1996, 11) says, 'In the case at hand the debt is intended to supply a domestic demand for assets denominated in the domestic currency, and in the absence of a norm such as a gold clause, there can be no question of the ability of the government to make payments when due, albeit possibly in a currency devalued by inflation. Nor can there be any question of balking by domestic lenders as long as the debt is limited to that needed to fill a gap created by an excess of private asset demand over private asset supply.'
11. The philosophical considerations of a system that deliberately denies a large number of its working-age population employment were considered in Mitchell and Burgess (1998b, 1998c). That work covered the ethical aspects of unemployment and argued that in the context of the Universal Declaration of Human Rights (1948), governments in countries like Australia are systematically violating each of the clauses contained in Article 23. The Universal Declaration of Human Rights was unanimously agreed on December 10, 1948. Article 23 of the Universal Declaration of Human Rights states:

    1. Everyone has the right to work, to free choice of employment, to just and favorable conditions of work and to protection against unemployment.
    2. Everyone, without discrimination, has the right to equal pay for equal work.
    3. Everyone who works has the right to just and favorable remuneration, ensuring for himself and his family an existence worthy of human dignity and supplemented, if necessary, by other means of social protection.
    4. Everyone has the right to form and to join trade unions for the protection of his interests.

REFERENCES

Bank of International Settlements (1994), *Annual Report 1993/94*, Basel: BIS.

Barro, Robert J. (1993), *Macroeconomics, 4th edn*, New York: John Wiley.

Bispham, J. (1988), 'Rising Public-sector Indebtedness: Some More Unpleasant Arithmetic,' in M. Boskin et al. (eds), *Private Saving and Public Debt*, Oxford: Blackwell.

Bullock, M., S. Grenville and G. Heenan (1993), 'The Exchange Rate and the Current Account,' in A. Blundell-Wignall (ed.), *The Exchange Rate, International Trade and the Balance of Payments*, Reserve Bank of Australia: Sydney.

Burgess, John, William F. Mitchell, Duncan O'Brien and Martin J. Watts (1998), 'Unemployment: Promises, Policies and Progress,' *Labour and Industry*, 9 (2), 103–22.

Christiansen, Hans and Charles Pigott (1997), 'Long-term Interest Rates in Globalized Markets,' *OECD Working Paper No. 175*.

Dwyer, Jacqueline and Christopher Kent (1993), 'A Re-examination of the Determinants of Australia's Imports,' *Discussion Paper 9312*, Reserve Bank of Australia: Sydney.

Friedman, Milton. (1968), 'The Role of Monetary Policy,' *American Economic Review*, 58, March, 1–17.

Glyn, Andrew (1997), 'Paying for Job Creation,' in Jonathan Michie and John Grieve Smith (eds), *Employment and Economic Performance: Jobs, Inflation and Growth,* Oxford University Press: Oxford, pp. 221–33.

Gordon, Wendell (1997), 'Job Assurance – The Job Guarantee Revisited,' *Journal of Economic Issues*, 21 (3), 817–25.

Graham, B. (1937), *Storage and Stability*, McGraw-Hill: New York.

Hawken, Paul (1997), 'Natural Capitalism,' *Mother Jones*, March/April.

Indecs (1995), *State of Play 8*, Allen and Unwin: St. Leonards.

International Labour Organization (1999), 'The International Labour Organization and the Promotion of Full, Productive and Freely Chosen Employment,' international consultation concerning follow-up to the World Summit for Social Development, Geneva, November 2–4.

Kalecki, Michal (1971), 'Political Aspects of Full Employment,' in *Selected Essays on the Dynamics of the Capitalist Economy*, by Michal Kalecki, pp. 138–45, Cambridge University Press: Cambridge.

Kasman, Bruce and Anthony P. Rodrigues (1991), 'Financial Liberalization and Monetary Control in Japan,' *Federal Reserve Bank of New York, Quarterly Review*, 16 (3) (Autumn), 28–46.

Lloyd, A.G. (1965), 'Reserve Price for Wool: a Defence,' in D.E. James and C.D. Throsby (eds) (1973), *Introduction to Quantitative Methods in Economics*, Sydney and New York: John Wiley & Sons Australia.

Lovens, Amory B., L. Hunter Lovens and Paul Hawken (1999), 'A Road Map to Natural Capitalism,' *Harvard Business Review*, May–June, Reprint Number 99309, 145–58.

Mitchell, William F. (1987a), 'The NAIRU, Structural Imbalance and the Macroequilibrium Unemployment Rate,' *Australian Economic Papers*, 26 (48), 101–18.

Mitchell, William F. (1987b), 'What is the Full Employment Unemployment Rate,' *Australian Bulletin of Labour*, 11 (1), 321–36.

Mitchell, William F. (1994), 'Restoring Full Employment: A Problem of Policy Balance,' *Australian Economic Review* 0 (105) (January.–March), 24–30.

Mitchell, William F. (1996), 'Inflation and Unemployment: A Demand Story,' paper presented to European Unemployment Conference, sponsored by the European Commission, at the European University Institute, Florence, November 21–2.

Mitchell, William F. (1998), 'The Buffer Stock Employment Model and the NAIRU: The Path to Full Employment,' *Journal of Economic Issues*, 32 (2) (June), 1–9.

Mitchell, William F. (1999a), 'The Causes of Unemployment,' in S. Bell (ed.), *The Unemployment Crisis: Which Way Out?*, Cambridge: Cambridge University Press.

Mitchell, William F. (1999b), 'Full Employment Abandoned – the Macroeconomic Story,' in M. Carman, and I. Rogers (eds), *Out of the Rut*, St. Leonards: Allen and Unwin.

Mitchell, William F. (2000a), 'The Job Guarantee in a Small Open Economy,' in William F. Mitchell and E. Carlson (eds), *The Path to Full Employment*, Syney: Centre for Applied Economic Research, pp. 89–116.

Mitchell, William F. (2000b), 'The Job Guarantee and Inflation,' *Employment and Labour Relations Review*, forthcoming.

Mitchell, William (2001), 'The Job Guarantee and Inflation Control', *Economic and Labour Relations Review*, 12, 10–25.

Mitchell, William F. and J. Burgess (1998a), 'Eight Propositions about Unemployment: An Australian Perspective,' *Forum on Unemployment: New Visions, International Industrial Relations Society World Congress proceedings*, Bologna, Italy.

Mitchell, William F. and J. Burgess (1998b), 'Employment, Unemployment and the Right to Work,' *Australian Journal of Human Rights*, 4 (2), 76–94.

Mitchell, William F. and J. Burgess (1998c), 'Unemployment, Human Rights and a Full Employment Policy in Australia,' in M. Jones and P. Kriesler (eds), *Globalisation, Human Rights and Civil Society*, Sydney: Prospect Press.

Mitchell, William F. and M.J. Watts (1997), 'The Path to Full Employment,' *Australian Economic Review*, 30 (4), 436–44.

Mitchell, William F., C.E. Mitchell, M.J. Watts and A. Butterworth (1995), *Women's Prospects in the Economic Recovery*, Canberra: AGPS.

Mitchell, William, Martin Watts and John Burgess (2000), 'Job Creation, Unemployment and Inequality in Australia,' Centre of Full Employment and Equity, Working Paper No. 03, 2000.

Mosler, Warren (1997–98), 'Full Employment and Price Stability,' *Journal of Post Keynesian Economics*, 20 (2) (Winter), 167–82.

Ormerod, Paul (1994), *The Death of Economics*, London: Faber and Faber.

Parish, R.M. (1964), 'Reserve Price for Wool: A Critique,' in C.D. Throsby and D.E. James (eds), *Introduction to Quantitative Methods in Economics*, Sydney and New York: Wiley & Sons Australasia.

Phelps, E.S. (1967), 'Phillips Curves, Expectations of Inflation and Optimal Unemployment over Time,' *Economica* (34), (August), 254–81.

Sawyer, M.C. (1985), 'On the Nature of the Phillips Curve,' *British Review of Economic Issues*, 7 (16) (Spring), 63–86.

Throsby, C.D. (ed.) (1972), *Agricultural Policy: Selected Readings*, Ringwood: Penguin Books.

Vickrey, W. (1996), 'Fifteen Fatal Fallacies of Financial Fundamentalism: A Disquisition on Demand Side Economics,' Columbia University Economics Department web site.

Von Weizsacker, Ernst, Amory B. Lovins and L. Hunter Lovins (1997), *Doubling Wealth – Halving Resource Use*, Allen and Unwin: New York.

Wray, L. Randall (1998), *Understanding Modern Money*, Cheltenham, UK and Lyme, US: Edward Elgar.

PART VI

THE FINAL HOUR

The employer of last resort (ELR) has been the subject of discussion in many sessions. Here my chapter on Automatic Stabilizers spells out its macro implications in detail. It is shown that an ELR is superior to an unemployment insurance policy costing the same. Both provide automatic countercyclical movements demand, expanding in the slump and contracting in the boom, but the ELR also generates output, not to mention giving people a sense of self-worth from doing useful work. Moreover, it provides support for the currency, and the pattern of countercyclical changes in employment also tends to stabilize the lower end of the money wage scale.

This sets the stage for the 'final hour,' the discussion that pulls it all together.

17. Short-run macroeconomic stabilization by an employer of last resort

Edward J. Nell

In contrast to supply-side dogma, modern economies appear to be subject to strong fluctuations in demand. This at any rate will be our premise. Moreover, there do not appear to be, in the modern world, any strong, market-based forces leading to stability. So there is a need for stabilization policies.

Investment spending appears to be a major source of demand variation. Yet if the purpose of investment were simply to be a corrective – moving the actual capital/labor ratio to its optimal level – stabilization would hardly be needed. Such a long-run position would be stationary, or, if the labor force were growing, the economy would expand uniformly. This is the picture presented by neoclassical theory, articulated, for example, by Hayek (1941).

But both Keynes and the older classicals, especially Ricardo and Marx, offer a different view: investment is the accumulation of capital, a process by which productive power is created, organized and managed. Driven by the desire for power and wealth, there is no definable 'optimum' investment. Investment expands productive power but does not move the economy towards any definite destination. Given such motivation and the important role of technological innovation, the urge to invest will sometimes be strong and widespread, but at other times weak and uncertain. This may help to explain the need for stabilizing policies that arise from the demand side.

In postwar mass production economies (Nell, 1998a), constant returns appear to prevail in the short run; to put it differently, unit costs are broadly constant.[1] Workers need only be semi-skilled and teams can easily be broken up and re-formed; processes can be operated at varying levels of intensity in response to variations in demand, and can be easily shut down and started up. It is likewise easy to lay off and recall workers.

Models can be developed based on an aggregate utilization function[2] with distinctive properties.[3] The mass production economy will be characterized by a straight line rising from the origin. As a first approximation, consumption can be identified with wages and salaries,[4] while investment can be taken as exogenous. As employment rises, the wage bill – and so consumption spending – will rise at a constant rate, namely the normal wage rate. The wage bill

– assumed equal to consumption spending – is represented by a straight line rising to the right from the origin; its angle is the wage rate. Investment spending will be treated as exogenous in the short run, so will be marked off on the vertical axis. Aggregate demand will then be the line C + I, rising to the right from the I point on the vertical axis; its slope is the wage rate.

ADJUSTMENT TO DEMAND FLUCTUATIONS IN THE MASS PRODUCTION ECONOMY

The origin, here in Figure 17.1 and in later figures, is the point at which labor cost absorbs all output. Employment in such an economy will depend only on effective demand; there is no marginal productivity adjustment.[5] Output will increase with the amount of labor employed (capacity utilized); all and only wages will be spent on consumption, and all profits will be saved as retained earnings. Investment can be taken as exogenous as a first approximation.[6] Expenditure is given by the C + I line. (This ignores G, government spending, for the moment, although in the modern world it will be much greater than in the earlier forms of the capitalist economy.) But the output function will be a straight line rising from the origin with a slope equal to the average productivity of labor. Suppose investment is exceptionally high; then employment will be increased, and consumption

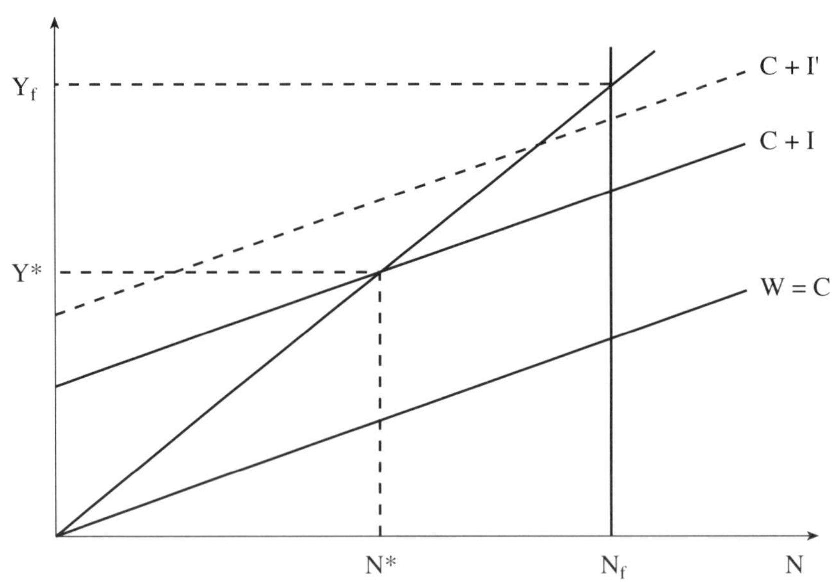

Figure 17.1 Adjustment in the mass production economy

will also be exceptionally high. Conversely, if investment is low, employment will be low, and thus so will consumption. Consumption adjusts in the same direction that investment moves.[7] When investment rises, consumption, output and employment also increase in a definite proportion.

The effect of government can be illustrated with a flat tax on wages and government spending on unemployment insurance, Figure 17.2. Tax revenues rise with N, and welfare spending falls. Rates can be adjusted so the budget balances at full employment. If Investment spending falls below the level required for full employment, tax revenues decline and welfare spending rises, providing a stimulus. If investment booms, taxes rise and spending falls, and the resulting surplus acts as a drag on the economy.

In modern economies, investment and consumption tend to move in the same direction, so that fluctuations are enhanced rather than dampened. The system is volatile, and will be even more so if investment responds to changes in output through an accelerator. But the government budget automatically moves counter-cyclically.

AN UNSTABLE LABOR MARKET

In the labor market in modern economies, we find that money wages tend systematically to be driven in the wrong direction. The labor demand function – or employment function – is derived by plotting the components of the employment multiplier, namely the real wage and employment, against each

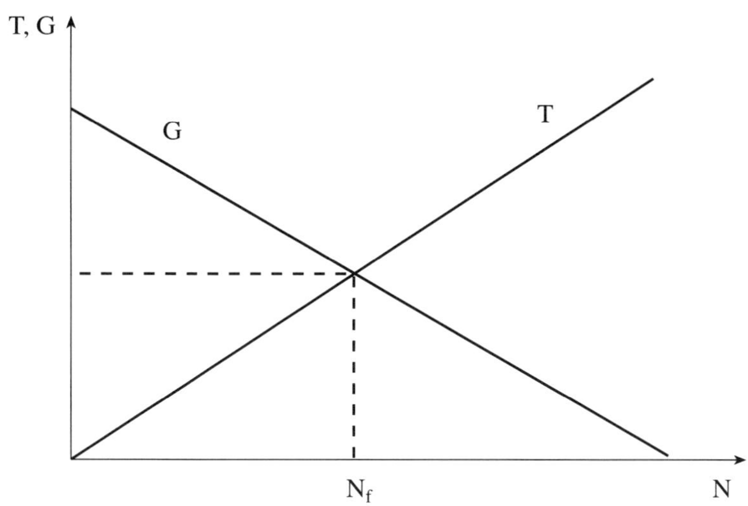

Figure 17.2 Government stabilization in the mass production economy

other. Assuming profits to be retained and saved, and wage income spent, ignoring both household saving and household spending financed by credit, the curve will show the employment generated (measured on the horizontal axis) by consumption spending at each level of the real wage (on the vertical axis). The intercept on the horizontal axis shows the employment generated by investment spending; then the curve rises at a falling rate from left to right, approaching the line 1/n asymptotically, where n is labor per unit of output[8] (Nell, 1988, 1991; Rowthorn, 1982; Lavoie, 1992).

This curve can be combined with either of two hypotheses about labor supply. Households may be supposed to defend a certain target level of consumption. If the real wage falls, the household will then have to offer more labor. In the extreme case, this may take the form of a rectangular hyperbola. Alternatively there is the more conventional view that higher wages will call forth greater labor force participation.

In Figure 17.3, it is clear that if the *real* wage is too high, labor demand will exceed labor supply, and there will be a tendency to bid *money* wages up. (If labor is in short supply, so that goods are not being produced, there will also be pressure on prices and inflation will result.) If the real wage is too low, labor supply will exceed labor demand, and the labor market will be slack, putting downward pressure on money wages. But in the modern economy, money wages are likely to be sticky, so may not drift down. Nevertheless, there will be

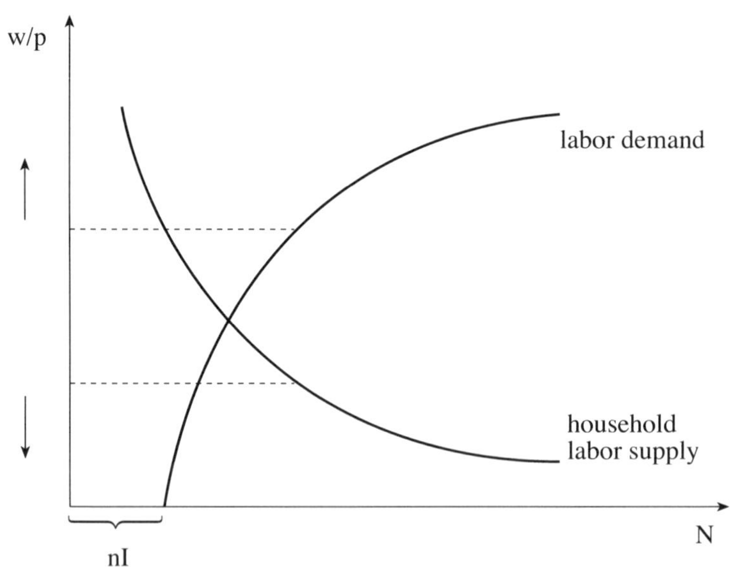

Figure 17.3 Mass production labor market: lifestyle defense

no tendency for the market to make a correction. The same clearly holds in Figure 17.4, with a conventional labor force participation function.[9]

The development of mass production (Nell, 1998a), then, besides vastly increasing productivity and raising normal growth rates, has also brought us a system in which volatility is self-augmenting, in both product and labor markets.[10]

The problem is that mass production labor markets tend to generate inflation. To control inflation, governments in the advanced economies have typically resorted to slowing down the economy, that is, to creating unemployment. In this case, the automatic stabilizer would tend to undermine the effort to control inflationary pressures. Consequently, such stabilizers have been neglected or even dismantled.

CONSTRUCTING AN AUTOMATIC STABILIZER THAT COVERS INFLATION

Automatic stabilization has significant advantages. It is not necessary to wait on policy makers to reach decisions and act. Policy need not wait on legislation

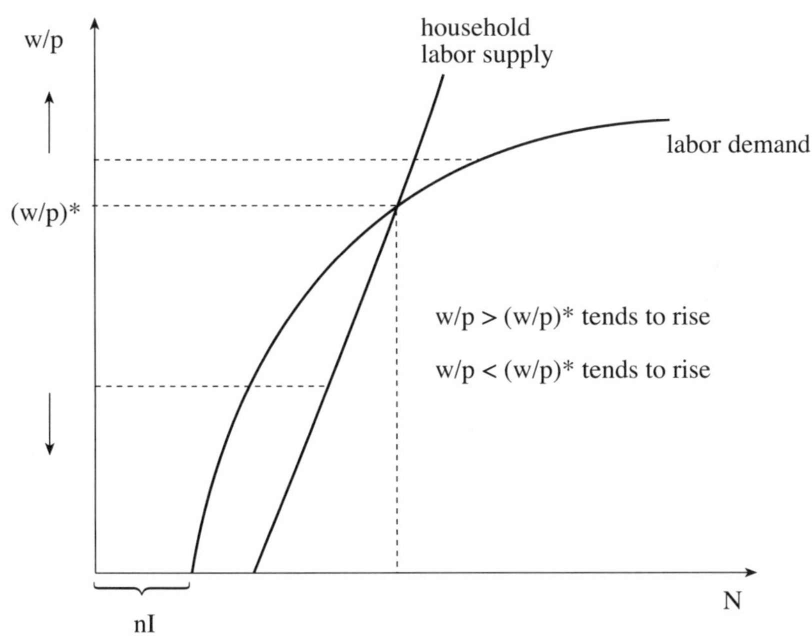

Figure 17.4 Mass production labor market: rising participation

by Congress, or upon decisions by courts. Stabilization will not depend on which party is in power. Nor does it rest on the frequently weak and unreliable effects of interest rates and monetary policy.

'Automatic stabilizers' expand in the slump and contract in the boom, thereby providing the economy with a tendency to self-regulation. To date, these have been largely transfer payments to the jobless. But the program could be combined with the 'buffer stock' principle and operate so as to stabilize wages as well as the level of output.[11] This would largely dispense with transfers; it would become a stabilizing public sector employment program, expanding in hard times and contracting in good, at a fixed wage. Such a program will be superior to one based on transfer payments – it will be shown here that, when other aspects of the economy are the same, it will produce a larger output with the same level of private sector employment. It will also help to stabilize the money wage.

This is the idea behind the proposals for an employer of last resort (ELR) program. A public service sector will be created that will offer a job at a basic living wage to anyone who is able and willing to work.[12] These workers will not only do useful and productive work; they will also keep up their skills and work habits, perhaps even receiving extra training. This sector will then provide an effective labor supply to the private sector when the latter expands, and will absorb excess labor when the private sector contracts. Labor will move from the ELR to the private sector, first, because the latter offers a higher wage, but also because it offers opportunities for advancement, not generally available in the ELR. Full employment – employment of everyone who wants a job and is able to work – will thus be maintained, and the basic wage will be stabilized since the ELR acts as a 'buffer stock' (Mitchell, 1998). Moreover the ELR supports and develops 'human capital' – the skills and habits of the labor force – independently of the level and fluctuations of investment in the private sector. And it provides income for families, reducing poverty and benefiting children, all of which can be expected to reduce crime and social disorder.

The Working of Automatic Stabilizers

An automatic stabilizer will change the mass production employment adjustment by raising consumption at every level short of full employment, while reducing its range of variation. This can be seen in Figure 17.5, which plots income on the vertical axis and employment on the horizontal. Private employment runs from the origin to N_f here (and in subsequent figures). At full employment, N_f, transfers will be zero; as employment falls, transfers rise, until at zero employment transfers reach their maximum at the intercept of the line T. The aggregate household income function will be the sum of wages

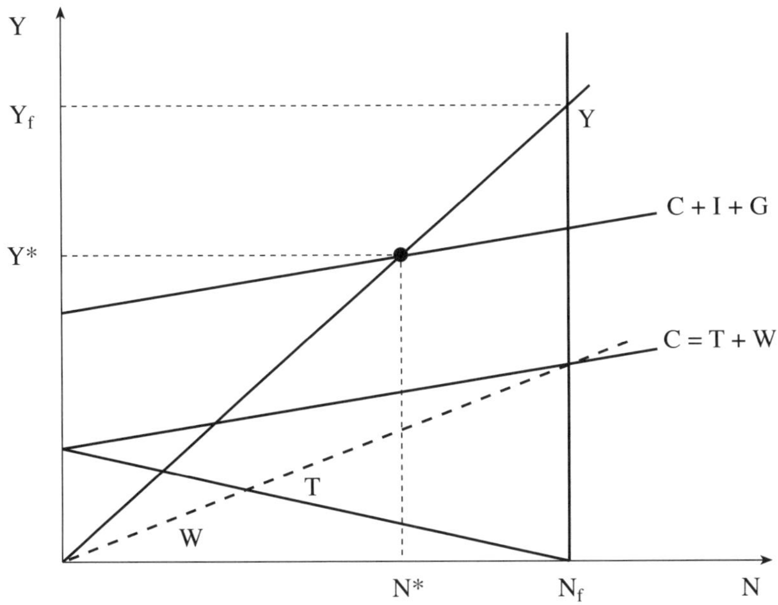

Figure 17.5 Employment and output with transfer payments

plus transfers, and by assumption, this will equal household consumption, C = T + W. When investment (and government spending on goods and services) are added, the result is aggregate demand, which intersects the utilization function to determine employment and output.

Now consider an ELR (Figure 17.6). As above, private employment will be measured from the origin running to N_f; ELR employment will be measured from N_f moving back towards the origin.

So a diagram for total output can be constructed in a way similar to the above aggregate household function. Output will depend on ELR employment as well as on private sector employment. The latter will normally be more productive. ELR output will be at its maximum when private sector employment is zero; private sector output will be at its maximum when ELR employment is zero. As private sector employment increases, ELR employment will fall, until all labor is employed in the private sector. The aggregate output line labeled Y is the linear combination of these two. Provisionally ELR output will be taken as equal to ELR costs, here assumed to be only wage costs.[13]

As in the case of unemployment insurance (continuing to ignore both household saving and household credit), total consumption demand will consist of two parts. There will be consumer spending out of private wages.

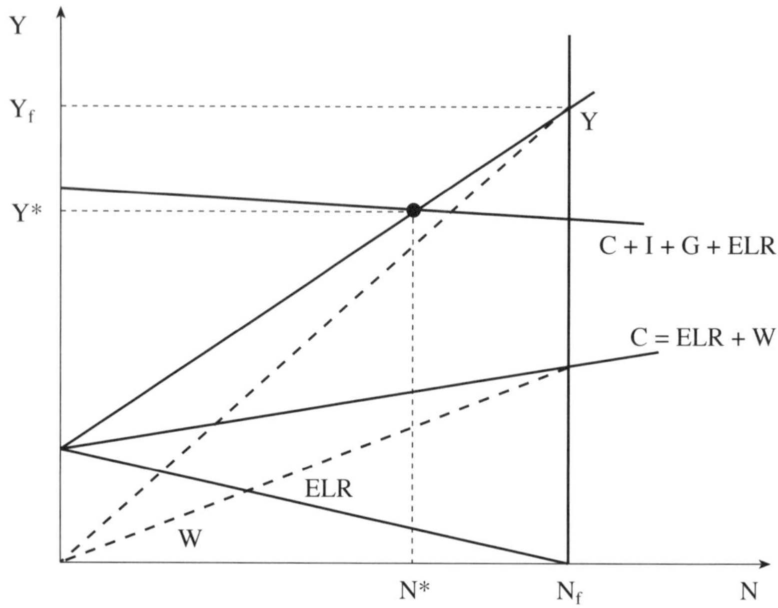

Figure 17.6 Employment and output with an ELR

This will be augmented by consumer spending out of ELR wages, in the same way that transfer payments supported consumption above. ELR wages will lie substantially below the private sector average, making it possible for the private sector to always be able to attract labor from the ELR.[14] As private sector employment rises, ELR employment falls; hence as private consumer spending rises, ELR-based consumer spending falls. Once again, the total is the combination of both, again indicated by the line labeled C = ELR + W. To get total spending, investment and government spending must be added to this.

However government spending must include ELR spending in addition to its normal spending on goods and services. The ELR produces socially useful goods and services that are paid for by the government and provided free to the community at large. This spending will fall as private sector employment increases, starting from a maximum when private employment is zero. So total spending will be private sector consumption and investment, ELR consumption plus government spending which 'purchases' the ELR output. The slope of aggregate spending depends on whether or not the decline in government spending, as private employment rises, outweighs the rise in household spending as workers shift from the public to the private sector.[15] If it does, the slope will be negative; if the differential between public and private wages is large enough, the slope will be positive. If they just balance it will be flat. Equilibrium occurs at the intersection of this line with the Y line, as indicated by the dot. Private employment is N*, ELR employment is N_f – N*. ELR output is given by the intersection of the vertical line rising from N* with the ELR output line.

COMPARING UNEMPLOYMENT INSURANCE WITH THE ELR

Now compare the ELR and a transfer payment system as answers to the problem of unemployment arising from insufficient aggregate demand. In the simplest case, with no markup on the ELR and ignoring taxes (they can be designed to be neutral), the answer is simple. This can be seen in Figure 17.7, which superimposes Figure 17.6 on Figure 17.5, by drawing the ELR solution on the unemployment insurance diagram. At every point on the employment axis, output will be the combined output of the private sector and the ELR. But government spending will exactly cover the output of the ELR. Therefore private spending will depend only on investment and the consumption supported by the combined private and public sector wage bills. But this will be the same as the consumption demand in an unemployment insurance

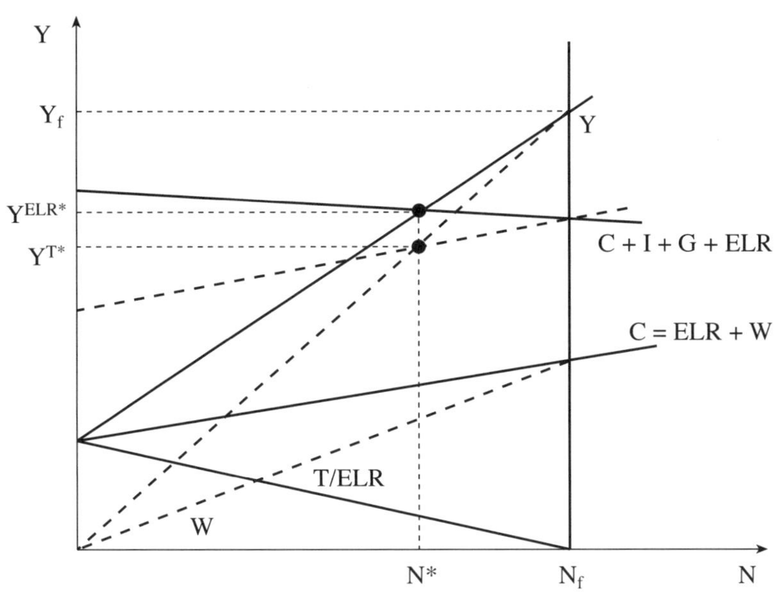

Figure 17.7 Employment and output: transfers versus ELR

system, where the transfer payments were at the same level as the ELR wage. So if investment is the same in the two systems, private employment will be the same. But output will be greater by the amount of the ELR output, which will be the same as government ELR spending.

The expenditure equilibrium of the economy will then be given by the intersection of the output function and the aggregate spending function, each including the ELR. The total output function will show the combined output of the ELR and the private sector; the total expenditure function will show the combined spending of ELR and private sector workers, plus investment (and normal government spending), plus government spending on the ELR.[16] Output will be higher in the ELR economy than under a system of unemployment insurance, but employment will be the same. (This conclusion will have to be modified if the output of the ELR has the effect of increasing the productivity of the private sector. In that event output would be even higher, but employment would be lower.)

However this is a 'stripped down' version of the ELR. The higher level of employment ensured by the ELR is likely to stimulate private investment; after all, the ELR creates a new set of active economic agents.[17] Moreover, in addition to private sector investment there will have to be ELR investment, since the ELR program will have to grow to keep pace with the rest of the economy. Such additional investment would then raise employment in the ELR above that of the corresponding 'transfer payment' system. Moreover, the ELR will very likely make purchases from the private sector, which will generate additional private employment. Further, many ELR services, for example, child-care, teaching assistance, Legal Aid, might be marketed to local governments and the private sector. These services would be sold at a markup over costs, earning profit. This profit would be a withdrawal, to be offset by ELR investment.

DIGRESSION: IMPLICATIONS FOR THE CURRENCY

An old argument against welfare asserts that if it is sufficiently large-scale, it 'undermines the currency.' This has never been a problem in practice even with very large welfare programs. But there is a logic to the argument, even if it has been abused by ideologues. Why work for money if you can get it for free? In an ELR everyone has to work to get money. The implications for incentives can be shown, using the same diagrams, by comparing the two systems at the point of zero private sector employment (Figure 17.8). Assume no investment and that government spending will be exclusively welfare payments in the one case, and ELR payments in the other. In the transfer economy, all economically active agents will be receiving welfare payments; in the ELR, all will be working in public sector jobs.

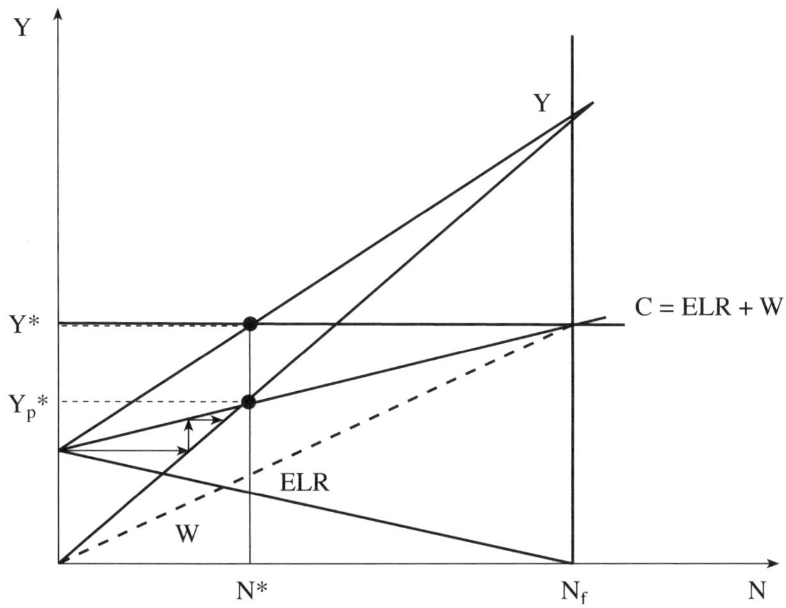

Figure 17.8 Spending ELR wages

Initially we suppose that everyone works for the ELR, producing the maximum public sector output, which the government pays for, providing ELR wages. These, however, are then spent on household consumption. But consumer goods are produced by the private sector, which must bid away labor from the ELR. The initial ELR spending purchases an output from the private sector, as indicated by the arrow in Figure 17.8, which, in turn, requires employment. Anticipating the spending of ELR wages, consumer sector firms will draw down their lines of credit to offer employment. These new private sector workers, in turn, will spend their wages on consumption goods, leading to further private sector hiring, and further spending. There will be fewer ELR workers, and more private sector workers, but total spending will go up, since private sector wages are higher. Eventually this converges on N* employed in the private sector, and $N_f - N^*$ in the public. The spending of ELR wages on consumer goods generates employment and provides the profit for consumer goods firms. Total output equals ELR output plus private sector output.

Now consider this same process in the transfer payment economy. *Ex hypothesi* everyone is receiving payment, for doing nothing, in fiat currency issued by the government.[18] Recipients of transfer payments try to spend them to purchase consumer goods. But why would anyone give up useful goods for paper or accounting units that everyone is already receiving for nothing? Why open the shop to sell goods for the same paper or accounting units that can be had by staying home and doing nothing? Why go to work in the private sector? True the private sector wage is, say, twice the level of transfer payments – but that means working for half a week in order to get the same payment that one could have by staying home and taking it easy!

In the ELR economy, the fiat currency has value because everyone has to work for ELR wages to earn the currency in which taxes are paid. For labor to shift to the private sector is reasonable because the private sector pays twice as much for the same hours. But such a shift does not make sense in the transfer economy. This is not an argument against transfer payments or welfare systems; but it is a reminder that a currency rests on contrived scarcity. Transfer payments cannot become *universal* without undermining the incentives on which a fiat currency rests.[19]

MONEY WAGES, THE ELR AND THE LABOR MARKET

Money wages will be stabilized very simply (Figure 17.9). There is no longer any interaction between demand and supply of labor that could put pressure on money wages. The average wage level of the private economy will simply be a markup over the ELR wage. Labor will be available to the private sector at

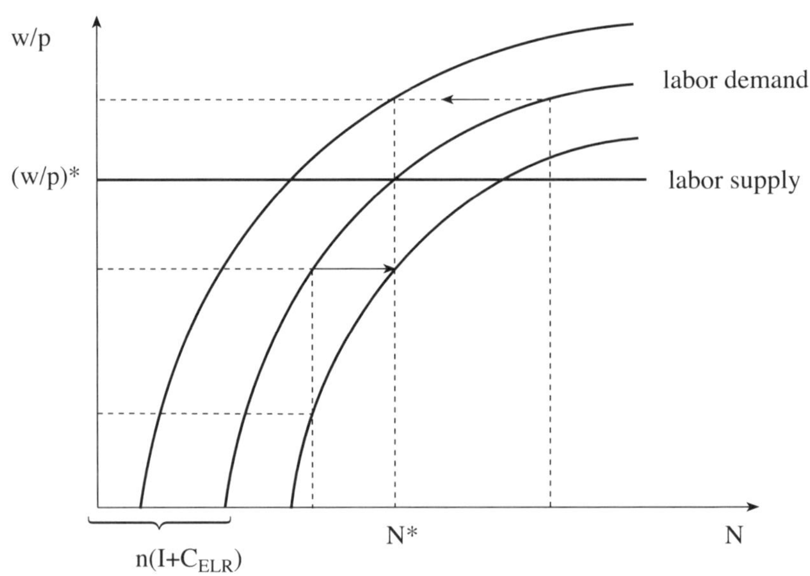

Figure 17.9 Stability of the private sector labor market in an ELR economy

that wage; so the 'supply function' will be a horizontal line starting from the vertical axis at a point indicating the markup over the ELR wage. That is, at the wage (w/p*), any workers needed will be willing to move on short notice from the ELR to the private sector. (We assume that there is no point at which additional inducements will be needed to attract further workers.) The horizontal line at this wage will intersect the labor demand function.

Suppose the wage offered by the private sector is too low, resulting in $N < N^*$. Employment in the ELR will rise and ELR output will increase. As the additional ELR wages are spent, demand for private sector goods increases, and the intercept on the horizontal axis will shift out, increasing the demand for workers at all levels of the wage. However, at too low a wage the private sector will find that it has trouble attracting adequate labor; it will have to raise the wage it offers. As it does it will hire more labor and N will rise towards N*.

Alternatively, suppose it pays too high a wage. Labor will flow out of the ELR, swamping the private sector, which will hire $N > N^*$. The ELR wage bill will decline, and so the intercept will shift in, reducing the private sector demand for workers at all wage levels. At the same time the private sector will be facing an oversupply of labor; it will find that it can easily cut back and still have enough workers. As it does so, N will fall towards N*.

Clearly this intersection will be stable at any point, since the ELR treats the labor it employs as a 'buffer stock.' That is, it absorbs labor from the private sector at the ELR wage while supplying it to the private sector at a fixed markup over that wage. There is no longer any 'household labor supply' to the private sector, so there cannot be a real wage that is 'too high' or 'too low,' that is, such that it would set up destabilizing market pressures on the nominal wage.

Now consider what happens when both the ELR wage and the private sector wage are changed together.[20] This is a change in the wage structure of the whole system and it has a significant impact on the economy. The effects of such a change can be decomposed into two parts. First, there will be a change in household spending, and consequently, in employment and output. Suppose the wage increases; then spending and employment will be higher. But the new level of the wage now means that the labor force will be smaller, if households typically defend a target standard of living, or larger, if higher wages attract new participants in the labor force. Taking the latter as an example, we can draw in the equilibrium level of employment and output at the new wage, exactly as in Figure 17.6. Now however, in Figure 17.10, we mark off the new level of full employment. The additional workers will now be employed in the ELR, so the household consumption function will have to be redrawn to reflect this. Their employment will now generate additional ELR output, so the output function will likewise have to be redrawn, as will the government ELR spending function.

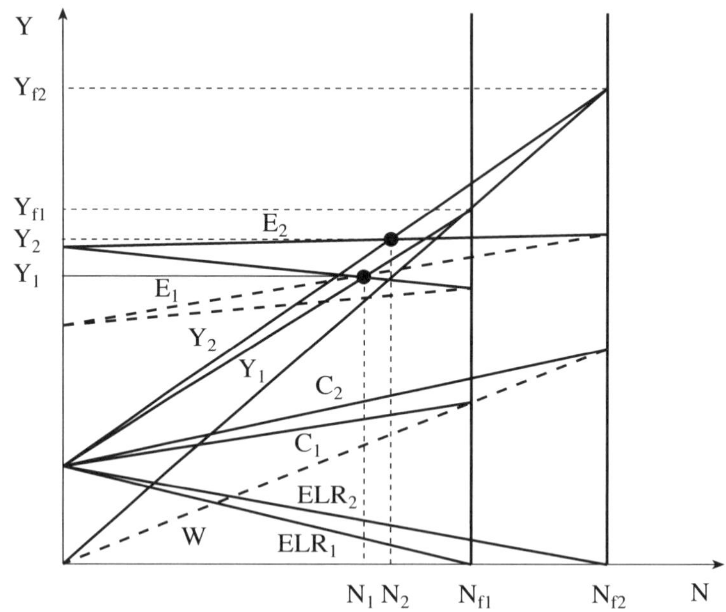

Figure 17.10 A change in the level of full employment

The additional ELR employment, matched by additional government ELR spending, must lead to an increase in household consumption spending by ELR-supported households. This increases private sector employment, leading to further respending of wages. So, as Figure 17.10 clearly shows, both output and private sector employment will increase, when the level of full employment rises as a result of an increase in the real wage. Of course, if the level of full employment *fell* when the wage rose – as it would if households uniformly aimed at target incomes – the opposite conclusions would follow. The impact of a change in the wage structure depends on the *nature and shape* of the labor supply function.

CONCLUSIONS

Technological developments in the modern economy have replaced the stabilizing price mechanism with a more volatile adjustment process, based on the multiplier (and accelerator). But automatic stabilizers embedded in government policy can be designed to reduce these fluctuations and restore a measure of stability. These have important advantages over discretionary policies, stemming from the fact that policy responses do not have to await successful political action.

But, to date, automatic stabilizers have largely been built around transfer payments, which do not put unemployed factors to use. Nor can a transfer payment system help to control inflation. By contrast the ELR puts the unemployed to work for a basic wage, and it stabilizes that wage.

In terms of short-run comparisons, the ELR appears to be superior to a transfer payment system in two ways. First it generates additional output. So an economy operating an ELR, but otherwise identical to an economy with a transfer payment system, will at least have a higher level of output but the same private sector employment. Since the ELR will also require regular investments, and may well market part of its output to the private sector, this conclusion must be considered minimal – the ELR economy might well be substantially better in both employment and output. Since the higher level of activity is likely to stimulate productivity growth, it might also have higher productivity. Secondly, the ELR will help control inflation. In contrast to the craft economy, the money wage in a modern economy is arguably unstable, generating inflationary pressures. The transfer payment system does not affect this one way or the other. But the ELR exerts a stabilizing force on money wages.

Finally these comparisons obviously concern the short-term aspects of the macroeconomy. We have taken investment as exogenous. But it could be argued in addition that an ELR could be designed to provide workers for venture capital projects promoting innovation, that it could provide services for cleaning up the environment, and that provision of worker training and public goods would tend to raise productivity. Large sections of the disadvantaged population could be brought into the economy on a permanent basis, thereby creating large new markets for consumer durables. In the long run, then, an ELR system could be designed to grow faster than an otherwise similar economy stabilized by transfer payments. But that is another subject.

NOTES

1. The widespread existence of constant unit costs came to light beginning with the debate on prices and pricing in the 1930s and 1940s (Hall and Hitch, 1937; Andrews, 1949). The suggestion here is that constant costs were the result of technological developments in manufacturing processes (Hunter, 1985). The evidence for constant costs is summarized and discussed in Lavoie (1992, Ch. 3).
2. To move from individual firms to the aggregate it is not necessary to hold the composition of output constant, so long as the movements are small. The aggregate function, of course, oversimplifies. When proportions of capital to consumer goods change in mass production, the degree of utilization changes but unit costs and prices are not affected.
3. The Penn World Tables provide data making it possible to plot output per head against capital per head with a large number of observations. When this is done for the advanced OECD economies, the scatter diagram shows no evidence of curvature. The same plot for the backward economies exhibits pronounced curvature, for middle range economies moderate curvature. Of course this can be considered no more than suggestive.

4. Wages and salaries in the aggregate are closely correlated with consumption spending, but do not fully explain it. Some obvious adjustments are easily made. Consumer spending also depends on the terms and availability of consumer credit. In addition it reflects transfer payments. Wealth and profitability are significant variables. But for the present purposes, which are purely illustrative, a simple 'absolute income' theory will suffice.
5. That is, employment is *not* determined in the labor market. It follows directly from the demand for output, given the output–employment function (as in Kalecki). Hicks, following Keynes, initially modeled effective demand by setting up the IS–LM system together with a labor market and a conventional production function. Later he came to feel that this was a mistake (Hicks, 1977, 1989).
6. On these assumptions investment determines – and equals – realized profits. When households save a certain percentage out of wages and salaries, the consumption line will swing below the wages line and profits will be reduced. When wealth-owning households (or businesses subsidizing top managers) add to their consumption spending in proportion to the level of activity, this swings the C + I line upwards, increasing profits.
7. The output multiplier in this simple example will be 1/(1–wn), where w is the real wage and n is labor per unit of output.
8. And money? Let household saving increase with the rate of interest (as consumer durable spending declines), while business investment declines as the rate of interest rises. (Neither influence is likely to be very great.) We can then construct a downward-sloping function (an analogue to the traditional IS) relating the rate of interest, i, to employment, N. It will intersect a horizontal line representing the level of the rate of interest as pegged by the central bank; this will determine the level of employment.
9. Why do unit wage increases at higher levels of the wage generate larger increases in overall employment? Because at higher levels of the wage, the respending effects will be greater. A higher wage here functions like a higher marginal propensity to consume in conventional theory.
10. If the intercept of the labor supply line were to the left of the intercept of the labor demand, there could be two intersections, one stable, the other unstable.
11. By contrast, it has been argued that the price mechanism provided pre-World War I economies with a built-in system of self-regulation – although perhaps it did not always work very well. This suggests a new way of looking at the debate over the amplitude of the business cycle (Nell and Phillips, 1995; Nell, 1998b). In spite of a much larger government sector, managed with an explicit intent to stabilize the system, the postwar economy has not been significantly less unstable than the economies prior to World War I. This is not a failure of Keynesian policies; it is rather that Keynesian policies have been needed to dampen down the volatility inherent in the new patterns of adjustment
12. Such a stabilization program would require 'functional finance,' but financing questions have been dealt with in earlier chapters, for example, 10, 11 and 12. For more on how to pay for an ELR, see Nell and Majewski (forthcoming); Mosler (1996); Wray (1998a, 1998b).
13. Jobs doing what? Many socially useful programs can be imagined; suggestions have included environmental cleanup, community service, education and school assistance including day care and home day care, home nursing and elder care, simple construction and home repair, and many other projects. Organizing the work to be effective will require managerial skill, particularly given that the workers may be untrained and undereducated, and that the better ones are likely to be bid away by the private sector. A good part of the effort will go into training, both formal and informal. Problems include possible competition with the private sector and 'substitution' of ELR workers in projects that local governments ought to be doing on their own budgets. See Wray (2000); Forstater (1998); and Nell and Majewski (forthcoming).
14. Changing this assumption makes the diagrams a little more complicated.
15. This does not necessarily imply that they are deliberately set at a low level. If they are set at a high level, then private sector wages will be driven up until the private sector is able to attract the labor it needs. The ELR is a *market* system; a basic wage is set, and the rest of the economy has to adapt to it. Since this wage is stabilized it will act both as a floor to money wages, and as a drag on rising wages.

16. Assuming all ELR output is 'purchased' by the government, and ignoring any other government spending, then $E = I + C + G$, where $C = w_pN_p + w_e(N_f - N_p)$ and $G = w_e(N_f - N_p)$. Under these assumptions $dE/dN_p = w_p - 2w_e$. If w_p is less than twice w_e then the aggregate spending line will slope down; otherwise it will rise. If some ELR output is sold commercially to the private sector, as might be plausible, or if there are other elements of government spending that depend on the level of employment, the equation will have to be modified.
17. Munnel (1990), Aschauer (1990) and others have presented evidence that government capital spending is strongly correlated with increases in private sector productivity. ELR spending, if properly designed, might well have the same effect.
18. A fiat currency is issued as a way of transferring resources to the state; it is 'tax-driven,' (Wray, 1998a). The treatment of taxes is presented in the appendix.
19. Thanks to Warren Mosler for discussions regarding this section.
20. The effect of changes in the real wage on investment are not considered here. A rise in real wages increases demand; it may even lead to a virtuous cycle of self-improvement in some set of households leading to a regular *growth of demand.* This would surely stimulate Investment (Nell, 2002; Nell and Argyrous, 2002). On the other hand, as Marglin and Bhaduri (1990), and Taylor (1991), have emphasized, a rise in wages reduces profits. Business at some times might be more responsive to changes in demand, at others to changes in profits. The evidence is not strong for this, however, and the impact of wage changes on investment will not be considered here.

APPENDIX

To keep the diagrams simple, taxes and savings were excluded. It is easy to show that the results do not depend on this assumption, either for the case of unemployment insurance or for the ELR. First we take investment as fixed exogenously, since the analysis is for short-period effective demand. Then we write the equation for consumption in a system with unemployment insurance, followed by the equation for consumption in an ELR economy. Output in an economy with unemployment insurance will simply be the private sector's output; but in an ELR economy, ELR output must be added to that of the private sector to determine total output. Government spending on goods and services will be lumped together with investment; but ELR government spending will equal ELR output.

$\mathbf{I} = \mathbf{I}^*$	Investment given
$\mathbf{C} = (1-h)[\mathbf{w}_p\mathbf{N}_p + \mathbf{w}_u(\mathbf{N}_f-\mathbf{N}_p)]$	Consumption in unemployment insurance case
$C = (1-h)[w_pN_p + w_e(N_f-N_p)]$	Consumption in the ELR case

Here **h** is the tax rate on wages (alternatively, it could be interpreted as savings), $\mathbf{w}_p$ the private sector wage, $\mathbf{w}_u$ unemployment benefit, $\mathbf{w}_e$ the ELR wage, $\mathbf{N}_p$ private sector employment, $\mathbf{N}_f$ full employment, **z** output per worker employed by the private sector and **u** output per worker employed by the ELR.

$Y = zN_p$ Output in the private sector; unemployment insurance case

$Y = zN_p + u(N_f - N_p)$ Output in the ELR case

$G_e = w_e(N_f - N_p)$ Government spending in the ELR case

Expenditure in the two cases will differ by the amount of government spending

$E = I + C$ Expenditure in the unemployment insurance case

$\mathrm{E} = \mathrm{I} + \mathrm{C} + \mathrm{G}_e$ Expenditure in the ELR case

In both cases equilibrium requires that output equal expenditure.

Assuming that there is the same private economy in both scenarios, so that h, I, w_p, N_f, and z are the same and that $w_u = w_e = u$, then, in equilibrium:

$Y = E$

$\mathbf{N}_p = [\mathbf{I} + (1-\mathbf{h})\mathbf{w}_u\mathbf{N}_f] / [\mathbf{z} - (1-\mathbf{h})(\mathbf{w}_p - \mathbf{w}_u)]$ The unemployment insurance case

$N_p = [I + (1-h)w_eN_f] / [z - (1-h)(w_p - w_e)]$ The ELR case

Private employment will be the same in both scenarios. So we find from the utilization functions that output in the ELR case will be greater than output with unemployment insurance as long as:

$$zN_p + u(N_f - N_p) > zN_p \text{ , or } N_f > N_p$$

Output in the ELR case will be greater as long as the economy is at less than full employment.

$\mathrm{Y} = \mathbf{z}[\mathrm{I} + (1-\mathbf{h})\mathbf{w}_u\mathbf{N}_F] / [\mathbf{z} - (1-\mathbf{h})(\mathbf{w}_p - \mathbf{w}_u)]$ The unemployment insurance case

$Y = uN_f + (z-u)[I + (1-h)w_eN_f] / [z - (1-h)(w_p - w_e)]$ The ELR case

REFERENCES

Andrews, P.W.S. (1949), *Manufacturing Business*, London: Macmillan.

Argyrous, George (2002), 'Endogenous Demand in the Theory of Transformational Growth', in M. Setterfield (ed), *The Economics of Demand-led Growth*, Cheltenham, UK and Northampton, MA: Edward Elgar.

Aschauer, D. (1990), *Public Investment and Private Sector Growth*, Washington, DC: Economic Policy Institute.

Forstater, Mathew (1998), 'Flexible Full Employment: Structural Implications of Discretionary Public Sector Employment,' *Journal of Economic Issues*, 32, 557–563.

Hall, R and C.J. Hitch (1937), 'Price Theory and Business Behavior,' in Andrews (ed.), *Oxford Studies in the Price Mechanism*, Oxford: Oxford University Press.

Hayek, F.A. (1932), 'A Note on the Development of the Doctrine of Forced Saving,' *Quarterly Journal of Economics*, 47, 123–133.

Hayek, F.A. (1941), *The Pure Theory of Capital*, London: Routledge and Kegan Paul.

Hicks, John (1963), *The Theory of Wages* (2nd edition), London: Macmillan.

Hicks, John (1977), *Economic Perspectives*, Oxford: Clarendon Press.

Hicks, John (1989), *A Market Theory of Money*, London: Macmillan.

Hunter, L.C. (1985), *A History of Industrial Power in the U.S. 1780–1930, Vol II: Steam Power*, Charlottesville: University Of Virginia Press.

Keynes, J.M. (1940), *How to Pay for the War*, London: Macmillan.

Kurz, H. and N. Salvadori (1995), *The Theory of Production*, Cambridge: Cambridge University Press.

Laibman, D. and E.J. Nell (1977), 'Reswitching, Wicksell Effects and the Neoclassical Production Function,' *American Economic Review*, 63, 100–13.

Lavioe, M. (1992), *Foundations of Post-Keynesian Economic Analysis*, Aldershot, UK and Brookfield, US: Edward Elgar.

Malthus, T.R. (1811), review of Ricardo's *High Price of Bullion*, *Edinburgh Review*, February.

Marglin, S. and A. Bhaduri (1990), 'Profit Squeeze and Keynesian Theory', in S. Marglin and J. Shor (eds), *The Golden Age of Capitalism*, Oxford: Oxford University Press.

Mitchell, William (1998), 'The Buffer Stock Employment Model and the NAIRU: The Path to Full Employment,' *Journal of Economic Issues*, 32, 547–57.

Mosler, Warren (1996), 'Full Employment and Price Stability,' *Journal of Post Keynesian Economics*.

Munnel, A. (1990), 'Why Has Productivity Growth Declined? Productivity and Public Investment,' *New England Economic Review*, Jan–Feb, 3–22.

Nell, Edward J. (1988), *Prosperity and Public Spending*, New York and London: Unwin Hyman.

Nell, Edward J. (1991), *Transformational Growth and Effective Demand*, London: Macmillan and New York: New York University Press.

Nell, Edward J. (1998a), *The General Theory of Transformational Growth*, Cambridge: Cambridge University Press.

Nell, Edward J. (ed.) (1998b), *Transformational Growth and the Business Cycle*, London and New York: Routledge.

Nell, Edward J. (2002), 'Notes on the Transformational Growth of Demand,' in M. Setterfield (ed), *The Economics of Demand-led Growth*, Cheltenham, UK and Northampton, MA: Edward Elgar.

Nell, Edward J. and Raymond Majewski, *Leviathan's Wallet* (forthcoming), Transformational Growth and Full Employment Program, New School University Mss.

Nell, E.J. and T. Phillips (1995), 'Transformational Growth and the Business Cycle,' *Eastern Economic Journal*, 21, 125–42.

Ricardo, D. (1810), *The High Price of Bullion*, in P. Sraffa (ed.) (1953), Vol. III, *Works and Correspondence*, Cambridge: Cambridge University Press.

Robertson, D. (1926), *Banking Policy and the Price Level*, London: P.S. King and Sons.

Rowthorn, R. (1982), 'Demand, Real Wages and Economic Growth,' *Studi Economici*, Siena, 18, 2–53.

Taylor, L. (1991), *Income Distribution, Inflation and Growth*, Cambridge, MA: MIT Press.

Thornton, H. (1802), *An Enquiry into the Nature and Effects of the Paper Credit of Great Britain*, reprinted (1939), George Allen and Unwin.

Wray, Randall (1998a), *Understanding Modern Money*, Cheltenham, UK and Lyme, US: Edward Elgar.

Wray, Randall (1998b), 'Zero Unemployment and Stable Prices,' *Journal of Economic Issues*, 32, 539–45.

Wray, Randall (2000), 'Public Service Employment: Full Employment without Inflation,' in Carlson and Mitchell, *The Path to Full Employment and Equity*.

18. Transformational growth project members and conference participants in open conversation

EDWARD NELL: Most proposals for public sector employment have treated it as a fiscal stabilizer, or as an anti-poverty measure. If it is to act as a fiscal stabilizer, the public sector should expand in a slump and contract in the boom. This is just what is needed to set up a 'buffer stock' approach to labor – to offer a labor supply in a boom and to hire in the slump, in both cases at a fixed wage. This will provide a stabilizing effect on the wage structure. We start by setting a fair, but low, wage at which labor will be absorbed in the slump and be released when private sector employment expands. Keeping the wage reasonable but low makes it easy for people to be bid away from public employment by the private sector. (This wage will become the market-imposed minimum wage.) In other words, the public sector wage will be chosen to make adjustment easy, and to help stabilize the wage bill. Of course, this has a direct impact only on the low end of the wage bill, but because the wage structure doesn't change easily, a very large part of the wage/price complex is stabilized. It can be expected that many of the jobs most likely to be created will be training jobs. At the same time we provide for full employment.

Warren Mosler likes to call this 'full employment with loose labor markets,' as it prevents upward pressure on the wage bill while at the same time maintaining a fully trained labor force.

RAY MAJEWSKI: I have two suggestions. The first concerns a problem central to this proposal and a way of dealing with it. Among the big headaches we face are not so much the technical and analytical issues of functional finance – although there are certainly challenges there – but the 'political economy' issues of functional finance. For example, when I see the employer of last resort proposal made here, I think of the last attempt at a jobs program in this country – CETA – and how that was summarily swamped by charges of corruption, inefficiency and so on. Certainly there may have been some of those problems in that program, but they were, in reality, of no serious consequence. There is, however, a strong set of political economy presumptions – popular presumptions – against jobs programs and the kinds of arguments made for them. We must find ways of dealing with these issues, including ways of presenting our ideas that will further our ability to institute programs.

One suggestion is that we take a lead from our friends the pragmatist philosophers. Among the things taught by the pragmatists is that progress comes not only in finding new answers, but in forgetting old questions. When old questions can't be immediately forgotten, one of the key ways of dealing with them is through evasion. Indeed, the subtitle of one of the books of a current, leading pragmatist is 'The American Evasion of Philosophy.' That's what their pragmatism is all about: If you don't like the old questions, don't talk about them.

There is one old question that I think we should no longer discuss, but forget and evade: the question of debt and deficit. One of the things functional finance teaches us is that debt and finance are not the point. Rather, the point is a set of macroeconomic policies that meet a set of goals. It's about how you spend, and what you spend on; about how you tax, how you borrow; and both the macroeconomic effects of these things and the ways in which you meet responsibilities by taking such measures. If we are going to get beyond academic meanings, the rhetoric we need to adopt is not that of debt, nor of deficit, but of responsibility. We need to discuss how using the tools of functional finance will allow us to better meet government's responsibilities.

I might add that, even politically, the deficit is not the point. I thought that was one of Professor Musgrave's very sharp comments: current political arguments are dominated really not by anti-deficit, but by anti-tax rhetoric and suspicion of government. The deficit discussions are, in some ways, symptoms of this. If we are going to try and address them politically, we must address those issues. We must find another way of talking about this, and stop putting the deficit discussion ahead of everything else.

LOUIS-PHILLIPE ROCHON: For me, the discussion of functional finance involves, not issues of economics, but issues of social philosophy. The question is, 'What kind of society do we want to live in? What values do we share?'

Answers tie into state responsibility. If, in the old trade cycle of the late 1800s and before, the GDP ratio was 5 per cent, we have to ask ourselves why. The state at that time did not have the responsibilities that we want it to have today. Whether it would have had the ability to execute such responsibilities is an open-ended question, a question of the responsibility of the state, the issues of unemployment, social safety nets and so on. From a political economy perspective, the problem is one of backward thinking.

In 1980 when the Republicans took office, Dan Rostenkowski, Chairman of the Ways and Means House Committee at the time, stood up during Reagan's first budget speech announcing the era of deficit reduction, and held up a credit card. Rostenkowski said, 'Would you want to live constantly with your credit card at the limit?' That image crystallized in the public imagination, creating the notion that governments are like households or individual workers. The issue has evolved to become a public conviction that government income should be managed like household income is managed. 'You cannot live beyond your means,' was the message. Behind that discussion is the notion that state responsibility is reduced. This has been lost in our discussion. Discussions as to whether unemployment was 2 or 3 per cent are, for me, secondary. Functional finance must deal first with the social responsibilities of the state, and then be applied as a means for achieving those goals.

JOHN SMITHIN: I am struck by your reference to 'loose labor markets.' I would like you to expand on this a bit. I realize that the policies someone like myself would put forward for full employment – having to do with fiscal policy, monetary policy, cheap money, running the deficit and so on – would actually lead to full employment with *tight* labor markets. It struck me that, in my world, there will be high employment, high real wages and the private sector will be bearing the cost of training. There may be more inflation than in your world, but I' m not particularly worried about inflation, especially if real interest rates are positive because even the rentiers are indexed.

In your world then, real wages will presumably be lower because you are pricing at the minimum wage. The cost of training is borne, as it were, by the public sector, though granted, it is not much of a cost if there is a deficit. I am asking, 'Which is the more attractive outcome?' The distinction is between a traditional Keynesian approach – such as I would have – and the buffer stock approach that you are now advocating.

NELL: A preliminary response to that statement is that the buffer stock approach is designed to provide a sort of double-duty automatic stabilizer – meant to stabilize or at least reduce volatility – that impacts on both the price level and the level of employment (and, therefore, the level of output). Even though it is aimed at both employment and prices, it is *not* claimed that it would eliminate all causes of inflation. It would eliminate or reduce some inflationary pressures. However, others will remain. For example, any kind of reasonably complex labor market is going to have important relativities to maintain. If productivity goes up in one section of that labor market, and wages or salaries follow productivity, there will be pressure on sectors that have not increased their productivity to raise wages to maintain the customary relativities. This will be an inflationary pressure, one that the ELR would probably not affect.

SMITHIN: But what are the costs of inflation? Bill Mitchell was talking about backward thinking and forward thinking. We decided to worry about that instead of the deficit.

NELL: Why should we worry about inflation?

SMITHIN: Yes, why should we, particularly if everybody is indexed? In other words, suppose real interest rates remain low but positive, real wages rise and we can index pensions. Isn't that a more effective proposition than the 'loose labor market' idea? What's wrong with inflation in that case?

NELL: That's a good question that I won't attempt to answer. For a long time I argued that inflation was not particularly important; that as long as it was single-digit, there was no danger. Even accelerating, double-digit inflation could be handled. Countries have, of course, endured very high amounts of inflation. Inflation certainly creates inconvenience, although the actual costs are hard to estimate. But it isn't just that inflation is inconvenient. It is also intensely disliked. The case of the United States is quite interesting. The US, by world standards, is really a low inflation country. The inflation that came in the 1970s, however, was intensely and widely disliked. Reaction to inflation in the US is possibly a cultural phenomenon. There is a difference in order of magnitude when the costs of inflation are measured against the far greater costs of unemployment. Though unemployment is much more serious, inflation is much more hated.

PHIL HARVEY: I have some thoughts on the choices represented by the two models – Smithin's Old Keynesian proposals and the ELR – that includes a response to Louis-Phillipe Rochon's suggestion that we need to discuss the social responsibilities of the state in this context.

Hearing the presentations today, I am not clear as to what people mean when they use the term 'full employment.' There is obvious agreement that full employment is unemployment less than the rates that now prevail. But what do we mean, in a positive sense, by full employment?

In the back of our minds when we speak of 'full employment' is the notion that government or society has a responsibility to ensure that work on reasonable terms is available to all who want it. That condition makes possible what we mean by full employment. As to the choice between the traditional Keynesian strategy of achieving that goal and the strategy that Ed Nell outlines, one of the functions of Nell's proposal is the creation of circumstances that provide strong political incentives for using the other strategy – traditional Keynesian policies. Right now, it is easy for policy makers to avoid striving for full employment (as I have defined it), based on any number of political or economic considerations. If there were an express statutory obligation in Nell's proposal requiring the achievement of full employment by means of an ELR program, then policy makers would have to choose whether they dislike government employment more than they dislike expansionary macroeconomic policies, and the public would have to decide whether it preferred traditional Keynesian policies that might increase inflation, or the maintenance of a large public employment program.

Coming back to my starting point, if full employment implies government responsibility for providing work, an ELR program makes good sense, but it probably should follow a different model than the one Nell proposes. For example, I see no reason to accept the minimum wage limitation in Nell's proposal.

As Ingrid Rima noted earlier, there is not *a* labor market, there are lots of labor markets. If we are talking about providing an alternative source of employment for people in all of those labor markets, then all that is really required is that wages and other conditions of employment be set at a level where it is possible to free up the relevant stock of labor when the private sector is prepared to employ it. Offering only minimum wage employment certainly is not required to satisfy that condition. Abandoning that limitation would also move Nell's model in the direction of the traditional model. I think that is desirable.

JAMES DUESENBERRY: I have a number of mundane questions. As you suggested, it may be of some value to look at numbers. When we talk about full employment, we base full employment on the definitions of unemployment from official statistics hovering around 4.9 to 6.5 per cent.

If looked at carefully, the numbers should be qualified in two directions. Out of that roughly 6.5 million, it turns out that the number of people who will have more than a short spell of unemployment is something like 2 rather than 5 per cent, indicating a large number of people who have relatively short spells of unemployment. We may wish to do something for these unemployed, but running them through a whole program may not be the optimum thing.

On the other hand, we know that a person is officially defined as unemployed if she works one day in a survey week, or part time, and so on. Whenever anybody expresses satisfaction in the employment situation, there are always a lot of people saying, 'What about all those part-time people? What about all those discouraged workers?' While 6.5 million is the official definition, if upper level qualifications are taken, that figure could be run up to ten million. I don't want to argue with the figures, but a substantial upward adjustment is needed to affect this aspect of unemployment statistics. We also need a downward adjustment because of short-term unemployment. These qualifications, of course, vary with circumstances, but we have to think about just what kind of definitions we want, and a little bit about objectives.

If there are marginal people who work when everything is nice, and will not work if things are not nice, we have to determine qualifications for getting them into the program, and think about the numbers that are involved in various kinds of employment.

Another aspect I want to raise is that I hear two different circumstances described in relation to this program. The simple one supposes that there is no problem with the present level of unemployment in the US. One way of thinking about the buffer stock program takes 5 per cent unemployment as a zero point; whenever unemployment, however defined, is more than that due to a slump, or slowdown, then the buffer stock picks up the extra unemployed workers generated by that slowdown.

Another way of looking at it is to think about the up side, where, given the labor force, we have jobs vacancies and unemployment existing side-by-side. The vacancies and the unemployment coexist because the vacancies are in the wrong place or the unemployed have the wrong skills. We might begin by asking what is a tolerable level of vacancies, from an inflation point of view. (Although we do not currently measure vacancies.) We decide that a certain vacancy index is okay, that it won't produce much wage pressure. From there, we start to work out what the total labor force would be and to determine how much special employment is necessary, not because there is a slump, but as a kind of normal, baseline situation. And that is the necessary buffer. Because, as it turns out, the demand for this kind of labor changes.

That is one way of looking at the buffer stock in relation to the NAIRU problem. The other way is to just look at the slump going downward away from that position. In your exposition, either or both could be done. You seem to be talking about one and then talking about the other. Probably models ought to be worked out for both, with some sense of the kind of numbers involved, which can then generate an idea of cost.

The last thing I want to say is about CETA. We have had a number of experiments over the years with various kinds of ELR elements. We have had programs with industry operations. In the late 1960s, we had a program in which all kinds of business firms – especially the large ones – were going to sign up and cooperate with programs to employ the difficult-to-employ. They actually had some success when the demand for labor was very high. Under that condition, they were willing to try anything. As soon as things slacked off, the program collapsed. At any rate, we have had a lot of experiments. I think it is a good idea for your project to look at the records and critiques of all past programs.

NELL: Those are three very valuable comments, especially in relation to the study of the labor force and the definitions of the unemployed. As I'm sure you know better than me, this recent expansion, because it has attracted more and more people into the labor force, has reduced unemployment rather slowly compared to the amount of jobs it has created.

DUESENBERRY: The participation rate has gone up by 2 per cent in less than two years.

NELL: This is an example of a neglected topic that needs careful study. I would expect that a training program would focus attention on Beveridge Curves, because an ideal way of contributing to the labor market's efficiency is to match skills with vacancies. The ELR could indeed make a contribution in that respect.

It is perfectly true that we could define what might be called a full-scale version of the program, and a crisis- or recession-management version. However, earlier I presented a basic textbook diagram to show that there is an orderly way of thinking about this in terms of effective demand. The choice between the two is quite significant. I am interested in working both versions. I am attracted to the full-scale version, but I think it would be worth while to study a minimalist version as well.

Concerning CETA, I was always rather enthusiastic about the program, and I've never joined in its criticisms. Actually, it didn't last long enough to have its bugs worked out. Further, some of those bugs didn't have that much bite.

DUESENBERRY: CETA did run into problems in part because of attitudes toward public employees. It became difficult to put CETA workers into any job already covered by community budgets. So people were in jobs for which the test seemed to be, 'Nobody thinks it's worth while to pay for this.' In my town, for instance, we had a person who wrote a history of the public library, something that was definitely not a high priority.

But maybe three things are needed. First, concerning the up side, having a buffer stock of labor when dealing with shortages; second, there are always people who can't read or who didn't finish school, so there needs to be a program for what we call the 'hard-to-employ.' Finally, we need programs for recessions.

NELL: In a certain sense, our educational system has not lived up to its responsibilities, as Ray Majewski and Louis-Phillipe Rochon have pointed out. I don't have much experience in government administration, but I think our proposal has a certain rough simplicity: we aim to establish a comprehensive program to deal with the hard-to-employ and those with major deficiencies in fundamental skills like reading and writing, while at the same time offering retraining and upgrading of skills, all included in a program that offers public service jobs to anyone who wants one.

One comprehensive piece of legislation, then, can make fiscal policy virtually automatic. That is to say, it is a countercyclical fiscal policy; when there is a recession, there must be an increase in public hiring. Workers have a right to a job. Hiring and retraining or re-educating must be administered through the same mechanism, so that the same procedures will handle the worker who cannot read *and* the high-skilled worker thrown out of a job because of downsizing. I am suggesting that there be one piece of legislation to handle a variety of conditions. Such a program could not be made to work comprehensively the first year or even the first two or three years. We could expect that there would be plenty of problems to work out.

MAJEWSKI: As James Duesenberry tells us, numbers help. Let me use them to sketch out how it might work. At the Transformational Growth Program, we have added an ELR to FairModel in order to get some idea of the scale, costs and impact of the program. We imagined the program starting gradually in early 1989, becoming fully operational in 1994 and projected in simulation to 2004. At any given time the ELR, employing between 400,000 and 1.6 million workers including administrators, would be roughly twice the size of CETA in the 1970s. Net costs, including a significant expansion to job training programs, would vary from around 0.5 per cent to 0.9 per cent of GDP. This has an effect on the deficit, but not a large effect. In the simulation without the ELR, the budget goes into surplus in late 1997. The ELR delays this by 11 quarters. Its indirect effect on unemployment is significant. Even if we count ELR workers as 'unemployed,' the program still lowers the rate of unemployment between 0.75 and 2 per cent. Extra private employment and the output of the ELR workers raise GDP. If we subtract the net costs from the extra output we find, correcting for inflation, that we are ahead between $4 and $10 billion for each quarter that the program is fully operational. For the period that we simulated, the extra output would have exceeded cost by around $400 billion. The program pays.

The main 'cost' of the program is that it slows the disinflation that occurred in the early 1990s. This slower disinflation is a consequence of the effectiveness of the ELR as an automatic stabilizer. To see this we simulated the effect of a 10 per cent increase of the T-bill rate (from 5 to 5.5 per cent) during the first quarter of 1994, and compared it to the outcome without the shock. In both – the plain FairModel and the ELR – the interest rate increase caused prices to be lower than they would have been without the shock. But the ELR reduced the sensitivity to the interest rate increase. Figure 18.1 shows the effect on prices.

This stabilizing effect also occurs for output. The interest rate increase causes real GDP to fall relative to the 'no shock' case. But once again the ELR makes the economy less sensitive to the change as shown in Figure 18.2.

The automatic stabilizers are also effective with demand shocks, as in this 10 per cent increase in Federal purchases from the private sector as in Figure 18.4. The stabilization also occurs for real GDP.

The area where the stabilizing effects are less clear is for price shocks. For some sorts of shocks, such as an increase in farm prices, the ELR stabilizes both price and quantity, as shown in Figure 18.3. For other sorts of shocks,

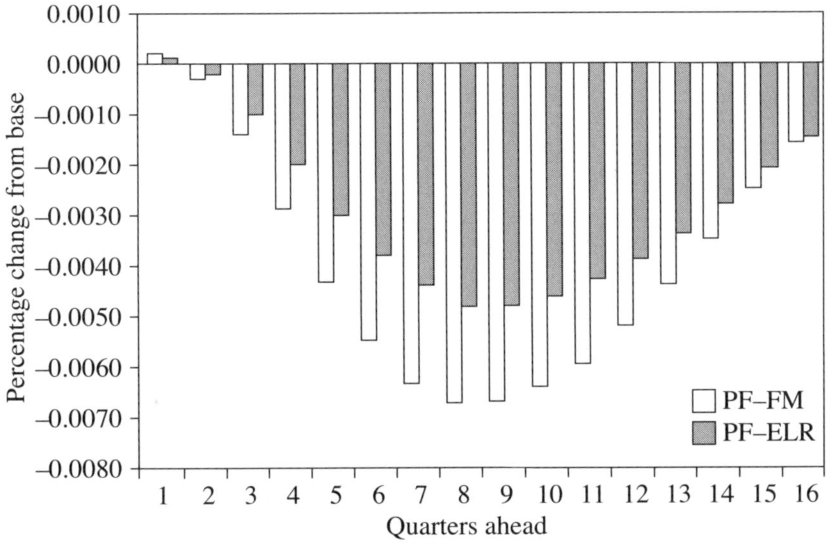

Figure 18.1 Firm sector prices response to a 10% increase in the T-Bill Rate

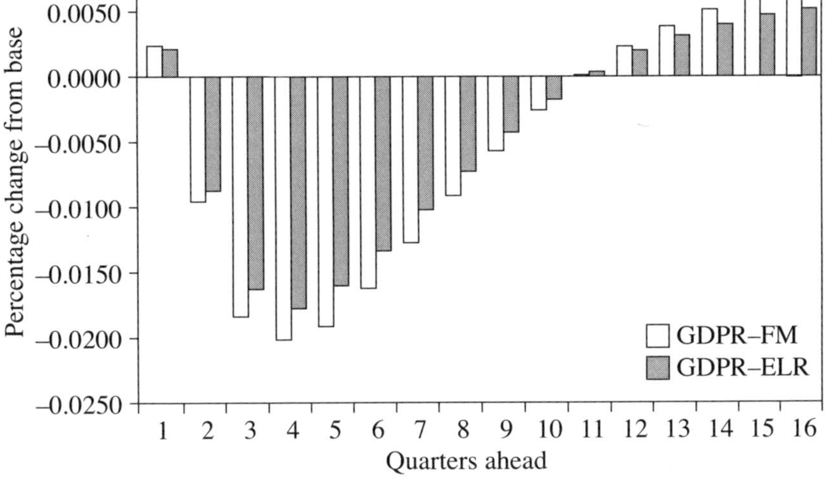

Figure 18.2 Real GDP response to a 10% increase in the T-Bill Rate

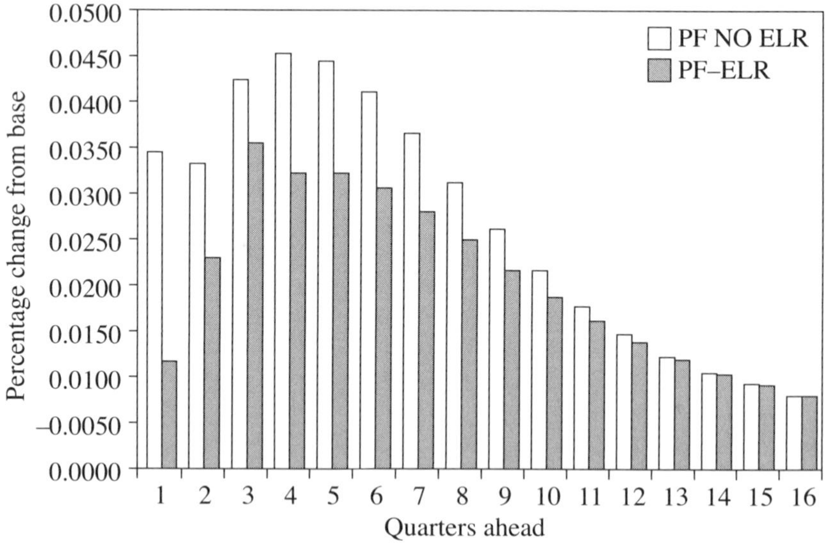

Figure 18.3 Firm sector prices response to 10% change in Federal purchases (COG)

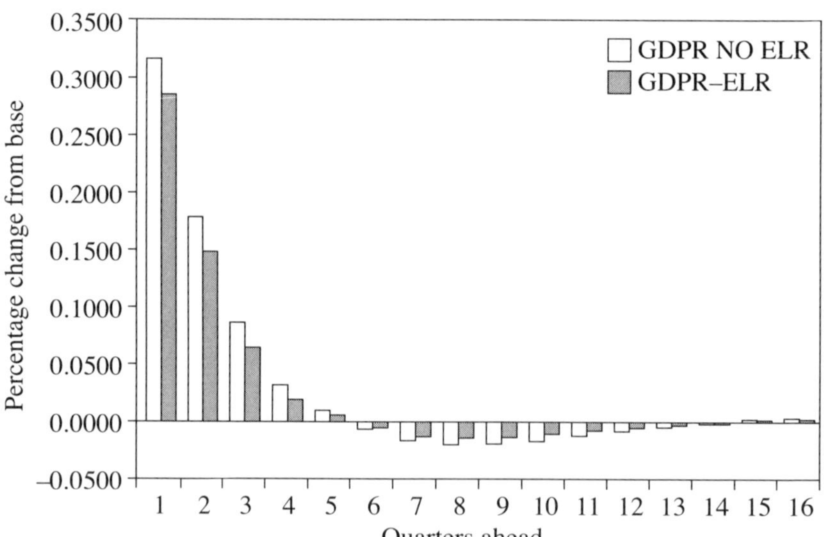

Figure 18.4 Real GDP in response to 10% increase in Federal purchases (COG)

such as to import prices, the ELR reduces the response of real GDP with a larger response in firm sector prices.

These results are preliminary, involving a number of assumptions about participation in the ELR: the wages it pays, its material costs, job training costs and so on. They suggest, however, that macroeconomically, an ELR can work and that it would pay to introduce one.

SMITHIN: Ray Majewski's simulations of the ELR within FairModel are very interesting. I think they confirm what most of us agree, that ELR would certainly 'work' in the sense of reducing unemployment and stabilizing output. Nor would it be costly in the conventional sense. There are still a couple of questions I would like to ask, however. Namely, what is the effect on real wages (as well as employment) of the ELR as compared to the 'Old Keynesian' program? I would not like to buy higher employment with lower real wages. Secondly, presumably the FairModel has a built-in 'natural rate' as most econometric models do. So are we stabilizing output around a given growth path? What would be the impact in a model in which effective demand has a permanent effect?

NELL: Real wages are pretty slow to move, both in reality and in the FairModel. And consumption demand tends to move the same direction as wages. Plus there's no natural rate there either. Ray, how would you answer?

MAJEWSKI: If we look at employees in the private sector, the ELR has the same, rather small, effect as an Old Keynesian stimulus. However, there is a composition effect. The ELR's workforce is paid a low wage and *ceteris paribus* this will (slightly) lower the average real wage. FairModel does not have a 'natural rate' of unemployment. This is one of the things that attracted us to the model. While FairModel's theoretical start is an income constrained Keynesian model, the interactive process of specification yields a result close to Post-Keynesian work. The model does tend to return to trend after short-term shocks. But in our simulations the ELR permanently increases output and employment without a continuous acceleration of inflation.

This simulation is not meant to stand on its own. It is suggestive, but not much more than that; it has to fit into a larger picture. James Duesenberry reminds us that we should look at the history of CETA and other similar programs. Phil Harvey reminds us that there are legal and political aspects to an ELR. And of course there is macroeconomic theory to be considered, especially Post-Keynesian and Old Keynesian. Our simulations must interact with and be adjusted in the light of all of these, informed by them and informing them. Simulations can be a useful tool in a historical, institutional macroeconomics, and when treated as part of a more complete story, they can give us a better idea of the potential consequences of a policy.

AUDIENCE MEMBER: I would like to play the devil's advocate for a moment. Leaving aside the purely economic questions to turn to social issues, if there were full employment guaranteed by this government employer of last resort, what would be the impact on worker discipline in the government sector? That is, if there were no chance to be unemployed from a job, what would become of worker productivity in the government sector?

NELL: I think worker productivity would be low. You absolutely have to have a right to a job, but not the right to fool around on a job.

AUDIENCE MEMBER: How would the right to a job be enforced?

NELL: With a corresponding right to fire. Otherwise, given that the idea is to train workers, especially sections of the population that haven't successfully worked for a time, training has to be in real work. It can be training work but it has to be disciplined.

AUDIENCE MEMBER: That has nothing to do with the business side of things.

NELL: That is perfectly true. But as I said, the program is like a Swiss army knife – very dangerous, perhaps, but a proposal with many facets. That is perhaps its strength as well as its weakness.

AUDIENCE MEMBER (1): I want to respond to what has been said about the CETA program. People involved in CETA twenty years ago were students. A lot of them had Masters' degrees. The work they were doing involved real property assessment for New York City. This program, in my opinion, worked very well because these people were very conscientious and devoted to their work. When they eliminated CETA, I wondered why. Your assessment is pretty much on target.

AUDIENCE MEMBER (2): In Sweden, they've had a manpower policy through the years, which was initiated by unions and the socialist democratic party. The idea was put forward by solidarist work policies in low profit industries and the need to make low profit rates into higher profit rates. As these companies closed down, they realized they had to retrain displaced workers for new jobs in other companies. Sweden had a complete manpower policy program that was part of their full employment program, but also part of their structural change support. They saw their country had not been very responsive to technological advances and was not keeping up with the world market. So they produced an entire program to support improvements.

Studies that were done in the 1970s showed that the flexibility of the work force, in a social democratic state, was actually much higher than in the US in what we think of as the ossified public sector. But actually, the turnover of people moving from job to job was higher than in the United States. This program actually *created* flexibility in the job market. To support actual change in the economy is a government responsibility. In Sweden they targeted full employment instead of inflation. They developed an entire series of policies to support unemployment, and, at the same time, to support investment. That's the kind of policy we also need to think about.

AUDIENCE MEMBER (3): Since this section of the conference refers to 'the future' in its title, I would like to read something. 'We need to take planned government actions on a larger scale to defend our environment. But even if we came to develop a theory for such planning, I mistrust both the will and the capacity of government to decide upon and effectuate such planned policies to the extent needed.'

This is not a comment on the recent Kyoto summit. It was written by Gunnar Myrdahl around 27 years ago. It seems to me that it is very applicable to the present situation because microeconomic policies completely ignore environmental issues.

NELL: One of the suggested categories of employment for an ELR is work on environmental cleanup. Such areas should be opened for ELR where there is no existing private business or public service. Otherwise, we would be doing what Giuliani is doing with Workfare, namely, displacing city employees with Workfare employees and, basically, driving down wages. Environmental cleanup is indeed an area that is in need of attention. But as I said, this proposal is a Swiss army knife and that is one little blade, though not at all its main *raison d'être*.

WALTER EBERSTADT: Please help me with this one: Downsizing. Where does it fit into this model? The downsizing theory goes like this: I have to be more efficient in order to compete, which exercises pressure on prices. I get the product more cheaply. I'm the customer; therefore presumably, if I buy it more cheaply, I have money left over to buy something else and give employment in another place because I've got more spending power. At what point is this overdone?

NELL: Assuming that it is done well, downsizing is an increase in productivity. Presumably afterwards the company is still able to accomplish its objectives, whatever they are.

EBERSTADT: One guy's loss is another guy's gain.

NELL: For any given company, downsizing, if it is done correctly, can't be anything but 'good.' For the company, of course; for those dismissed it is another story. On the other hand, if you install a computer system and fire a lot of people because computers are going to do their jobs, there is always the possibility that the system will crash.

EBERSTADT: But somebody had to make those computers – even if they do crash – and got employment out of it.

NELL: If those computers are worth while, their total labor cost is going to be less than the cost of labor that they displace, because that's what you're using them for. And so, I don't think that the employment in making them can offset the labor they displace.

Surely, for any given company, downsizing represents an increase in productivity. However, taking all companies together, what has happened is that a large number of salaried people have been displaced. They are no longer able to maintain their consumption at the same rate. So there is a falling off of demand; this is what puts the drag on the economy. If the downsizing were to stimulate an investment boom, then this drop in demand would be replaced. But if downsizing simply takes place with a given rate of growth of aggregate demand, and displaces enough people to create a downward drag, then, in fact, far from stimulating investment, downsizing is likely to have a negative 'accelerator' effect, pulling investment down.

AUDIENCE MEMBER: In Europe, we have a system where it is much more difficult to downsize because it is expensive to let go of labor. Should we be moving in that direction here?

DUESENBERRY: When unemployment has been absorbed without creating inflation, there has most likely been an investment boom. If not, there must have been some fiscal or monetary action to increase aggregate demand and create a situation in which total output could become higher because displaced people are now working in new jobs and producing something else. That is, there is a bigger total demand and a bigger total supply.

Though I don't know the whole causal sequence in the US, that is actually not so far from what has actually happened in the last few years. After all, we now have higher employment and lower unemployment than we had when the downsizing surge began. That's the good news. But there were a lot of highly specialized and highly paid individuals who lost jobs. It took them a long time to find new jobs, and they were forced to accept pay lower than their previous earnings. So it is not a happy outcome for absolutely everybody. That's the basic story, but we have the added option that, if the private boom doesn't come off, we can do something in the public sector, that is, if we are sticking to our public sector labor project.

NELL: The employer-of-last resort proposal we are considering would make it possible to absorb any amount of downsizing. But it does demand a big wage cut. The president of Eastman Kodak, I think, was downsized. The camera division merged into their parent company and he was out of a job. I think he eventually ended up selling cars.

EBERSTADT: So be it.

NELL: But in my scheme he would have gotten a minimum wage job right away. The object, again, in this proposal, is to make policy automatic. If you have to rely on fiscal policy to go through Congress, to be formulated into the budget, to be presented in the budget speech, to go through Congressional committees and so on, by the time the legislation is passed, the need will have changed.

It is better, therefore, to institute something that acts automatically and has multiple possibilities. Now, as Jim Duesenberry said earlier, there could be a full-scale version and a sort of stripped-down version in which we really stick to the counter-cyclical aspect and drop everything else. It seems to me an open question as to which way to go. Both are probably worth exploring.

MAJEWSKI: I want to stress once again the importance of political economy. Alvin Hanson who – besides being a significant popularizer – was a policy entrepreneur and had an advantage we don't possess. That is, he had a network of Wisconsin School economists in the Labor Department that, though not necessarily Keynesians, were of a similar mind. He also had administrators experienced in the things necessary to the construction of bureaucratic programs.

One of CETA's difficulties was the lack of a similar policy network. The Labor Department, by the time CETA came around, lacked the same orientation and, in some ways, had lost the bureaucratic skills and organization the Labor Department possessed in the late 1930s and early 1940s. So in trying to construct these programs, we have to start thinking about the network and the government capabilities necessary for their implementation. It is a mistake to be projecting them without that.

NELL: That's a good point concerning a network of like-minded and similarly trained personnel. At the least, a pool of such resources is important.

AUDIENCE MEMBER: Luckily, the innate structure of the population has made us build more colleges and primary and secondary schools. If the population declines somewhat, we'll have some spare buildings. Perhaps we already have some spare intellectuals that could be used.

I don't have a quarrel with the proposal. It's wonderful. It's been tried in a lot of societies. But I wonder why no one has spoken of the variant of the employment of *first* resort. I think you are stepping around the possibility that public employment might trample on the sacrosanct private right to become extremely rich on other people's lack of skills.

Isn't the issue, rather, what people want to do with their lives? Once they become unemployed, they suddenly have a choice. Isn't one of the goals to get people to exercise choices and go in directions advantageous to themselves, in addition to simply stabilizing the economy? I think your grand program should be, not a government guaranteed job, but guaranteed work for everyone, somehow, some way.

NELL: Well, it's perfectly true that the best thing for people's sanity is a good war. World War II saw an enormous reduction in alcoholism, suicide and drug addiction.

AUDIENCE MEMBER: That's because the war was elsewhere. If it had been on site, that wouldn't have happened.

NELL: It is certainly not true that sanity is winning in Yugoslavia right now. But a good war that is fought somewhere else, as an example of massive mobilization for some kind of purpose far grander than the personal self . . .

EBERSTADT: I never drank more than I did in World War II.

NELL: But you didn't become an alcoholic. I read that in statistics. I didn't drink at all during World War II.

EBERSTADT: You were too young.

HARVEY: In response to Ray Majewski's comment, the policy-interested network that he describes is in place and has become increasingly active in the past eighteen months, largely in response to welfare reform and the counter-responses of people who think along the same lines as most people in this room.

This is the second conference I've attended this week. The first was in Washington DC, with discussion focusing on immediate political and policy issues. There are a number of people who have been working in this area for some time. My own book, *Securing the Right to Employment* [Princeton University Press, 1989] addresses a number of questions raised here today, including Jim Duesenberry's question about how such a program would look. The book also considers issues such as worker discipline, downsizing and international trade – where an economic benefit to the economy as a whole nonetheless hurts particular groups of workers. Economists say that the benefit compensates for those who are hurt. The problem is to design institutions that ensure those who are hurt also share the benefit. A well-designed public employment program is the blade of the Swiss army knife that can help provide that answer. So I encourage you to look at my book and other people's work in this area, because some of the groundwork has already been done.

NELL: It's a great book. Any comments?

AUDIENCE MEMBER: The important issue of the environment has been mentioned. For example, looking at the infrastructure of roads, couldn't there be a joint project between securing a cleaner environment and having better roads? In just about every borough there are potholes that do terrible things to cars, like putting the wheels out of alignment. I think that the infrastructure needs to be reviewed.

NELL: Wait until the big water mains break. This is the question with which we began. John Smithin raised the question of full employment with a tight labor market, with massive public works projects and strong stimulation of investment. Why go, instead, to the kind of thing I'm proposing? My answer, in one phrase, is that a Swiss army knife not only has all of these features, but is also very easy to operate. Large-scale investment in the infrastructure would push the economy toward full employment, with a large, active, private sector, plus a private and public investment mix. That would be highly desirable. But maintaining full employment and controlling inflation would still need automatic counter-cyclical buffer-stock employment policy.

EBERSTADT: I'm against potholes, but how do we finance fixing them? Do I pay through taxes, or do I buy a government bond?

AUDIENCE MEMBER: Maybe a combination of both, depending on how the program comes out of the government committees.

EBERSTADT: But instead of that particular government bond, which I buy to fix those damn potholes, I might have been buying an IBM bond because IBM wants to employ all sorts of people. How does this get allocated?

AUDIENCE MEMBER: I just want to call attention to the soft underbelly of all this. One major problem is that there are millions of people in the United States who work for less than the minimum wage, with miserable jobs in households and so on. I'm not sure that this program addresses the problems of the lowest tenth of the population.

NELL: It definitely does. That is certainly one of the larger blades of the Swiss army knife. The answer to Walter Eberstadt's question (which Walter will not like) is that the potholes – and all the rest – are addressed through deficit spending.

HARVEY: I have two responses to that answer. First, for people who believe that deficits do not matter, Ed's answer is adequate. But for people who believe that deficits *do* matter, there is an alternative answer. My own research supports the conclusion that a comprehensive jobs program would, in fact, save more money than it spends. The costs of unemployment – including transfer payments, lost taxes and indirect costs associated with the effects of unemployment on illness, mortality and so forth – are great enough that it probably would be cheaper for governments to put every unemployed worker to work than to pay for joblessness in the many ways we currently do. You wouldn't have to choose between the IBM bond and the government bond. You would simply have to transfer funds from one government account to another.

EBERSTADT: But deficit has to be financed somehow.

HARVEY: There is no deficit. That's my point. An ELR program could be fiscally neutral. My proposed program doesn't pay minimum wages. It pays market wages, well above the minimum. And my research suggests it would still be fiscally neutral.

NELL: With this tangle, we have now come full circle, back to where we began yesterday morning. The unemployed are falling into the potholes. Can we afford, instead, to hire them to fix the roads? It might cause a deficit, says Walter Eberstadt. Ruin our finances. No, Phil Harvey tells us, if we plan it right and do it on a sufficient scale, it will pay for itself. Phil is surely right. If there is enough public spending it will set off an expansion in the private sector, and the resulting tax collections will pay for the public sector programs. This shows up in our simulations, too. But the reason is that at full employment, we don't want the government still providing a stimulus; we don't want excess demand pressure. It's *not* because in the boom we have to have a surplus to pay down the debt we ran up in the slump. The debt just doesn't matter that much. Randy Wray, Mat Forstater and I – and many others here – have all argued that Abba Lerner was right: the deficits and debts of the sovereign government need not pose a problem in the modern world. They are easily managed. As Warren Mosler has pointed out, the burden of the debt is largely a matter of interest rate policy. Deficits and debts, the whole panorama of 'sound finance,' should be put to one side, so the focus of policy can be to achieve prosperity – full employment without inflation.

I would like to say that this has been a marvelous session. I've enjoyed it very much. And I would like to declare our conference closed.

AUDIENCE: Bravo!

Index